ADVANCE PRAISE

"A long overdue book outlining the importance of deeply understanding and incorporating our patient's total experiences with their world. It is absolutely in the best Kurt Lewin tradition; unraveling the intricacies of bi-directional person–environment interactions so fundamental to effectively helping people coming to us for therapy. This book untangles the complexities of the Bio–Psycho–Social–Existential approach by updating Engel's original 1977 formulation with the knowledge we have gained from twenty-first-century data. "

—**Barry Nierenberg, Ph.D., ABPP,** Past President, APA Division of Rehabilitation Psychology, Board Certified, Rehabilitation Psychology, Distinguished Professor, College of Psychology, Nova Southeastern University

"Aldrich Chan has taken an incredibly complex set of topics and distilled them into an easily readable text. It is at once practical and theoretical, leading the reader to both understand the topics through relevant examples and envision how these models could impact future neuroscience and behavioral research. It is an enjoyable and thought-provoking read for anyone trying to better understand what drives human behavior."

—**Kenneth D. Hartline, Psy.D., ABPP-CN,** Board Certified Clinical Neuropsychologist, Los Angeles, CA

"Where is our self? What is its existence? How is it related to the world? Can we provide therapy to the self? These are the questions that this book addresses. It does so in a novel and highly innovative way. The author simply says: there is more to the self than we can see, observe, and demarcate in our third-person perspective in science. That 'more' hints upon a deeper layer; beyond the veil of the visible towards the invisible. Chan does remarkable work in unravelling a deeper layer of our self and its existence. Where does this deeper layer of our self lead us? To the world within which our brain and its body continuously align and integrate us—and it is this alignment and integration that makes for our existence. A wonderful book that opens the deeper layers of our existence and provides novel inspiration for better psychotherapy."

—**Georg Northoff, M.D., Ph.D.,** University of Ottawa, author of *Neurophilosophy and the Healthy Mind: Learning From the Unwell Brain* and *The Spontaneous Brain: From the Mind-Body to the World-Brain Problem*

"This outstanding book explores the ways that our perceptions of our own reality are colored by our personal experiences and the 'veils' of our minds. Dr. Chan is an expert in the default mode network, and as an erudite and versatile neuropsychologist provides a concise overview of contributions by major philosophers, psychologists, and neuroscientists on how the mind, consciousness, and brain work together. In addition, he shares new, exciting, integrated therapeutic conceptualizations and techniques to help patients."

—**Carolyn Drazinic, M.D., Ph.D., MBA,** Chief Medical Officer, Florida State Mental Health Hospitals; Associate Professor of Clinical Sciences, Florida State University; named Best in Medicine, American Health Council; featured in Leading Physicians of the World, International Association of Healthcare Professionals

REASSEMBLING
MODELS OF REALITY

THE NORTON SERIES ON INTERPERSONAL NEUROBIOLOGY

Louis Cozolino, PhD, Series Editor
Allan N. Schore, PhD, Series Editor, 2007–2014
Daniel J. Siegel, MD, Founding Editor

The field of mental health is in a tremendously exciting period of growth and conceptual reorganization. Independent findings from a variety of scientific endeavors are converging in an interdisciplinary view of the mind and mental well-being. An interpersonal neurobiology of human development enables us to understand that the structure and function of the mind and brain are shaped by experiences, especially those involving emotional relationships.

The Norton Series on Interpersonal Neurobiology provides cutting-edge, multidisciplinary views that further our understanding of the complex neurobiology of the human mind. By drawing on a wide range of traditionally independent fields of research—such as neurobiology, genetics, memory, attachment, complex systems, anthropology, and evolutionary psychology—these texts offer mental health professionals a review and synthesis of scientific findings often inaccessible to clinicians. The books advance our understanding of human experience by finding the unity of knowledge, or consilience, that emerges with the translation of findings from numerous domains of study into a common language and conceptual framework. The series integrates the best of modern science with the healing art of psychotherapy.

REASSEMBLING
MODELS OF REALITY

·····································

THEORY AND CLINICAL PRACTICE

·····································

Aldrich Chan

W. W. NORTON & COMPANY

Independent Publishers Since 1923

Note to Readers: Standards of clinical practice and protocol change over time, and no technique or recommendation is guaranteed to be safe or effective in all circumstances. This volume is intended as a general information resource for professionals practicing in the field of psychotherapy and mental health; it is not a substitute for appropriate training, peer review, and/or clinical supervision. Neither the publisher nor the author(s) can guarantee the complete accuracy, efficacy, or appropriateness of any particular recommendation in every respect. As of press time, the URLs displayed in this book link or refer to existing sites. The publisher and author are not responsible for any content that appears on third-party websites.

For information about permission to reproduce selections from this book, write to Permissions, W. W. Norton & Company, Inc., 500 Fifth Avenue, New York, NY 10110

For information about special discounts for bulk purchases, please contact W. W. Norton Special Sales at specialsales@wwnorton.com or 800-233-4830

Manufacturing by Lake Book Manufacturing
Production manager: Katelyn MacKenzie

ISBN: 978-1-324-01597-0

W. W. Norton & Company, Inc., 500 Fifth Avenue, New York, N.Y. 10110
www.wwnorton.com

W. W. Norton & Company Ltd., 15 Carlisle Street, London W1D 3BS

1 2 3 4 5 6 7 8 9 0

Contents

LIST OF TABLES

LIST OF FIGURES

Foreword

BY LOUIS COZOLINO

Reassembling Models of Reality is an exploration and meditation for thinking people concerning the nature of human experience. It takes us bottom-up from sensation, to perception, to cognition; outside-in from culture, to relationships, to the individual; and top-down from abstract thinking, questions of meaning, and the construction of self. It could also be called the deconstruction of human experience and the destruction of the myth of reality, but that might be a bit much for a title.

As a cross-disciplinary field of study, interpersonal neurobiology has always brought together many perspectives in an attempt to understand the nature of human experience. If you are familiar with the Norton Series on Interpersonal Neurobiology, you are already aware of the breadth and depth of the authors and topics which have been explored. This is both a new kind of work for us while at the same time resting well within the worldview and mission of the series. The reader will find a clear through line from the work of Dan Siegel, Allan Schore, and myself over the past two decades.

Clinical psychology and the allied fields of psychotherapy and counseling have come to suffer from an overemphasis on technique and a lack of understanding of the mechanisms of action of our work. Dr. Chan's work speaks directly to this gap and fills in some missing pieces. This is a smart, ambitious work filled with the best references from the right people and an excellent source book for students who want to expand their horizons into the fields of neuropsychology, philosophy, and cross-cultural studies. *Reassembling Models of Reality* is an ever-shifting kaleidoscope of ideas, research findings, and images, an admixture of scientific theory, philosophy, and clinical application that will expose you to new ideas and stimulate you to think in new ways.

Chan's work also fits well with the contemporary stream of thinking guided by Amos Tversky, John Bargh, and Donald Hoffman, works which reflect the growing appreciation of the distortions of human perception, reasoning, and judgment. It is becoming increasing clear that evolution has selected and shaped our perception in ways which enhanced our survival as primitive animals and later as hunter-gatherers. We now face a global-technological world with a new set of problems for which our paleolithic perceptual and analytic apparatus is ill-equipped. As Jonas Salk famously said, "evolution is both a problem solving and problem creating process." The problems our brains and minds were shaped to solve are mostly gone, and new problems such as cross-tribal cooperation, prejudice, and climate change require new evolutionary adaptations; adaptations which will have to take place via cooperation and acts of will rather than the twists and turns of natural selection. There appears to be a race occurring between the evolution of consciousness and the forces which threaten our survival. The practice of psychotherapy sits at the intersection of these forces.

While this perspective on human experience can be confusing and demoralizing, it also opens a window as to how we can improve our lives by learning to not accept anything and everything that bubbles up into consciousness. We need to learn to be wary consumers of our own minds and the beliefs and biases they so generously offer us. While humans have evolved to believe and not to analyze, skepticism, fact-checking, and doubting is exactly what we need to be doing with what comes from around us and inside us. This book, and the current generation of thinkers exploring the building blocks of perception and cognition, make it clear how important it is for us to learn to be skeptical of the offerings of our minds.

I found Dr. Chan's discussion of the default mode network (DMN) especially informative. It is clear that he has a deep grasp of this topic, as well as its implication for human experience and healing. His coverage of the DMN is a good introduction and overview for those who are new to this interesting and extremely important area of neuroscience for psychologists and anyone interested in subjective experience. Another treat for the reader with an interest in Buddhism will be the numerous ways in which its perspectives and philosophy are explained and reinforced via Chan's review of the neuroscience of sensation, perception, and cognition.

Perhaps more important than any topics he discusses is what *Reassembling Models of Reality* implies: the more we know, the more we are able to think about our clinical work, and the more we can view our lives from multiple perspectives, the better equipped we are to love, work, and heal others. I predict we are going to hear much more from Aldrich Chan in the years to come.

Acknowledgments

The perpetual support I have received from my father, mother, brother, and grandparents is unparalleled. I am very fortunate to have been born and raised into such a loving family. The diversity of experiences I have had growing up as a Chinese-Canadian in Costa Rica has undoubtedly influenced my disposition and thought. With the same profundity of respect and love, my deepest gratitude to Jessica Shraybman for assisting with edits, inspiring me and putting up with my madness throughout the process of writing this.

I thank Drs. Louis Cozolino and Daniel Siegel for their endless wisdom, guidance and encouragement that has endured ever since I was a young doe-eyed doctoral student. From the ground of my being emanates a deep warmth and appreciation for their connection and support throughout my professional development and the publication of this book.

I would also like to express my thanks to the interns of my practice, the Center for Neuropsychology and Consciousness. These students include: Sydney Sroka, MA (+ assisting with Appendix B and C), Ryan Karasik, MA (+ assisting with Appendix A), Nadine Robertson, MD, Kayla Garrison, MA, Kate Williams, BA, and Jason Ouyang, BA, for providing constructive feedback toward the development of this book.

This list of acknowledgments would be incomplete without thanking Deborah Malmud, a vice president at Norton, for seeing the potential in my initial manuscript, providing constructive feedback and for being flexible towards my requests throughout the process of publishing this book. Thanks, as well to the rest of the Norton group who has assisted me throughout: Mariah Eppes, Megan Bedell, Kevin Olsen, Kelly Auricchio, and Sara McBride Tuohy.

Special thanks to Rebekka Helford and Irene Vartanoff for playing a major role in editing this book and providing me with great feedback. I must also give acknowledgment and thanks for suggestions and thoughts about select aspects of the book that came from Georg Northoff and Terry-Marks Tarlow.

Finally, I am profoundly grateful to Costa Rican artists and friends Daniel Icaza and Devindar Aulakh. Daniel for allowing me to use his artwork for the front cover and Devindar for collaborating with me on a musical project in service of promoting this book. My gratitude to James Widener for his assistance with the development of Gestalt artwork.

Introduction

....

Life is a child playing, moving pieces in a game:
kingship belongs to the child.

The hidden harmony is superior to the visible.

—HERACLITUS

There is more to our selves than we can ever know, more happening in any relationship than we can ever be conscious of, and more to reality than we can ever comprehend. The reaches of nature extend into a vanishing point, a continuity far beyond what we can sense and perceive. We say, "Seeing is believing," yet what is it that we see? Our visual system registers less than 1% of the known electromagnetic spectrum (Sliney, 2016) and less than 5% of the known universe (Panek, 2011). We are relational animals, ever so confident in our judgment of others, overlooking that every relationship is partially imagined. Interpersonally, we rely on inferences challenged by context and predictions refracted by our minds. We think we know ourselves, yet we enter the world amnestic, ever forgetful of our rootedness in nature; with our actions determined by multiple pre-existing narratives continually streaming in and out of consciousness. Our minds are populated by selves, processes that exist on their own accord, expressing their desires in spite of our aspirations. We like to think we are directors, yet much of the time, the actors have already been cast and their roles acted out even before we have envisioned the play. We are each a brief happening in nature's diffuse penumbra, a spark of light striving to illuminate a path back to its source and forward into the unknown.

What do we know about our psychological experience of reality? How might this impact the way we think and live? Is there a "right" direction? How can we better prepare ourselves for the challenges that lie ahead?

In less than 1/12 of a second, we actively register millions of bits of information triggering a neural cascade of electrochemical interactions, generating our experience of all that surrounds us. Our brain constructs a dynamic map of the world, limited by our senses, selectively filtering what we experience. This leads me to ask, is the presumed clarity of what we sense an accurate indicator of what is known? What *invisible* processes are influencing our daily decisions and actions? The purpose of this book is to delineate the filtration processes that curate our reality, what insights may be gleaned from what we believe we know, how systems within each process may influence everyday experience, and how we might work with them to improve well-being for our clients and ourselves. In this book, I offer thoughts that build on a model of biopsychosocial-existential (BPSE) processes, each of which are inextricably intertwined, and actively involved in the turning of becoming into being. I begin with the presupposition that these active layers of organization exist and add that parts of these layers receive, shape, distort, interpret, and/or reinterpret information into a particular reality. While the rest are self-evident, I refer to an existential process merely as a descriptor for systems of meaning concerning existence. The attempt here is to incorporate an underlying process that may capture atheism, religion, and spirituality. In the context of this book then, it is important to release the word *existential* from its usual associational confinement to apricot cocktails, cigarettes, coffee, and freedom. Although what will be presented may appear as a system of thought, it is critical to note that my intention is only to expand awareness and multiply the tools available for clinical use because systems are, oftentimes, the harbingers of rigid thinking.

In this book, I explore ideas that converge from many sources, including science, philosophy, and clinical experiences. For those philosophers who believe I am trespassing, let me be clear that I am not claiming to be a philosopher, but would consider myself philosophically informed. I acknowledge that much of psychology has its roots in philosophy, and I have a deep admiration for the thinkers who have paved the road for many of us to live *an examined life*. In the spirit of interpersonal neurobiology, this work stresses Edward O. Wilson's (1999) suggestion of *consilience*, or the act of integrating knowledge from different specialties in service of finding common truths. The purpose of integrating fields is not only to seek areas of agreement when different paths are pursued, but also to address the limitations found in each to generate a more complete picture.

In this context, I do not adhere to any particular psychotherapeutic approach. Furthermore, randomized controlled trials have determined that various psychotherapeutic modalities are equivalent in their outcomes for several disorders (Cuijpers, Reijnders, & Huibers, 2019), with the relationship being the most important factor. I am aligned with Cozolino's (2010) proposal that "from the perspective of neuroscience, psychotherapy can be understood as a specific kind of enriched environment designed to enhance the growth of neurons and the integration of neural networks . . . all forms of therapy regardless of theoretical orientation, will be successful to the degree to which they foster appropriate neuroplasticity" (pp. 25–26). Each theoretical approach capitalizes on different entry points to plasticity. These include the senses, emotions, thoughts, behaviors, imagination, and movement. I thus gather the essential ingredients of many approaches to elucidate fundamental concepts that may promote well-being. Humans are complex, and I have always found it wise to open ourselves up to many forms of thought so as to address individual differences effectively. It is my belief that integrating knowledge from different disciplines may advance divergent thinking and our existing conceptual frameworks. In this way, we may cultivate a greater foundation of knowledge and experience that will enhance our adaptive potential. This book aspires to intellectually stimulate, stir creativity, increase awareness, and be a helpful clinical guide. Throughout this work, you will find that I define certain words in order to defuse semantic confusion, as it is often the culprit of misinterpretation and at its worst offense. I humbly invite the reader to align with the attitude presented and attend to the semantic clarifications throughout. With any luck, these additions may help us steer clear from muddy waters.

Some of the content of this book may seem suggestive, and I foresee two possible biases to which I would like to add a cautionary note. On the one hand, some individuals may utilize the upcoming knowledge as proof to further their ideas of realities beyond what we experience. On the contrary, I only address realities that are within the realm of what people have experienced, as documented by science, and inferences elaborated by particular iconoclasts whose work has influenced our current paradigms of thought in a progressive direction. There now exists an abundance of literature supporting claims grounded in wild generalizations and misinterpretations of scientific findings. I do not take this lightly, nor do I endorse the sort of magical thinking that goes with it.

On the other hand, science itself has produced a line of thinking that may be forcing nature onto a procrustean bed.* Science is about following nature's lead through the various clues it leaves behind. Suggestive results may be meaningful, but not absolute. Richard Feynman (1988) characterized science as a "satisfactory philosophy of ignorance" (p. 248). I do not know of any other method more effective in investigating so-called objective truth than science, but that does not mean there are no weaknesses. From my experience the Achilles heel of *scientism* is less known, and so I will spend a brief time describing some of it. A substantial part of science's influence comes from its productivity and the very fact that, theoretically, any scientific claim can be challenged and potentially falsifiable† (Chalmers, 2013; Popper, 1968), thus exempting it from the status of dogma. The irony is that when these two are combined, it has produced many minds that take science as dogma. It is easy to attribute the success or productivity of a theory to its accuracy, but that is a fallacy. It is important to remember that despite its advances and assistance to humanity, even science, though a very powerful tool, is a work *in progress*. Results from scientific studies can be interpreted in different ways, and *truths* are partially defined by consensus among members of the scientific community. This space for interpretation also allows for the introduction of the researcher's subjective opinions. Internal models of reality are subject to differences that result in competing views of reality. Kuhn's (2012) famous introduction of the term *paradigm shift* aptly noted that the introduction of new models results in new questions, some being asked of old data, resulting in the revision of previous models and providing a refined landscape for subsequent research. One example of this includes research on the brain's resting state, which used to be considered *noise*. It was not until the publication of two comprehensive reviews, one by Shulman and colleagues (1997) and a second by Raichle and colleagues (2001) that internally oriented cognition and resting-state activity rose to the forefront of research.

---

* Greek mythology: Procrustes, son of Poseidon, lured travelers to his home. He had a penchant for amputating or stretching individuals in order to make them fit his bed of death.

† Falsifiability in the logical sense (Popper) is controversial; nevertheless there are adherents. There also exists sophisticated falsificationism among others, which is observational and experimental (see Chalmers, 2013).

There are, of course, other examples that have resulted in an expansion of knowledge rather than contradicting or invalidating existing findings. Science also rests on fundamental assumptions about the universe and is limited to objective evidence; thus, it cannot make value judgments or offer meaning, both of which are critically important facets of the human experience. Science may therefore provide information about how something works but not give you a why to your existence, and even the *how* can be limited, such as attempts to define the nature of consciousness. The quest for causation is not the same as a quest for meaning. Logic is another means by which we gather information that is critical to science, yet, as we will see, logic is also subject to skepticism. Any system with presuppositions is limited by those presuppositions. Therefore, any argument put forth would then be redundant in that it would only be used to prove itself, because the initial argument ultimately stems from the very presuppositions from which it is arguing. Although technology and techniques have been able to overcome many of the limitations we once faced, we are still susceptible to errors.

Science accrues information through observation. Yet even observation of phenomena may elicit different responses from individuals. Figure-Ground such as Rubin's Vase (see Figure 1.1) is an example demonstrating how "two normal observers viewing the same object from the same place under the same physical circumstances do not necessarily have identical visual experiences, even though the images on their respective retinas may be virtually identical" (Chalmers, 2013, p. 5). How does the observer effect from quantum mechanics play a role? How objective can we be if the mere observation of a phenomenon (and the observer does not even have to be human) inevitably influences its state? Does this phenomenon suggest that, on a fundamental level, we are unable to disentangle ourselves from any experiment?

It is important to note that although this book will be exploring the brain, many of the findings presented herein are based on statistical truths, which are not *complete* truths. Rather, we are looking at correlations and averages, neither of which offer a direct representation of reality. The presence of phenomenology in science, which focuses on experience and takes on a first-person descriptive approach, may very well complement current scientific trends, which have a tendency of taking a third-person explanatory approach (Carman, 2012; Merleau-Ponty, 1945/2014). Why is it that we deny the importance of subjective experience when the very facts that we encounter are housed in it and when there are methods that may move us closer to truth? After underscoring the importance of objectivity, Oliver Sacks (1998) also emphasized the importance of subjectivity, noting that "a living creature, and especially a human being, is first and last active—a subject, not an object" (p. 177). Lastly, there is a boundary that we are unable to cross when exploring the mind as it relates to matter: namely, that any conclusions drawn about matter, mind, and their relationship are themselves mental constructs. I believe that we can only move closer to the truth if we integrate findings from several fields, and herein lies the importance of consilience.

A *veil* is a piece of fine material used to protect and conceal the face. I use the word *veil* (interchangeably with *filter*) for its symbolism, referring to its ability to filter, limit, and distort our immediate experience of reality. I have intentionally separated *processes* from *veils* because processes course through the very fabric of human beings. Humans are, after all, processes within processes; we are not stagnant models. Veils are active modules emerging from processes that may interfere with a balanced judgment. For example, memory is a component of cognition that can inaccurately bias a decision. Memory may thus act as a veil in certain circumstances.

As a neuropsychologist, experiment and experience are equally important to me. Objective truths may be analyzed, whereas experiential truths are actually lived. In addition to education, psychotherapy, and research, my core task as a neuropsychologist is to assess the integrity of an individual's cognitive architecture, as it is informed by sensation, perception, cognition, and emotional functioning. What distinguishes neuropsychology as a specialty is in its vivisection of the brain-mind relationship. First, the neuropsychologist administers assessments that are validated by research and correlated to brain structure or functioning. Data is generated, winnowing a vast range of diagnostic possibilities into a narrow range of probabilities. The neuropsychologist however must give life to the data, so to speak, through the interpretation of data in the context of an individual's unique context and history. Without the client's experiential and historical input, data reduces the individual to a set of numbers; analogous to someone attempting to know a plane solely through its instrument panel. Thereafter, the client is given a comprehensive report, with a diagnosis, prognosis, and recommendations. Broadly speaking, my job is to: (a) help my clients see an accurate representation of their brain-mind relationship (which leads to a diagnosis) and (b) use this information to prevent undesirable consequences and maximize the chances of living optimally. We are required to deepen our understanding of both, in relation to one another, if we hope to advance our potential.

The eight chapters in this book cover a vast amount of territory and is structured to be an introduction to various lines of thinking and research. Each chapter could easily have been expanded into an entire book, I have tried my best not to vitiate the work of those cited, but any condensed and pragmatic approach often requires certain sacrifices. The first five chapters dismantle the seeming accuracy, reliability, and stability of our sensory-perceptual, psychological, and sociocultural experiences. These chapters are written with the intent of demonstrating the filtration systems within each dimension of existence. When we become aware of the processes that determine many of our decisions, it creates a necessary disruption, granting space for possibilities. I caution the reader that an internal apocalypse may ensue, although I hope it does not go beyond its technical ancient Greek translation *apokalupsis,* as *an unveiling,* or to "uncover, reveal" (New Oxford American Dictionary, 2010, p. 73). In any case, I have applied safety measures by introducing ways of working with the shortcomings of each veil at opportune locations. These sections are labeled *applications, dialogue,* or *reflections and applications,* and are intended to inspire attitudinal shifts and materialize concepts in service of diagnosis, treatment, and enhanced well-being. In addition, I describe representative clinical populations to illustrate the importance of these processes and how veils operate in our existence and everyday functioning. Each process is a necessary component of human experience, now requiring additional scaffolding from other capacities to offset evolution and the rapid growth that has taken place in society and in technology.

The sixth chapter focuses on the concept of meaning, specifically how we currently define it and its therapeutic applications. Thereafter I assert that what has been lacking in current investigations on meaning is their discovery through specific psychophysical experiences. This is the focus of the seventh chapter, where I elaborate on self-transcendent experiences and their counterpart, self-other–oriented moral emotions as *vital signals.* This is followed by an examination of mystical experiences, as currently understood in chapter seven. Finally, the eighth chapter summarizes the veils in a hypothetical scenario, tracing the route of information as it becomes distorted from its inception as a sensed thing to its digested experience in consciousness. It then recapitulates the previous chapters into a list of potential deceptions that lead to self-inflicted suffering.

The chapter is exploratory, diving further into concepts and methods that may supplement existing approaches in therapy.

I conclude this introduction by offering the following propositions, succeeded by a subjective account, in first person, of how a healthy mind might appear in this model.

I. A fraction of information from the objective world, selected by evolutionary pressures, is actively registered and influenced by our nervous systems. The objective world is experienced through consciousness in a highly processed form: Perception.

II. Perception is highly influenced by intrinsic activity in the brain, which includes predictive neural circuitry. Expectations interact with sense data to form the phenomenal world: a model of reality in which we would best function.

III. The confluence of complex nonlinear interactions within and among our brain, body, and relationships (Siegel, 1999) are in dialogue through spatiotemporal dynamics with the world (Northoff, 2018). This gives rise to a conscious mind; a relational and embodied process that regulates the flow of energy and information (Siegel, 2012).

IV. Mind and Matter are descriptions of a single process. Put together, they are more accurately understood as occasions of experience, or events, not substances (Whitehead, 1927–28/1978).

V. The conscious self-process has a limited capacity and is disproportionately outweighed by non-conscious/unconscious* processing. The unconscious process is not a passive storehouse, nor is it merely reactive and automated, but a dynamic regulatory process actively selecting, organizing, and guiding contents into and out of consciousness.

VI. Conscious and unconscious processes are governed by primary affective systems that promote survival, procreation, and flourishing while maximizing conservation of energy. These include: SEEKING,

---

* Non-conscious refers to neural processing, whereas unconscious refers to psychological dynamics.

CARE, LUST, PANIC, FEAR, RAGE, and PLAY (Panksepp, 1998; Panksepp & Biven, 2012).

VII. The sum self-process is open and active, consisting of three core layers: proto, core, and autobiographical (Damasio, 2010). These three layers are informed by primordial self-processes that are assembled around primary affective fields (Panksepp, 1998), and complex self-processes* (Jung, 1948/1981) that cluster around secondary and tertiary emotions (which are derived from primary emotions). The conscious self-process is necessary for the development of novel adaptive strategies and the organism's experiential enhancement.

VIII. There are biological, psychological, sociocultural, and existential (BPSE) processes with shared and unique components. There exist as many models of reality as there are humans.

IX. These systems may conflict, disposing us to a foreground that veils a background of potential interior and exterior experiences.

X. Survival is contingent upon short-term and long-term predictive neural circuitry.

    a. Short-term circuitry alerts reflexive behaviors necessary for real-time adjustments due to conduction or processing delays.

    b. Long-term circuitry involves developing executive functions (e.g., inhibition, delayed gratification, self-control) in service of improved prospection and consideration of variance.

XI. Bottom-up and top-down processes (via attention and executive functions) converge and select information that is valued, perceived, and stored in memory.

XII. Memory is flexible and primed to prepare us for the future; it is not intended to record an accurate history of the past.

XIII. As we develop through time, we implement acquired and learned strategies to increase our chances to meet evolutionary pressures.

---

* Jung (1948/1981) called these *feeling toned* complexes.

XIV. As demands increase in complexity, non-conscious and conscious self-regulatory strategies may become insufficient in their ability to successfully manage our functioning in relation to the changing world.

XV. Improved adaptation and well-being require advancing models of reality via the continual expansion and integration of conscious and non-conscious processes to improve self-regulation and predictive success.

XVI. Expansion and integration are contingent on plasticity for assimilation or accommodation of information.

XVII. Awareness (A) allows us to *feel* congruence and incongruence in psychophysiological processes (Solms, 2017) thus prompting meta-cognition (M) to regulate its own mental states and behaviors as is appropriate. AM is responsible for the meeting of needs, management of variability, the confirmation/updating of pre-existing knowledge, and individuation.*

XVIII. Self-transcendent experiences (STE) and their counterpart, other- and self-oriented moral emotions, are *vital signals*, psychophysiological reflexes that orient the individual toward experiential truth.

XIX. Experiential truth begins as a *feeling* of congruence (or incongruence), transitions into a meaningful relation, and matures into propositional truth values that we recognize as the still small voice of conscience. These developments correspond to anoetic, noetic, and autonoetic levels of consciousness (Vanderkerckhove, Panksepp, 2009).

XX. Conscience is a relational process rooted in the interactions between primary affective systems identified as SEEKING and CARE (Panksepp, 1998) and its environment. Psychologically, it may be rooted in early attachment-based experiences related to experiences of nurturing (Sagan, 1988; Carveth, 2013). Conscience is a compass, and vital signals are akin to amplifications of magnetic fields, orienting one toward truth values.

---

* This term comes from Jung (1954), it is to develop ". . . the most successful adaptation to the universal conditions of existence coupled with the greatest possible freedom for self-determination" (p. 171).

XXI.   The living person is a process of internal and external relating. Healthy functioning is contingent upon the quality of these
relationships.

Reassembling models of reality (R-MOR) approaches the practice of therapy as a dynamic relationship. Its core purpose is to collaboratively *unveil*
biased and maladaptive processes to facilitate the maturation and expression
of experiential truth. Processes occluding maturation may include unmetab-
olized somatic experiences, dysregulated emotional systems, antiquated psychological representations, sociocultural discord, and/or existential dread.
Insight and *experiences* promote novel solutions that are *congruent* with one's conscience and vital signals, corresponding to beneficial structural and functional
reconfigurations (unique to every individual) between and among neural systems, the body, and the environment. The process of unveiling promotes the
establishment of symbiotic relationships within and between biopsychosocial–
existential processes. Therapy aims at maximizing the number of advantageous
symbiotic relationships within and between the self-processes that compose
the individual. Increased frequency of embodied symbiotic actions facilitates
their consolidation into implicit systems. This generates novel or reconfigured
neural ensembles that support adaptive functioning. States become a form
of *pre-reflective mutualism* corresponding to integrated neural systems (Siegel,
2010) and Jung's idea of wholeness over "perfection." Beyond the movement of
unconscious processing to conscious experience, integration requires energy
and information to be appropriately (dis)charged and/or metabolized. Clinicians assist with these processes, with the goal of cultivating consciousness,
congruence, meaning, and tolerance for suffering. The mind-brain strives to
minimize conscious resource expenditure through increasingly veridical predictive models of the world.

a.   Healthy differentiation must include consideration of environmental pressures and individualistic tendencies.

b.   Healthy differentiation requires *conscious* suffering due to the
necessity to sacrifice conflictual behaviors that are problematic to
the whole.

The goals of psychotherapy are varied, and there seems to be a vague consensus as to what healthy mental functioning looks like. So long as traits, thoughts,

feelings, or behaviors do not interfere with domains of functioning (e.g., social, occupational, personal, etc.) they are not clinical symptoms. There are, of course, several descriptors used (e.g., well-being, peaceful, happy), yet I have found them somewhat difficult to ground in everyday functioning. What does well-being look like? This is partially due to the need to be slightly elusive in order to respect individual differences. Nonetheless, I propose one example of what healthy mental functioning might look like in someone who has successfully overcome some difficult habits. The following is a fictitious journal entry, intentionally vague for relatability, of Emrys, an individual who has consciously taken a *leap* into the process of integration and embodied symbiosis.

JOURNAL ENTRY

It has been some time since I have been able to overcome some dysfunctional habits. It is easier now, but at times, temptation still beckons. I trust the tension will naturally subside, as it is recycled into energy that I can reuse. I recall my values and remind myself that I no longer wish to submit to commands that may harm me. I acknowledge them as echoes from the past, a distant part of me, now acquired by a larger process that continues to mature into the future.

I am more productive and better able to nurture relationships that I value. I no longer feel like Jekyll and Hyde; I no longer feel fragmented. I feel more complete, and my responses are whole, embodied, and effective. They come from the depths of my being as much as the heights of my principles. There is much more coherence and stability. I am anchored, and every part of me has a say: precedence dependent on the context.

This does not mean I am not without challenges. The difference is, I can better adapt to situations, with focus and resolve. I am fully present with the experience at hand, for it is in the present that my actions can birth new truths about who I am and where I am headed.

I do not shy away from stress; my patience and tolerance for it grows. I am aware that, sometimes, new conclusions from the mind take time to settle in the body. Whereas the body is the first to receive information from the environment, the intellect is the first to learn from it: the body—the last. I show my respect by consciously suffering, giving it the time and space needed to assimilate or accommodate this new information. I have found that when I accept the suffering I experience, I become more empathic with others around me, knowing that this is shared suffering. I trust that my body will adapt, as to the best of my ability I have considered responses from all parts of my being.

There are moments when I feel negative or positive emotions, but I no longer identify with them. I do not become them; I do not act them out, nor do I push them away. I am detached, yet connected. I sit with them, feel them, and allow the emotions to circulate my system. I allow them to play their role in guiding and fueling my behaviors that ensue. Outside their proper place and time, sadness resolves as introspection, anxiety as motivation, confusion as curiosity, chaos as spontaneity, and aggression or sexuality as assertiveness. The containment of these feelings enlivens and empowers me.

There are times I think about the past and future, yet I am always present with them when I do. I am conscious when my mind wanders. I watch nature unfold from the inside. I have become more sensitive to what occurs in my inner world and what is happening around me, without any loss of efficiency. When there is a mismatch between my expectations and the reality of a situation, I reflect. I identify any potential biases and put them aside so I can make a more objective decision. This takes some time, but I find that my reflections on action slowly but surely become reflections in action.

I make sure to cultivate the important aspects of my life, distributing energy as needed to work, play, relationships, and health. There is much uncertainty, much unknown, yet the mystery of nature energizes me and feeds my curiosity. Every process is an exploration and every exploration is an inner and outer journey. Although the unknown certainly scares me, I place trust in my entire organism's ability to cope with what will happen. I actively gather knowledge, connect it with my experiences, and act in ways that best represent this relationship in response to my current situation. I strive to keep an open mind, knowing that I have been wrong many times before.

I pay attention and examine experiences that *move* me both physically and psychologically. I derive my values from these experiences, seeing them as signals that promote my vitality. I follow nature's lead, I listen to my conscience, and as a result find meaning in my daily life, whether I am suffering or happy. I am appreciative and increasingly fulfilled by what others might call daily *mundane* experiences. I find that there is something to be learned from every person I encounter. There is much inspiration to be found in the shared tendency humans have to actualize in the midst of so much challenge. I nurture this striving for potential, enjoying the co-creation of increasingly connected and resilient narratives in support of it.

• •

Similar to all other professionals, I am not without influences. I am particularly indebted to the historical work of Jaak Panksepp, Alfred North Whitehead, Carl Jung, Wilfred Bion, William James, and Karl Jaspers. Contemporary thinkers include Daniel Siegel, Louis Cozolino, Georg Northoff, Mark Solms, and Antonio Damasio.

Studying the complex, nonlinear dynamics of the mind requires the continual incorporation of new research, consilience, and dialectical thinking. Antiquated theories are being discarded, updated, or revised, new theories are developed alongside research, and novel syntheses are accumulating throughout the literature. All the while, practitioners are responsible for translating this knowledge into practice. This demand makes the profession increasingly difficult, yet more commendable in its pursuit. No longer can we be satisfied with two-dimensional models for a four-dimensional reality!

REASSEMBLING
MODELS OF REALITY

CHAPTER 1.

Sensing, Perceiving, and Conscious Processing

He who sees with his eyes is blind.

—SOCRATES

Awakening from a deep slumber, you find yourself in a pocket of chaotic associations, somewhere between the narrative of a fantastic dream and the stability of waking consciousness. You hear multiple voices, and see flashes of images. This nonlinear sequence settles into a linear experience, as your self is reconstituted into a sense of continuity. In an instant, it is quiet, and you are only aware of your internal dialogue. After a brief stretch, you blink, sit up on your bed, and notice yourself in a mirror. Light traveling at 186,000 miles per second is recognized by your visual sense mechanisms and an image of yourself flickers into view. What you see is light reflecting off of you, but humans actually emit light as well, albeit one thousand times below the sensitivity that our eyes can detect (Kobayashi, Kikuchi, & Okamura, 2009). Our eyes are actually part of the brain, and each eye harbors a structure called the retina, which transduces or translates external stimuli into electrical signals. Two upside-down images are formed on the retina because of the refraction of the cornea. The information journeys through the optic nerves, some of which

1

cross at the optic chasm, into the lateral geniculate nucleus and is ultimately processed in the visual cortex at the back of the brain. In this process, the image is flipped right side up and the two images are combined into one. Information is encoded, the world is given order, and specific images are assembled into visual-spatial perception* (Blumenfeld, 2010). You close your eyes again as you yawn. At this moment, the world outside does not exist as you perceive it; some would argue it does not exist at all with no one to perceive it, only to come back into existence when your eyes open.

Much of what we see and feel is selected by complex filtration systems, resulting in our perception of the wondrous world around us, at the cost of several illusions and limitations. Some of these costs are gladly paid for, whereas others are not. We begin with the very experience of time and space. The first illusion is our temporal orientation to the present. Although it may *feel* as if we are living in the now, the fact is that our perception lags behind real time by approximately 350 milliseconds, during which time information from the outside world is sensed, perceived, and interpreted by neural structures before being registered in conscious awareness. If we include our subsequent behavior, the estimation rises to 550 milliseconds–1 second (Haggard, 2008; Libet, 1973, 1999; Libet, Wright, & Gleason, 1982). This means our conscious selves are actually perpetually living in the past. To compound this illusion, space is expanding (Bahcall, 2015; Hubble, 1929) and the Earth is moving rapidly, yet we do not feel as if the space we inhabit has changed, nor do we feel as if we are moving. We become accustomed to the constants in our lives, and it becomes easy to simply trust how we *feel*.

Maybe you believe what you see is accurate, but, as the previous and ensuing discussion demonstrates, that belief is incorrect. We all have a blind spot where our optic nerves are located, and it is in fact our brains that impose the most likely of structures on this uncertainty. Despite the fact that up to one third of the brain is involved in producing vision, much remains unseen, because we are only capable of seeing within a narrow band of light, with updated sources indicating a span of 310–1100 nanometers (versus 380–780; Sliney, 2016). Humans are considered *trichromats*, possessing three types of cone cells, whereas avian vision is *tetrachromatic*, having four single-cone types,

---

* This is the traditional account of visual perception, which is seemingly undergoing a revision (see section: Bayesian Brain).

which allows them to see a whole extra dimension of color. Varela noted that the proper comparison of a bird's vision to a human's would be like a two-dimensional creature trying to imagine three-dimensional space. He went on to say that "it's not that they see more colors, it's not that they see better colors, it's that their color space is unimaginable for us" (as cited in Solano, 1983, 11:31–11:40). Perhaps a less accurate but more digestible comparison is imagining an attempt to explain the color green to someone who can only see in black and white.

There are full patterns on flowers not visible to the naked human eye, privy only to certain insects. Technology has been able to override some of these limitations and also play with them, such that we now have the capacity to take pictures of flowers in certain frequencies of light enabling us to detect such patterns. What this also means is that we are not seeing reality as it is; rather, we see the spectrum of light that is most useful to our survival and, as we will come to understand, impose patterns to further help organize the sheer amount of information presented to us.

To be clear, we do not see *raw* matter; all the information outside of us is interpreted and transformed through sensation and perception. Another fallacy is that we are passive recipients of sensory data surrounding us. This is quite far from the truth. We are in fact quite active in our selection of information. Although they may appear motionless, our eyes actually move quite frequently and rapidly. One common type of eye movement is saccadic movements, which occur in service of mapping out the territory around us and determining what parts of a scene are of interest. Saccadic movements also maximize the efficiency of our use of physiological resources. It is estimated that our brain can process anywhere between 2–60 bits of information per second (bps) when perceiving, attending, and deciding and 106 bps for processing sensory information. However, we are only estimated to be able to consciously manipulate 3–4 bps (Wu, Dufford, Mackie, Egan, & Fan, 2016).

Two studies evaluating sex differences in vision concluded that men overall were better at detecting fast movements and fine detail, whereas women were better able to distinguish among hues, such as blue, green, and yellow (Abramov, Gordon, Feldman, & Chavarga, 2012a, 2012b). It turns out that women and men, in fact, *do* see things differently. This finding also supports the assertion that our perception has been shaped by our hunter-gatherer history and evolutionary necessity.

Our brain is capable of perceiving 10–12 frames per second, with anything faster resulting in the perception of motion. Today, motion pictures have at minimum 30 frames per second. Stationary images can also induce the illusion of motion, in particular when shapes and colors are modified strategically and placed in a specific sequence. There exist many other optical illusions that play with how images are imprinted on the retina and neurologically processed.

These limitations and illusions translate to every sense that we have. Sound travels at 330 meters per second and our auditory range is equivalent to 20–20,000 Hz, yet technology has enabled us to detect bands outside these zones, including what we call infrasounds (which range from 0–20 Hz, such as the sounds of elephants) and ultrasounds (which range from 20,000– >160,000 Hz, such as the sounds of dolphins and bats). It is estimated that we register 100,000 bits of auditory information per second (Markowsky, 2017). One fascinating illusion is the tritone paradox, whereby individuals who are played exactly the same Shepard tones (tones containing both higher and lower frequencies) will have differing responses as to whether the next tones in a sequence are higher or lower. This occurs because our brains select tones that they prefer, which has been found to be influenced by both language and culture (Deutsche, Henthorn, & Dolson, 2004).

Bushdid, Magnasco, Vosshall, and Keller (2014) estimated that human olfaction is capable of distinguishing over one trillion scents. However, this claim has not been without argument (Gerkin & Castro, 2015). When it comes to olfactory sensitivity, dogs are estimated to be able to detect odorant concentration levels of up to 100,000 times that of a human (Walker et al., 2006). Although there is clear evidence for olfactory hallucinations, the experience of olfactory illusions is still up for debate (Batty, 2014). Similar to other senses, our capacity for identifying odors diminishes as we age; typically, by age 70, humans are able to identify only 30–45% of common odorants people can smell at age 20 (Purves et al., 2001). Neurologically speaking, olfaction is unique among the senses, having a direct pathway to our limbic system rather than being routed through the thalamus. It is estimated that we register 100,000 bits of olfactory information per second (Markowsky, 2017).

Our gustatory system is intimately entwined with other senses, such as vision, audition, touch, and especially smell. In their literature review, Auvray and Spence (2008) concluded that flavor is more accurately understood as a perceptual modality in which information from all these senses are integrated by the very process of eating. Indeed, many attribution errors occur in the perceptual blurring of boundaries when we attempt to distinguish what sense is detecting the specific taste (Stevenson, Prescott, & Boakes, 1999). In fact, taste is considered our weakest sense. It is estimated that we have 10,000 taste buds, with the ability to detect combinations of five primary tastes, including sweet, salty, sour, bitter, and umami. It is estimated that we register 1,000 bits of gustatory information per second (Markowsky, 2017). This pales in comparison to the gustation of a cow, for example, which has an estimated 25,000 taste buds. Cows are hypothesized to have such a well-developed gustation system to allow for the enhanced detection of toxins in plants (Molyneux & Ralphs, 1992).

Our sense of touch arises when sense receptors are activated by a stimulus, with sensory neurons relaying information to an area of the brain called the somatosensory cortex. Our sensitivity to touch ranges throughout our body and is partially dependent on the bodily area's relative amount of representation in our somatosensory cortex. These representative regions differ among species. It is estimated that we register 1,000,000 bits of tactile information per second (Markowsky, 2017). We also experience a wide variety of tactile illusions. To begin with, a widely known fact from the field of physics is that because of electrons repelling one another, nothing is actually ever touched, and in fact it is estimated that we are made up of 99% *empty** space! One somatic illusion is called the cutaneous rabbit illusion (Geldard & Sherrick, 1972). Rapid sequential tapping on two areas separated by an area with low representation, such as the forearm, results in the illusion of taps *hopping* up the intermediate area. Neuroimaging research has since confirmed this illusion as being registered in the primary somatosensory cortex (Blankenburg, Ruff, Deichmann, Rees, & Driver, 2006). In one fascinating study, Miyazaki, Hirashima, and Nozaki (2010) were able to extend this effect onto one experiencing taps on a stick balanced on subjects' index fingers, signifying that the illusion may even occur outside of us.

Sense information is integrated in association areas of the brain, regions separate from primary areas initially elicited to interpret sense data. These regions are also communal areas where senses engage and are incorporated with one

---

* The space is empty in the sense of some "thing" being there. There are, however, forces at play within these spaces.

another. Further illusions may arise when the expectation of a particular experience does not match our reality. Such is the case with the McGurk effect, whereby visual information can influence our perception of what we hear (McGurk & MacDonald, 1976). The intermingling of visual and auditory information has shed light onto the mechanisms involved in integration. Why is it, for example, that we see lightning before hearing the thunder clap? The answer lies in their relative arrival time. Auditory stimuli are processed faster than visual stimuli, but visual stimuli travel faster. At 10–15 meters distance, these differences are canceled out; this has been termed the *horizon of simultaneity* (Pöppel, 1988). However, we are able to continually match asynchronous stimuli beyond this range. Why is that? The best theory is that we have neural mechanisms that bind visual and auditory stimuli within a relatively large window for multisensory synchronization (Morein-Zamir, Soto-Faraco, & Kingstone, 2003; Spence & Squire, 2003). Sugita and Suzuki (2003) suggested that as distance increases, the window for temporal integration actually accommodates auditory information with the expectancy for visual stimuli to arrive first.

Theoretically, the spectrum of sensory data has no known limits; the experiences are *ad infinitum*. Simply because no known living organism on earth can detect an ultrasound range >160,000 Hz does not mean that it does not exist.

PERCEPTUAL GROUPING

Every man takes the limits of his own field of vision
for the limits of the world.

— ARTHUR SCHOPENHAUER

Our senses *feel* the world, whereas our perceptual faculties render what is meaningfully observed or experienced. The world appears to us as ordered, rather than disjointed. When perceiving objects, we automatically simplify the information around us by organizing and grouping the objects into patterns. This underlying process is not something that we can physically change. As Merleau-Ponty (1945/2014) so aptly put it, "Perception is not a science of the world, nor even an act or a deliberate taking of a stand; it is the background against which all acts stand out and is thus presupposed by them" (p. xxiv).

The traditional laws of categorization were first proposed by Max Wertheimer, including: proximity, similarity, continuity, connectedness, common fate, and closure (Wagemans et al., 2012). These are all fairly self-evident. We non-consciously group objects together when they are close to one another (proximity), when they appear like one another (similarity), when they appear to follow an order like a curve (continuity), when they share visual properties (connectedness), and when they move in the same direction or speed (common fate). In addition, when we perceive an incomplete form, our brains may complete its appearance as an estimation of what is likely there (closure; see Figure 1.1).

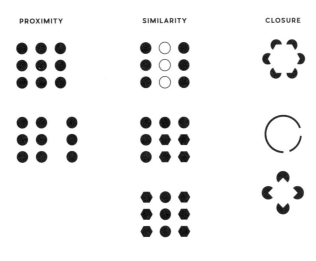

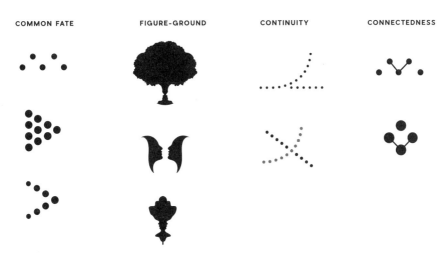

Figure 1.1: Traditional Laws of Categorization *Source:* James Widener

One important perceptual phenomenon is figure-ground organization, whereby we focus on figures that stand out to us, sometimes at the expense of the background. Our processing has evolved in such a way that we can only focus on one perceptual experience at a time; any attempts at seeing both simultaneously result in alternation (see Figure 1.1, Figure-Ground). These are also examples of how two people may see an identical object but describe a different experience.

In life, our perceptual and organizational tendencies can be either troublesome or useful. The extent to which a trait is adaptive, has been passed down from generation to generation. This includes the use of camouflage, enabling them to remain hidden in the background. For humans, failing to notice something in the background can be quite costly. Gestalt Psychology draws parallels from these perceptual findings into human psychological functioning. From this perspective, we exist as dynamic interconnected systems in a semi-structured field. We are both composed of the field and necessary for its emergence. Each element is dependent on the other. As conscious organisms, we sense, perceive and organize experiences through their subjective sensation — or meaning. What we are psychologically conscious of (the figure) is a derivative of a background that extends spatially (actual environment) and temporally (past, present, future) into an incalculable range (Gold & Zahm, 2018).

Evolution's creative expressions of adaptation can be further witnessed in forms of mimicry, including: Mullerian, Batesian (Sherratt, 2008), and aggressive (Jackson & Cross, 2014). Mullerian mimicry is a form of mimicry involving the evolution of truthful appearances to warn predators that they should be avoided. Frogs with yellow stripes warn predators that they should be approached with caution because this appearance has developed in tandem with their poisonous defenses. Similarly, it would be wise for a human to approach groups of armed uniformed soldiers in any territory with caution. Batesian mimicry occurs when a species mimics the appearance of another dangerous species, but in reality it is harmless. Both Mullerian and Batesian mimicry are effective means of protecting oneself from predators. In contrast, via aggressive mimicry, a parasite may mimic a harmless species to enhance its potential to find a host. Thus, although evolution has supported the necessity for perceptual grouping, it has also supported the counteracting of these perceptual biases, generating a spiral that promotes complexity and diversity.

It follows, that sense-perception itself becomes insufficient. For materialists, the evolutionary pressure to adapt may have played a role in the development of higher consciousness. These tendencies extend into everyday human experience, spanning from uniforms to better identify help, to scam artists who swindle money through their exploitation of our general trust and basic tendencies.

SENSORY GATING, INTERPRETIVE LOOPS, AND REFERRED PAIN

The brain is the organ of destiny. It holds within its humming mechanism secrets that will determine the future of the human race.

—WILDER PENFIELD

The limitation of our senses is further amplified by a process known as sensory gating (SG). Our brains have automated processes that filter redundant sensory stimuli to prevent irrelevant information from overwhelming the cortex (Cheng, Chan, Liu, & Hsu, 2016). Researchers have found dysfunctional gating to be associated with schizophrenia (Toyomaki et al., 2015), bipolar disorder (Cheng et al., 2016), and autism (Chien, Hsieh, & Gau, 2019).

When two identical auditory stimuli are sequentially presented close enough in time, for example, the brain will suppress the second stimulus. This phenomenon corresponds to an event-related potential (electrical activity) occurring around 50 ms after the presentation. Researchers call this auditory P50 SG. P50 is considered a preattentional biomarker, whereas others, such as N100, are theorized to be involved with the triggering of attention; P200 may correspond to selective attention (Chien et al., 2019). Multiple areas of the brain have been correlated to sensory gating, suggesting an intricate process; these regions include the thalamus, specifically the pulvinar nuclei (Green, Hernandez, Bookheimer, & Dapretto, 2017), the prefrontal cortex, and the hippocampus (Grunwald et al., 2003).

Information in the brain flows in many different directions, but for the sake of functional utility, let us review two main pathways of information flow: vertically, from subcortical to cortical (bottom-up) or from cortical to subcortical (top-down); and horizontally, from left hemisphere to right hemisphere and vice-versa. Generally, bottom-up processes include sensory-perceptual or emotional data that may bias higher order cognitive processes. The use of experimental methods such as binocular rivalry* or backward masking† have repeatedly demonstrated that emotional stimuli processed below conscious awareness may still trigger the amygdala, superior colliculus, basal ganglia, and pulvinar (Tamietto & Gelder, 2010). This in turn may influence our decisions and actions. Top-down pathways incorporate organismic expectations that may exist below or within awareness. For example: when a person is attending to a specific task, visual stimuli deemed irrelevant may be registered by the visual cortex but subsequently suppressed and even completely removed from sight via frontoparietal regions (Beck et al., 2001). From a conscious perspective, one may be required to inhibit an impulse due to the situation they are in. This relates to increased orbitofrontal activity in connection to the limbic system (N. He, Rolls, Zhao, & Guo, 2019; Kober et al., 2010).

Furthermore, before information reaches awareness, it is involved in several feedback and feedforward loops. To be clear, feedback is reactive, correcting for a problem that has already happened, whereas feedforward is predictive in nature and contingent upon previous knowledge. It thus anticipates problems that may arise and corrects them beforehand. To illustrate how information is further filtered neurally, I will introduce two pathways that information can take. The first, the *perforant* pathway, is involved with learning and memory; it has been studied in detail with rats (Witter et al., 2000). Early psychology students are often taught that the hippocampus is involved in the formation of memory and spatial maps. Specifically, the right hippocampus is related to visual memory and the left is verbally mediated (Papanicolaou et al., 2002). To understand the perforant pathway, however, the hippocampus can be understood more specifically in terms of its substructures.

This hippocampus is composed of the dentate gyrus, the Cornu Ammonis 1 (CA1), CA2, CA3, and the subiculum. *Cornu Ammonis* means the horn of Amon, in reference to the ancient Egyptian deity Amun-Ra, because its structure looks like the horn of Amun-Ra. The following table describes functions associated with these regions alongside other regions of interest:

---

* Presenting different stimuli to each eye, resulting in perceptual alternation.

† Sequential presentation of stimuli, resulting in the latter to mask the former.

TABLE 1.1: The Hippocampus: Areas and Functions

AREA	STUDY	FUNCTION
CA1	Kraus, Robinson, White, Eichenbaum, and Hasselmo (2013)	Time and distance coded by CA1 neurons
	Bartsch, Döhring, Rohr, Jansen, and Deuschl (2011)	Retrieval of episodic autobiographical memory, mental time travel, and autonoetic consciousness
CA2	Caruana, Alexander, and Dudek (2017)	Social memory and recognition (processing)
CA3	Farovik, Dupont, and Eichenbaum, (2009)	Spatial information and shorter (than CA1) memory sequencing for events
Dentate Gyrus (CA4: "Deep polymorphic layer of DG")	Jonas and Lisman (2014)	Preprocessor of incoming information for subsequent processing in CA3
	Blackstad (1956)	Pattern separation: transforming similar input patterns to different output
		Formation of new episodic memories
Subiculum	O'Mara (2005)	Dorsal: processing spatial information, movement, and memory
		Ventral: major regulatory role in inhibition of HPA axis.
Entorhinal Cortex	Schultz, Sommer, and Peters (2015)	Encoding and retrieving of object and spatial features
Perirhinal Cortex	Brown and Eldridge (2008)	Recognition memory, paired associate learning, reward sequence learning

As can be seen in Table 1.1, each hippocampal subfield has distinct functions, and there are a variety of pathways through which information gets filtered within this tiny region of the brain. Information does not pass through these fields once but many times, being processed and reprocessed through loops connected to cortical regions in the brain. Many of these loops exist in a variety of regions. After the brain constructs information to form the perceptual world we experience, it then appears to consult our memory to improve our potential for survival.

A second fascinating theory was proposed by Hawkins and Blakeslee (2004), who described the input and output processes that occur within the six layers of the neocortex. These layers differ by the types of cells that populate them. As a result, they are all connected in distinct ways. In general, sensory data is first processed in the lower layers, 6 and 5, of the neocortex and are then relayed to layers 1 and 2, where perception may arise. Interestingly, information is then sent back down to be reprocessed in layers 3 and 4, where information from layers 1, 2, 5, and 6 is integrated. The meeting of information in layers 3 and 4 may be an area where learned expectational biases influence the bottom-up neutrality of sensory data. Expectations help us anticipate problems and make sense of our environment, which is necessary for survival. However, problems arise in other contexts in which the biases of our expectations negatively influence our objectivity or ability to live in the moment. In such moments, it is important for us to suspend top-down influences in order to perceive the world with more objectivity, through bottom-up processing.

A bodily example of how the interpretation of information can become misguided is in the phenomenon of referred pain. Referred pain occurs when pain in one area of the body is sensed in another. This occurs because there is no direct sensory representation of internal organs in the spine. The spinal cord interacts directly with sympathetic ganglia, which are collections of cells that regulate internal organ functioning. A "convergence of visceral and somatic sensory afferents [occurs] in the spinal cord" (Sengupta, 2009, p. 5), and by the time the data is received by the brain, there is a loss of precision as to the source of the pain, resulting in it being referred elsewhere. Pain in the heart, for example, can be felt in the left shoulder or arm.

SENSATION AND DECISION-MAKING

Color has a significance all its own, and in a realm all its own. Just as music has, color is the music of light.
—FRANK LLOYD WRIGHT

Research continues to demonstrate ways in which biology plays a major role in influencing behavior and decision making. Many scientists would go on to assert that we have no real ability to determine how we act (for a current review, see Haggard, 2008). Libets's (1973, 1999) classic studies on free will show evidence that before we make any decision there is already electrical activity occurring in the brain, not only before a behavior is implemented, but even before we are aware of the desire to act (350 milliseconds). He does suggest, however, that there also exists a 200-ms gap enabling us to *veto* the decision. The study is controversial, and other researchers have argued that the work has many factors and limitations to consider. Although free will is not the focus of this book, I include this finding simply to further the conclusion that non-conscious processes influence our decision making.

Many studies have been conducted using animal models to help us better understand human behavior and functioning. In addiction research, rats have been shown to prefer cocaine over food (Perry, Westenbroek, & Becker, 2013), and some even starve themselves. In fact, rats and pigeons will prefer cocaine to a sexual mate. Lisle and Goldhammer (2003) attribute these behaviors to the organism's tendency to seek pleasure, avoid pain, and conserve energy. From a biological standpoint, the immediate pleasure from cocaine indicates to the biological system that one is achieving one's goals while conserving maximal energy. Technology has gifted us with many advancements, yet like a Trojan horse, some of these gifts may have a negative impact. What feels good to our nervous systems may thus not actually be good for us. Other examples of artificially induced pleasures might include other substances, fast food, and excessive technology use (e.g., gaming, social media, pornography). The other important factor to consider is the intensity of the pleasure received. Overstimulation via artificially induced pleasures can occur, resulting in the blunting of naturally induced pleasure; however, with time and effort, this blunting may likely be partially reversed.

Building on the potential deceptions of our very instinctual drives, many studies have since arisen demonstrating the differing ways that sensory experiences may influence our decisions. Some of these are noted in Table 1.2.

TABLE 1.2: Sensory Influences on Decision Making: Relevant Literature

SENSORY INFLUENCES ON DECISION MAKING	SOURCES
Vision and Behavior	
Color is symbolic and affects mood, cognition, and behavior	Elliot and Maier (2014)
Visual organization positively correlates with feelings of pleasantness and disorganization is negatively correlated with feelings of pleasantness	Langeslag (2018)
Taste and Behavior	
Aspects of the genome related to taste differ in liberals and conservatives	Hatemi et al. (2011)
Taste sensitivity and greater fungiform papilla density are associated with greater conservatism	Ruisch, Anderson, Inbar, and Pizarro (2016)
Sour taste predisposes an individual to risk-taking behavior	Vi and Obrist (2018)
Taste sensitivity is associated with consuming different food types	Puputti, Hoppu, and Sandell (2019)
Touch and Behavior	
Tactile sensory input influences judgment	Ackerman, Nocera, and Bargh (2010)
Physical pain increases likelihood of engaging in guilty pleasures	Bastian, Jetten, and Stewart (2013)
Skin receptors have direct access to emotional responses	Auvray, Myin, and Spence (2010)
Brief touch correlated to increased tips, "signing a petition (Willis & Hamm, 1980), returning lost money (Kleinke, 1977), helping to pick up dropped items (Gueguen & Fischer-Lokou, 2003), volunteering for charity and looking after a dog (Gueguen & Fischer-Lokou, 2002)" (Sin & Koole, 2013, p. 8)	Sin and Koole (2013)

SENSORY INFLUENCES ON DECISION MAKING	SOURCES
Smell and Behavior	
Aspects of genome related to smell differ in liberals and conservatives	Hatemi et al. (2011)
Disgusting smells influence severity of moral judgment	Schnall, Haidt, Clore, and Jordan (2008)
Possibly due to perceived presence of another, body odors increase prosocial behavior and affect moral decisions	Cecchetto et al. (2019)
Odors are associated with emotions and can alter mood	Herz (2005)
Body odor disgust sensitivity is associated with authoritarianism	Liuzza et al. (2018)
Congruent and incongruent odors are related to time perception	Zhou, Feng, Chen, and Zhou (2018)
Sound and Behavior	
Happy music promotes cooperation in decision-making groups	Kniffin, Yan, Wansink, and Schulze (2017)
Irrelevant sounds are associated with reduced cognitive performance	Schlittmeier, Hellbrück, Thaden, and Vorländer (2008)
Sexuality and Misattribution of Arousal	
Adrenaline mimics and promotes attraction	Allen et. al. (1989)
Exposure to attractive female faces in heterosexual men is associated with improved memory	McKinney (2011)
Exposure to attractive women in heterosexual men is associated with temporal discounting	Baker, Sloan, Hall, Leo, and Maner (2015)
In women, romantic desire (RD) is associated with the tendency to help others publicly but not privately (not noticed by others). In men, RD relates to spending more resources on luxuries and less on necessities.	Wilson and Daly (2004) Griskevicius et al. (2007)
Sexual arousal is related to reductions in executive function, though not in suppression group	Suchy et al. (2019)
Sexual arousal in gay and bisexual men is related to increases in risky sexual decision making, although unrelated to cognition	Rendina, Miller, Dash, Feldstein, and Parsons (2018)

SENSORY INFLUENCES ON DECISION MAKING	SOURCES
Hunger	
Hunger is associated with improved decision making in times of uncertainty	de Ridder, Kroese, Adriaanse, and Evers (2014)
Hunger is associated with decreased risk taking in economic decisions (controversial)	Levy, Thavikulwat, and Glimcher (2013)
Hunger helps mediate the effects of sexual arousal and risky financial decision making	Otterbring and Sela (2020)

These are important findings that shed light on the fact that we use lower level physiological processing when making judgments, much of the time out of awareness. We may believe we are making decisions based solely on higher order thinking, but this is simply untrue. It is especially important to be aware of this fact in ambiguous situations when we simply cannot consider all of the facts.

Bearing in mind that sensory experiences are *first to the scene*, it is not too surprising that they should play a role in influencing our thoughts and behaviors. From the perspective of survival, there is likely a great deal of benefit in becoming very alert if you are in the wild and you can see and smell freshly rotting flesh. However, this becomes more confounded when you are in safe environments requiring complex decision making that may influence many others in the process. Of course, it would be silly to expect anyone to dissect all their experiences sequentially every moment in search of potential biases. However, it may be beneficial to spend time shifting your awareness to this domain and narrow down the search to significant factors. Moreover, once biases become learned, their awareness may become embedded in neural structures that correspond to intuitive decision making.

CLINICAL APPLICATION

Be aware of your sensations and surroundings:

What experiential state are you in? What about your client? Might either of your states of arousal be influencing your mental processes and behaviors (MBs)?

Check in with all of your senses. Is there anything you find disagreeable around you (e.g., a foul smell, a bad taste in your mouth, an uncomfortable seat)?

Are you in any direct physical discomfort? If so, how much might this discomfort be affecting your MBs (e.g., having back pain and feeling short-fused)?

GENE–ENVIRONMENT INTERACTIONS

At the bottom every man knows well enough that he is a unique being, only once on this earth; and by no extraordinary chance will such a marvelously picturesque piece of diversity in unity as he is, ever be put together a second time.

—Friedrich Nietzsche

At a deeper level exist gene–environment interactions. To begin with, we are influenced by intergenerational transmission of information beyond our own parents at a genetic level. One of the most fascinating discoveries is that of epigenetics, the study of how experience modifies gene functioning. Our diet, lifestyle, and major health issues contribute to the turning on and off of specific genes, altering our phenotype, or gene expression. The two main ways epigenetics manifest are through DNA methylation and histone modification (Masterpasqua, 2009). In fact, the process of epigenetics has been found to extend beyond our own lifetimes and be inherited by future generations. Challenging conditions may elicit epigenesis if they persist for two generations or more (Lacey, 1998). In humans, studies on famine indicated that an induced defense was carried onto the next generation, causing a restriction of physical growth as a response to food shortage (Harper, 2005). Other traits, such as inhibitive capacity in temperament, have been found to be partially a result of epigenetic inheritance (Fox & Henderson, 2000). Thus, in congruence with evolutionary theory, epigenesis tends to have adaptive value. Epigenetics opens up a dialogue about how our decisions and experiences in our lifetime may affect ourselves and future generations and how our current generation has been affected by our ancestors. It is as if there are potential gene sequences *pending* to be actualized, should our lifestyles meet the right internal and external conditions. The past very much affects the present, and so too do our present experiences directly affect the future.

During early development, genes guide the migration of neurons. At one end of the spectrum there are genetic anomalies, some of which can lead to neurodevelopmental problems. Disorders such as Fragile X syndrome, Turner syndrome, and Klinefelter syndrome are examples of chromosomal abnormalities. More multifactorial cases arise when we consider degenerative brain disorders such as early onset Alzheimer's disease, whose risk increases to 60% when an individual has multiple family members afflicted with the same disease (Bekris, Yu, Bird, & Tsuang, 2010). Outside those severe cases, do genes influence our behavior? An entire field of science, behavioral genetics, is dedicated to the exploration of these problems. Plomin, Defries, Knopik, and Neiderhiser (2016) reviewed ten replicated findings from this field and concluded that:

1. All psychological traits show significant and substantial genetic influence.

2. No traits are 100% heritable.

3. Heritability is caused by many genes of small effect.

4. Phenotypic correlations between psychological traits show significant and substantial genetic mediation.

5. The heritability of intelligence increases throughout development.

6. Age-to-age stability is mainly due to genetics.

7. Most measures of the environment show significant genetic influence.

8. Most associations between environmental measures and psychological traits are significantly mediated genetically.

9. Most environmental effects are not shared by children growing up in the same family.

10. Most common disorders are at the genetic extreme of the spectrum of normal trait variation (pp. 3–10).

When we begin examining the extent of genetic contributions to daily life, we find that they are actively interacting with the environment to varying degrees. We are filled with propensities, many of which are biological in nature.

CLINICAL APPLICATION

Personal

- Construct a family tree that includes medical and psychological history.
- Have genetic testing done if you are worried about inheriting genes that place you at risk for a particular disease or disorder.

Therapist

- Ask clients about ancestral history. Explore familial history for potential epigenetic inheritance (e.g., survivors of extreme circumstances; such as prisoners of war, famine, holocaust).
- Be sure to gather personal and family psychiatric, psychological, and medical history.
- If risks are found, look into factors that may protect you from the expression of diseases. Nothing is guaranteed, but there may be methods to mitigate risk factors.

SPLIT-BRAINS STUDIES

The brain has millions of local processors making important decisions . . . you are certainly not the boss of the brain. Have you ever succeeded in telling your brain to shut up already and go to sleep?
—MICHAEL GAZZANIGA

Neuropsychologist Roger Sperry won the Nobel Prize for his studies on *split-brain* patients in the 1960s. As is commonly recognized, the brain is divided into two hemispheres. For patients with a condition known as intractable epi-lepsy, electrical storms occur in the brain that are medication resistant and unmanageable. In these cases, the procedure for relieving these symptoms had been to split the corpus callosum, or the bands of nerve fibers that connect the two hemispheres and act as a highway of information flow from one hemi-sphere to the other. One of the fears is the phenomenon of *kindling*, whereby seizure activity may begin to spread to neighboring regions.

In one study, Gazzaniga, Bogen, and Sperry (1962, 1965) flashed visual stimuli for 1/10 of a second to either the right or left visual field of split-brain subjects. The timing was done strategically so as to prevent the projection from being perceived in the other eye field due to natural eye scanning. Sub-jects were quite confident that their experience of everyday life was ordinary. When the stimulus was shown to the right visual field (processed by the left hemisphere), subjects were able to report seeing the stimulus and point to the spot where it was shown. When the stimulus was shown to the left visual field (processed by the right hemisphere), the subjects reported not seeing any fig-ure, but were able to point to where the visual stimulus was shown (the latter finding was not replicated in a second study with more stringent controls). This phenomenon occurs due to the disconnection between the right hemisphere, which relates to visual functions, and the left hemisphere, which relates to language-based functions in the majority of individuals. Importantly, it has been found that although the majority of right-handed individuals have lan-guage lateralized to the left hemisphere, language may be lateralized to either hemisphere, or both. One study (Khedr, Hamed, Said, & Basahi, 2002) found that 87.5% of right-handed individuals have left hemisphere dominance, 8.2% have bilateral cerebral representation, and 4.2% have right hemisphere lan-guage dominance. On the other hand, pun intended, 70% of left-handers have language represented in the left hemisphere, 15% of left-handers have language represented in the right hemisphere (anomalous representation), and 15% of left-handers have language represented in both hemispheres. Microprocessing of information thus occurs in the left and right hemispheres of the brain, con-nected via the corpus callosum, producing related yet distinct views based on their specialized operations.

These findings suggest that split-brain clients have two autonomous percep-tual accounts working simultaneously. From this finding emerged the concept of the left-hemisphere interpreter (Gazzaniga, 2005), referring to the tendency for the left brain to provide explanations for events, even in the absence of any real explanation.

In modern times, doctors take utmost caution before recommending surgical procedures for clients with intractable epilepsy. Given the variations of language lateralization, clients may undergo a neuropsychological evaluation invented by Japanese physician Juhn Wada called Wada testing (Sever, Vivas, Vale, & Schoenberg, 2018). In efforts to help determine the risks involved with a procedure, clients undergo temporary anesthetization of half of their brain through the injection of sodium amobarbital in their left or right internal carotid artery. As the left (or right) hemisphere sleeps, clients are given the Wada test to determine where language is lateralized and the extent to which memory is affected.

Split-brain studies demonstrate that perception involves multiple processes working in tandem to produce a coherent, unified field. We now know that the left and right hemisphere overall specialize in construing the world differently. As explained by Iaian McGilchrist (2009), the right hemisphere tends to approach the world pre-reflectively, engaging with it as a whole, interdependent process of which we are an intimate part. It is exploratory, open to possibilities, and ever on the lookout for predators. The left hemisphere represents the world as categories, divisions, and fragments, allowing us to generate predictions. It seeks certainty and is ever on the lookout for prey. Despite these seemingly disparate qualities, these systems remain integrated, resulting in what we experience as a single, unified whole. Receiving and projecting information back to a wide range of cortical real estate, Crick and Koch (2005) believe this unification occurs in an area of the brain called the *claustrum,* a neural structure nested beneath the cortex neighboring the insula.

In reaction to the overly *left-hemispheric*–based focus of society, many authors have written on the importance of recognizing right hemispheric nonconscious signals (Marks-Tarlow, 2012; McGilchrist, 2009; Schore, 2019). Right-brain approaches (Schore, 2019) align themselves with affective neuroscience, attachment, and intuition, characterized by "primary sensory, emotional, and other body-based experience as the foundation for organizing immediate response and higher-order perception" (Marks-Tarlow, 2012, p. 12). Intuition arises in response to an internal query, or is evoked through a particular circumstance. It may present as visceral reactions, hunches, or immediate internal facts that emerge without prior deliberation (Marks-Tarlow, 2012).

This is in contrast to impulses that arise from our basic drives, such as hunger and lust. They are continuous, and they reemerge within a short amount of time after a need has been met. In decision-making, Bechara, Damasio, and Damasio (2000) posited that the ventral medial prefrontal cortex may be "a repository of dispositionally recorded linkages between factual knowledge and bioregulatory states" (p. 296). This proposal led to the *somatic marker hypothesis*, which describes our decision making as a "process that is influenced by marker signals that arise in bioregulatory processes" (p. 295). Indeed, Schore's (2019) extensive research repeatedly emphasizes the importance of right-brain to right-brain synchrony within the intersubjective field. This synchrony, typically below awareness, expresses itself through rapport and rapid somatic-affective–based communications underlying attachment-based transactions.

APPLICATIONS: SOMA AND AFFECT

Feeling without symbolization is blind;
symbolization without feeling is empty.

—Eugene Gendlin

There currently exist several approaches specialized in intervening at an affective[*] and physiological[†] level. In addition to sensory-motor processes, these approaches owe much to interoception, our ability to sense a vast array of inner bodily signals ranging from an increased heart rate to the discomfort felt in an intense or awkward social situation. Our interoceptive system monitors our homeostatic balance, and any potential disruptions to it. Its core anatomical node relates to the insula within the parietal lobes (Duquette, 2017).

One philosopher and therapist whose thinking was much ahead of his time was Eugene Gendlin (1962/1997), who noted long ago the importance of *felt experience*. He posited that in any meaning that emerges there is a symbol in relation to an object and our *experience* of the meaning. Gendlin offers a simple exercise to notice this: ask yourself what the definition is of any symbol or word, you will find that there is a sense of knowing what it is before any

---

[*] Psychoanalysis, Psychodynamic, Emotion Focused Therapy, etc.

[†] Gestalt Therapy, Focusing, The Hakomi Method, Somatic Experiencing, Sensorimotor, EMDR, Limbic System Therapy, etc.

internal articulation of it. Language is not necessary for knowing. Many times, it is even too difficult to verbally express what an experience was like, and others where language simply does not "do justice" to the experience felt. For the majority of people, language expression and comprehension are lateralized to the left hemisphere, whereas their homologous functions in the right-hemisphere are emotion, prosody, context, and meaning. Conventional therapeutic approaches stress left-hemisphere expression, whereas Gendlin's method emphasizes right-hemisphere expression.

"The living body," Gendlin (1962/1997) states ". . . includes 'unfinished' or 'potential' patterns for certain preordered interactions with objects in the environment" (p. 25). What we articulate is but a fraction of that which exists within the preconceptual world. He offers *focusing* (Gendlin, 1996) as a method to explicate these felt experiences. Broadly, "it begins with the body and occurs in the zone between the conscious and unconscious . . . a bodily sense of any topic can be invited to come in that zone, and one can enter into such a sense" (p. 1). A felt sense is not simply attending the sense of pain, rather it is a "physical sense of something, of meaning, of implicit intricacy. It is a sense of a whole situation or problem or perhaps a point one wants to convey. It is not just a bodily sense, but rather a bodily sense of . . ." (p. 63). Unlike a felt emotion, it has a distinct quality shared by all. It is thus an "edge of experience" on which one focuses (see Gendlin, 1996, for more information). As an example: when an individual is upset with their significant other, and is unable to express their emotions, it is commonly said that there is a "tension in the room." Qualities used to describe this tension might be a "thickness," "heaviness," or a "restlessness." This perceived tension can be a target of intervention for focusing.

Focusing is likely recruiting information from the anterior insular cortex, which has been described as a zone where information from frontal, limbic, and sensory regions converge, integrating one's homeostatic state with cognitive, social, and emotional information (Harrison et al., 2010). Focusing points toward a potential reservoir of concrete bodily experiences that have yet to be articulated, or brought to full maturity.

There is more information within us than we immediately give voice to, and even some of what might be known nonverbally, has not yet been thought of. A similar, yet distinct concept was proposed by Bollas (1987) in a psychoanalytic context. He termed this the *unthought known*. Although the approach is vastly different, he also spoke of preverbal states "awaiting that day when they can be understood and then either transformed into symbolic derivatives or forgotten" (p. 5). The possibility for nonverbal knowns that have yet to be thought of, likely also occur at the border of unconscious and conscious, that continually drive certain behaviors until they have been symbolized through thought.

The necessity for clinicians to look beyond psychological processing, to assist clients with the ingestion, digestion, metabolization, and/or discharging of energy and information has led to novel approaches. Conceptually, there has been much development in the overall recognition that certain somatic experiences must undergo assisted metabolic processes within the nervous system. We know, for instance, that traumatic memories are salient due to their somatic and affective-based qualities. They are consolidated differently, and current interventions on trauma have been focusing on processing symptoms in their respective domains of nervous system absorption (Levine, 1997; Van der Kolk, 2014).

This line of thought may be bridged to the work of Wilfred Bion, a psychoanalyst (1965/1984) whose life, creativity, and thought led him to develop a grid (with a vertical and horizontal axis) tracking different stages of thought formation in clinician and client and how they may be engaging them (Bion, 1963/2018). From the clinician's viewpoint, this grid is useful in localizing the development of maturity level of a client's experience in relation to a particular problem. The vertical axis begins with two theoretical elements he labeled as *beta* (β) and *alpha* (α). β elements "represent the matrix from which thoughts can be supposed to arise" (Bion, 1963/2018, p. 22). They are sense impressions in the form of emotionally and somatically based signals where thoughts and things are indistinguishable. They may be projected or expressed through nonconscious action (Vermote, 2019). These may relate to post-traumatic experiences whereby somatic-affective expressions correspond to limbic activity and autonomic arousal.

The "alpha-function" transforms β into α elements, which are "products of work done on the sensa believed to relate to such realities" (Bion, 1963/2018, p.22). They can be understood as a proto-thought, feeling, or image. In Bion's model, the evolution of thought is theorized to advance from alpha elements to dream thought/dreams/myth. Bion believed that we are always dreaming, and that it is a prerequisite for thinking (Grotstein, 2007). This form of thinking then progresses into preconception, conception, scientific deduction, and algebraic calculus. Thus, there is a progression from "raw" data to higher levels of abstraction and integration. This echoes Schore's (2003a) suggestion to direct "therapeutic technique toward the elevation of emotions from primitive presymbolic sensorimotor level of experience to a mature symbolic representational level, and a creation of self-reflective position that can appraise the significance and meanings of these affects" (p. 280). Refer to Appendix A to find descriptions, relevant citations, and possible neural correlates that correspond to Bion's vertical axis.

The following is a traditional example of how this may be of use in practice. Unconscious defenses that minimize or avoid intolerable affective states may be projected onto the clinician. This projected affect may induce a select internal state within the clinician, resulting in a temporary identification with said state (*projective identification**). Bion uniquely contributed the view that this a form of communication, not simply defense. The clinician must first become aware of this occurrence, and to subsequently help *contain* affective information that the client cannot bear or think themselves. As therapy progresses, the client gradually gains the tolerance necessary to contain and symbolize these contents.

In the example of trauma, a clinician may first notice the inability of an individual to share their traumatic memories without the expression of uncomfortable somatic experiences. This may be understood as an inability to contain β elements. This very acknowledgment guides the clinician toward the use of a somatic-based intervention to assist with discharging and subsequent metabolization. Once limbic-autonomic activity has been regulated, one may begin processing said experiences at a symbolic level, increasing discernment and decreasing excitotoxic affect.

Yet another novel right-brained intervention that may be stimulating activity in Bion's alpha function is focusing, especially in situations whereby the feelings for a situation may be less than clear. This is an active developmental

---

* Schore (2003a) considers projective identification a right brain defense, along with dissociation. Experiencing these intense affective states runs the risk of disorganizing the system. This is one of the reasons why individuals come to therapy. "It requires two minds to think a person's most disturbing thoughts" (Ogden, 2008, p.1).

framework that seeks to promote the maturation of intrinsic processes. In each moment, the clinician tracks affective shifts indicative of states that are developmentally arrested. For Bion the grid is inherently neutral, one's thoughts may evolve or devolve. The grid is a way "Bion investigates the process through which truth evolves and the process through which truth is blocked" (Symington & Symington, 1996, p. 3). The clinician may ask themselves: (1) Where in the developmental process is my client's experience in relation to the presenting problem? (2) What can I do to facilitate this process toward maturity? This might be followed by the questions: What needs to be discharged, metabolized and/or integrated? What method would best address these needs? (3) Are they (or am I) doing anything that might be degenerating development?

One line of localizing early stages of thought formation may be through degenerative brain diseases and traumatic brain injuries (TBI). In particular, TBI victims typically have their frontal-temporal lobes compromised, which highlights the role of these regions when considering the development of mature thought and behavior. For example: many patients I have seen with frontal lobe lesions present as impulsive and without filter. Freud's ego and reality principle would be contingent upon frontal lobes for inhibitive actions. Severe TBI victims in the state of post-traumatic amnesia (PTA) suffer from a discontinuity of memory characterized as anterograde[*] and retrograde[†] amnesia. From my clinical experience, thoughts and actions are characterized by incoherence. Truth statements are inconsistent, attention is easily derailed, and information is not assimilated appropriately. It seems that state of PTA may be a window into a primordial stage of thought formation, and Bion's alpha function, which may very well correlate to areas of the frontal and temporal lobe. Patients in PTA have a defective alpha function, and present as a stream of beta and alpha elements (perhaps another window into *balpha elements;* Ferro, 2005) that have yet to be metabolized into linear coherence suitable for consciousness.

Nonverbal experience such as soma and affect predate verbal expression. Somatic and affective experiences may elicit complex, coordinated, goal-oriented motoric movements. Many times, this may be beneath consciousness. Marion Goodman (1982) noted that "body movements . . . can be understood

---

[*] Inability to create new memories.

[†] Inability to remember old memories.

as a waking dream. In its spontaneous movements the body is like an infant crying out to be heard, understood, responded to" (p. 79). There have been multiple cases in my clinical practice in which giving voice to affected areas of the body has resulted in reductions of pain or as a cue for a particular memory. As a culture so focused on verbal communication, we have lost touch with information housed within these primordial domains. These domains have been evolving long before the development of any formal language. In fact, they continue to evolve, alongside newer mammalian circuits.

As therapists we may help individuals reestablish a stronger line of communication, with right hemispheric biased circuits, emphasizing experiences of the world as a process rather than an entity to be dissected, a living interconnected whole rather than mechanical, the broader picture over details, the personal over the impersonal, cooperation over exploitation, flexibility over rigidity and the need for certainty, willpower and self-motivation over greed and the desire to manipulate, and meaning over meaninglessness (McGilchrist, 2009). These descriptions match well with an anecdote from Jill Bolte Taylor (2016), a neuroanatomist who suffered from a stroke in her left hemisphere:

> As the language centers in my left hemisphere grew increasingly silent and I became detached from the memories of my life, I was comforted by an expanding sense of grace. In this void of higher cognition and details pertaining to my normal life, my consciousness soared into an all-knowingness, a "being at one" with the universe. . . . I found it odd that I was aware that I could no longer clearly discern the physical boundaries of where I began and where I ended. I sensed the composition of my being as that of a fluid rather than that of a solid. I no longer perceived myself as a whole object separate from everything. Instead, I now blended in with the space and flow around me. (pp. 41–42)

This dimension of human experience is of grave importance and its lack of emphasis in culture is concerning. I have encountered many clinical cases with high functioning individuals whose logic has resolved many practical concerns, yet they continue to feel as if something remains unresolved. Sometimes, the problem is rooted outside of logic's jurisdiction. This discomfort is frequently described as feeling "stuck," "uneasy," or "heavy." Unable to think beyond logic, there remains nonverbal experiences waiting to be sensed, *and then* processed through bodily experiencing or through articulation.

THE EMERGENT MIND

O, what a world of unseen visions and heard
silences, this insubstantial country of the mind! . . .
A secret theater of speechless monologue and
prevenient counsel, an invisible mansion of all
moods, musings, and mysteries, an infinite resort
of disappointments and discoveries . . . where each
of us reigns reclusively alone, questioning what we
will, commanding what we can . . . where we may
study . . . what we have done and yet may do. An
introcosm that is more myself than anything I can
find in a mirror . . . what is it? And where did it
come from? And why?

—JULIAN JAYNES

From a neuropsychological perspective, the mind emerges from complex systems in the brain in relation to the environment in which it is immersed (Beaumont, 2008). It is, however, more complex than we had previously thought. It is important to be aware that the notion of the brain as the sole contributor to psychological functioning is now outdated. In a review of the literature, Carabotti, Scirocco, Maselli, and Severi (2015) found ample support for the existence of a reciprocal relationship between our gut and brain, now called the *gut-brain axis*. The microbiota in our gut have been found to be intimately related to symptoms of autism, anxiety, and depression. Our gut microbiome is made up of over 1,000 different bacterial species, cumulatively containing over 3 million genes. Interestingly, it may even relate to our personalities. For example, Kim and colleagues (2018), found that higher levels of gammaproteobacteria have been correlated to high neuroticism, whereas higher levels of proteobacteria and lower levels of lachnospiraceae have been correlated to low conscientiousness. Another study found that sociability correlated to higher gut flora diversity, and anxiety and stress correlated to reduced gut flora diversity (Johnson, 2020). In fact, greater than 90% of serotonin receptors are synthesized in the gut's auxiliary nervous system, known as the *enteric nervous system* (Yano et al., 2015). Only two hours of exposure to a social stressor has been shown to alter the representative profile of core microbiota phyla (Galley et al., 2014).

Beyond the gut-brain, we have also been finding that cardiovascular difficulties are highly associated with deficits in attention, learning, memory, psy-
chomotor speed (Leto & Feola, 2014), and especially executive functioning
(Stenfors, Hanson, Theorell, & Osika, 2016). It may further result in the production of inflammatory cytokines and depressed mood (Leto & Feola, 2014),
which is logical given that our heart pumps blood into arteries that provide our
brain with the necessary oxygenation and nutrients to continue its functions.
The list goes on to include different organs in the body, each impacting the
neuropsychological functioning in discrete ways. In truth, the whole body may
be best understood as an interconnected web of differentiated systems, with
the mind an emergent phenomenon resulting from interactions from relationships within and between the individual and their environment.

In interpersonal neurobiology, the mind is further conceptualized as a
complex system that emerges from the brain, body, and relationships (Siegel,
1999). This is somewhat echoed in neurophenomenology, a scientific approach
termed by Laughlin (1990) and championed by Varela et al. (1996, 2016). In
this framework, cognition is *embodied*, meaning it is shaped not just by the
brain but by many features of our entire organism, further defined by enaction.
This means that "the living body is self-organizing" (p. xxxviii) and cognition
is also dependent on the interplay between the organism and its environment.
From this perspective, the mind cannot be understood by simply examining
the brain; rather, the mind must include the *entire organism* (e.g., enteric nervous system, motor systems), the *environment* in which it is situated, and the
experiences that arise as a result. "The lived body, the lived mind and the lived
environment are all thus part of the same process, the process by which one
enacts one's world (. . . brings forth a world)" (p. xxxviii).

As a complex system, the mind is considered *nonlinear,* in that a small input
can lead to vast changes. For example, we know from Jean Piaget's (Piaget &
Cook, 1952) work that when we learn new information, sometimes we need to
alter our existing belief systems to accommodate it. The system is *open* because
it is influenced by its surroundings; *chaos-capable*, as is evident in unpredictabil-
ity; and *self-organizing,* meaning it can change that from which it arises, formally known as recursion. Self-organization is seen in the ability to harness our
awareness to alter our mental states, brain, and behaviors. Further encapsulat-
ing the extent of the psychological fabric, one must consider that the emergence
engages with not only mental representations of the immediate external world,

but also how they interact with the underlying inherited neural processes that evolved through time. The process of mind, being an emergent gestalt, is highly influenced by—but cannot be reduced to—neural processing.

All of these approaches stress that reductionism is outdated. If we are to have an accurate depiction of human functioning, we must consider a variety of perspectives. One domain that has been overlooked is the importance of human experience as it is captured in phenomenology. Imagine if an alien race with an interest in humans decided to examine multiple brains, how much would they learn about what it would be like to be a human? Phenomenology began as a philosophical method by Edmund Husserl (1900/1999), to investigate the world that we perceive from a first person rather than third person perspective. This greatly enhances an investigation's proximity toward reality by adding our actual human experience to the equation. In his view, everyday experience is described as a *life-world,* or a *pregiven* experience, an immediate perception intertwined with sociocultural narratives and history. It is simultaneously a ground for validation and an indefinite horizon for exploration (Moran, 2015). Husserl (1900/1999) states that in every experience there is "a perception of something, recalling of something, thinking of something, hoping for something, fearing something, striving for something, deciding on something;" further elaborating that "the basic character of being as consciousness, as consciousness of something, is *intentionality*" (p. 323). In this sense, within experience exists an *infinite dialogue* between one's innumerable sets of intentions and its horizon. In his words, we exist in "a world that pulsates according to our life's interests" (Husserl, 1954: 500). In order to access the phenomenological field, Husserl (1900/1999) developed a method of *phenomenological reduction*: "1) . . . the methodical and rigorously consistent *epoché* of every objective positing in the psychic sphere, both of the individual phenomenon and of the whole psychic field in general; and 2) in methodically practiced seizing and describing of the multiple 'appearances' as appearances of their objective units and these units as units of component meanings accruing to them each time in their appearances" (p. 325). In summarizing *epoché,* Van Deurzen (2010) suggested *bracketing* presuppositions, describing rather than explaining the observed, unbiasing aspects, contextualizing them (horizontalization), and verifying all observations.

There are currently two major shifts rippling out from humanity in this technological era: the importance of human experience and social-affective neuroscience, both of which are related to a right-hemispheric account of the world. These are likely connected, and a necessary compensatory shift in reaction to the mechanical, isolated, impersonal, and productivity-based focus in today's society. Phenomenology as a disciplined and structured research method has been active (for concise summary, see Neubauer, Witkop, Varpio, 2019), albeit, a bit of a neglected child. We have become so enamored with third person objective findings, that we have forgotten one of the major reasons these findings are important to us—to enhance our present-day experience.

From eastern traditions, mindfulness-based practices have become increasingly popular in their relation to mental health. Inherent to these practices is the emphasis of developing increased objectivity and equanimity. This clearly has implications for improving research as well and has been adopted in Varela's (1996) framework of neurophenomenology, which includes mindfulness, introspection, and phenomenological methods with neuroscientific findings; an attempt to combine first, second, and third person perspectives of experience.

THE COGNITIVE RESERVE HYPOTHESIS

The events of inner experience, as emergent
properties of brain processes, become themselves
explanatory causal constructs in their own right,
interacting at their own level with their own laws
and dynamics. The whole world of inner experience
(the world of the humanities) long rejected by
20th century scientific materialism, thus becomes
recognized and included within the domain of
science.

—ROGER WOLCOTT SPERRY

In 1991, David Snowdon began a longitudinal study of aging, following 678 Roman Catholic nuns, all of whom were members of the School Sisters of Notre Dame congregation. The participants' ages ranged from 75–102 years, with the oldest member reaching 107 years of age by 2002. The study used three primary sources of information: (1) convent archives on their history; (2) annual examinations to document changes in cognition and physiology; and (3) postmortem studies on the nuns' brains, since they all agreed to donate their brains at death. The postmortem studies showed brains diagnostically indicative of Alzheimer's disease, a degenerative brain disorder characterized by the deposition of amyloid plaques and neuro-fibrillary tangles, accompanied by a loss of memory and other cognitive functions.

However, for some reason, some nuns who exhibited the classic biological signs of Alzheimer's remained functioning within normal limits, showing no outward indication of the disorder. A substantial proportion of participants in the mild to moderate stages of Alzheimer's disease pathology showed no symp-toms of memory impairment. Even 8% of participants with the most severe symptoms of Alzheimer's disease pathology failed to show any symptoms of memory impairments.

In "Lessons from the Nun Study," Snowdon (1997) reported:

> Sister Mary, the gold standard for the Nun Study, was a remarkable woman who had high cognitive test scores before her death at 101 years of age. What is more remarkable is that she maintained this high status despite having abun-dant neurofibrillary tangles and senile plaques, the classic lesions of Alzhei-mer's disease. (p. 150)

How is this possible? The leading theory is the cognitive reserve hypothe-sis (CRH), which speaks to the mind's endurance beyond neurologic injury. The finding was that education and enriched experience can increase *reserve* and protect one against the expression of symptoms following brain disease or injury. Higher cognitive reserve does not prevent neurologic insults, but it can modify the functional and clinical expression of such conditions. Research supports the notion that cognitive reserve is acquired through quality of education, IQ, literacy, occupational attainment, complexity of leisure activities, healthy lifestyle, integrity of social networks, learning his-tory (Scarmeas & Stern, 2013; Wu et al., 2016), and conscientiousness in particular responsibility (Sutin, Stephan, & Terracciano, 2018). All of these factors may promote flexible strategy usage, an ability thought to be captured by executive function tasks. Many subjects with high cognitive reserve also demonstrate greater neural efficiency, greater neural capacity, and the ability to compensate for affected functions via the recruitment of additional brain regions. Thus, high cognitive reserve has a tendency to be accompanied by the presence of more efficient synaptic networks or pre-existing cognitive abilities. Accompanying the CRH is the brain reserve hypothesis. This passive model theorizes that neuronal count and brain size (structure versus function) protect one from the expression of symptoms; however, this has not been a consistent finding.

This leads to the question, does the mind extend beyond the brain? In the *DSM-5* there is a specific category of disorders characterized by physical distress with either no medical etiology or symptoms that are far beyond what would be expected from findings (American Psychiatric Association, 2013). To what extent? From psychologically induced visual blindness to losing control of an arm due to psychogenic nonepileptic seizures, psychophysiological expressions are wide-ranging and very real. Naturally, a clinician would be suspicious that the client must be exaggerating or lying. One of the criteria for psychosomatic disorders, however, is that the individual must not be exaggerating or lying or have any potential reason to do so. With the polygraph in decline, forensic psychology and neuropsychology have since developed many tools with high sensitivity and specificity in detecting individuals who may be feigning symptoms for some alternative benefit (Walczyk, Sewell, & DiBenedetto, 2018). These tools have been used successfully in many legal cases. Is it possible that the emergent mind extends beyond the mere addition of physical processes? Science does not yet have an explanation, but what we do know is that psychological experience may certainly affect physiological functions. Beyond the mind influencing the brain-body without leaving traces commensurate with expected symptoms, there exist mental disorders that may create widespread dysregulation of brain systems, such as post-traumatic stress disorder (PTSD; Chan, 2016). PTSD is an example of how a psychosocial experience can completely alter physiological processes. If our bodies can be affected to such an extent, to what degree might we be able to influence it *positively*?

CONSCIOUSNESS

Suddenly, my consciousness was lighted up from
within and I saw in a vivid way how the whole
universe was made up of particles of material which,
no matter how dull and lifeless they might seem,
were nevertheless filled with this intense and vital
beauty.

—ALDOUS HUXLEY

In medical circles, consciousness is mostly used to describe a person's degree of responsivity and alertness. For example, the consciousness of victims of vehicular collisions is assessed using a point system called the Glasgow Coma Scale. Subtleties as basic as the ability to open the eyes in response to speech; the orientation to time, place, and person; and the victim's motor responses are examined. The victim is then given a score that helps classify the severity of their injury. In these circumstances, basic arousal, alertness, and coordination directly relate to cerebellar, basal ganglia, temporal, and brainstem functions (Lezak, Howieson, Bigler, & Tranel, 2012). In its most complex form, consciousness is "a process that involves at least three aspects: a subjective felt sense, a knowing and a known" (Siegel, 2012, p. 51). I am also partial to Nagel's (1974) emphasis that "there is something it is *like* to be that organism" (p. 436).

Many theories have been developed to account for higher states of consciousness, what I am referring to as awareness. Crick and Koch (1998) hypothesized that conscious experience results from synchronized neuronal firing generating 40 Hz oscillations. In support of this notion, Lachaux and colleagues (2000) found that gamma oscillations are emitted in the recognition of ambiguous patterns. Gerald Edelman (2003), a biologist and Nobel Prize winner, adopted a Darwinian approach to explain consciousness. Edelman's approach is Darwinian in the sense that it promotes consciousness as arising in humans as a result of higher order natural selection. Put simply, he asserted that the development of consciousness was unintended, but that evolution promoted the selection of neural systems that coincidentally gave rise to consciousness. In his view, the systems supported are necessary for the brain to process vast amounts of sensory-motor information in parallel. These systems integrated further with processes such as memory, learning, and prospection, providing an adaptive survival advantage. The morphology of the brain, with its 100 billion neurons and over 100 trillion connections, need not localize consciousness outside of biology. Edelman espoused the notion of *reentrant signaling*, "an ongoing process of recursive signaling among neuronal groups taking place across massively parallel reciprocal fibers that link mapped regions" (p. 5521). In other words, neuronal groups are mapping out the world simultaneously, and there are many that recategorize maps of the world; these maps are layered until the eventual emergence of coherent, stable, and continuous experiences. Eventually, they reach the stage of consciousness. In Edelman's view, the thalamocortical system is of greatest importance in regulating dynamic interactions among distributed groups of neurons. Many other models have been proposed in order to clarify levels of consciousness and their biological substrates (Brown, 1976; Damasio, 1999; Farthing, 1992; Neisser, 1997; Newen & Vogeley, 2004; see also the global workspace theory, proposed by Smallwood, Brown, Baird, & Schooler, 2012). Currently, Tononi (2012, a student of Edelman) and his colleagues (Oizumi, Albantakin, & Tononi, 2014; Tononi, Boly, Massimini, & Koch, 2016) have been working on *integrated information theory*, which bases its premise on integrated information being the foundation for yielding consciousness and seeks to mathematically quantify the effects of consciousness.

Tononi views consciousness as a conceptual mathematical structure, emerging from integrated information, and the collapse of an infinite series of possibilities. The structure is defined by quales, shapes that determine qualia space or particular subjective experiences. The mathematical symbol representing consciousness, a whole that is greater than the sum of its parts, is what they call Phi. They begin with five core axioms from a phenomenological viewpoint, which is summarized as: ". . . every experience exists intrinsically and is structured, specific, unitary, and definite (Tononi, Boly, Massimini, & Koch, 2016, p. 1).

Panksepp (1998) and Solms (2017) assert that the beginnings of consciousness is highly associated with the extended reticulothalamic activating system (ERTAS), which is a very deep subcortical structure in the brain. This runs counter to mainstream associations of consciousness as a higher-level function correlated to cortical networks. "Ironically, it turns out that consciousness is lodged in the inmost interior of the brain. Consciousness is an endogenous property of the brain; it does not stream in through the senses" (Solms, 2017, p. 91). This conclusion is supported by the existence of continual consciousness despite large swaths of cortical damage in humans, the loss of consciousness in humans with epileptogenic activity around ERTAS, and interspecies studies. Contrary to Edelman, Solms (2017) notes that consciousness arose in reaction to the necessity to *feel* states of arousal propogated by drives. These feelings inform us of our needs, and in turn signal us to work toward fulfilling those drives. In his model, affect is primary, preceding perception and cognition. In fact, emotional systems do not undergo any form of gating, like perception. They continue to interfere regardless of their irrelevance, which supports their prioritization (Tamietto & Gelder, 2010). "The secondary (perceptual and cognitive) form of consciousness is achieved only when the subject of consciousness *feels* its way into its perceptions and cognitions, which are unconscious in themselves" (Solms, 2017, p. 92).

One interesting model championed by Hameroff and Penrose (1996) has been receiving more attention after receiving years of criticism. Hameroff and Penrose knit together quantum theory and neuroscience to explain consciousness in what they termed the *Orch OR model*. They suggested that "aspects of quantum theory and of a newly proposed physical phenomena of quantum wave function 'self-collapse,' are essential for consciousness, and occur in the cytoskeletal microtubules and other structures within each of the brain's neurons" (p. 453). Hameroff and Penrose believe that tubulin's crystal-like structure, its organization, and its role in information processing make it a particularly good candidate for the quantum activity necessary for global binding of consciousness.

In philosophy, it is an *easy problem* when we examine relationships between mental processes and brain functioning. There are even great models that account for how we construct our sensory world and perceive objects. It is safe to say that much of mental functioning is mirrored in brain processing. Even so, what we have are still models, models that can change, and it is important to remember that when we are looking at brain functioning, we are looking at statistical truths and correlations, not causation. In this context, is there any evidence to suggest that there may be something beyond physical processing? A computer may create a display out of 1s and 0s, but it has no subjective experience and no quality of experience, such as the sight of blue, the feeling of love, or the smell of a green space after rainfall. We have *qualia*, an experiential dimension to everything from thoughts, to feelings, to perception. Where, why, and how does this all happen? The inability to account for this dimension of existence is called the *hard problem of consciousness*.

Edelman (2003) asserted that it was an evolutionary necessity for higher order neural systems to produce discriminatory capacities. In his view, these capacities account for qualia. William James (1904) had an interesting view. From the presupposition that everything stems from *pure experience*, the problem of consciousness can be better understood in terms of how we are relating to the information. In short, there are *percepts*, objects appearing in consciousness, and *concepts*, or our understanding of what they are. The world beyond a percept is re-presented in concepts; thus, there are concepts parading as percepts. He believes that we are making an error in adding an extra component and trying to explain it away, when truthfully, what is observed and what exists outside of our observations rest on the same continuum.

Despite seemingly convincing arguments, physiological models are still less than satisfactory for many philosophers of mind. David Chalmers (1996) asked the questions,

> How could a physical system such as a brain also be an experiencer? Why should there be something *it is like* to be such a system? . . . We do not just lack a detailed theory; we are entirely in the dark about how consciousness fits into the natural order. (p. xi)

Materialism and physicalism are metaphysical frameworks that have unsuccessfully accounted for consciousness, leading to a serious reconsideration of panpsychism, who some categorize as a form of idealism. Metaphysical accounts are interpretive frameworks, and they do not negate science in any way. To be clear, metaphysics does not depend on scientific proof, it interprets scientific results alongside other disciplines with the purpose of maximizing coherence for all the phenomenon experienced in the world. Materialism and physicalism are not synonymous to science by any means. In science the dominant model is physicalism, which, put simply, asserts that everything can be reduced to physical entities.

In the East, idealism has roots in Chinese, Buddhist, and Vedic philosophies and in the West is associated to figures such as Plato, George Berkeley, Immanuel Kant, and F. H. Bradley. Broadly speaking, all idealist accounts share a common thread, and that is the mind as the ground of nature, not matter. Beyond this ontology, there remains many differences within the umbrella of idealism. Other related conceptions include, but are not limited to, monistic panpsychism, pluralistic panpsychism, panexperientialism, and cosmopsychism. There are volumes of literature in relation to idealism and its different forms.

Here I will simply summarize, using a Q and A format, a few naïve assumptions and arguments against idealism drawing from Bernardo Kastrup's (2019, pp. 128–150) conceptualization of objective idealism. To begin with, his hypothesis is: "There is raw experience—qualia, pure and simple—associated with the universe as a whole, which does not require anything like the kind of information integration underlying human self-reflection" (p. 149). He further asserts that we are dissociated conscious systems from a larger encompassing consciousness.

> **Question (Q):** A brain lesion will lead to alterations in mental processing. How can the world be consciousness?
>
> **Reply (R):** Since reality is generated by consciousness, the brain is an image of consciousness, meaning correlations between brain functions and consciousness are to be expected. There is no negation of science, everything we call physical are expressions of consciousness.
>
> **Q:** So, the world is a dream?
>
> **R:** Materialism views consciousness as constructed by the brain, idealism views the brain as embedded in consciousness.
>
> **Q:** Why is it that we cannot manipulate the world through thought?
>
> **R:** Consciousness exists on a spectrum, much of which is outside of ego volition (e.g., dreams, implicit processes, the physical laws of the universe). The world is not a personal dream, in fact objective idealists posit that "there is a world outside and independent of their personal psyche" (p. 146).
>
> **Q:** But the world is clearly made of solid objects, it is not all in the mind!
>
> **R:** Solidity, however, is a property of sense-perception, making it a quality of experience. Outside of perception, these solid objects are

assumed to be abstract. We may also use dreams as an example; in dreams objects may be solid.

Q: Would the world cease to exist without perceivers? That would be absurd!

R: No. In Berkeley's time, God takes the place of observers collapsing the wave function. Kastrup (2019) attributes this role to mental contents inside an alter of universal consciousness.

Q: But the universe evolved long before consciousness emerged.

R: That is a materialist assumption. Idealism does not posit that consciousness emerges from the physical universe; it precedes it. The universe is an expression of consciousness.

We can be more certain of consciousness than we can be of the physical world, as consciousness is directly experienced, whereas the world is secondarily co-constructed. There are many contenders in consciousness debates. Some of these include: whether consciousness can be reduced to mindless matter (materialist); whether it emerges from synergistic interactions (emergentist); whether it is an illusion, as supported by Daniel Dennett (1991); whether consciousness is the primal stuff of our universe (panpsychist), as supported by Chalmers (1996) and Kastrup (2019); or whether the fundamental stuff is neither entirely matter nor mind, and perhaps something that contains both (neutral monist), as Nagel (2012) would argue. Volumes of literature have been written on these topics and variations thereof, all of which remain hotly debated and unresolved.

SPATIOTEMPORAL DYNAMICS AND CONSCIOUSNESS

Billy Pilgrim has come unstuck in time.

—Kurt Vonnegut

A radical, novel, and exciting new paradigm was introduced by Georg Northoff (2018), who implores us to reconsider the question of the mind-body problem. In its place, he recommends readdressing it as the *world-brain* problem. By this he stresses that what needs to be studied is the relationship between the phenomenal world and the brain's alignment to it. This led to the development of what he termed a neuro-ecological model, which views the reduction of existence to physical elements or mental properties as incomplete. He specifies: "The existence and reality of consciousness consist in complex organization of relation, that is, the linkage and coupling between different space-time relations such as those of the existence and realities of the world and brain" (p. 274).

The introduction of spontaneous neural activity and the Default Mode Network (DMN, "resting" state network) as an important topic of research marked a new frontier for understanding human functioning. Instead of viewing the brain as a passive recipient of information, sufficient evidence supports the brain's resting spontaneous activity as significant, actively influencing and producing information. The one-way highway became a two-way multi-lane highway. Researchers (Menon et al., 2011) have since revealed several other networks* exhibiting spontaneous activity in continuous interaction with the DMN, revealing a functional *spatial structure* greater than its anatomy (Northoff, 2018). Electrical fields generated by interactions within and between these networks fluctuate and are described through frequency bands (i.e., alpha, delta, theta, beta, gamma) forming a *temporal structure*. It is well known, for instance, that long-range gamma waves may synchronize neuronal assemblies across the brain, integrating and coordinating information. For this reason, it has been found during activities that involve learning (Miltner et al., 1999), attention (Gregoriou et al., 2009), and conscious perception (Melloni et al., 2007).

Research has since encountered cross-frequency coupling between the gut-brain axis in resting state (Rebollo et al., 2017), the brain-heart axis (Park, Correia, Ducorps, & Tallon-Baudry, 2014), and naturally, in order to function in harmony with the world, humans must synchronize with external events. Together, Northoff (2018) describes this as a *spatiotemporal alignment* of the brain with the body, relationships, and the surrounding world; which, in his view, is a requisite for consciousness. Thus, consciousness is no longer located in the brain, nor the mind, but in the relation between the synchronization of internal and external spatiotemporal dynamics. This is what he calls the *ontological predisposition of consciousness*. He places a particular emphasis on studying

---

* The default mode network is more active at rest, though there also exist several spontaneous activations in the salience network, central executive, and sensorimotor (Klein, 2015).

the brain through spatiotemporal terms, given that space and time may be considered the "common currency" between neural and mental functioning (Northoff, Wainio-Theberge, & Evers, 2019). Following Kant's lead, his methodology incorporates what he terms as *concept-fact iterativity*, whereby scientific data and philosophical concepts are continuously in dialogue.

There has been a significant quantity of research supporting obstructions in neural synchrony in schizophrenia (Spellman & Gordon, 2015). One result of disturbance in healthy oscillatory rhythms and frequency fluctuations is a failure to properly adapt to external stimuli (Northoff, 2016). An example of this may be the misperception of a causal relationship, such as an individual with schizophrenia believing that their movements were causing a leaf to fly, when in fact it was a gust of wind. Other deficits have included correlations to the severity of hallucinations and reductions in working memory (Spellman & Gordon, 2015). There exist many other disorders where these sorts of disruptions are found, including (but not limited to) bipolar disorder (Kim et al., 2013), traumatic brain injury (Wang et al., 2017), PTSD (Misic et al., 2016), autism spectrum disorders, and Williams syndrome (Castelhan et al., 2015).

THE BAYESIAN BRAIN

The character of a sensuous perception depends not
so much on the properties of the object perceived
as on those of the organ by which we receive the
information.

—HERMANN VON HELMHOLTZ

Building on the brain as a receiver *and* producer of information, there has been a recent surge of research in predictive processing, which suggests the brain is not idle, passively receiving information, but produces perceptual expectations influencing how sensory information is ultimately interpreted. This view actually has its origins in philosopher Immanuel Kant and German scientist Hermann von Helmholtz (Swanson, 2016). Kant (1781/1929) promoted the role of the human mind in perception by espousing the idea that objects *conform* to cognition and that even space and time were cognitive properties. Building from these ideas, Helmholtz applied the model of the brain as an organ of statistical computation into the realm of science (Swanson, 2016).

The idea that our experience of reality is highly influenced by our expectations—that neural predictions inform what is sensed and perceived—is currently known as the *Bayesian brain* (Seth & Friston, 2016). As with most models in science, this paradigm has not gone unchallenged (Bowers & Davis, 2012), yet it continues to garner immense attraction from researchers in the fields of psychology, neuroscience, and artificial intelligence. Passive models of perception view information as constructed by bottom-up processing, whereas predictive influences introduce the importance of top-down processing. For vision, expectations appear to inform sense data during the early stages of visual processing, with a proclivity to occur during alpha wave activity in the occipital lobe (Sherman, Kanal, Seth, & VanRullen, 2016). Predictions also seem to influence the speed at which visual information is presented to us in awareness (Pinto, van Gaal, de Lanage, Lamme, & Seth, 2015). Their experiments further endorse the hypothesis that "the timing of conscious access depends on validation of perceptual predictions rather than on mismatches between predictions and sensory input" (p. 13). Examining research on "why can't you tickle yourself," Blakemore, Wolpert, and Frith (2000) conclude that non-conscious sensory predictions are the reason. Studies demonstrate that when a discrepancy is introduced between predictions and sensory feedback there is "an increase in tickliness" (p. R11).

Predictions require probabilistic constraints, otherwise what is possible would overwhelm a system. These include *affordances*, which can be defined as what the environment has to offers us (Gibson, 1979). Gibson (1979) goes on to propose that perception is not simply about stimulus-response, rather about distinguishing the variety of ways stimuli can be related to, enriching our relationship to them. These relationships can modify our perception of value in relation to what is available and play a direct role in how we engage with world. As humans we actively modify the environment to reap higher degrees of affordance, and we cannot understand ourselves without considering the environment. From the perspective of artificial intelligence, something as complex as a human requires multiple levels of constraints, which may include space and time (Clark, 2013). What might these predictions seek to accomplish? Friston's (2009) response would be the conservation of energy and management of variability.

If we change the environment or our relationship to it, sensory input changes. Therefore, action can reduce free-energy by changing sensory input, whereas perception reduces free energy by changing predictions . . . free energy is not used to finesse perception, perceptual inference is necessary to minimize free energy. (p. 295)

The Bayesian model may be conceptualized with Siegel's 3P model of the mind (2018), adding specificity. The 3P model asserts that at the base of mental experience is a *plane of possibility*. What limits the possibilities of perceptual experience are constraints (or priors) that allow for predictions to be possible. These constraints interact with accrued experiences through time to form *plateaus of probability,* narrowing the field of perceptual (a priori) and psychological experience (a posteriori). This then feeds into a specific action, or what he calls a *peak of activation*. Identifying constraints may assist us in deepening our capacity to revisit the plane of possibility that we initially had as a child, giving us a more objective view of a particular situation. When we lack the knowledge to confront a challenge, we encounter difficulties through life. In this conceptual framework, the constraints we have are not sufficient; meaning we need to engage in activities that broaden our horizon of possible responses.

The convergence of top-down and bottom-up processes meet where statistical systems are in a continual process of being updated. This has been termed the Markov blanket, which "defines the boundaries of a system in a statistical sense . . . a partitioning of a system into internal and external states where the blanket itself consists of the states that separate the two" (Kirchoff, Parr, Palacios, Friston, & Kiverstein, 2018, p. 1). In psychotherapy, the Markov blanket may be where observation decouples top-down and bottom-up processing to enable an expansion of possible responses. Holmes and Nolte (2019) note that the *free energy principle* and the Bayesian brain provide a deeper understanding of psychopathology, and psychodynamic approaches including mentalizing, free association, dream analysis and projective identification. They further draw parallels to theories from Freud,[*] Bion,[†] Fonagy,[‡] and Laplanche.[§]

---

[*] Free association.

[†] Minus K, unconscious decision not to know and similar to the brain's blood-brain barrier, we have Bion's contact barrier, which "emphasizes the establishment of contact between conscious and unconscious and the selective passage of elements from one to the other" (Bion, 1962, p.17).

[‡] Mentalizing, belief updating.

[§] Transference.

The primacy of endogenous influences on external stimuli is further espoused by neurologist Jason Brown (2019) who developed the *microgenetic theory of perception* through clinical studies. This theory inverts traditional paradigms of perception, suggesting that object formation begins as a whole subcortically with its parts being differentiated cortically. In his model, the optic nerve meets signals at the brainstem, generating a two-dimensional spatial map of a pre-object. The pre-object traverses into the limbic temporal regions, interfacing with memory and becoming elaborated in dream space. This is followed by its rendering in a three-dimensional Euclidean space in parietal regions, and it is only at the end that features are analyzed at the occipital lobe. Thus, "early stages in visual processing do not combine into object representations, but rather carve out final objects from pre-object categories that develop over successive fields of space representation. Categories are innate templates that are specified to diversity" (p. 9). He provides a variety of disorders that may be better accounted for by this model, including aphasia, agnosia, blindsight, palinopsia, cortical blindness, and visual neglect. In this view, "the world of perception, though for the most part indistinguishable from the objective reality to which it refers, is in itself nothing other than an image that is generated within the mind" (p. 3). In line with German idealism, the noumenon remains unknown.

Brown (2019) finds much inspiration in Whitehead's (1927–28/1978) work. Perception considered in *Process and Reality* (PR) is unique, in that there is no subject-object dichotomy, but a subject-superject. In his theory, perception is secondary to *prehension* (Griffin, 1989), which may be defined as the process of bonding within and between individual units of process. Superjects are bonds that are synergistic, in that their bonding generates more than their added components. Processes from the objective world are prehended or appropriated by processes in the subject, continually catalyzing superjective states (i.e., a sensory-perceptual gestalt) into the present. This ultimately allows for self-determination over determined processes. The process of perception is not under our control, it just happens to us. This is the first stage of perception, which Whitehead termed *causal efficacy*, possibly linked to the right-hemisphere biased circuitry (Roy, 2017). Non-conscious physiological processes conform to the world, just as the world conforms to our body. We are dependent on these underlying interactions. What follows is the world as it is constituted in our immediate experience, which is what he labeled *presentational immediacy*, possibly linked to the left-hemisphere biased networks (Roy, 2017). We experience ourselves as subjects in a spatially extended world populated by objects. As mentioned earlier, there is a delay in time before the world is perceived in consciousness. The immediate presentation of the world is thus always in the past, making the past the ground on which the present may operate. In this phase we have relative independence in the ability to relate to the world. This phase however is inherently meaningless without *symbolic reference,* marking the third phase. Notably, our attribution of meaning arises from the previous two modes, and is fallible due to its interpretive nature (Roy, 2000). From this viewpoint, PR asserts that while we see only bits of reality in the present, those select portions are nonetheless accurate.

In close proximity is *experiential realism* (Hass, 2008), which is an interactionist account of reality, viewing it as emerging from the synergy between the organism's body and the world surrounding it. Nothing is re-presented in the mind, rather, the interaction produces a presentation that everything else is contingent upon; and contrary to naïve-realism, we do not see things-in-themselves because of the influence from our sensory-perceptual mechanisms. Our perception of reality is thus not a filter hiding another reality, rather our perception of reality is "real" yet there is more to it than can ever be recognized at any given moment. As Merleau-Ponty (1968) put it "perhaps 'reality' does not belong definitively to any particular perception, that in this sense it lies always further on . . . what each perception, even if false, verifies, is the belongingess of each experience to the same world" (p. 40–41). This would follow the idea that "experience is not a veil that shuts man off from nature; it is a means of penetrating continually further into the heart of nature" (Dewey, 1958, p. x).

In contrast, Hoffman (2019) asserts that a radical shift in the current scientific consensus of perception needs to be made. He suggests that sense-perception is shaped by evolution, favoring fitness over truth. This goes against the hypothesis that we do in fact view an accurate, albeit limited version of reality (what philosophers call direct realism, or naïve realism). Through the use of evolutionary game theory and genetic algorithims, Hoffman and Prakash (2020) adduce reasons to support that veridical perceptions do not in fact confer any advantage to the organism. They begin by a discussion on object permanence,* and question the idea that consciousness emerges from the brain, as in the absence of a perceiver, brains and neurons may not even exist. Insights derived from these games include: (1) true perception results in the expenditure of more energy; (2) time; (3) the structure of the world and fitness are not monotonically related; (4) valuable information for survival may be lost for truth; and (5) complex perceptual systems aligned with the real world structure would require far more complexity to create, which would be unnecessary to the survival of an organism. They conclude "in short, natural selection does not favor perceptual systems that see the truth in whole or in part. Instead, it favors perceptions that are fast, cheap, and tailored to guide behaviors needed to survive and reproduce" (p. 3).

Hoffman and Prakash's (2020) research supports what philosophers call *indirect realism,* or that experience is a veil, and what we see is not even close to what objective reality would really appear like beyond human perception. According to their computer interface analogy, what we see is akin to desktop folders, when what truly underlies their manifestation is actually code. We may even use a magnifying glass to see that everything is composed of pixels (which he compares to neurons), but this still prevents us from viewing the truth of what actually exists in the world beyond our sense-perceptions. In their theory called *conscious realism,* the world prior to perception is populated by conscious agents. Therefore, Hoffman (2019) quipped, "I take my perceptions seriously, but not literally" (p. xiii). In this context, we find that the very world we experience is but a model conditioned by the pressures of evolution and the brain. We are shackled to these fundamental conditions, without which the form and quality of matter may appear quite different.

With all these models in mind, what evidence is there that our brains may contain pre-existing impressions of objects before we even encounter an object? It has long been supposed that people with congenital blindness only dreamed of sensory experiences to which they have access (Hurovitz, Dunn, Domhoff, & Fiss, 1999). Bertolo and colleagues (2003) conducted sleep studies with individuals who were congenitally blind. Using an EEG, and waking them up

---

* A term from Piaget, who proposed that in development there is a phase during infancy characterized by object impermanence, or "out of sight, out of mind" (which is why peek-a-boo is so fun for infants up to a certain age). Eventually, the capacity for object permanence is developed and a child may know that when an object is out of sight, it may still exist.

every 90 minutes, they found that many dreams involved visual imagery. Subjects were even able to draw the visual images they experienced. Neuroanatomically, this may be a result of "cross-modal reorganization of extrastriate cortical areas, but not of the primary visual cortex . . . the identification of particular sensory perceptions can be considered as a predetermined property of specific cortical areas" (Lopes da Silva, 2003, pp. 329–330). This supports the potential existence of sense data that may exist independent of perceptual experience. Whether there may be a low-level statistical rendering of an image or more is still up for debate.

Hallucinations also challenge the notion that some relation needs to exist between observer and object, as an object may appear without any elicitation from some actual existing object. Yet this argument does not hold sway, when you consider that objects often hallucinated have already been perceived in the past, thus the relationship has already been stored in memory. If one hallucinates an object that is not familiar, it is likely a combination of features from varying objects perceived, which relate to the constructive simulation hypothesis as discussed earlier. In any case, hallucinations and dreams inform us that the brain has the capacity in and of itself to create experiences just as vivid as what we perceive in the environment. Considering these examples, is it not too much of a stretch to think that when an object is perceived, the brain may have altered what is being perceived?

TRUTH

Truth is one and many at the same time. It is one when it is considered as reality itself. It is many when it is considered as a property of our knowledge of things.

—CHUANG TZU

As nature's vanishing point* becomes a source of projected beliefs, individual differences erupt into a plethora of models. This is evident in the multicultural world in which we live, but is best highlighted in areas less exposed to westernization. As anthropologist Wade Davis (2009) stated, "Just to know that, in the Amazon, Jaguar Shaman still journey beyond the Milky Way, that myths

---

* I am defining the vanishing point as anything beyond the current limits of objective knowledge.

of the Inuit elders still resonate with meaning, that the Buddhists of Tibet still pursue the breath of the dharma is to remember" (p. 1) that our reality is just one system among many others that have successfully endured through time.

We can only experience the world through our body and sensations. With the very basis of experience being challenged, where might we find truth? Are we destined to live out a Sisyphean* fate? I approach this section with some trepidation, yet I find it important enough to share some conception of where my general thoughts rest, so as not to leave the reader in complete darkness after pulling the rug out from under. This is by no means supposed to be a comprehensive account of truth.

The first step in answering this question is to define truth. There are two competing theories of truth: the correspondence theory of truth, and the coherence theory of truth. In general, the correspondence theory of truth literally refers to how well a statement corresponds to the objective world, in contrast to how well a statement coheres with existing sets of propositions believed to be true. I build on Siegel's (2012) definition of truth as an "integrated coherence, of how something flexibly connects many layers of facts and experiences into an interwoven whole" (p. 88). Truth by nature is timeless. Whereas consciousness is complimented by the unconscious, the phenomenon is complimented by the noumenon. In philosophical terms, the world that we experience is called the *phenomenon* (Kant, 1781/1929). The phenomenon arises from a relationship between the observer and the unknown world that exists before it is actively perceived. Kant (1781/1929) used the term noumenon, in the negative sense, to signify "things in themselves, which lie beyond its [cognition] province" (p. 79). He then asks, "If we abandon our senses, how can it be made conceivable that the categories have any sense or meaning at all, inasmuch as something more than the mere unity of thought, namely, a possible intuition, is requisite for their application to an object?" (p. 79). For Kant the "thing in itself" is more a mental property as opposed to any type of tangible material; for it is our senses that give objects their appearance and concreteness. One has to wonder what sort of experience he may have had if he entered a sensory deprivation tank.

Assuming there is a world that exists beyond observers, or vice versa, each side may have its own truth, but we are not directly privy to those perspectives.

---

* From Greek mythology: As a punishment Sisyphus was forced to push a giant boulder up a hill just to have it roll back down when he reaches the top—in perpetuity.

What we are privy to is what emerges from the relationship. The truth accessible to humans are the phenomenon (the appearances); this is the truth directly accessible to us in scientific inquiry. Do we have any way of observing things in themselves beyond human perception? Not directly, because the very act of observation requires perception. Yet there may be indirect ways, possibly reached through mathematics, physics, coherence, and invariance. The closest we may be able to approach these truths would be through interdisciplinary consilience.

Parallel to objective truths are experiential truths. I use the term experiential, as opposed to subjective, because subjective truths are associated with a sort of solipsism, when in reality subjective truths are relational. I conceptualize experiential truth as a maturational process beginning with feelings of *congruence** (or incongruence), agreement, consonance, and/or harmony. In this frame, experiential truth begins as a feeling, and is elaborated into specific ideas and behaviors as it ascends neural systems into the cortex. Problems arise when experiential truth does not follow its maturational trajectory and is subsequently not expressed. Thus, it may be understood as required nourishment for the mind, without which the person may begin to deteriorate (Bion, 1965/1984).† As will be discussed in Chapter 8, my position is that the individual's conscience is a cortical representation of experiential truth. I add conscience to Grotstein's (2007) ideas on truth: conscience as a compass for truth, consciousness as a truth drive, and curiosity as their right hand. Facilitating the acknowledgment and maturation of truth is a fundamental goal in psychotherapy. How is experiential truth being veiled or obstructed? How does one best express an experiential truth? Many decisions we make are based on value systems embedded in right-hemisphere biased orbitofrontal–limbic networks (Schore, 2019), which are further influenced by our genes and history. In addition, there is now ample evidence that moral decision making is at least partially a biological reflex, not just arrived at rationally. In fact, McGilchrist (2009) believes they are completely reflexive responses:

---

* Rogers (1951) used the word *congruent* in relation to the therapeutic stance of being completely genuine, and in relation to the client's degree of alignment between their perceived self and actual experience. Discordance is produced through conflicts between the actualizing tendency and self-actualizing tendency.

† Bion's work refers to emotional truth. I use experiential, as it encompasses emotions to behavior.

Moral values are not something we work out rationally on the principle of utility, or any other principle for that matter, but are irreducible aspects of the phenomenal world, like colour . . . moral judgments are not deliberative, but unconscious and intuitive, deeply bound up with our emotional sensitivity to others . . . Empathy is intrinsic to morality. (p. 86)

It is just as important to live in accordance with one's highest conception of truth as one's *experience* of truth. We cannot disentangle these sorts of facts from becoming, which would subsume moral decision making. The interplay of our natural predispositions, superimposed by consciously formulated narratives are in a continual movement of co-construction. What is of interest however, is that although a moral judgment may be experienced in the moment, collectively they need not be followed. The fact that we may choose to live with or against them suggests a flexible process. Every decision selects from a spread of possible responses with varying degrees of congruence and incongruence. Congruent decisions are seldom the easiest to make, many times carrying with it the need to sacrifice some immediate gain. Experiential truths require a corresponding behavioral expression to complete its maturity. Behavioral truths are contingent on time, continually born in the present, made true by their happening, "recorded" in history. Behavioral activation may be the end or beginning expression of experiential truth, as each expression becomes a truth impressed on one's being. Continual acts forge habits through plasticity, as the passage of time acts as midwife, helping you birth new truths through your actions.

At a non-conscious level, our brains have sensory-perceptual "faith," everytime it projects information based on the probability of what information might exist, such as our visual blind spots. At the conscious level, our limits force upon us a conceptual faith. When I speak of faith, I am speaking of a form of trust, trust in something that transcends the importance of our immediate needs (such as our systems of meaning); trust one must place in their beliefs of truth in order to act with intention, meaning, and stability. Although faith is often attributed to those who believe in God(s), atheists are just as faithful to their own perspective, as there is currently no definitive resolution to this matter.

We all strive to project our very best understanding and conceptualization of truth into the vanishing point, and act accordingly. Living in accordance to a consciously constructed belief system is to have faith in something beyond the reflexive instinctual reactions endowed by nature. Whether we can keep these beliefs in abeyance, regard them as a process open to change, yet live up to these beliefs as if they were absolutely true (knowing they could be completely false) until proven otherwise, is the challenge faith poses. Many of us may find it necessary to take what existentialists call a Kierkegaardian *leap*, or a "leap of faith" to laymen. Jaspers (1971) adds that a "leap is decisive for my freedom. For freedom exists only with and by transcendence" (p. 25). To live in accordance with that which we consider highest within us, is to simultaneously *transcend* any contradictory experiences we may feel in the moment. To be free, our decisions cannot be made by instinctual needs, but by our highest experience and conception of truth (which may involve meeting needs, in the right context). Consistently living in this manner builds upon the biopsychosocial world of the individual, placing one's existential process as the center of gravity; with the gravitational field increasing in its strength and radius with every investment. For this reason, I am aligned with Jaspers's belief that "faith is a direct awareness not of some 'thing' designated as God or as Being but of a process through which one expands the world of truth, will and feeling" (Owsley in Jaspers, 1971, p. 4). It is thus not in the truth itself, but in the striving for truth that sets us free.

Kierkegaard (1843/1985) is considered a progenitor of existentialism. In his book *Fear and Trembling,* his character Johannes de Silentio describes "movements of faith" (p. 67) through the *slaves of misery* (p. 71), the *knights of infinite resignation* (p. 71) and the *knights of faith* (p. 68). He describes how faith is expressed in each of these characterizations in the context of a love that is unable to come into fruition. For our purposes, I will be providing a modern adaptation in the context of our desire to live in accordance with truth that is not entirely accessible to us. The following would be a personal take, much stripped of religion—perhaps we can rephrase them as movements of trust. I apologize in advance for those Kierkegaardians who may feel insulted by the intentional contortion of these ideas.

The slaves of misery would abandon the quest for truth altogether. They do not take any leap and default to their natures' non-conscious directives; a reactive organism living on instinctual impulses and society's input in response. They may follow the herd and believe in what everyone else believes, or decide to live a life satisfying pleasures and avoiding pain. There is no trust in beliefs, as there is only existence, which vacillates between nihilism and basic responsibilities necessary to survive in a social world. One is thus not contributing in any way to the domain of truth arrived at through freedom. They may tell themselves "there is no way of knowing whether there is a point to life. Any reason is as good as another. I will do what I feel like." Filled with inconsistent and often conflicting beliefs and behaviors, the slave lives a life unexamined, adapting beliefs to what may be most advantageous in the moment, and settling for a potential far below their actual capacity. Their capacity for a response beyond reactivity is not mature, and their potential to flourish in the social world diminishes. As Kierkegaard (1843/1985) noted: "The mass of humans live disheartened lives of earthly sorrow and joy, these are the sitters out who will not join in the dance" (p. 70). Being is thus not explicated, rather stunted.

Infinite resignation is the renouncement of something very important for a transcendent purpose, and its reconciliation in the suffering involved. People who give up a particular type of food because of their beliefs, despite their craving for it (with biological health implications not involved), may be a concrete and relatable form of infinite resignation. To Kierkegaard (1843/1985), infinite resignation is a precondition for faith. For one to act on faith, one must consciously sacrifice a longing that is very challenging, possibly "impossible" to meet. This sacrifice itself builds faith and expands the domain of freedom, as the pain involved becomes spiritually expressed, " . . . only in infinite resignation does my eternal validity become transparent to me, and only then can there be talk of grasping existence on the strength of faith" (p. 75). The strength of the belief will only increase with greater investment. This is intuitive, given that saying one has faith is not the same as someone who actually sacrifices pleasurable experiences for the sake of a belief. In our discussion of truth, we renounce rigid, absolute certainty for an open process subjected to continual examination and renewal. Existential dread would be the suffering one must reconcile.

The knights of infinite resignation live an ethical life and are conscious of their beliefs systems. They act in a way that is in congruence with what they believe to be true. They surrender to and suffer through uncertainty; experiencing the suffering of unmet needs as a way to empower their freedom (or meaning-systems, character). This subsequently spurs continued evaluations of their system of belief. They are however "quiet" or "dismissive" (p. 71) when their actions are not reciprocated. This is because they lack trust in the "strength of the absurd" (Kierkegaard, p. 67); as a result when they dance, "they make the upward movement and fall down again . . . but when they come down they cannot assume the position straightaway . . . they waver an instant and the wavering shows they are nevertheless strangers in the world" (p. 70).

The knights of faith (KoF) perform a *double movement*, containing all the qualities of the knights of *infinite resignation*, with the added *strength of the absurd*; meaning they act with the complete trust that eventually their efforts will be reciprocated, even when the odds are completely stacked against them. As such they resign "everything infinitely, and then [take] everything back on the strength of the absurd" (Kierkegaard, 1843/1985, p. 70). An example: they may be immensely suffering in the moment, but contrary to giving up, their suffering empowers them, as they completely trust that living in accordance with their highest experience of truth will reap benefits. It is because of this, that the KoF continues striving for truth in the face of suffering, and still passionately engage fully with the world. This is also why the knights of faith are the only ones that end up maximally flourishing. As dancers they "transform the leap in life to a gait, to express the sublime in the pedestrian absolutely—that is something only the knight of faith can do—and it is the one and only marvel" (p. 70).

Faith is objectively groundless, and given ground only through subjective belief. "It confers no secure knowledge, but it gives certainty in the practice of life" (Jaspers, 1951/2003, p. 51). In psychotherapy, there must be a desire to change. This desire really comes from trust. Trust that:

1. There are greater streams of consciousness than that which one is currently inhabiting;

2. They will know when becoming is oriented in the right direction;

3. They can endure the challenges that will confront them and access a greater stream of consciousness if they continue to do so.

Trust or faith is always in relation to the unknown, the degree to which they exist depends on many variables. Science and logic that can be quite supportive of certain directions or behavioral changes. It is well known that repetition breeds habits, which are reflected in neural pathways. There are also different personality dispositions, leading to variations in one's capacity to operate under uncertainty, and this has been found in neuroscience, with heighted reactivity to uncertainty correlating to the anterior insula, amygdala (Tanovic, Gee, & Joorman, 2018), and the bed nucleus of the stria terminalis (Buff et al., 2017), among other regions. Presently, the leading model for addressing challenges with uncertainty comes from Dugas, Gagnon, Ladouceur, and Freeston (1998), which highlights the intolerance of uncertainty as a core dimension of worry, further emphasizing that avoiding anxious thoughts, thinking that worrying is useful, and one-sided pessimistic outlooks on problems exacerbate symptoms. One should rather learn to tolerate emotional experiences, challenge inaccurate projections of the future, and engage in exercises that increase emotion regulation skills and discernment of real threat (Tanovic, Gee, & Joorman, 2018).

REFLECTIONS: PHILOSOPHY OF THE ORGANISM

Doubt is the origin of wisdom.

—Descartes

To exist is to change, to change is to mature, to mature is to go on creating oneself endlessly.

—Henri Bergson

I am walking down a beach. I can see the sun setting in the horizon; hues of orange, pink, purple, and blue coalesce into different patterns throughout the sky. Some of these colors are projected onto altocumulus clouds, with others filling the spaces in between. The ocean, a light shade of turquoise in the morning, has now a darker tint, with less visibility due to the reduction of light. Is vision what reality is composed of? If I close my eyes, vision as reality is removed. I can hear the waves crash, people chatter, the laughter of children, music, and the birds above. Perhaps reality is auditory? Yet if I put on noise-canceling headphones with my eyes closed, the world continues. I can feel the sand beneath my feet, the wind caressing my skin, and the sun's warmth trailing off, preparing for the cycle of night to initiate. Maybe the sense of touch is reality? To think that these sensual experiences compose reality is an error. What we can see, hear, touch, smell, and taste are interpretations of the subject, not entirely the properties of the object. Without sense impressions, what might things be like?

In my view, reality is akin to a Möbius strip, with the objective twisting into the subjective; and the subjective simultaneously twisting out into the objective. The body is in continuity with the mind, as much as the mind is in continuity of the body. Everything is relationship. Conservatively, I support

Galen's (2006) *realistic physicalism*, which endorses *micropsychism*. This view supposes a plurality of physical ultimates, some of which, *at minimum*, must be experience laden. The fatal flaw, he asserts, is our acceptance that everything can be measured by physics or neuroscience, and that which cannot be measured (i.e., experience), must not exist as physical. Examples of emergentism (e.g., H_2O), though enticing, have simply been insufficient in their complexity to account for inner experience emerging from nonexperiential physical properties. Liberally, I am particularly fond of Alfred N. Whitehead's (ANW) *Process and Reality* (1927–28/1978) as a metatheory, which has Buddhist and Taoist flavors (Fang, 1980), and in Western philosophy, influences from Heraclitus, Plato, Leibniz, Henri Bergson, William James, and John Dewey. This line of thinking stresses creativity, process, and relationship, bringing ideas to life. The position endorsed in this theory is in between physicalism and idealism: panexperientialism.* Similar to Solms (2017), Panksepp and Biven's (2012) notion of dual-aspect monism, panexperientialism views mind and matter to be two sides of the same coin, this is in fact what Whitehead (1927–28/1978) calls *dipolarity*. The "primal stuff" of the universe in this view is not consciousness or matter, but units of pure potential and matter-mind *processes*, which in their final relational configurations form an *experience*. Matter-mind processes are events, actualized occasions of experience, or in short, *actual occasions*.† Actual occasions are described as having spatial volume, and although their growth into more complex processes may extend as quanta of time, their respective phases are not temporally successive (Roy, 2000). The entire process of an actual occasion occurs simultaneously, meaning every phase influences and occurs within one another. In two publications, Northoff

---

* Panexperientialism was a name given to Whitehead's PR (1927–28/1978) by Griffin (1997). As a metatheory, it has demonstrated to be quite compatible with many different approaches. It has been allied with the theoretical foundations of neuropsychology (Brown, 2001; 2018), neuro-ecological theory (Northoff, 2016); integrated information theory (Oizumi, Albantakin, & Tononi, 2014), cerebral laterality (Roy, 2017), quantum mechanics (Epperson, 2004; Eastman & Keeton, 2003), and many more (see Weber & Desmond, 2013).

† Whitehead (1927–28/1978) called them *actual occasions* or "actual entities," which "are drops of experience, complex and interdependent" (p. 18). The descriptor phrase "drops of experience" is particularly useful as it brings to mind the image of raindrops building upon one another as opposed to two independent entities conversing. At times, I use the word *event* as a general term that may describe all levels of experience, from complex relations between quantum events forming a stable entity, to a storm (Cobb, 2008).

(2016a, 2016b) acknowledges the compatibility between his neuro-ecological approach and ANW's metaphysics. In his work, the spatiotemporal occasions continually composing the brain are nested within the world's spatiotemporal process (i.e., what he terms *spatiotemporal nestedness).*

In ANW's (1927-28/1978) *Process and Reality* (PR) there is a perpetual cycle of movement, where an underlying conceptual process* collapses pure potentials (what he refers to as *eternal objects*), which condition actual occasions with an ideal aim, directing how they may integrate and organize to realize them. This occurs through additive and synergistic bonds with a unique variety of emergent occasions resulting in pluralistic expression. How do non-sentient occasions bond? Through a process he called *prehension.* Prehensions may be understood as basic bonding capacities that become more complex with greater connections. Northoff (2016a) summarized prehension into three core features: prehensions mediate between two occasions allowing for a potential emergence of a novel occasion, the novel occasion has a non-symmetrical temporal relationship with previous occasions, allowing the present occasion to incorporate the past occasion, without the past determining the present, and thirdly, prehensions generate temporal coherence and novelty through their continual process of linking. The earliest process of prehending may manifest as a basic interior experience of approach/avoidance or to include/exclude. In other words, prehensions are guided by feelings, which can be found in the concept of *hylopathy,* from the work of Charles Sanders Peirce. Peirce (1891) believed that in all matter there may exist a primitive form of *feeling.* As complexity increases, protofeeling states may eventually pass into conceptual feelings with intention (Brown, 2017); ". . . feeling seeks closure and recurs in a direction toward the future. This direction is the seed of purpose and the subjective aim" (Brown, 2019, p. 166).

Events increase in complexity through novel combinations of occasions with one another, eventually forming the physical world. "It lies in the nature of things that the many enter into complex unity . . . the many become one, and

---

* This conceptual process has a primordial nature, which he defines as the "unlimited *conceptual* realization of the absolute wealth of potentiality" (Whitehead, 1927–28/1978, p. 343) and a consequent nature, which is the physical universe. Consistent with his metaphysics, the entire process of reality is dipolar, with the conceptual needing the physical to actualize, and the physical happenings informing the conceptual. Superseding this conceptual process is a creative striving for actualization leading to evolution.

are increased by one" (Whitehead, 1927–28/1978, p. 21). This idea coheres well with emergence in complexity theory. In its most basic form, an occasion "feels as it does feel in order to be the [actual occasion] which it is . . . it is *causa sui*" (Whitehead, 1927–28/1978, p. 222). Consciousness emerges from complex levels of integrated processes leading to the formation of gestalts. A rock would also be composed of actual occasions, however these occasions differ, and though enduring, culminate in a "non-social" additive grouping. The interiority of a rock is reduced to "that of the individual molecules" (Griffin, 1989, p. 23). Thus, at its most basic level, interiority is not conscious, but can be, as interiority ascends with gradations of complexity in interaction. Consciousness is not the same as experience; one can have a completely non-conscious experience. This is evidenced in figure-ground perception. The figure and ground are experiences, yet we may only be conscious of the figure. The idea that a non-conscious ground of experiences can be registered outside of awareness is no longer questioned by researchers. Similarly, most of the time, we only become conscious of dreams after we wake up. This can only happen if they had some form of prior experience that was likely not entirely conscious. ANW (1927–28/1978) notes: "Consciousness flickers; and even at its brightest, there is a small focal region of clear illumination, and a large penumbral region of experience which tells of intense experience in dim apprehension. The simplicity of clear consciousness is no measure of the complexity of complete experience" (p. 267).

ANW (1927–28/1978) states "process and individuality require each other. In separation all meaning evaporates" (p. 97). How does individuality and being fit into this picture? Individuality is held together by epochality and the process of percolation (Weber, 2008). The epochal theory of time conjectures that time is not altogether continuous, but formed through discontinuous processes. In this case, those processes are the continual bonding of individual occasions, the outgrowth of which are distinct durations. In other words, it is the relationships between occasions that construct the space-time continuum (Cobb, 2008). This harks back to James's (1890) *specious present,* which suggests that there are varying degrees of depth to our experience of subjective time of the present. Our experience of the present, or the *remembered present* (Edelman, 2003), does not simply flit about, but may vary in duration. In humans, duration has evolved to become more extensive, as can be seen in the duration of mental states. "Duration is not an addition to nature, but an inherent feature that expands over the evolutionary sequence" (Brown, 2018, p. 115). Duration may be understood through the differing lifecycles of complex spatiotemporal occasions. This cycle consists of becoming-perishing-being (or concrescence-satisfaction-transition), which Weber (2008) refers to as *percolation*. Once a complete novel occasion has been generated through concrescence (becoming), they satisfy the aim of their process and perish into objectivity, or transition into being. They are subsumed back into potential, remaining as a possibility. Datum, now objectified in being, provides information for successive superjective[*] states of becoming. Thus, "how an actual entity becomes constitutes what that actual entity is" (Whitehead, p. 23, 1927–28/1978). In every new occasion is the presence of a creative advance, echoing Bion's idea that every time you meet with your client, you are meeting somebody new. This model refutes determinism, granting individuality and freedom.

In PR, *creativity* is considered *the ultimate*, it is amoral, "a process of bringing new occasions out of old ones" (Cobb, 2008, p. 67). The idea that it is creativity that permeates every level of analysis is why Weber (2006) calls this philosophy Pancreativism. Every moment is an instance of creativity. Our bodies are constantly changing, and every moment experienced in our lives is different from the next. There is no destiny that has been written. As Mesle (2008) put it, "The future does not exist . . . we are always on the verge of falling forward into nothingness; but, in each moment, the world becomes anew, and the creative advance continues" (p. 5).

One excellent example of creativity in biological processes can be found in exaptation. Exaptation is a term coined by Gould and Vrba (1982), which are extensions of adaptations. They are currently understood through *preaptation* and *nonaptation* (Ferriera et al., 2020). A trait that is selected for evolutionary purposes is an adaptation. Some of these traits, however, may be co-opted for other functions that increase fitness. The classic example here are birds, whose feathers are thought to be selected for thermoregulation in their ancestors, and were eventually co-opted for flight (Reuter, 2010). Nonaptation refers to extended applications for a particular adaptation, that is outside of natural selection. An example of this may be improved perception of motion adapted for hunting, is now being used for playing racquetball. These have also been called *co-opted adaptation and co-opted spandrel* by Buss et al. (1998). As you can

---

[*] Superjects: are emergent events greater than the sum of their parts, similar to a gestalt. They are informed by their past but not determined by it.

imagine, many of the evolutionary traits we have inherited no longer serve their original purpose. As a result, there exists a plethora of novel spandrels being adapted to the modern world.

Jason Brown's (2001) microgenetic theory (MT) approaches neuropsychology through process philosophy. MT explores the moment-to-moment morphogenesis of mental processes as they erupt "like the surge of a fountain" (Brown, 2018, p. 112). He views them as a successive rhythmic progression of mental states moving from "potential to actuality, past to present, unity to diversity and simplicity to complexity" (Pąchalska et al., 2007, p. 243). In other words, "mind consists of a single process of whole-to-part or category-to-member transition that partitions over phases in the mind/brain state" (Brown, 2017, p. 37). If we were to isolate a slice of time associated with a single mental state, we would find that it is accompanied by distributed electromagnetic fields generated through neural activity. In MI, mental states begin at the brainstem, incorporating emotion through the limbic system and distinction as it continues traversing up the cortex. Importantly, these three nested spatiotemporal systems harbor different experiences of consciousness and time. A mental state is not well differentiated until it has reached the cortex, and temporally, the brainstem may react in a fraction of a second, whereas the cortex may take several seconds. The development of a mental state is determined by inherited predispositions from the species (phylogeny, measured in eons), the individual development (ontogeny, measured in years), and microgenesis (moment to moment arising and perishing, measured in milliseconds). "The mind in microgenetic theory arises from the becoming of the brain" (Pąchalska et al., 2003, p. 231).

The role of the clinician rests in an interstitial space between mind-matter and potentiality-actuality. We are a relational factor, a prehension between these realities. This role does have consequences, specifically an isolative factor, as we act as guardians of the secretive struggles from people on all walks of life. There is simultaneously an intimate connectivity as a result of being privy to the expression of nature in all its varying forms. This incurs a responsibility of the highest order, not just to the client, but to oneself and society. The wisdom gained must be lived out if one wishes to evolve in their efficacy, and the coded rhythms of life must be shared for the benefit of others; without which one stagnates like puddles of water collecting impurities.

Humans can be described in terms of atoms and space; distributions of elements; electrochemical discharges; inner beliefs, thoughts, and feelings; or the interconnected relationships and social structures in which they are embedded. Each description would be just as valid as the other, yet each one of these descriptions are also realms beyond which we could immediately see. Many of us base reality on our senses; however, we only see certain features of people and things. The image analogous to Freud's theory of the unconscious is an iceberg with 10% (conscious) above water, and 90% below. If we focus on what we are consciously aware of in relation to the world and what is happening all around it, that likely drops to ≤ 1%. Our limitations are simultaneously gifts, enabling there to be a process of indefinite exploration. Awareness expands ever deeper into the vanishing point of nature. While perception opens up its hidden recesses for exploration, imagination untethers us from space-time as it allows our thoughts to move through possibility and into actuality. A plurality of perceptual experiences and directions for personal maturation are born, superimposed upon the ground of nature and being.

Information arising from the senses is in no way discrete, their method of communication is immediate, and blatant. This only accentuates its allure. Our senses cannot be used as a reliable tool for all that we do in this world. For example, our senses might convince us that any country in the world is farther away than the stars above. Why? Because we can see the stars but not other countries around us. According to our senses, we could also watch a motion picture and assert that it depicts a continuous, uninterrupted flow of movement, rather than a rapid succession of still photographs, but that is not the case. Likewise, it would not have been *common sense* that the past, in the form of stars, lights up our night sky. It is our ability to reason that has allowed us to "see" beyond the visible and create technologies that assist in the process. It is thus in combination with other faculties, does the act of sensing become valuable.

Just as the majority of the universe is composed of what we currently term *dark energy* and *dark matter*, and on a smaller scale, the majority of the Earth is unexplored ocean territory, there is also far more happening within and between us than we can immediately sense. In Theaetetus, Socrates proposed that people who rely entirely on their senses for information are *eu-amousoi*, which translates to *living happily without muses*, referring to access to inspiration he and others encountered as a result of being acquainted with this invisible world. Data retrieved from our senses is important, but it can be a source of deception without input from other stratums of experience.

CHAPTER 2

Feeling, Mental Imaging, and Thinking

....

Let us, therefore, try and find out by experiment
whether we shall not make better progress on
the problems of metaphysics if we assume that
objects must conform to our cognition.

—IMMANUEL KANT

I begin with feeling to emphasize its process as one that precedes thinking. In fact, as will be elaborated (in Chapter 4), emotions form the core through which all self-processes are organized. This theory supported by Panksepp (1998) and Damasio (2010) is in stark contrast with LeDoux and Brown (2017), who believe emotions to be a higher order cognitive construction. In this debate, I side with the former, the surmounting evidence of which resists the interpretations and theoretical logic of the latter. This section is followed by our imagistic faculties. There is a non-conscious process of mental imaging that precedes imagining. It likely generates a partition, enabling there to be a subject-object dichotomy, or the experience of yourself as an individual separate from the environment. It is only after these abilities that higher order cognition is possible.

Cognition, which in common parlance is synonomous to thinking, is an umbrella term for the various mental processes related to the acquisition, maintenance, regulation, and implementation of information. Although cognition includes many capacities, this chapter will focus specifically on the domains of attention, memory, language, prospection, executive functioning, and inhibition and delayed gratification. Neuropsychological assessment currently focuses on what is called *cold cognition*, or cognition supposedly devoid of emotion. More research is currently being conducted on *hot cognition*, or cognition that is personally relevant and highly influenced by emotions (Harvey & Penn, 2010).

EMOTION: I FEEL, THEREFORE I AM

What comes first in each of us is rather feeling, a state
as yet without either an object or subject . . . there is
here no difference between the state and its content,
since, in a word, the experienced and the experience
are one. And a distinction between cognition and other
aspects of our nature is not yet developed. Feeling is not
one differentiated aspect, but it holds all aspects in one.

—F. H. BRADLEY

In psychology, *emotions* are understood as objective processes that occur in our body that result in the subjective experience of *feelings*. *Affect* refers to how emotions are observed to be expressed in another person, and sometimes is used interchangeably with feelings. There has been a lot of development in the field of emotions in the recent years. Corticocentric models demand that the cortex is necessary for the interior experience of a feelings. These models, however, have been inverted by substantial evidence from affective neuroscience (Panksepp, 1998). Congenital anencephaly,* animal decortication studies and aphasic stroke victims are just a few examples of individuals who continue to feel and display affectivity (Panksepp & Biven, 2012). Language and higher order cognition are not necessary for affect, there are affective states that are nonverbal and purely experiential. Damasio (2010) has also since changed his position on animals having feelings in light of recent research, noting somatic-affective features to his idea of a protoself (Damasio, 2003). Feeling has not

---

* Children born with almost no neocortex.

only been found at the most primitive area of the brain (brainstem), but has been suggested to be a core function of consciousness itself (Solms, 2017).

Emotions act as signals that elicit approach or avoidance behaviors. They help us survive, even before we are aware of a situation being dangerous, and also help guide us toward new behaviors and away from maladaptive behaviors. In ambiguous situations, our conscious selves continue to *feel* a certain way, triggering us to think of novel solutions to a problem that may not be rooted in the present. As our complexity increases with maturity, emotions become coded into what we determine as advantageous, filtering and selecting that which fits into its organism's identity and value. Emotions have the power to trigger us to fight with ferocity instantaneously, make us stutter with fear, or cause us to faint without a second's thought. As Panksepp (1998) so aptly summarized, "Emotive circuits change sensory, perceptual, and cognitive processing, and initiate a host of physiological changes that are naturally synchronized with the aroused behavioral tendencies characteristic of emotional experience" (p. 49). Through a host of brain stimulation studies, he identified seven instinctual affective systems considered to be *primary processes*. These raw affective experiences are highly connected to sensorimotor systems. They are followed by a *secondary process* associated with learning and emotional control, and a *tertiary process* that includes reflection on what has been learned and social emotions. Primary processes can be found in the chart below:

SEVEN PRIMARY AFFECTIVE SYSTEMS	NEURAL CORRELATES —Panksepp and Biven (2012)
SEEKING*/expectancy	Ventral tegmental area, dorsolateral hypothalamus, Nucleus accumbens, Periacqueductal Gray (PAG)
LUST/sexual excitement	Arises from hypothalamus, septal region, hypothalamic nuclei
CARE/nurturance	Anterior cingulate, BNST, VTA, preoptic area, PAG
PLAY/social joy	Dorso-medial diencephalon, parafascicular area, PAG
FEAR/anxiety	Trans-diencephalic. Lateral and central nuclei of amygdaloid complex, hypothalamus, PAG
PANIC/GRIEF/sadness	Anterior cingulate, BNST, preoptic area, dorsomedial thalamus, PAG
RAGE/anger	Medial nucleus of amygdala, BNST, hypothalamus, dorsal PAG

* These are capitalized to emphasize that they are primary-process systems of emotion.

Depending on the primary process emotion(s) that move through the secondary system, which emphasizes the upper limbic system, an individual may experience empathy, trust, blame, pride, shame, and/or guilt. Continuing up into the tertiary process which is largely neocortical, one becomes capable of metacognition (think about thinking), labeling their feelings, tolerating them, and delaying gratification (Panksepp & Biven, 2012).

Contrary to perceptual stimuli that may be blotted out of sight during one's engagement on a task, emotional systems seem to be prioritized, evidenced by their continual interference regardless of their irrelevance to the task at hand (Tamietto & Gelder, 2010). One important aspect of emotional experience is the notion that we are governed by both *fast and slow systems* (Cozolino, 2010). Imagine, for example, that you are walking in a forest and notice a snake out of the corner of your eye. In this moment, the fast system takes action; information from your senses is relayed straight to the thalamus, then to your amygdala. In 50 ms, your brain reacts to the threat. You jump back, your heart races, and you feel a layer of cool sweat. As you reorient yourself, the slow system is engaged; you now discern that what you thought was a snake was simply a vine hanging from a tree, posing no threat at all. Your breathing slows down, accompanied by a sense of relief. During the process of discernment, the brain reprocesses information in the hippocampal-cortical circuitry. In this particular scenario, although the initial experience is protective in nature, it can actually be framed as an emotional illusion because a stimulus that appeared to be real was not, and you acted as though it was. However, in the event that the offending object was indeed a snake, your limbic system might have saved you from being attacked.

Emotions and consciousness seem to have an inverse relationship in that, as emotions arise, there is a corresponding narrowing of consciousness, resulting in impulsive decisions. Pierre Janet (as cited in Jung, 1973) described this phenomenon as *abaissement du niveau mental* ("lowering of the mental level"). Indeed, we know today that poor emotion regulation may lead to impulsive decision making, higher levels of cortisol (the key stress hormone), and behavioral disinhibition. Our frontal cortex can be overridden by limbic activity in response to actual, illusionary, hallucinatory, or imagined stimuli. Our species' struggle to survive has endowed us with the capacity to imagine potential predators lurking in a future space that has yet to exist. This ability allows us to plan effectively, but may also overwhelm our daily lives, resulting in obsession, rumination, and anxiety: core reasons people seek or are referred for psychotherapy. In clinical practice, emotional experiences may amplify the therapeutic alliance. When working with maladaptive emotional experiences, the clinician may challenge the validity of overwhelming emotional experience (e.g., CBT, solution-focused therapy) or increase the capacity to bear emotional experience (e.g., psychoanalysis, existential therapy, mindfulness).

Emotional illusions are prevalent in humanity, from irrational phobias to unfounded feelings that result in violence to infatuations leading us to ignore all flaws in another person. Without a doubt, emotions may act as a veil, effectively clouding our judgment. One of the lesser known emotional illusions with high impact is known as *affective forecasting* (Wilson & Gilbert, 2003). Humans are notorious for being poor predictors of their future state of mind. In their review, Wilson and Gilbert found that the intensity and duration (impact bias) of future emotional reactions are usually over- or underestimated. Further, they indicated that this phenomenon occurs mainly because people fall short in their consideration of the impact of unrelated events (focalism); people are not aware that they may substantially reduce emotionality when they make sense of events (ordinize). Many of our decisions are based on what we imagine the future to be. In individuals who are ridden with anxiety, the imagined future may be a distorted one, preventing them from ever becoming what they aspire to be. Emotions are foundations of our experience and can lead us to do great or regretable deeds. How we feel may be very important in our survival, but it is just as important to know that our feelings may deceive us and lead to our downfall.

CLINICAL CASE

Mr. L was a transplant client with one functional lung and other medical challenges. In addition, he had lost some functionality in his legs. He was referred to me due to his less than optimal effort spent, and sometimes complete refusal to partake in physical therapy (PT) appointments. After discussing his condition, he made it clear to me that just thinking about trying to walk, even with assistance, resulted in anxiety about not having enough oxygen or falling. Given that he was stationed in a physical reha-bilitation center, his time for treatment was to be short-lived, and I had to triage interventions for him. In his case, his anxiety, both anticipated and immediate, needed to be mitigated in order for him to maximize his recovery and time in rehab. This was not only his complaint, but also the concern of other professionals who had to work with him.

I knew through my research that responses to threat are medi-ated by the amygdala, and anticipatory anxiety is mediated through the bed nucleus of the stria terminalis (BNST; Buff et al., 2017; Yassa, Hazlett, Stark, & Hoehn-Saric, 2012). Thus, my inter-vention needed to elicit frontal circuitry so as to increase con-nectivity and help inhibit his overactive amygdala and BNST. One of the interventions I began with was affective forecasting. On a 0 to 10 scale (10 being the highest), I first asked him to rate his level of anxiety regarding his PT session. He rated himself at an 8. His FEAR/anxiety circuits were clearly active. Before beginning, I noticed his arms were crossed, and he was in a rigid posture. Understanding that these primary feelings were in direct relation to sensorimotor systems, I took some time to have him uncross his arms and examine if this had an impact for him. I taught him breathing exercises prior to his engagement, and I had him engage in these exercises. I spoke to him encouragingly after-wards, reassuring him that I would be there literally every step of the way. He provided positive feedback, and gestured he was ready. My hope at this point was that my care for him, alongside the PT's touch and encouragement, would trigger an activation of his endogenous opioids and oxytocin. We also decided to add in a component of play. His goal was to walk a certain distance with assistance. We decided to make it partially a game, with every step earning him points. The reward was one-night increased screen time (his wife limited his TV consumption in the room). The hope was for him to reconsolidate this experience with his PLAY system active, thus developing emotional resilience and increase his inclination to continue with treatment. After walking with assistance from one corner of a room to the other during the session, I asked him how anxious he felt; he rated himself at a 4. By the end of the session, he reported that his anxiety was at a 3. I compared the differences in ratings and then educated him on emotional forecasting. Thus, I tailored my treatments to activate the systems of PLAY and CARE, to counter FEAR; and utilized affective forecasting to update his biased expectations. It may additionally be helpful to normalize their experience by educating them about the biological nature of affective systems, especially if they are expessing secondary insecurity. This may shift their perspective into neutrality and/or acceptance.

MENTAL IMAGERY AND THE IMAGINARY

The will to look inside things makes vision piercing and penetrating . . . it detects the crevices, clefts, and cracks through which we can violate the secret of hidden things.

—GASTON BACHELARD

Imaginative activity rests along a continuum between perception and conceptual understanding. It allows us to temporarily untether ourselves from space and time to focus on projects of our choosing; the purpose of which may range from survival, to play, to problem-solving, and empathy. Neuroanatomically, imagination (in the form of mental imagery) has been found to elicit descending signals from the parietal cortex to the occipital cortex (top-down) contrary to visual perception which tends to be bottom-up (Dentico et al., 2014). Imagination is not limited to any sensory modality, but its most frequent association is to mental images. Mental imagery is fascinating for many reasons. On the first count, mental images may be non-conscious, such as their role the Bayesian brain. Projected images in the blind spot of our eyes, and possibly even the phenomenological experience of colored peripheral vision (there are very few cones in these areas), may all be related to imagistic activity attempting to provide us with a coherent image of the world.

Consciously, mental images are not perceived, but they are experienced. They present to us as nothing, outside phenomenon, inside the stream of consciousness. Without the phenomenal bond, inner images may exist and cease to exist at our will. Mental images may be deconstructed into various properties. One is vividness; images vary in their vividness and important patterns have been replicated: (1) vividness positively correlates to unexpected memory recall and (2) vividness inversely correlates to image latency (vivid-is-fast relation) (D'Angiulli et al., 2013). If I were to ask you to imagine an apple, and rate its vividness, versus imagining curiosity, there would likely be a measurable difference in vividness, the speed at which an image comes to mind, and memory recall. This suggests that vividness may play a direct role in mediating memory retrieval. Another property examined is familiarity. Interestingly, visual imagery defies the rule that the DMN and the task-positive network (TPN) are entirely anti-correlated. Low vividness ratings and low familiarity judgments tend to elicit DMN activity, whereas high ratings elicit the TPN, yet if you have an item with high vividness but low familiarity, you would have competing signals from both networks resulting in the reduced memory performance (Lefebvre & D'Angiulli, 2019). These sorts of findings have been important for elucidating the important role of mental imagery, and practically, for formulating strategies to improve memory recall. Mental imagery is not only related to memory recall, but frequently used in working memory. Anytime we are rotating objects in our minds in order to put together a piece of furniture, enjoying a guided imagery meditation or mentally rehearsing for a sport, our imagistic faculties are active.

The importance of imagination in well-being is often underestimated, and this also rings true for its problems that arise as a result of undisciplined or overactive imaginations, specifically in relation to anxiety. Our culture favors verbal expression as an indicator of intelligence, but this is a polarized and incomplete view. Inner dialogue and imagery have an asymmetrical relationship, with the presence of visual imagery encompassing tasks eliciting conscious verbal or visual thought, as opposed to visual thought, which does not require verbal input (Amit, Hoeflin, Hamzah, & Fedorenko, 2017). This serves as further support to the fact that the stream of images that course "behind" our immediate phenomenal experiences not only develop earlier in humans, but evolved before verbal expression. It may be a more primal medium through which all conceptual forms operate. Preceding any thoughtful response is an imaginary one; predating any major creative work was one that was imagined. From an existential vantage point, the ability to untether ourselves from space and time into this partition in consciousness affords us an entryway into freedom and self creation (Sartre, 1940/2004; 1936/2012). Freedom means possibility, which indicates what could be and what is not, in contrast to what is. It may be that what *is* relies on us knowing what is *not*, in order to be experienced as real. Seen this way imagination is not only the source of freedom, but is also intimately connected with our very understanding of what we call real (Sartre, 1943; Hopkins, 2016).

APPLICATIONS: THE USE OF IMAGERY

When a living system is suffering from ill health, the remedy is found by connecting with more of itself.

—FRANCISCO VARELA

It is of interest here to note that nested within the parietal lobes are three areas of psychotherapeutic significance. These include the insula, which corresponds to interoception (Duquette, 2017); the precuneus, which relates to memory and imaginative functions (Cavanna & Trible, 2006); and the somatosensory cortex, which is associated with our bodily sensations. Information processing can follow a path of "external" bodily sensations, "internal" bodily experience (interoception), imagery and then verbal expression (temporal lobes), and action (motor cortex, frontal lobes). What follows, then, is a pathway to assist therapists in facilitating the full maturation of experiential information. It seems that information that remains "unprocessed" does not discriminate between any of these phases.

Based on the current models of therapy, it is my view that the use of mental images has not been given sufficient attention. Neuroanatomically, the precuneus is a convergence zone receiving from and relaying information to a vast network of subcortical and cortical regions (Cavanna & Trible, 2006). In addition, it harbors a reciprocal relationship with the claustrum, which may relate to the unification of perceptual experience (Crick & Koch, 2005). Imagination overall has been found to elicit descending signals from the parietal cortex to the occipital cortex, contrary to visual perception, which tends to be from the bottom up (Dentico et al., 2014). Considering the influence that imagery and networks of expectation have on perception itself, it may be worth integrating its use into practice.

Furthermore, asking clients to focus on spontaneous images that arise in relation to any given challenge may be quite insightful. Consider the following:

CLINICAL CASE

The patient was a twenty-year-old woman with severe depression and anxiety. She presented to my office feeling hopeless, as she had been treated by several clinicians and psychiatrists and had "been on every medication." She presented as articulate and intelligent. There were many moments where she was unable to even speak due to excessive crying. Her previous therapist used CBT, yet the client remained feeling anxious and depressed, even though she knew "logically" she "should not be feel that way."

After typical safety measures, and engaging her in ways to process affect, I realized that her excessive emotionality was actually working against her treatment. I decided to try a different approach. I asked her to close her eyes and simply allow any image to come to mind. She arrived at the image of a sailboat caught in a storm. While describing the image in great detail, she began to calm down. She said it helped to put feelings into a visual presentation. Suddenly, there was an eruption of emotion again as she shifted from the image back to her current emotional duress. Trigger words such as feeling *helpless, useless, alone*, and *undeserving*, pulled her out of the exercise. After facilitating her emotional expression, I asked her to revisit this image, but this time to stop the rain, still the ocean, and silence the thunder. In between each request, I had her attune to her sensory and affective experience, followed by any thoughts. She succeeded in regulating her emotions, and gained access to a new technique. This allowed us to discuss deeper underlying issues that had been obstructing her progress.

• •

ATTENTION

Each of us literally chooses by his way of attending
to things, what sort of universe he shall appear to
inhabit.

—WILLIAM JAMES

Attention enables us to nurture or be nurtured by what we are focusing on. The time spent attending any particular subject tends to correspond to our value of it. In a similar vein, attending to anything in particular corresponds to the neglect of something else. Attention is a prerequisite for any form of intelligent behavior. It can also be the cause of poor decision making.

Attention can be further understood as having five different subtypes: simple, selective, sustained, alternating, and divided. First, we must be alert, in order to orient ourselves toward an external stimulus. We then *select* an object of focus, and if it is important, we *sustain* the attention for a prolonged period of time. Sometimes, complex environments require us to shift or *alternate* our attentional processes between multiple task demands. At other times, we must focus our attention on a few tasks at once, and so we must be able to proportionally *divide* our attention.* These subtypes depend on three core neuroanatomical systems identified by Petersen and Posner (2012): alerting, orienting, and executive control. Signals around us vary in importance. If a particular threshold is met, a signal may instantiate adrenergic projections from the locus coeruleus in the reticular activating system in the brainstem to the forebrain to alert us of the need to process and prepare for the signal in question. Orienting is further divided into two networks: the ventral- and dorsal-orienting network. These relate to the frontal eye fields, temporoparietal junction, pulvinar nucleus, superior parietal lobes, and superior colliculus. The ventral (bottom-up process) decides on which competing input should be given priority and the dorsal network (top-down process) synchronizes visuospatial-orienting activity. Finally, there is the dual executive network, which is also divided into two: the dorsolateral prefrontal cortex–parietal network involved with task initiation, switching, and adjustments; and the

---

* Of note, there is still some controversy over the existence of divided attention, with some researchers arguing that divided attention is really just alternating attention at a great speed.

anterior cingulate cortex–anterior insular network (or cingulo-opercular), which allows us to sustain our attention.

What we attend to essentially determines what we *see*. One of the most popular examples of this phenomenon comes from a study by Daniel Simons and Christopher Chabris (1999), demonstrating what they called *inattentional blindness*. In their study, subjects are asked to view a video clip of a group of people passing a basketball back and forth. Subjects are then asked to count the amount of times the ball was passed; at the end, people are prompted to give an answer and then asked if they witnessed anything unusual while counting. Despite the fact that 90% of subjects will claim that they would have witnessed a gorilla if one had appeared in the video, about half of the subjects will not have noticed that a man in a gorilla suit walked through the group of basketball players, paused, pounded on its chest, and exited the scene.

One demonstrative neurological condition quite popular in neuropsychological circles is hemispatial neglect (HN). An individual afflicted by a lesion or tumor in their right parietal lobe may develop HN. This condition may cause the person to behave as if the left side of the world does not exist. This however has nothing to do with sensory input (as would be found in homonymous hemianopsia), rather it is about interpreting and attending to the information in the left visual field. This is why it is also known as hemispatial inattention. What is more, this condition not only occurs during perception, but may also extend into a person's imaginative space. Thus when asking a person to imagine a scene in their mind, they will only be able to describe the right field, that is unless you subsequently ask them to rotate the image.

The ability for attention to select what is consciously seen can be quite shocking, especially with the amount of variables that can influence our attentional capacity. Another clinical population of interest are individuals diagnosed with attention deficit hyperactivity disorder (ADHD). ADHD is characterized by inattentive symptoms, hyperactive or impulsive symptoms, or a mix of both. I am often asked, why are overly hyperactive people given stimulants? Stimulants increase dopamine (DA), epinephrine (EPI), and norepinephrine (NE) to address *deficiencies* in DA (Blum et al., 2008), EPI, and NE (Lee, Lee, & Park, 2015). Two particular neural areas related to these changes are the dorsolateral prefrontal cortex, which is associated with working memory, and the anterior cingulate cortex, which is associated with selective attention and error monitoring. Generally, both areas have been found to be smaller (i.e., reductions in volume) in individuals with ADHD (Seidman et al., 2006). Functional imaging revealed diminished activity in frontostriatal circuitry, an area necessary for inhibition and attention (Epstein et al., 2007). Deficits in these areas as a whole are thought to contribute to problems in attention, conflict resolution, and goal-directed behavior.

It is common knowledge that in order to learn effectively, we must be able to attend to the information being taught. Most people are quite familiar with the diagnosis of ADHD in children and the necessity for structure, medication, and other appropriate interventions to help them pursue a promising educational trajectory. One common thread I have heard from patients is, "I know what I'm supposed to do, I see others doing it, but for some reason I just can't. There's something wrong with me." Importantly, it is well known that overall performance on IQ tests is quite similar for individuals diagnosed with ADHD and individuals who have not been diagnosed with it (Schuck & Crinella, 2005). However, given the host of other problems they experience, they feel, and are frequently, misperceived as having suboptimal intellect, which may contribute to higher rates of depression (Daviss, 2008).

Fewer people are aware of adult ADHD. Unmedicated adults with ADHD may have problems with procrastination, disorganization, forgetfulness, tension, restlessness, sleep disturbances, impatience, and time management. Hyperactivity and impulsivity may be expressed in tendencies for thrill seeking (e.g., unprotected sex, speeding) that can endanger their well-being (Ben-Naim, Marom, Krashin, Gifter, & Arad, 2017). It is easy to understand why attentional deficits can result in dysfunctional relationships and difficulty maintaining occupation. One longitudinal study conducted by Moffit and colleagues (2015) followed 1037 individuals from birth. First, traditional trends of ADHD were found, with 6% of the sample being diagnosed with ADHD as children and a reduction of 3% as adults. Surprisingly, however, a significant portion of adults with ADHD did not actually overlap with children diagnosed as ADHD, challenging the current diagnostic criteria for ADHD and suggesting that ADHD is not lifelong and may not need to be diagnosed in childhood. Is this truly the case? Or might these be false positives?

During the first year of my fellowship, I and my colleagues often found adults presenting with ADHD-like symptoms without any diagnostic history of ADHD or familial corroboration for childhood ADHD symptoms. Many reasons could account for this phenomenon, such as not being diagnosed as a child due to a tolerant family believing symptoms to be mere manifestations of the person's character, cultural differences, incorrect diagnosis in youth, lying, or very high functioning individuals who could *mask* symptoms until they were challenged sufficiently for the symptoms to be present. After screening out these variables, we found a number of ADHD candidates who did not seem to fit the profile. Upon further investigation, we found that many of them suffered from obstructive sleep apnea (OSA). Individuals with OSA suffer from chronic disruptive pauses or shallow breathing during sleep that interrupts sleep quality, resulting in excessive daytime sleepiness. In moderate to severe cases, symptoms of OSA mimic ADHD, including impaired attention, learning, and executive functioning. Like ADHD, OSA also affects the dorsolateral prefrontal regions, parietal lobule, and hippocampus (Joo et al., 2010).

Diagnosis guides treatment, and it is possible that treating an incorrect diagnosis would lead either to no improvement or even to harm. Luckily for those suffering from OSA, cognitive symptoms are at least partially reversible when their condition is properly treated.

APPLICATIONS: ADHD

Each person is an idiom unto himself, an apparent
violation of the syntax of the species.

—GORDON ALLPORT

Psychological difficulties may arise when we are negligent of the other factors that may exist in the background of what we have chosen to focus on. Awareness of attentional limitations may serve to shift attitudes from rigid ideas about a presenting problem to curiosity about it. This allows for the exploration of possibility. Indeed, "relaxation . . . favours creativity because it permits broadening of attention, and, with the expansion of the attentional field, engagement of the right hemisphere" (McGilchrist, 2009, p. 41). There simply may be things in plain view to which a client has not yet attended. Fritz Perls, the founder of Gestalt therapy, was well known for shifting clients' attention to their nonverbal gestures and asking them to express what they might be suggesting (Yontef & Jacobs, 2010). Psychotherapeutic techniques have since evolved to include training a client's attention via mindfulness exercises, as well as focusing attentional systems on interpersonal, external, internal, and bodily experiences in service of gaining new insights or processing underlying emotions.

When working with someone with attentional deficits, clinical acumen becomes very important in discerning the source of symptoms as biological or psychological in nature. Simply because one has deficits does not mean they have ADHD. If there is any question about the existence of ADHD, the current gold standard is neuropsychological testing. This entails several hours of interview, objective testing, and obtaining collateral evidence to support the diagnosis. Many of the symptoms in adult ADHD overlap with those of bipolar disorder, depression, and anxiety-based disorders; it is important to remember to assess and diagnose carefully, because doing so guides appropriate treatment. As Arthur Conan Doyle (1985) noted, "It is a capital mistake to theorize before one has data. Insensibly one begins to twist facts to suit theories, instead of theories to suit facts" (p. 27). Medication, education, expectation management, and the implementation of appropriate structures will benefit non-ADHD individuals in a relationship with someone diagnosed with ADHD. The simple mismatch of what one would normally expect the other to attend to can be easily perceived as hurtful, even if it was completely unintended. These are all factors to be considered in the clinical setting when working with individuals with attention deficit problems.

I have often wondered if there are evolutionary benefits to ADHD. Group survival could only increase with various members attending to and engaging the world differently. This could be noticing a camouflaged predator, helping find different food sources, locating shelter or refuges for safety, or even the accidental (or not) creation of useful tools. Society today is quite different, with traditional occupations bounded by structures. It could be of benefit for individuals with treatment resistant ADHD to seek out occupations that offer a wide-range of stimulating responsibilities. Minor changes like switching from driving automatic to driving manual may be helpful in keeping ADHD afflicted individuals from drifting off.

MEMORY

Memory never recaptures reality. Memory reconstructs reality. Reconstructions change the original, becoming external frames of reference that inevitably fall short.

—FRANK HERBERT

The type of reality that we inhabit is anchored by our attention and further defined by our memories. Neuropsychologists divide memory into stages. The first stage of memory is *sense memory*, which can register vast amounts of visual information for up to 200 milliseconds. Information may then be selected to enter *short-term memory*, which stores information for 30 seconds to a few minutes, with a capacity of about seven plus-or-minus-two bits of information. Sometimes we use short-term memory not only to store information but also for problem solving. When this is the case, we call it *working memory*, due to the added component of executive functioning. Research has supported the notion that information is maintained through reverberating neural circuits (Lezak, Howieson, Bigler, & Tranel, 2012). If information does not undergo the electrochemical processes involved with storing information into *long-term memory* (LTM), a process called *consolidation*, the reverberation naturally ends and the memory is lost. LTMs are hypothesized to be stored throughout the cortex and not in any single location, via processes creating changes within and between neurons and their dendrites. Most popular neuropsychological examinations estimate LTM to begin around 20–30 minutes after first exposure. Memory exists for every sense that we have and also includes *recent* and *remote memory*, terms used for autobiographical memory. *Explicit memories* can be retrieved consciously, whereas *implicit memories* are non-conscious by nature. This would include memories such as how to ride a bike, a skill that would be further classified as a *procedural memory*.

Overall, memory can be categorized into four stages: encoding, storage, consolidation, and retrieval. Forgetting may occur at any stage, whether it be poor encoding or a failure to retrieve information. The popular Ebbinghaus (1880, 1885a, 1885b) forgetting curve, which has been replicated several times (Murre & Dros, 2015), found that after 20 minutes, we are able to recall 58% of information presented; 1 hour results in 44%, 1 day results in 33%, and

6 days result in 25% of material retained. Memory across the lifespan tends to follow an inverted U-shape. We begin amnestic, and around age three we begin to have some ability to consciously retrieve memories, with memory becoming most accurate for events that have occurred during adolescence and early adulthood and subsequently declining with age (Hertzog & Shing, 2010).

The most commonly known reason for forgetting is lack of usage; yet there are three other important ways forgetting occurs. One way is through interference. Processing new information may interfere with previously learned information, especially if the information is similar to information that was learned already. We call this *retroactive interference*. Similarly, information that has been learned already can interfere with information being learned. We call this *proactive interference*.

One famous example of how unreliable memory may be is found in eye-witness testimonies (Malmberg & Xu, 2007). In fact, most police forces no longer attempt to identify suspects in a photo array of six to nine photographs; instead, they present photographs sequentially (one by one) in an attempt to improve accuracy. This is due to potential retroactive interference, as victims or witnesses may begin to confuse details in their attempt to identify the correct individual when presented with several faces that have similar features. However, the efficacy of this protocol has not yet been determined conclusively (Carlson, Gronlund, & Clark, 2008). Indeed, a meta-analysis concluded that 75% of wrongly convicted individuals involved mistaken eyewitness identification (Wells, Memon, & Penrod, 2006). Accuracy diminishes further when people are attempting to identify faces of people from a different ethnic background, resulting in what is called *cross-race bias* (Benton et al., 2006).

The phenomenon of false memories has been well documented. One way this occurs is through what is called the *misinformation effect* (Loftus, 2005). People can be misled by suggestive questions and information. The very wording of a question can result in overestimations or underestimations of events. For example, when individuals were exposed to a video of a car accident and asked, "How fast were the cars going when they hit each other?" estimates of speed were typically 20% less than when asked, "How fast were the cars going when they smashed into each other?" False memories of shattered glass also were more likely to emerge when the word *smashed* was used (Loftus, 1979).

The second reason for forgetting is a direct insult to the brain, such as a traumatic brain injury (TBI) or a neurological disorder that results in the degeneration of brain processes. In severe instances, it may result in antero-grade amnesia (the inability to formulate new memories) or retrograde amne-sia (the inability to recall events from the past). One fascinating phenomenon related to disruptions in brain functioning is *confabulation*, or unintentional lying, which may occur as a result of disorders such as Alzheimer's disease, Wernicke's aphasia, Korsakoff's disease, TBIs, or aneurysms. The leading neu-ropsychological theory to account for confabulation is that retrieval of infor-mation has been disrupted, as is the case of people with severe frontal lobe compromise. The frontal lobes have been associated with executive function-ing, and because of this, some theorize that there is also a failure to evaluate the output of information, as well as poor reality monitoring.

The third reason for forgetting was proposed by Freud, who asserted that memories of a disturbing nature may be repressed as a defense to protect one's psychological integrity. In fact, memory for traumatic events in particular may be poor (Odinot, Wolters, & van Koppen, 2009), and forgetting details of traumatic events is actually a symptom of post-traumatic stress disorder, as listed in the *DSM-5* (American Psychiatric Association, 2013). Our confidence in the happenings of the past can be quite troublesome. When we experience a significant event, especially something traumatic, it is easy to become defined by it. Yet one study found that as confidence in memory for a traumatic event increased, the accuracy of that memory decreased (Hirst et al., 2009). As Lacy and Stark (2013) so aptly summarized, "Accuracy produces confidence, but confidence does not necessarily indicate accuracy" (p. 650). However, the relationship between accuracy and confidence is not especially well defined.

Currently, neuroscience supports the flexibility and fallibility of memory, demonstrating that our brains do not function like precise computers do when storing information. In fact, our brain reconstructs the memories through *memory traces*, and our present experience necessarily influences our memories every time they are retrieved. Although this may sound maladaptive, it may be necessary to integrate these memories flexibly to help us imagine and plan for the future, as suggested by the constructive simulation hypothesis (Schacter & Addis, 2007a, 2007b). This appears to prioritize our memories in service of planning for the future, in contrast to keeping an accurate record of the past.

Memory is thus open to distortion, addition, omission, and reinterpreta-tion. Given this information, it is with great misfortune that we base so much of our well-being on our memories. Humans evolved to remember the gist of the situation, but when details are involved, we become far less reliable. This is called *fuzzy-trace theory* (Reyna & Brainerd, 2005). Though inescapable and useful in many circumstances, memory remains a veil insofar as we allow it to drive the very foundations of who we are.

APPLICATIONS: TRAUMATIC BRAIN INJURY AND ALZHEIMER'S

A man does not consist of memory alone. He has feeling, will, sensibility and moral being.
—ALEXANDER LURIA

Similar to working with clients with attention deficits, the first step in working with individuals who have disorders characterized by memory impairments is to consider whether those impairments are biological or psychological. When working therapeutically with people who were medically compromised, I found myself having to navigate the question of whether a problem was a neurologic deficit or a psychological defense. These two situations are approached very differently and elicit different reactions from others. In ambiguous cases, it is extremely important to be engaged actively with others in treatment, such as family members, in order to gain collateral information and medical records on their prior functioning. How have they changed since the accident? Or were they always like this? If this is not possible, a neuropsychological evaluation will be necessary. In the best-case scenario, the client should have both a thorough history and an evaluation, but, unfortunately, this will not always be the case.

False memories are unavoidable. However, to tell such individuals that the accuracy of their memory is unreliable would likely have the effect of invalidating their perspective. Therefore, it is more important for the clinician to work with the underlying affect beneath the content. When clinically engaged with clients, we are taught to use open-ended questions and the reiteration of the words the client is using to prevent the imposition of beliefs and further distortions. This suggestion loses its strength when working with memory disorder patients. Just as challenging the existence of hallucinations can be futile, challenging what a client believes to be true may do more harm than good.

Two major diagnoses associated with memory impairment are moderate to severe TBI and Alzheimer's disease. Interestingly, though different in etiology, classification, course, and recovery, among other qualities, both diagnoses have substantial overlap in terms of the ways a person can work with ensuing memory difficulties. As a mechanism intimately tied with identity and daily functioning, memory results in profound changes when it has been compromised. Typically, following a severe TBI is a phase of post-traumatic amnesia (PTA). During this time, the person experiences severe confusion, and a discontinuity of memory characterized by retrograde and anterograde amnesia. A neuropsychologist determines the length of PTA via specific examinations, and its length helps determine the severity of the TBI.

In many cases, memory disorders do not initially include loss of awareness. Clients, aware of their deficits, may experience sadness, anger, or emotional outbursts. In extreme cases, their own identities come into question, especially if they were achievement oriented and high functioning in the past. Untethered from memory, there is no longer any anchor for their selves in the present. Reactivity increases, as attention flits about in different directions. Life becomes more difficult for them and burdensome to caregivers. In the most severe cases, clients may completely lack awareness of their own deficits and may become completely aphasic.

With this demographic, it is paramount to work with caregivers, educating them to be aware of what to expect and how to work with agitation. For safety reasons, someone with TBI and Alzheimer's should be given an identification card with their name, address, phone number, and other important information in the event that they become lost. Difficulty finding words, getting lost, and forgetting names or objects become common occurrences.

Dialogue

Situation: If the afflicted person's memory is severely affected, caregivers must learn to alter their behaviors, such as utilizing cues in the structuring of their sentences.

- *"Don't you remember who this is?"* (may elicit agitation)
- **Instead say,** "This is our nephew, Michael."

Situation: When an action has been performed incorrectly,

- *"No, that is wrong,"*
- **Instead say,** "How about we try it like this?"

Situation: Open-ended questions should be balanced with simple, closed-ended questions, depending on the severity of the memory disorder.

- **Open-ended:** "How are you feeling right now?"
- **Closed-ended:** "Are you feeling sad?"

Moreover, one may be creative and provide the client with a memory book that includes pictures and information to further support remembering. It is also important to remember that a client's memory having been affected does not mean they are incapable of understanding a situation. Talking to others about the client as if they are not there or using "baby talk" with them may be very degrading. It is important for caregivers to phrase feedback in a form that accounts for cognitive deficits. If a client can do something, even if they are struggling, it will be important to let them do it so they can contribute and, if possible, begin to relearn certain responsibilities (especially in the case of TBIs). Doing so may even help reduce the rate of decline in their capacity to function. To take away all responsibilities may negatively affect the client because networks involved with action may be lost to disuse. If the client can still do a task, caregivers should let them. One never knows when a capacity may simply be lost.

When working with an individual with a memory deficit, it may be beneficial to summarize the challenges discussed previously and be more active in sessions. Ask clients to keep a journal so they may read to remind themselves about daily events and their experiences. Given the degeneration of their memory systems, clinicians should begin extending clients' memory to the environment, inviting them to use calendars, notes, or digital phone reminders. It can be extremely helpful to simplify their lives, reducing responsibilities to an appropriate level, and arranging support to be context congruent, such as leaving a sticky note on the car dashboard reminding them to lock the car and take their keys with them (if they are able to drive). Routine is vital to this population; clients should not be isolated to mundane tasks. A structured schedule with varied content will help reduce avoidable frustrations. Repetition of stories or facts is to be expected, and there is not much use in reminding them that they are repeating something; for this reason, when working with clients who have Alzheimer's, the clinician or caretaker must develop patience and tolerance.

When working with neurologic clients with memory disorders or individuals seeking assistance with memory, mnemonic devices may be very helpful. Clinicians can teach clients to better categorize lists in order to improve their memory for verbal information; one practical example is that organizing grocery lists by their category ("condiments, meats, dairy") will be more effective than a disorganized list of food items. The more meaningful an experience is, and the more a person can relate it to their everyday life, the more likely it will be remembered. Chunking numbers or creating a story involving numbers may help with remembering strings of numbers. Using extreme associations may help with remembering names. In higher functioning individuals, clinicians may use the method of the loci, combining familiar imagery to facilitate memorization, such as in the use of a memory palace. If the clinician believes there is a memory deficit or confusion interfering with a client's daily life, and it is not due to some sort of psychological phenomenon, the client should be referred for a medical or neuropsychological evaluation. In these cases, it is the clinician's duty to help clients generalize these mnemonic devices to relevant areas of their life.

From a neuropsychological perspective, many interesting studies have been conducted on the predictive validity of certain constructs. During my time at the University of Miami, we conducted neuropsychological research that has extended the utility of proactive and retroactive interference in its potential for improving early detection for individuals at risk of developing Alzheimer's. One measure yielded a sensitivity of 84.6% and specificity of 96.2% in distinguishing people with mild Alzheimer's disease from normal older adults (Loewenstein et al., 2004). These sorts of predictive paradigms are cost-effective and may be extremely valuable in their ability to improve prognostic outcome. If we subscribe to the notion of emergent materialism, which states that the mind emerges from brain activity, then naturally, another way of examining neurophysiological decay or dysregulation associated with neurological disorders (other than neuroimaging) would be through analyzing clients' neurocognitive correlates.

LANGUAGE

The unnamable is the eternally real. Naming is the
origin of all particular things.

—LAO TZU

Language has the ability to veil or unveil reality. Language can be used to tell the truth or to deceive. Fundamentally, we use words to represent objects in the natural world, and thus words abstract what we perceive. Importantly, as perceptions become conceptions (ideas that exist secondary to perception), representations become increasingly subject to interpretation. One word can be defined vastly differently from one person to another. This phenomenon becomes even more complex when multiple languages are being translated or when people from different cultures are communicating. Language in the form of thought plays a large role in reducing the amount of information around us, which in some cases may be strategic and in others may be detrimental. Buddhism offers a famous analogy of the finger pointing at the moon, the purpose of which is to suggest that the pointing finger is not the moon itself. In this case, the finger pointing would be language, because a word represents some object in the environment and is not the object itself. With this in mind, language may also help unveil experiences. This may apply to the overflowing of emotional dams that occur during arguments in relationships. Conflicts do not resolve themselves, but are resolved through revealing truths.

Edward Sapir was the first to empirically propose the notion that language may play a role in the very foundations of human mental experience. He formulated the concept of *linguistic relativity*, ultimately asserting that language shapes our perception. This notion was further elaborated by Benjamin Lee Whorf, resulting in the development of the Sapir-Whorf hypothesis. Whorf was highly influenced by his examination of Hopi linguistic structure, which indicated that this group of Native Americans view the world as a process rather than a set of objective structures to be measured (Hussein, 2012). Consistent with this observation, the concepts of past, present, and future do not exist in the Hopi language; in contrast, their universe is divided into that which is manifest, such as concrete objects, and that which is manifesting, which generally refers to their subjective lives (Von Franz, 1992). Current evidence supports the weak argument of the Sapir-Whorf hypothesis, which suggests that language *influences* thought processes; in contrast, the strong argument, which asserts that language *determines* cognitive processes.

Lera Boroditsky's (2001) studies have suggested that language influences cognition and essential aspects of reality, such as time, space, causality, and relationships. She stated that "languages force us to attend to certain aspects of our experience by making them grammatically obligatory. Therefore, speakers of different languages may be biased to attend to and encode different aspects of their experience while speaking" (p. 2). For example, she noted that an aboriginal community called the Pormpuraaw do not have words for right or left; rather, they use cardinal directions of north, east, south, and west. As a consequence, their orientation to these cardinal directions is better developed than that of English speakers. In another interesting linguistic comparison, Boroditsky noted that English speakers and Mandarin speakers conceptualize time differently. Whereas both tend to describe time as a linear, horizontal process, Mandarin speakers do so with the addition of describing time vertically from up to down when ordering time units such as weeks or months. Boroditsky concluded that these tendencies result in differences in mapping time, thus demonstrating a unique cognitive signature.

The Ethnologue Organization, the world's lead authority on cataloging languages, estimated that throughout the entire human population there exist approximately 7,097 languages. This incredible diversity poses a real challenge when people who speak different languages interact. Many individuals are now bilingual. Does this alter a person's brain and functioning? Kroll and Dussias (2017) noted that contrary to popular belief, evidence supports languages as activating similar neural networks in fluent bilingual speakers as opposed to others. In solving problems, bilinguals recruit the same brain areas as monolinguals but appear to utilize these regions more efficiently. In addition, children are not confused if they are exposed to multiple languages early on. In fact, they develop specific mechanisms to discriminate languages. This phenomenon may relate to findings that bilingual children initially exhibit lower receptive language, although they outperform monolingual children for executive control. The frequent use of cognitive switching (from one language to another) may even relate to a better developed ability to ignore irrelevant information and to achieve higher attentional control.

Moreover, learning two languages may result in enhanced neural activity in areas of the brain related to executive function, due to higher demand for information-processing efficiency compared to learning only one language. Among the many benefits, bilingualism in children in low SES families seems to decrease the risk of academic failure; bilingualism has been documented to serve as a protective factor for the elderly, delaying the onset of Alzheimer's symptoms by 4–5 years when compared to monolinguals. Bilingualism opens opportunities for social interactions; it may be economically advantageous and increase cultural sensitivity, broadening a person's perspective of the world. There seem to be cognitive advantages of bilingualism, regardless of when another language is learned.

APPLICATIONS: NAME IT TO TAME IT

A language is not just words. It is a culture, a tradition, a unification of a community, a whole history that creates what a community is.

—Noam Chomsky

Language is one of the primary vehicles of healing in psychotherapy. The therapist-client relationship is a foundation that language helps build. Clinicians aim to ask questions that give space for a voice within the client that has not yet been heard but perhaps only sensed or felt. They facilitate the maturation of psychological experience through improving inner faculties of reason. "Reason . . . sets in motion everything it touches. Because it questions and confers language, it creates unrest. Thus, reason makes it possible for all origins to unfold, to open, to become clear, to find speech and to relate themselves" (Jaspers, 1971, p. 57).

One of the goals of psychotherapy is to utilize communication to *stimulate neuronal activation and growth* (SNAG) in order to promote integration (Siegel, 2012). Given language's capacity to act as a veil, a critical piece of advice is to ask clients to define abstract words or concepts that the therapist and client may understand differently. We should never assume we understand, especially if a conversation appears to be going in circles. As opposed to a defense, circumlocution may be something more fundamental. Not making assumptions is especially important if we are working with an ethnically diverse population. This goes hand in hand with asking clients to elaborate on the contents of their speech, because sometimes specific words used may be reflective of their state of mind, gateways to deeper experiences. Language can be used as a shovel, a tool to dig deeper into psychological experience. Thoughts are automated movements in the mind, like gravel to be sifted through, with occasional discoveries in the underground. Alongside the basic skills of active listening, paraphrasing, and attending to the clients nonverbal and verbal communication, note that the primary language a person uses may be accompanied by a fundamentally distinct conceptualization of the world. Be sure to approach each client with an open and exploratory attitude.

It is a commonly held notion that verbalized emotion or clarification of ambiguity can create a calming effect. A study by Matthew Lieberman and colleagues (2007) demonstrated that *affect labeling* decreases activity in the limbic regions while increasing activity in the right ventrolateral prefrontal cortex, thus regulating negative affect. Of particular interest, this relationship has been found to be mediated by the medial prefrontal cortex, which contains descending inhibitory tracts to the amygdala. As Dan Siegel (2010a) would say, one must "name it to tame it." When clients are experiencing emotion dysregulation, the goal is to strengthen the descending inhibitory tracts between frontal systems and the limbic system. Clinicians may accomplish this via Socratic questioning, asking clients to keep thought records, enhancing expression of affect, making interpretations, promoting mindfulness, and implementing other methods that enhance the client's capacity to bear suffering.

Neurological conditions offer a window into the specialization of specific areas of the brain and what may be occurring in everyday experiences. For example, the basic mechanics of language may be highlighted when aphasia occurs. Aphasia, the inability to comprehend or formulate language, tends to arise in conjunction with some insult to particular regions of the brain, such as Broca's area, Wernicke's area, and a bundle of fibers connecting them called the arcuate fasciculus. Even though they will understand language perfectly well, individuals who have suffered damage to their Broca's area may be unable to produce speech, or their speech may come out jumbled, even if in their minds the meaning is clear. In contrast, damage to Wernicke's area may result in an inability to understand speech with the concomitant ability to speak fluently. One of the symptoms arising from problems with the arcuate fasciculus is the inability to repeat simple sentences.

Tillfors and colleagues (2001) conducted a PET study on individuals with social phobia, finding that when presented with stressful scenarios during which they needed to speak, cerebral blood flow was redirected from cortical and speech-based areas to the limbic system, likely resulting in their inability to present in a calm, collected manner. Indeed, language and emotionality have quite an intimate connection. A few words from the right person may trigger either an inflammatory response or a sense of security and well-being.

Lastly, it is critically important for clinicians to convey ideas that are experientially relevant to clients. Language used in the form of metaphors grounds abstract concepts in lived experience. According to McGilchrist (2009),

> The right hemisphere can see that metaphor is the only way to preserve the link between language and the world it refers to . . . for the left hemisphere consequently, language can come to seem cut off from the world, to be itself reality. (p. 118)

This effect can extend to similes, analogies, and narratives that additionally elicit images, a more impactful form of thought. They may be used to paraphrase what a client has just expressed to elicit a more visceral experience or to describe concepts that are difficult to comprehend (for a comprehensive list of useful metaphors, see Stoddard & Afari, 2014).

Dialogue

(**T** = Therapist, **C** = client)

C: I feel like I'm falling apart, like I'm breaking down. *(Reflects the need to feel whole, use of metaphor)*

T: I'm sorry to hear that. What parts of you are breaking down? *(Using client's language, elaboration, building on the metaphor)*

C: My wife just won't let me be me. She's always complaining . . .

I try to change but it's never good enough and I feel as if I'm becoming someone else.

T: What parts of you have you had to change? *(Asking them to make a vague comment more specific, identifying parts that are breaking down)*

C: I don't know, it's just too much. Its hard to express! *(Limbic activity may be narrowing his higher order cognition)* The other day I punched a hole in my wall *(Acting out)*, and I'm having those same feelings now.

T: What are the feelings you're having? *(Identifying the emotion to calm limbic activity, and teaching client to appropriately express themselves verbally, so they do not act out)*

C: I guess it's, it's rage.

T: I can see your fists are clenched right now. *(Drawing attention to physiology—usually clients will release or alter their reaction in response)* What does rage feel like to you, physically?

C: My heart and brain are going a mile a minute, and I'm sweating a bit. I feel like there's a lump in my throat and it's hard to speak *(Continuing processing images, thoughts, feelings, sensations)*

T: What's your experience like now?

C: I'm still irritated, but I'm calmer now that it's out of my system. *(Client has successfully regulated emotions via language that otherwise may have led to punching a hole in the wall)*

T: I'd like to revisit the feeling of falling apart. What parts of you were you referring to? Take your time. *(Decreased limbic activity should promote access to relevant frontal-temporal regions)*

C: I used to spend hours focused on creative projects, but she doesn't take them seriously, and because of this she interferes with my process, asking me to stop and do the dishes . . .

> The session continues, further identifying aspects of the client that are falling apart in order to develop clarity over vague descriptions of experiences. Clearly identified problems serve as a platform for specific interventions to help the client regain a sense of wholeness in the context of realistic life demands.

PROSPECTION

The ultimate value of life depends on awareness and the power of contemplation rather than upon mere survival.

—ARISTOTLE

The underlying cognitive capacity for affective forecasting is *prospection*, the ability to project oneself beyond the present moment and in an imagined future where one can plan and think about potential scenarios (Zheng, Luo, & Yu, 2014). Several studies in neuroscience have revealed a significant neural overlap between autobiographical memory (ABM) and prospection (Perner, 2000; Spreng, Mar, & Kim, 2009; Suddendorf & Corballis, 1997). In a study conducted at the Massachusetts Institute of Technology, autobiographical memory, prospection, and theory of mind were found to account for "81.42% of the covariance [the degree to which two variables have a linear relationship] in the data"; furthermore, ABM and prospection were dissociable from theory of mind, "accounting for 13.75% of the covariance in data" (Spreng & Grady, 2009, p. 1116). More specifically, Zheng, Luo, and Yu (2014) propose the overlap covers visual-spatial, self, and emotion processes which correspond to the hippocampus, mPFC, amygdala, and insula. Notably, these regions were found to be associated with a network of interacting regions of the brain called the default mode network (DMN), which will be revisited in detail later in this text. This correlation is intuitive, because we frequently use past experiences to help us better predict the future. It is likely that the ability to suspend mental time, reconsider the past, plan for the future, and imagine an array of potential scenarios emerged as evolutionary necessities. We evolve in the face of challenges, and it is not until our habitual tendencies are inadequate that other functions emerge in service of our needs. Suspension of internal stimuli and imagination thus move us beyond our necessity to act out instinctual reactions.

Of note, future events are associated with a prevalent positivity or optimism bias (Schacter et al., 2012). This tendency may be related to our use of this function to engage in effective coping by enhancing our capacity for emotion regulation and problem solving (Brown, MacLeod, Tata, & Goddard, 2002; Sheldon, McAndrews, & Moscovitch, 2011; Taylor, Pham, Rivkin, & Armor, 1998). Practically, positivity may be useful to prepare ourselves for unseen challenges that may arise, as well as a way to plan strategically when working with clients.

Naturally, future events that we deem personally relevant result in greater subjective feelings than events that are not. This is consistent with the *self-referential effect*, which shows that information relevant to the self is better remembered than information that is not. The intensity of emotions has been found to be greater in anticipated future experiences than in past experiences (Caruso, 2010; Caruso, Gilbert, & Wilson, 2008; Van Boven & Ashworth, 2007). This finding speaks to the relevance of including a future orientation in clinical settings, a nod to solution-focused therapists. Second, it intuitively matches the experience of how an idea that is embedded in our minds can be more motivating than an actual lived event. This highlights the level of significance of our psychological experience. It is easy for us to imagine ourselves being motivated by a tangible reward; however, much of the time we are driven by forces that exist only in our minds. This is a cornerstone of human experience: the capacity to act solely on the experience of an abstraction.

In addition to an optimistic bias regarding future events, we also have a tendency to diminish the importance of future rewards as they increase in their distance in time (Green & Myerson, 2004). A spatial analogy to this would be objects appearing smaller the farther we are from them. This phenomenon in future-oriented experience is known as *temporal discounting*. The resolution of temporal discounting entails magnifying the representation of emotional aspects of future reward in a way that overrides this bias so as to produce less impulsive and more farsighted decisions. The longer term the payoff, the stronger the incentive must be (Benoit, Gilbert, & Burgess, 2011; Peters & Buchel, 2010). Thus, from a clinical perspective, clinicians should help clients understand how the future reward may yield immediate benefit and how acting in ways counter to their desire is disadvantageous. It can be helpful to have the client list these out so that the benefit becomes concrete to them; should they feel a moment of weakness, they can refer back to their list.

INHIBITION AND DELAYED GRATIFICATION

Self-control is crucial for the successful pursuit of long-term goals. It is equally essential for developing the self-restraint and empathy needed to build caring and mutually supportive relationships.

—WALTER MISCHEL

One of the most important cognitive functions that has developed with the human frontal lobes is behavioral inhibition, the ability to silence immediate neural, typically limbic reactions in order to respond in a more adaptive manner. Inhibition occurs at a cellular level and may also be understood at a behavioral level. In relation to the latter, inhibition is our ability to say *no* despite a signal from our own minds that can lead to immediate gratification but poor long-term harmony. It may also mean inhibiting intrusive thoughts that propel more suffering. It is one of the most distinguishing features of the human mind when compared to other animals.

Just as our lives are very much defined by a unique balance of approach-avoidance behaviors, the brain's homeostatic balance is partly achieved by excitatory and inhibitory activity. Glutamate is the principal neurotransmitter for excitation, and gamma-aminobutyric acid (GABA) is the principal neurotransmitter for inhibition. Around 80% of glutamatergic cells in the cortex are excitatory and 20% are GABAergic interneurons (Buzsaki, Kaila, & Raichle, 2007). Inhibition can be *phasic* (short lived) or *tonic* (long lasting). Phasic inhibition occurs usually via active GABA receptors in the presynaptic interneuron, whereas tonic inhibition is mediated by GABA in extracellular space (Farrant & Nusser, 2005). Behaviorally, inhibiting an internal reaction initially relies on conscious thought, although it may eventually become second nature, resulting in an automated subconscious or non-conscious response to inhibiting the specified internal stimuli.

The very presence of inhibition suggests that there is something beyond that which is being inhibited. Inhibition directs us toward the very fact that there are systems within us operating without our consent. Our body has a mind of its own and communicates its needs to us, sometimes through impulses or dissonant experiences. What is it that can be inhibited? Anything from impulses to distasteful thoughts to emotional reactions. Inhibition is required in delayed gratification, which is our ability to implement abstract strategies to inhibit our immediate desires for a greater reward in the future. The difference between delayed gratification and immediate gratification lies in time. They are intertemporal choices, choices that can be made at different points in time, depending on the relative payoffs people assign to them. Delayed gratification is developed—it is not an innate capacity—and it has been associated with higher academic achievement, greater intellectual capacity, stronger decision making, and enhanced social responsibility and competence. It has also been identified as a protective factor for physical and psychological health (Twito, Israel, Simonson, & Knafo-Noam, 2019). In animal models, increased abilities for delayed gratification demonstrate higher white matter connectivity between the caudate and the right dorsal prefrontal cortex (Latzman, Taglialatela, & Hopkins, 2015) and higher levels of integration between the nucleus accumbens (the brain's reward center) and the hippocampus (Abela, Duan, & Chudasama, 2015). These findings lead me to ask, if inhibition and delayed gratification improve our metacognitive capacities (our ability to think about thinking), might our desires that continue to exist beyond procreation and survival serve a secondary function (i.e., namely, as stimuli to advance neural development and complexity)? What is of utmost importance for anyone to define is the purpose of inhibiting a particular internal experience. With proper use of this function, we can begin carving a path toward who we would like to be, as opposed to following the currents that seem to push us in the opposite direction. In my opinion, it is one of the most powerful abilities to help facilitate an individual's development.

On a final note, I find it necessary to stress that inhibition and delayed gratification are about suppressing intrusive thoughts to reap a higher reward. If you are feeling inclined to succumb to an outburst of anger at your boss, you would be reacting in an imbalanced, unintegrated manner. Inhibiting this reactivity would possibly benefit you in two ways. First, it may save you from unemployment, and second, the emotional surges may be better harnessed by asserting yourself with confidence and power in a logical and professional manner in the future. Thus, logic becomes integrated with emotion. The notion of having an integrated response will be elaborated further in a future chapter because it plays a crucial role in well-being and therapy.

REFLECTIONS: THE WHEEL IS NOT THE CAR

A knife has the purpose of cutting things, so to perform its function well it must have a sharp cutting edge. Man, too, has a function: unlike any other being he is capable of rational thought. So happiness consists in the rational exercise of the souls faculties in conformity with excellence or virtue.

—ARISTOTLE

Each domain of cognition is necessary for the functioning of human reasoning. Aristotle (4th century BCE/1943) believed that proper reasoning was necessary for one to lead a virtuous life and achieve *eudaimonia*, or human flourishing. Jaspers (1971) adds that the "basic characteristic of reason is the will to unity" (p. 54). He asserts that "reason . . . wants to bring into lucid being, to endow with language, to keep from disappearing . . . reason pushes on to wherever unity is fractured . . . to prevent metaphysical rupture, the disintegration of being itself, in this fragmentation" (p. 56). The unity achieved by reason subsequently finds its meaning in transcendence.

Yet cognition, the foundations of higher order reasoning, is susceptible to many errors. Moreover, consciousness also has a very limited capacity. Perceptual categorization is further amplified by the natural tendency for conceptual categorizing and objectification. If you think about it further, any object that is in view extends infinitely. If we look at a tree, we may notice its crown, its branches extending outward, with its leaves bristling in the wind. We see the steadiness of the trunk, and all the different colors that change with seasons. We call this whole image "a tree," but if we look at its bark under a microscope, the color may appear different, and we may see a host of differences from what we can sense without any technological assistance. This continues when we look at the atomic level, quantum level, and other potential levels yet discovered. Cognition limitlessly extends into everything we objectify (Jaspers, 1917). When we objectify any object or subject, we limit it, we lose the whole. Thinking itself also pulls us out of the whole, and into the intellect. Picture a car, if we removed all its parts and left only the wheels, would it still be a car? This is one of the weaknesses of any evaluation that focuses on particular aspects of being, and the necessity for there also to be a trained professional to help interpret the data in the context of the human as a whole.

CHAPTER 3.

Passive and Active Veil Systems

∙∙

All things are subject to interpretation,
whichever interpretation prevails at a given
time is a function of power and not truth.

—FRIEDRICH NIETZSCHE

In neuropsychology, decision-making faculties are categorized as a part of executive functioning. Decision making is influenced by implicit processes and conscious strategies. Clinically, certain neuropsychological tests enable us to examine the ways people process information. What we tend to find is that there are differences in individual strategy use, mostly without awareness, that may improve their ability to learn. These implicit strategies may improve other functions, such as memory. For example, client A, who initially performed worse than client B, may subsequently outperform client B with use of a strategy. Our ability to plan and strategize forms the basis of our approach to the reality that is presented to us.

Decision making is riddled with complications. Given the massive amount of information that our brains must process, we rely upon a series of heuristics or shortcuts to simplify information (Kahneman & Tversky, 1973, 1984). This is beneficial because it helps the organism conserve energy efficiently while making guesses based on history. If someone presents as extraverted and confident, it is more likely that we will assume that they hold a job that is in line with those attributes, such as being a public speaker, even though we know there are many exceptions to this rule. This heuristic is called a *representative heuristic*. Such a decision-making strategy can be dangerous in the clinical field, as we may be prone to negating individual differences and attributing symptomology to incorrect sources. A concrete example could be accidentally attributing racing thoughts and decreased sleep to mania as opposed to an anxiety disorder, each of which requires vastly different treatment options.

One of the easiest decision-making traps to fall into is *confirmation bias*: the selective tendency to focus only on information that supports our current beliefs while ignoring information that invalidates them. This heuristic can be particularly troublesome but is easy to indulge, because to accept invalidating information means we must use more neural resources to adjust our belief system. Unfortunately, the sacrifice of accuracy for efficiency in this scenario can lead to devastating consequences. A typical error made by a therapist may be an incorrect interpretation of a client's problem and the therapist's insistence that it is true. Being wrong may evoke countertransferential feelings from our past.

We function on efficiency; decisions following different lines of logic within us are constantly competing to be expressed. When making a prediction, we are most likely to base it on the judgment that elicits the least amount of effort. This *availability heuristic* is biased because we will incorrectly judge the frequency of an occurrence based on our familiarity with a specific occurrence. For example, the more accounts we hear of homeless individuals begging for money to spend it on drugs, the more likely it is that the next time we pass a homeless person, we will automatically attribute their begging to drug-related reasons. This may then directly influence our decision to give them money, even if many indigents have a different agenda altogether.

Counter to overlooking an individual difference for a statistical truth, we can also easily make the mistake of relying too heavily on the unique aspects of a case while ignoring base rate information. This is called a *base rate fallacy* (Pennycook & Thompson, 2017).

The *simulation heuristic* dictates that the easier it is to imagine an event happening, the more likely it is that we will predict that event to happen. This also has direct consequences; if what was visualized did not happen, levels of negative affect will increase with direct proportionality to the degree to which we believed what we visualized was likely to happen.

The nature of mental processes may further magnify distorted thinking by drawing a relationship between two unrelated variables. This may be exemplified as a result of the assumptions we make when we first set eyes on an individual. For example, we may assume that someone who is poorly or casually dressed is of low socioeconomic class. This *illusory correlation* is highlighted by the disproportionate amount of incorrect arrests of members of certain ethnic groups and genders. Superstitions appear to have some relation to this heuristic. In an experiment by B. F. Skinner (1948), pigeons were fed pellets at random intervals. After some time, pigeons began acting in strange ways prior to the release of a pellet. It was found that the pigeons' strange behaviors were in fact attempts to cause the pellet to be released. They had associated their random behaviors at the time with the release of a pellet.

The *false consensus effect* refers to our general tendency to use ourselves when attributing behaviors and beliefs to others. Despite the variety of natures and the ways people are nurtured, we still predict other people's behaviors based on ourselves. We act on the presupposition that under our shared human condition we can accurately predict why someone is acting in a certain way. The problem with this assumption is that a person can have any number of a seemingly infinite array of responses in any given circumstance. This is further contingent on the individual's biological, psychological, social, and spiritual disposition at a certain time. As we will discuss further, this phenomenon may be directly connected to a neural network in the brain called the default mode network (DMN).

The *gambler's fallacy* is the belief that the likelihood of a chance event increases or decreases as a result of previous events, such as in slot machines programmed to be random, when in truth there is no relationship between the events. This phenomenon is intimately associated with a variable ratio scheduling of reinforcement (i.e., intermittent reinforcement), which occurs when reinforcements (in this case money from slot machines) happen after an unpredictable number of attempts. Intermittent reinforcement yields persistent and rapid responding and is understood to be the most addictive form of reinforcement.

DEFENSE MECHANISMS AND SELF-REGULATING PROCESSES

Genius, like the inhabitants of the depths of the sea,
moves by its own light.

—SANTIAGO RAMÓN Y CAJAL

An aspect of psychodynamic formulations is the investigation of unconscious psychological defenses to threats, similar to how our immune system has automated reactions to external threats. Psychological research on emotion, priming,* stereotypes, and other implicit processes have uncovered an extensive network of non-conscious neural processing (Tamietto & Gelder, 2010). Clinically, when an individual has a lesion on their primary visual cortex, they may be cortically blind, but still respond to visual information being presented to them. This phenomenon is called blindsight, and along with hemispatial neglect (as discussed earlier), demonstrates that perception itself may occur unconsciously. Yet another condition includes prosopagnosia, or "face-blindness," which may occur as a result of an insult to the fusiform gyrus. Despite being unable to consciously recognize a familiar face, emotional responses through physiological measures have demonstrated significant autonomic responses (Tranel & Damasio, 1985). More popular cases typically involve individuals suffering from anterograde amnesia, as despite their inability to consciously recall learning a particular task, their actions and/or performance prove to be otherwise (Semenza, 2017). Indeed, Schore's (2019) extensive research has led to the proposal of a right-hemisphere biased hierarchical system of the unconscious. These include the preconscious, which houses implicit values and beliefs guided by the orbitofrontal-limbic network, and the deep unconscious, which he associates with the body and autonomic nervous system. He further asserts that the "cortical-subcortical limbic core thus reflect the early developmental history of the subjective self" (p. 190).

---

* Priming is a research method whereby a subject is usually exposed to a stimulus below their awareness. Consequently, the subject may respond differently to stimulus that follows (depending on what the previous stimulus was).

New research on functional and comparative neuroanatomy has favored select theories in psychoanalysis, resulting in the incorporation, revising, and updating of theories based on their mutual insights. This emerging field has been called neuropsychoanalysis (Northoff, 2011; Panksepp & Solms, 2012; Schore, 2019). This field has garnered support from Eric Kandel, Antonio Damasio, and Oliver Sacks. One major update includes altering Freud's notion that the id is unconscious. Although the Freudian id is associated with deep structures such as the brainstem, instinctual demands are considered to be at the very forefront of consciousness (Leuzinger-Bohleber, Arnold, & Solms, 2017). In line with Freud's descriptions, Solms (2015) describes the id as interoceptive and ego as exteroceptive. The upper brainstem (PAG) to the limbic system, corresponding to the internal body (id), "generates internal 'states' rather than external 'objects' of consciousness . . . it gives rise to a background state of 'being'" (p. 156). This state corresponds directly to the pleasure-displeasure, which subsequently prompts the exteroceptive or external body (ego) to come up with strategies to meet those needs.

Information is filtered through a vast amount of neural systems. The development of these systems were guided by our genes and molded by experiences. The content that is filtered, in addition to our biases, likely promoted our survival in some way. One useful model to consider was developed by a neuroscientist named Paul MacLean (1990) in the 1960s and further elaborated in 1990; this model is currently resurfacing in the work of other researchers in affective neuroscience. Its simplicity assists with a basic understanding of the brain for laymen, but it is an imprecise model and oversimplification for any serious professional in neuroscience. Nonetheless, it is useful tool for psychoeducational purposes for clients interested in the gist of what may be happening.

Put simply, MacLean categorized core neurological functions into three divisions that may be taught alongside the hand model of the brain. He begins with the *reptilian complex* consisting of the brainstem and cerebellum. This would include the lower palm of your hand, with your wrist and forearm representing the brainstem descending into the spinal cord. The brainstem is estimated to have evolved around 300 million years ago. It is the first part of central nervous system to develop in the womb, and it is almost fully formed at birth. Together these areas are important for wakefulness, arousal, breathing, reproductive drives, balance, coordination, and movement. The *paleomammalian complex* consists of the limbic system, which is partially developed at birth and evolved around 200 million years ago. It is important for homeostasis, olfaction, memory, emotion (HOME), and learning. This is represented by your thumb pulled 90 degrees inward into the upper palm. The *neomammalian complex* refers to the cerebral cortex, in charge of organizing conscious thought, problem solving, and self-awareness. This would be represented by the four fingers wrapping over the thumb. The relevance of this model enters when describing the conflicting evolutionary motives of these three brains that comprise the whole. Maclean viewed the repitilian brain as harboring our predatorial natures, our paleomammalian brain with self-preservation and neomammilian with advanced social behaviors.

The unconscious can be seen as the psychological correlate of non-conscious neural processing. As is implied in its name, the unconscious is not directly observable but must be inferred from dreams, psychological experiences, behavioral manifestations, or physiological studies. One famous manifestation is the Freudian slip, which occurs when someone speaks a different word than was intended in reaction to an inner drive. For example, I remember once arriving at a former professor's office when I was feeling hungry and telling the administrator, "I am here to visit Professor D's restaurant." Other manifestations include defense mechanisms, transference, and countertransference. The brain will impose structure on uncertainty, just as our brain adjusts for the blind spots in our eyes, providing us with a complete picture. The therapist initially presents as a question mark, or an unknown. As an unknown, the client's beliefs and paradigms are projected onto us. Stern (1985) called these projections *representations of interactions that have been generalized* (RIG). For instance, if a client has been mistreated by police officers, the client may suspect the next police officer encountered will have less than kind intentions. Countertransference occurs when the therapist begins to behave in a way that conforms to the client's projected contents. In these scenarios, it is always beneficial for the therapist to reflect on the event in service of better understanding the client's interpersonal difficulties as a result of their projections.

Freud (1894) coined the term *defense mechanisms* to describe phenomena that arise in direct defense of a psychological threat. Individuals are theorized to become arrested in certain stages of development and as a result exhibit different forms of defenses, categorized generally as narcissistic, immature, and neurotic. In contrast, healthy individuals harbor mature defenses. More recently, empirical research has indicated that the use of defenses is reduced when we become aware of them. This was found through research on developing children, whereby their defenses were less prevalent when their cognitive functions enabled them to understand what their defenses were and when the children were aware of them in the present (Cramer, 2015). This finding supports the psychodynamic framework of mechanisms involved with healing, specifically insight (the other being a corrective emotional experience; Shafranske, 2009). As would be expected, particular defenses have been correlated with specific diagnoses, and excessive use of defenses is related to psychopathology (Cramer 2015; Zanarini, Weingeroff, & Frankenberg, 2009).

Immature defenses, as the name implies, are considered primitive because they are defenses commonly used to cope with reality in the earlier periods of life. This does not mean adults do not have these kinds of defenses, but they are expected to use them with decreasing frequency as their frontal lobes become more developed. Acting out, for example, occurs when someone is unable to inhibit their impulses and as a result acts on them without regard for social appropriateness. It makes sense that infants and toddlers would engage in this defense because of the underdeveloped state of their prefrontal cortex, which is largely in charge of inhibiting inappropriate responses. As children's frontal lobes develop, the affect regulation strategies their parents teach them become embedded into this neural circuitry. Parents may, temporarily at least, analogously act as a prosthetic prefrontal cortex for their children (Cozolino, 2014). It is fascinating to track the interface between psychoanalytic defenses and biology. For example, in borderline personality disorder, self-cutting as a form of passive-aggression (an immature defense) can be more fully understood in relation to an opioid deficit. In this model, self-cutting generates a response from opioid systems, which is involved in not only regulating pain, but also reducing stress and negative emotional responses (New & Barbara, 2010). According to Vaillant (2011), these defenses tend to manifest in people with personality disorders, with adolescents, and with substance abusers.

Narcissistic defenses are termed as such because in them the self is idealized, and other aspects of existence are denied or eliminated from awareness. Such defenses may distort reality, reshaping it to fit the person's needs and grandiose thinking. Splitting is one of the foundational defenses for narcissists; it is related to polarized thinking, whereby people and situations are seen as all good or all bad. This may be accompanied by projection, which is the attributing of undesirable inner states onto outer people or events. According to J. Perry and Cooper (1986), these have been significantly correlated with antisocial psychopathology.

Neurotic defenses relate to each other via shifts in emotion and identity. They are neurotic because they arise from reactions to anxiety, major depression, and other mood-based disorders. Neurotic defenses include controlling, managing, or regulating the environment excessively to avoid anxiety; displacement, resulting in someone punishing a cat instead of an authority figure who has upset them; and dissociation, which results in perceiving oneself as an external object. Others include repression, inhibition, isolation, and intellectualization. According to Vaillant (2011), these occur most often in individuals with psychosomatic disorders, compulsions, phobias, and amnesias.

Mature defenses are ways we manage our impulses effectively as adults. These healthy manners of defense become more common with age. These include altruism, anticipation, asceticism, humor, sublimation, and suppression. These kinds of defenses are all about responding to inappropriate impulses and expressing them through different outlets. Examples of sublimation might be passionately engaging in dance, playing music, focusing one's extra energy on helping others, or telling jokes. Suppression is the immediate decision to postpone our attention to a conscious impulse. We are not avoiding the issue; rather, we are intentionally silencing it.

Gestalt therapists call the meeting of an individual and their environment a *contact boundary* (Gold & Zahm, 2018). They view defense mechanisms as self-regulating processes that occur in relation to events that may transpire at the boundary. Self-regulatory processes arise when the organism's homeostatic balance has been disrupted (Perls, 1947). These are a few ways in which an organism attempts to restore their balance. Table 3.1 summarizes these self-regulating processes.

TABLE 3.1: **Self-Regulating Process**		
SELF-REGULATING PROCESS (Gold, Zahm, 2018),* pp. 102–111)	**EXPLANATION**	**DISADVANTAGES (D)/ ADVANTAGES (A)**
Introjection	Complete identification with an exterior idea or stimuli. E.g., blind acceptance of societal rule, adoption as if part of the self.	**D:** Individuality is stifled. **A:** Many times, we learn through imitation.
Retroflecting	Energy needed for action is directed toward the self (anger, guilt) or the other (anger, critical). Needs must be met via relationship.	**A:** Proper self-control is equivalent to aware retroflection. **D:** When reflexive and unaware.
Confluence	Self-other boundary is dissolved.	**D:** Complacency, sumissiveness, or agreeableness. No expression of individual opinions. **A:** Social harmony
Deflecting	Contact intensity is mitigated. Example: during a vulnerable moment one "laughs" it off, or talks around a topic.	**D:** Deeper insight and processing of emotions is neglected. **A:** Social harmony, may protect a vulnerable self
Egotism	Procrastination of responsibility via unnecessary amounts of introspection.	**D:** Stuck, actions not made despite higher intellectual awareness. **A:** Preventative for impulsivity

* A more comprehensive description of each can be found in (Gold & Zahm, 2018, pp. 102–111). Projection was not included due to its controversial position in Gestalt therapy and redundancy with its psychodynamic counterpart.

APPLICATIONS: PROJECTION AND REPETITION COMPULSION

It is a joy to be hidden, but a disaster not to be found.

—D. W. WINNICOTT

Defense mechanisms operate without our full consent. Although they mean well (i.e., by protecting us from anxiety and self-disintegration), they also distort our feelings, desires, and decisions. At times, our aspirations can be overwhelmed by the urges that arise from these defenses, resulting in a reduced sense of personal autonomy (Shapiro, 2000). A comprehensive referenced chart of defense mechanisms can be found in Appendix B.

Two defenses I want to visit in more depth due to their salience in clinical encounters and everyday life are projection and repetition compulsion. The *objective world* plays a role in the elicitation of our senses, but a large part of it is constructed through non-conscious processes. The very act of perception is transformation; we transform the *code* of the universe to the world we see around ourselves. This code is uncertain to us, with new streams of thought suggesting that what we see is actually nothing like the code it is interpreting (Hoffman, 2019). The world, as we perceive it, is in part a mental projection. Not only is this code interpreted in accordance to pre-reflective expectations in the brain, but it is also colored by our reflective processes.

We populate the external world with our mental contents, and they tend to be ones we are unable to tolerate. Such a phenomenon occurs in moments of uncertainty, and our projections may be agreeable or disagreeable. For example, an encounter with a complete stranger may trigger a negative emotional reaction in us far beyond what would be expected. We automatically project disagreeable attributes unto them, when, upon further reflection, we find they have somehow become a representative of traits we dislike about ourselves. This may happen the other way around as well. Some people whom we highly respect become imbued by us with virtuous qualities that they never have exhibited. These people become larger than life and we become biased and easy targets for exploitation. In this situation, such virtuous qualities were perhaps qualities we wished to see more in ourselves but have been unable to live up to.

It is because of our tendency to project that we must help clients be present with all of their thoughts, especially in relation to us (via transference). Denying the existence of these projections robs clients of their potential wholeness and awareness necessary to become more balanced in their judgments (Woodman, 1982). To put it simply, in a sense, projection causes us to unknowingly give a piece of ourselves to someone else. These pieces must be re-owned; in doing so we reclaim a force that equates to the level of power that was directed toward the object of projection. This does not mean we must act on all thoughts; rather we should consent to some, cultivate others, and let others free themselves.

One of the most common and insidious challenges I have encountered in therapy are the maladaptive relational cycles that individuals repeat with others. Freud (1920) believed that feelings that have yet to be recalled consciously manifest in the form of these cycles. He called this *repetition compulsion*, and it may well transfer onto the therapeutic relationship. Repetition compulsion may arise in multiple levels of experience and may be a defense from a traumatic origin or an attachment-based strategy that is no longer of use (Bowins, 2010). The purpose of these cycles is interpreted as an organism's desire for mastery; thus, the reason why someone continues to sabotage themself may not be entirely related to some destructive drive. Rather, it may be the creation of an opportunity to find resolution. One way this can be worked through directly is Hanna Levenson's (2003) time-limited dynamic approach, in which she labels these dysfunctional relational patterns as a cyclical maladaptive pattern (CMP). In her therapeutic approach, the core goal is to identify these maladaptive patterns, their historical origins, and their associated expectations, and find ways to subvert their continued existence. Subverting would occur through insight and new experiences within the therapeutic relationship.

Overall, defenses are typically interpreted by a trained psychodynamic or analytic therapist. It is important to note that the image of the aloof and distant analyst is considered a misinterpretation. The function of the analyst's technical neutrality is to prevent the imposition of the therapist's value system and beliefs onto the client and is actually more about remaining neutral in the client's attempts to involve the analyst in their conflicts (Kernberg, 2016). Thus, the analyst should neither support nor denigrate the client's viewpoints. The appropriate therapeutic attitude is to be engaged with appropriate space so as not to promote maladaptive cycles. Psychoanalysis is more about process rather than about the specific content of information being presented. Although a client may be speaking about an incident that upset them, the underlying patterns of emotional experience are what interest practitioners. From the perspective of Kernberg (2016), the steps involved in interpretive intervention include: (a) clarification of mental processes; (b) confrontation of nonverbal behavior that may seem contradictory; and (c) interpretation, which is a hypothesis about the underlying unconscious process.

Dialogue

1. **Clarification:** It sounds as if you never felt "good enough" in your parents' presence, is that accurate?

2. **Confrontation:** You mentioned that you feel unfairly judged by your parents, and now you're telling me that you're receiving feedback from your partner that they feel judged by you. Might there be some relation?

3. **Interpretation:** It sounds as if you were criticized frequently by your parents, and they made you feel you were not "good enough." Now you are struggling with relational difficulties, partly because your partner feels judged by you. Might it be possible that by doing so, you prevent yourself from ever being in that position again, and perhaps even feel some solace in knowing your partner may understand how you felt?

In a therapeutic context, the therapist may point out the defense, confront a client on their psychological attempt at defending themself, and interpret the defense as it potentially relates to anxiety and its historical correlates. In this way, the analyst facilitates a gradual broadening of awareness. As the unconscious becomes conscious, individuals become more flexible and stable, capable of noticing these defenses arising before they hijack their system. In severe disorders, successful treatment is akin to the terraforming of a client's subjective atmosphere and landscape.

Two other successful approaches in working with rigidly resistant defense mechanisms include Bateman and Fonagy's (2010) mentalization-based treatment (specifically for borderline personality disorder), an approach whereby the clinician actively engages the client's ability to think through another person's perspective, and for those with shorter span of time for therapy, Davanloo's intensive short-term dynamic therapy, an intensive approach meant to break through the client's defenses (Johansson, Town, & Abbass, 2014).

Self-regulation processes from Gestalt psychology culminates in biased experiences resulting in a loss of information and inefficient investment of energy needed for an optimal response. Working with these processes includes reconnecting with experiences that clients may have avoided, helping them cultivate awareness for the use of a particular strategy, and re-incorporating new insights into the figure of their focus. Techniques might include pointing out incongruences between what a client is saying and nonverbal expressions, asking clients who deflect to stay with emotions that are uncomfortable, or giving voice to gestures or bodily experiences.

COGNITIVE DISTORTIONS

People are not disturbed by things, but by the view they take of them.

—Epictetus

We are riddled with illusions that haunt us daily. How often do we act in ways that are counter to our so-called beliefs? If our self is not in control of this physical body and mind, then who is? We have an inherent lie mechanism embedded in our systems of thought. By this, I refer to the phenomenon of *cognitive dissonance*. When we act counter to our values or feelings, it generates dissonance within us. In order to resolve this dissonance and feel better, we adjust our stance, often through a logic that rests on relativism and context. For example, let's suppose that you wanted to stay in one night because you have been spending lots of money lately. However, your friends are urging you to go out, and eventually they convince you to join them. You are temporarily mad at yourself for being unable to stand your ground, but then you tell yourself, "Well, life is short and I can die at any moment, so I might as well enjoy it while it lasts." You feel better and enjoy a night with your friends, only to feel bad the following day.

Beyond situations like this one, our cognitions are quite prone to error on an everyday basis. Evolutionary adaptation has generated heuristics or shortcuts that have allowed us to make fast judgments. Our brain is a parallel processor, meaning it is not like a computer that processes information serially (needing to sift through all information systematically). Despite the benefits of speed, survival, and protection, our cognitions may become maladaptive in different contexts.

Cognitive behavioral therapy (CBT) focuses on cognitions (thoughts), feelings, and behaviors. Beck, Rush, Shaw, and Emery (1979) developed cognitive therapy, which was inspired by stoicism. One of the foundational ideas of stoicism is that it is not a situation that results in negative psychological experiences, but rather a person's interpretation of the situation. These interpretations are under the person's control, whereas anything else should be approached with *amor fati* (love for one's fate). Generally, CBT focuses on mastering these interpretations by recognizing automatic dysfunctional thoughts, identifying their origins in core beliefs, challenging them rationally, and implementing behavioral interventions.

Cognitive distortions offer one way to justify our antisocial behaviors and cast ourselves in a positive light. Helmond, Overbeek, Brugman, and Gibbs (2014) conducted a meta-analysis with the aim of clarifying the relationship between (a) cognitive distortions and externalizing problem behaviors and (b) the interventions used in mitigating problem behaviors through improving the person's ability to combat these distortions. After reviewing data on 18,544 subjects, the meta-analysis of their first aim yielded a medium to large effect size ($d = .70$, $p < .001$, 95% confidence interval). However, the treatment yielded a much smaller effect size ($d = .27$, $p < .05$, 95% confidence interval). Thus, whereas the association between cognitive distortions and externalizing behaviors was quite high, the treatment for these distortions still has room for improvement.

Everyone will experience cognitive distortions from time to time. As we would expect, different mental disorders come with different profiles of cognitive distortions used (Rnic, Dozois, & Martin, 2016). When treating individuals who suffer from depression, we may commonly encounter distortions such as mental filtering, all-or-nothing thinking, mind reading, or catastrophizing.

People may cope with depression in different ways, one of which is substance addiction. In these sorts of cases, which I experienced frequently at the Union Rescue Mission, people may feel extremely guilty about the lies they told to obtain their desired substance. Many feel that they are inherently corrupt, focusing on all the bad behaviors they have committed while completely ignoring their positive actions. This sort of *mental filtering* leads to the continued cycle of shame, which on an extreme scale can truly incapacitate recovery. It is also common to find reasoning being skewed, as one relapse results in the identification of the self as a failure. *All-or-nothing thinking* also perpetuates this cycle. As attempts at recovery proceed, oftentimes a person's imagined interactions with others feel disheartening. The addict in recovery may assume that others are thinking negative thoughts and as a result react to those assumptions as opposed to the reality of the situation. This form of *mind reading* may further promulgate catastrophizing, the belief that there is only one future possibility for them—namely, the worst-case scenario.

We are not responsible for the automated thoughts or emotions that present themselves to us. Indeed, much of this can be biologically driven. What we are responsible for, however, is whether we believe in them or challenge them.

APPLICATIONS: ON BECOMING SOCRATES

You cannot know your real mind, as long as you deceive yourself.

—BODHIDHARMA

Fundamentally, I have always viewed the central role of the clinician in CBT to be that of Socrates. Challenging distortions comes in the form of collaborative empiricism, meaning the evidence supporting a client's output is examined in depth, and the process of examining invites the client's input throughout. Anyone who has read any Socratic dialogues will find that he does not debate his pupils, rather, he engages them in a dialectic. Thought oscillates between two opposing ideas, generating doubts. Doubts form new answers until truths from both sides are established, a third idea transcending its former position emerges. Rutter and Friedberg (1999) suggest that there are five steps which are important for Socratic questioning: "1) elicit the automatic thought; 2) link the automatic thought to feeling and behavior; 3) connect the thought-feeling-behavior sequence together with an empathic response; 4) enlist collaboration; and 5) Socratically test the belief" (p. 489). The subsequent layer of influence comes from Stoicism, particularly the notion that experiences in themselves are neutral, and that it is our interpretation of those experiences that bother us. This comes from the *Enchiridion* (translation by Long, 1877) by Epictetus, who subsequently relates this insight to Socrates, and his attitude toward death and decision to die via poisionous hemlock when he could have escaped. Interpretation or opinion is under our control, and Stoics advise that we exercise this intellectual capacity, as it may very well save us from self-inflicted suffering. In my opinon, teaching others how to think with intent, structure, clarity, and purpose is CBT's core strength.

When it comes to cognitive distortions, we may be prompted to examine the extremes of the situation, asking what is the worst and best reality of a particular interpretation, and what is the most realistic outcome based on the facts (e.g., automatic thought record). Taking a step back from becoming upset by writing out responses in detail allows the client to view different angles with more precision, and come to a more accurate conclusion mitigating dissonant affect. Behavioral interventions, such as "acting as if," have been successful in helping others align their thoughts and emotions through behaviors and adopt a mindset that helps them recognize that they do have the ability to act in ways that they believe to be best for them. Behaviors themselves can be considered thoughts, when viewed from an objective perspective. This will be further elaborated in Chapter 6. A comprehensive referenced chart for cognitive distortions can be found in Appendix C.

Defenses, self-regulatory processes, and cognitive distortions tend to be reactive, and protective expressions toward events that disrupt our balance. They attempt to protect, and if not, maximize the organism's efficiency. The problem is that in doing so, they may simplify reality maladaptively, resulting in inefficient engagements with the world and self. Mere exposure to the existence of this veil is a first step in becoming aware because awareness of an obstacle is the first step in evading it.

CHAPTER 4.

Self-Processes

···

We embody the world and through our senses
make it come to life, in the same way we also
are brought to life ourselves by being in the
world and by embodying it.

—MAURICE MERLEAU-PONTY

Notably, one third of our lives is spent sleeping, another third is focused on goal-oriented activities, and the final third is spent engaged with inner events. Broadly speaking, our range of experience varies within and among these three states of awareness in any given 24-hour day. In our primary state, sleep, our brains create dreams, fantastic storylines with streams of images and sensations. Dream objects are in constant flux; a cup has the potential to morph into a butterfly, and any imagined figure could become realized; dreams are a phantasmagoria, much of which is out of our control. In the secondary state, the *conceptual world*, we experience sensations, images, feelings, and thoughts. We experience a steady flow of subvocal articulation (inner dialogue) and possess the capacity to imagine, eliciting phantom-like projections: visual imprints just light enough not to overwhelm perception, yet strong enough to suspend and experience them in our purview. We can induce anything into psychological existence and nurture it until it becomes a part of our daily lives. This second state is an interface between the primary world and tertiary world, or the *perceptual world*, the world we refer to as *real life*, where much is constant: a cup remains a cup, and the sun will rise and set predictably. Indeed, physical laws continue to keep our objective world relatively fixed. These three worlds grew from, help create, and are embedded in an *objective* world, a continual mystery with a capacity for an infinite number of experiences beyond what we may even imagine.

We all inhabit fields of awareness that are perpetually expanding and contracting. They seem to expand in comfort, contract in moments of anger, dissociate from memory in deep sleep, and enter a reliable state in wakefulness. These fields of awareness are populated by an inner and outer world of fleeting impressions, sensations, ideas, and feelings that all help compose our very beings. We notice them because we have an experience of self, a spotlight of consciousness operating from an identity that is continually emerging and constructed through time. In our dreams, we find our self acting as a distinct actor-observer in narratives and worlds that our brain constructs. The important phenomenological hint here is that our psychological systems extend far beyond our experience of self. Parenthetically, we are not creating them consciously. In waking life, we feel as though we are an isolated entity located in our heads, inhabiting a body that interacts with a world.

We understand the self as *I* (representing the subjective experience of self) and *me* (the objective self). The subjective experience of self is measured by phenomenological means, such as self-reports and rating scales. Different means have been used in attempts to measure the objective self, such as correlations with brain structure and function. From the perspective of the brain, I am partial to Antonio Damasio's (2010) idea that there may be *protoself structures*, with primordial feelings, such as awareness of body, without language, capable of experiencing pleasure and pain. In line with this theory is Jaak Panksepp's (1998) idea of the simple ego-type lifeform (SELF) that may emerge from synchronized motor processes. There are many theories regarding the different layers of self, with the most advanced of them being aligned with Damasio's notion of an autobiographical self "defined in terms of biographical knowledge pertaining to the past as well as anticipated future. . . . The multiple images whose ensemble defines a biography generate pulses of core self whose aggregate constitutes an autobiographical self . . . the autobiographical self, whose higher reaches embrace all aspects of one's social persona, constitute a 'social me' and a 'spiritual me'" (p. 24).

Psychological researchers have a variety of definitions for the self, coming to no conclusive agreement on the subject. Similar to consciousness and the mind, the self is thought to be an emergent property of complex systems. Nowak, Vallacher, Tesser, and Borowski (2000) asserted that, "like a society of individuals, the self can be viewed as a complex dynamical system, with interactions among system elements promoting the emergence of macro-level properties that cannot be reduced to the properties of the elements in isolation" (p. 39). The self, conceptualized as emerging from multiple selves, is not new, but important, renewed in recent findings that they may be reflected by a rich collection of operating systems in the brain (visit the section on *embodied symbiosis* for more; p. 243).

This description leads to the question, what are these elements? Georg Northoff and Felix Bermpohl (2004) suggested several possible components, identified in Figure 4.1.

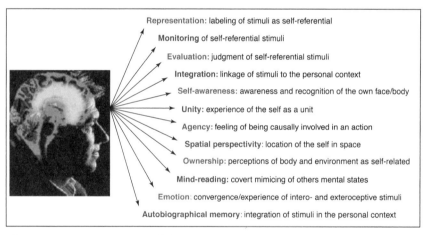

Figure 4.1: Components of the Self   *Source:* "Cortical Midline Structures and the Self," by G. Northoff and F. Bermpohl, 2004, *Trends in Cognitive Sciences, 8*(3), p. 103.

If we are to build on this model, we find several avenues through which our experience of an autobiographical self may become biased. A large portion of what determines the sorts of autobiographical memories are relevant to be integrated are the narratives about ourselves based on memories that we designate to be important. This designation process relates to evolutionary pressures and is unfortunately further influenced by unreliable memories and predictions.

This is an example of how a more advanced cognitive function may depend on incorrect information from previous layers. If one layer is not accurate, one that relies on it will not be accurate either. Even if we were to identify with metacognition,* our ability to monitor and regulate mental processes, we are still left with energy and information that arise from a particular self with its unique genetic dispositions, experiences, and environmental context.

From a developmental standpoint, it is interesting to note that during infancy (up to 2 years of age), humans lack an autobiographical self. It is an illusion to believe that our current sense of self has existed with us since our inception. Although a self may have been developing during those early years, with experiences becoming embedded into implicit memory systems, a stable and continuous sense of self that is capable of introspection simply does not exist during early infancy. Approximately 65% of the brain develops after birth (Knickmeyer et al., 2008), meaning 65% of our neural architecture forms in relation to interactions with family, friends, and the environment. This process plays a key role in settling the once prevalent debate between nature and nurture, with some aspects of life leaning more toward one end than the other. For example, physical characteristics are genetically driven, but proportions change when we begin to consider factors such as IQ, which seems to range from 57–86% (Bouchard & McGue, 2003; Panizzon et al., 2014). Consider also that in a twin study, genetic influence accounted for only 12% of the personality trait of agreeableness (Bergeman et al., 1993).

As time goes on the brain develops in interaction with its social environment, giving rise to a sense of self. Thus, humans "seem to emerge into self-awareness from an undifferentiated sense of membership and interrelationship with family and community" (Cozolino, 2010, p. 258).

Why do we develop a sense of self? Baumeister and Finkel (2010) suggested that the purpose of the self is to serve social needs, that is, to gain social acceptance and secure and improve our position within the social hierarchy. They identified three core functions: reflexive consciousness, the ability to turn in toward oneself; interpersonal relations, self as forming from interactions and relations; and making choices or exerting control. Even if this was not the complete story, it would be very difficult to argue that it is not part of it. We are social animals, after all, and the opinions of others do matter to us to vary-

---

* Traditionally defined as our ability to "think about thinking."

ing degrees. As a result, we may present ourselves differently in moments of solitude when compared to in large groups.

THE DEFAULT MODE NETWORK

A large fraction of the overall activity—from 60–
80 percent of all energy used by the brain—occurs
in circuits unrelated to any external event . . . our
group came to call this intrinsic activity the brain's
dark energy, a reference to the unseen energy that
also represents the mass of most of the universe.

—MARCUS RAICHLE

Returning to our experience of a self that is stable and continuous, might we find corresponding regions of the brain that are continually active? To the surprise of many scientists, we do not. A paradoxical yet intriguing hypothesis is that neuronal discontinuity may be key in leading to psychological continuity (Northoff, 2016; Schore, 2019). More specifically, multiple complex neural processes shifting rapidly may be required in order for the psychological experience of self as connected and continual to emerge. This would lend support to the notion that the self is a process, and its stability through time is an illusion.

When several regions of the brain are in constant interaction with one another, they form a neural network. We currently know of numerous neural networks, or *small worlds* (Long et al., 2013), that work together, and they correspond to multiple modes of engagement. We are constantly engaging with ourselves, disengaging from the environment, and vice versa. When neuroscientists think of correlates to the self, they think of the cortical midline structures, which have been subsumed into the *default network* (Raichle et al., 2001). This collection of structures has since been termed the *default mode network* (DMN).

The DMN is a vastly interconnected network of brain regions that are active during moments of *rest*; that is, when we are not engaged in any particular externally oriented activity. The irony here is that the brain is never resting; even when it is not actively engaged in a task, its consumption of energy is reduced by less than 5% (Raichle et al., 2001). Anticevic and colleagues (2012) labeled the DMN a task-negative network (TNN) in contrast to a task-positive network (TPN) because the DMN deactivates when we are engaged in an external task. However, this notion has been found to be incorrect because tasks involving self and social processes have been found to activate the DMN (Mars et al., 2012). What precise functions are active during rest? Sometimes we are intentionally recalling a personal memory (autobiographical recall), simulating a future event (prospection), developing our identity (self-referential processing), or thinking about an interaction that may have occurred (social cognition). Other times, our mind is simply wandering.

This finding means that the same network used in self-functions overlaps significantly with our capacity to understand others. It also means that the brain has an independent network, the DMN, that is dedicated to our inner lives. It is composed of the medial prefrontal cortex, hippocampal formation, lateral temporal, and parietal cortices surrounding the temporoparietal junction, the posterior cingulate cortex, and the precuneus. In addition, these cortical areas are connected to autobiographical recall and prospection, which are themselves connected by what Endel Tulving (2002) labeled "mental time travel" (p. 2). It turns out that the relationship between time and self-experiences may be elaborated further. Georg Northoff (2016) proposed that self is embedded in the experience of time, value, and reward—a fascinating hypothesis influenced by the inverse relationship between temporal discounting and self-continuity. This assertion makes sense, as we tend to lose the subjective importance of a reward as the future extends farther away from the present. It can be inferred, then, that there is a sort of discontinuity of the immediate experience of self. Neuroanatomically, the perigenual anterior cingulate cortex (PACC) links the experience of self-continuity and temporal discounting. Northoff suggested that this region may be where self is embedded in time.

The following list and Table 4.1 summarize relevant regions of the brain and their overall functions:

Anterior cingulate cortex (ACC) [2]
Bilateral inferior parietal and posterior temporal around the
   temporoparietal junction (TPJ) [5]
Hippocampal formation [2, 4]
Inferior parietal lobule [2, 7]
Insula [7]
Lateral parietal cortices [1, 4, 7]

Lateral temporal lobes [7]

Medial posterior cortex [5]

Medial prefrontal cortex (mPFC) [1, 2, 4, 5, 6, 7]

Middle temporal gyrus [3]

Posterior cingulate cortex (PCC) [1, 2, 4, 5, 6]

Precuneus [1, 5, 6]

Thalamus [7]

References

1 Bianconi et al. (2013)

2 Buckner, Hanna, & Schacter
   (2008)

3 Daniels, Bluhm, & Lanius
   (2013)

4 Fair et al. (2008)

5 Mars et al. (2012)

6 Raichle et al. (2001)

7 Spreng et al. (2009)

TABLE 4.1: **DMN Regions and Functions**

NEUROANATOMY	FUNCTION
Medial Prefrontal Cortex (Mitchell, Banaji, & Macrae, 2005)	Information processing relevant to self and considering the minds of other people
Parietal Lobes (Beaumont, 2008)	Somatosensory perception, bodily perception, visual-spatial orientation, memory, symbolic synthesis, and cross-modal matching
Temporal Lobes (Buccione, Fadda, Serra, Caltagirone, & Carlesimo, 2008; Kapur, Ellison, Smith, McLellan, & Burrows, 1992)	Role in memory for past events, affecting both autobiographical (i.e., episodic, semantic) and nonautobiographical (i.e., public events, general semantic knowledge) memory
Hippocampal Formation (Buckner et al., 2008; Fair et al., 2008)	Formation of new memories, spatial coding, contextualization of memory

NEUROANATOMY	FUNCTION
Posterior Cingulate Cortex (Maddock, Garrett, & Buonocore, 2003)	Evaluative functions and mediation of interactions of emotional and memory-related processes
Precuneus (Cavanna & Trible, 2006)	Mental imagery strategies related to the self, facilitation of successful episodic memory retrieval
Temporoparietal Junction (Saxe, 2006)	Theory of mind, empathy

Literature reviews have indicated that the DMN can be separated into subsystems that are differentially involved. Several models for this phenomenon have been proposed (Andrews-Hanna, Reidler, Sepulcre, Poulin, & Buckner, 2010; Christoff, Irving, Fox, Spreng, & Andrews-Hanna, 2016; Li, Mai, & Liu, 2014). The most recent review by Christoff and colleagues (2016) divides the DMN into three subsystems, as shown in Table 4.2.

TABLE 4.2: DMN Subsystems and Functions

DEFAULT NETWORK SUBSYSTEMS	ASSOCIATED REGIONS	FUNCTIONS
DN_{CORE}	Anterior mPFC Posterior cingulate cortex Posterior inferior parietal lobule	Self-referential processing
DN_{MTL}	Hippocampal formation Parahippocampal cortex	Autobiographical recall Prospection
DN_{SUB3}	Dorsomedial prefrontal cortex Lateral temporal cortex extending into temporopolar cortex	Emotion processing Theory of mind

It would be easy to assume that the DMN is the seat of the experience of self, but this fails to make sense when we consider its relationship to other brain networks. As a reminder, the DMN is inhibited when a person is actively engaged in a goal-directed activity (Anticevic et al., 2012). Thus, if the DMN was the neuroanatomical correlate of the autobiographical self, then it may simply vanish when we engage on a task.

The DMN functions in relation to other neural networks: specifically, the salience network (SN) and central executive network (CEN). The SN is a neural network that determines the importance of internal and external stimuli (salience) as related to an individual's context, further orienting an individual to internal activity or the environment. It is composed of the ventrolateral prefrontal cortex, anterior insula, anterior cingulate cortex (Sridharan, Levitin, & Menon, 2008), amygdala, and putamen (Patel, Spreng, Shin, & Girard, 2012). The CEN is activated when the brain is engaged in a task, and its central nodes are the dorsolateral prefrontal cortex and posterior parietal cortex (Sridharan et al., 2008). The SN has been found to be responsible for transitioning between the DMN and the CEN (Goulden et al., 2014). The following description comes from Antonio Damasio (2010), who suggested:

> Posteromedial cortices (part of the DMN) possibly [reflect] the background-foreground dance played by the self within the conscious mind. When we need to attend to external stimuli, our conscious mind brings the object under scrutiny into the foreground and lets the self retreat into the background. (p. 243)

More recently, research has suggested that the necessity to toggle back and forth amongst these networks plays an important role in contextualizing information (Smith, Mitchell, & Duncan, 2018). Specifically, our ability to navigate the world and its daily activities highly benefits from integrating temporal (i.e., memories, prospection) and self-other related information.

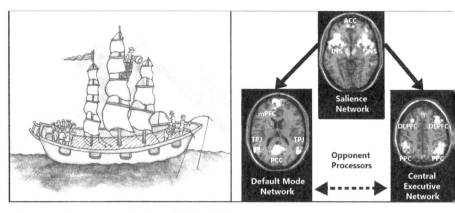

Figure 4.2: DMN and its Relationships

Left: The group of sailors in a huddle represents the social nature of the DMN. In addition, one individual is looking at where the ship has gone (autobiographical recall) and another is looking at where the ship is going (prospection). **Center:** The sailor on the mast represents the salience network. He may only direct the light at one side at a time, directing the focus of energy and information flow inward or outward. **Right:** The men fishing represent the CEN—as they are engaged on an external task.

Adjacent image to the right: The three networks as they are reflected in the metaphorical boat.

Note: Not all regions of the DMN, SN, and CEN are displayed in this diagram. mPFC: medial prefrontal cortex, TPJ: temporoparietal junction, INS: insula, DLPFC: dorsolateral prefrontal cortex, PPC: posterior parietal cortex.

Source: Reprinted from "Play and the Default Mode Network: Interpersonal Neurobiology," by A. Chan & D. Siegel, 2017, in T. Marks-Tarlow, D. J. Siegel, & M. Solomon (Eds.), *Self and Creativity: Play and Creativity in Psychotherapy* (pp. 39–50). New York, NY: W. W. Norton and Company. Reprinted with permission.

NEUROPLASTICITY AND SELF-PROCESSES

*What one commonly takes as "the reality," including
the reality of one's own individual person, by
no means signifies something fixed, but rather
something that is ambiguous—that there is not
only one, but that there are many realities, each
comprising also a different consciousness of the ego.*

—ALBERT HOFFMAN

We cannot locate the self in the brain, but we have been able to correlate some of its functions to the DMN. How stable is this network? Can it change and, if so, is change related to alterations in the experience of self?

To begin with, the brain continues to change throughout our lifetime through plasticity. Plasticity is the brain's natural ability to reorganize its structures, functions, and connections in response to its unique environment. There are many forms of plasticity including: short-term plasticity, long-term plasticity (LT potentiation, long-term depression), spike-timing-dependent plasticity, metaplasticity, homeostatic plasticity, and structural synaptic plasticity (Mateos-Aparicio & Rodriguez-Moreno, 2019). Processes that consolidate plastic changes tend to occur during sleep or restful waking states. Fortunately, the notion that our brain matures, stagnates, and declines is now regarded as a fallacy. Developmental processes related to the frontal lobes mature well into the twenties and myelination may continue up to forty years of age (Sowell et al., 2003). It is theorized that concomitant reductions in grey matter density may relate to greater myelination (as myelination increases conduction speed and efficiency of information distribution). Moreover, our brains grow with the expansion of existing synaptic connections as we get older, a process called *arborization*. Cozolino (2014) hypothesizes that our brains shift in their development from the necessity to learn to the necessity to specialize; which would be in congruence the continual development of myelination. The efficacy of psychotherapy owes much gratitude to our brain's plastic nature, as is supported by mounting studies finding that psychotherapy may result in neural changes (Mason, Peters, Williams, & Kumari, 2017).

Moreover, researchers have found that new neurons and glial cells continue to be born throughout our lifetime. Neurogenesis, or the birth of new neurons, has also been found in the dentate gyrus within the hippocampal formation, which is associated with learning and memory, and in the striatum, related to reward, aversion, and motor behaviors (Ernst & Frisén, 2015). Glial cells are known as the *supportive cells* in the brain. Estimates approximate a glial-neuron ratio of 1:1 up to a 10:1 ratio. The birth of new glial cells has been found in DG and the subventricular zone (Boldrini et al., 2018; Rusznack, Henskens, Schofield, Kim, & Fu, 2016).

It is no surprise that the DMN does in fact change. To begin with, the DMN does not actually fully stabilize until the ages of 9–12 years. Table 4.3 lists the developmental milestones leading up to metacognitive capacity and the stabilization of the developing self. Attachment and learned experiences form the basis of expression for these functions. It is possible that around the age of 7 years, there is an emergence and subsequent acquisition of a wider range of self-related and social capacities. It is not until the age of 8 years and beyond that these functions begin to take form and stabilize, which is reflected in DMN functioning.

TABLE 4.3: Human Developmental Milestones

DEVELOPMENTAL ABILITY	AGE OF DEVELOPMENT
Self-recognition (Rochat, 2003)	2 years old
Explicit memory (Siegler, 1998)	3 years old
Theory of mind (ToM; Saxe, 2006)	3 years old
Representational theory of mind	5 years old
Self-concept (Leflot, Onghena, & Colpin, 2010)	7–8 years old
DMN stabilizes (Thomason et al., 2008)	9–12 years old
Mature delayed gratification (Mischel, Shoda, & Rodriguez, 1992)	8–13 years old

One mental illness that has substantial evidence for alterations of DMN functioning is post-traumatic stress disorder (Chan, 2016). The general conclusion of my dissertation, which examined the impact of PTSD on the DMN, was that during a resting state the DMN exhibits intrusions from the SN, and when an individual is engaged in a task the CEN exhibits intrusions from the DMN. There were thus dysfunctional changes that occurred intra- and inter-network. Functionally, this may manifest as the struggle to focus on a task without experiencing intrusions from negative emotional experiences. Additionally, individuals diagnosed with PTSD may be unable to safely retreat into themselves without conflicting experiences and hypervigilance. In relation, Sood and Jones (2013) elaborated that "the DMN has a dark side to it. . . . [S]pecific DMN activity can produce mind wandering. Inability to suppress DMN activity can lead to attentional lapses and impairs task performance" (p. 138). These changes related to specific areas likely contribute to the manifestation of hyperarousal, intrusions, avoidance, and negative mood and cognitions.

In contrast, we also find that the DMN changes in response to mindfulness-based practices (as documented subsequently). More specifically, this may appear as the reconfiguration of the DMN, with increased resting-state functional connectivity to areas of the brain (e.g., dorsolateral prefrontal cortex) associated with working memory, decision making, and regulating attention (Taren et al., 2017). Other changes have also been documented relating to alterations in other regions and improved emotion regulation (Chan & Siegel, 2017).

The flexibility of self is further demonstrated in the recent resurgence of psychedelic research. The reintroduction of psychedelic substances into research parallels the ever-growing literature on meditation. Griffiths and colleagues (2016) encountered highly promising results in their randomized double-blind trials using psilocybin to improve quality of life in individuals with life-threatening cancer. Even six months after ingesting this substance, positive changes remained (e.g., decreased depression and anxiety, increased meaning in life and optimism). Specific alterations in DMN connectivity appear to be central to the overlapping experience of an expansion of consciousness (decreased self-consciousness and increased interconnectedness with others and the world) and in its extreme form, ego-dissolution, or the loss of self-identity (see Table 4.4).

TABLE 4.4: **Consciousness-Altering Experiences and Their Neural Correlates**

METHOD	RECEPTORS	NEURAL CORRELATES	SUBJECTIVE EXPERIENCE
Psilocybin	Carhart-Harris et al. (2012) 5HT2B agonist 5HT2C agonist 5HT2A agonist	Decrease DMN connectivity Decrease CBF in thalamus, ACC, PCC Indirectly increase D in BG	Ego dissolution Hallucinations Blissful
LSD	Carhart-Harris et al. (2016) 5HT2A agonist 5HT2B agonist D2 agonist	Decreased coupling mPFC–ACC Increase V1 CBF (decrease alpha), hallucinations Glutamate release in cortex Decrease DMN connectivity: Parahippocampal-retrosplenial cortex Decrease delta and alpha in PCC	Ego dissolution Hallucinations Chaotic, blissful
Meditation	(Brewer et al., 2011) In meditation compared to controls: Increased mPFC, fusiform gyrus, inferior temporal, parahippocampal, left posterior insula (Boccia, Piccardi, & Guariglia, 2015)	Decrease DMN connectivity: dACC Increased grey matter volume at PCC, temporoparietal junction, angular gyrus, OFC, hippocampus, subiculum, brainstem	Relaxation Regulating attention Detachment from thoughts Ego-dissolution in highly experienced meditators

TABLE 4.4: *Meditation* continued

Areas of Brain Active During Meditative State	Functional Modifications in Meditators	Structural Modifications
Functions (Fx) right hemisphere:	*Increased Activity* *Fx right:*	*Increased grey matter volume in:*
ACC	Medial frontal gyrus	Right ACC
Superior frontal	Parahippocampal gyrus	Left middle and medial frontal gyrus
Parahippocampal gyrus	Middle occipital gyrus	Left precuneus
Inferior parietal lobule	Inferior parietal lobule	fusiform gyrus right
Middle occipital gyrus	Lentiform nucleus	thalamus
Fx left hemisphere:	*Fx left:*	
Precuneus	Inferior frontal gyrus	
Middle and superior temporal gyrus	Precuneus	
Precentral gyrus	Caudate nucleus	
Posterior cerebellum	Thalamus	
Fx bilateral:	*Fx bilateral:*	
Caudate nuclei	Middle frontal gyrus	
Insula	Precentral gyrus	
	ACC	
	Insula	
	Claustrum	

At the very minimum, it is fair to say that there are indeed other states or flows of consciousness that exist and are accessible when the right filters are tuned out or when other processes are accessed. Structural and functional alterations in long-term meditative practitioners beyond the practice of meditation, in conjunction with self-reports, support this assertion. It is interesting to note, however, that even in experiences of ego dissolution, consciousness remains. The difference is that consciousness may seem to operate independent of the filter of self-identity and other flexible social constructions related to self. It is possible that these two systems may be dissociable. However, as Millière, Carhart-Harris, Roseman, Trautwein, and Berkovich-Ohana (2018) suggested, meditation and psychedelic experiences are not uniform; experiences range as a result of individual differences, meditation types, length of practice or, in the case of psychedelics, frequency, type, and dosage. People may encounter varying degrees of selfless experiences at different points in their development.

For this reason, it is a major mistake to confuse the stability of consciousness with the self. The difference in distinguishing the subjective experience of these constructs may be akin the difference between air (consciousness) and light gusts of wind (self). The self from the perspective of the brain is constantly changing; there is no self, but rather a process of *self-ing*, as Dan Siegel would say.

REFLECTIONS: DEPENDENT CO-ORIGINATION AND CONCRESCENCE

Every living being is an engine geared to the
wheelwork of the universe. Though seemingly
affected by its immediate surrounding, the sphere of
external influence extends to infinite distance.

—Nikola Tesla

Pratītyasamutpāda or Dependent Co-origination comes from Buddhist philosophy, recognizing that everything co-arises, or is dependent upon each other to be born. This runs in parallel with ANW's (1927–28/1978) notion of concrescence, meaning "the production of novel togetherness" (p. 21). Put another way, it is the process of growing together to become something new and concrete (Cobb, 2008). Our bodies and self-processes originate through relationships and continue to grow from relationships.

Both nature and nurture play a role in our becoming and a significant portion of the brain develops with contributions from our experiences, further influenced by experiences from previous generations. We have mirror neurons, neurons that fire in response to others performing an action, and we find that networks of areas related to self-processes overlap significantly with our understanding of others and our ability to navigate psychological time.

Objectively, the notion of an unchanging, isolated self is a mirage and to identify the self as an entity is an illusion. The autobiographical self is a continuous process with flexible boundaries that is intimately connected with its environment, building upon previous and imagined experiences. The autobiographical self seems to have developed in response to survival and social demands. The self-system, with its preferences and identity, selectively dictates what information is considered important and what is not. On the bright side, it simplifies information processing, but on the dark side, it may be a costly filter. From an evolutionary perspective, the self-system may help us develop distinct interests, prompting us to further differentiate and specialize, thus promoting novelty and subsequently promoting human interdependence.

The DMN and its intertwining self-social functions support the simulation theory of mind, suggesting that we use ourselves as a template for understanding others. This suggests that the DMN likely plays a role in our interpersonal biases. Projective mechanisms and transferential dynamics may be understood as potentially rooted in this network. The generalized templates elicited by uncertainty are likely useful to explore for the purpose of helping our clients develop a well-integrated DMN. Interestingly, the very act of self-reflection may have been made possible via mirror neurons, which allow us to reflect on an internal representation of self (Uddin et al., 2005).

The majority of the decisions we make have been influenced by others and every decision we make will influence others, either directly or indirectly, through themselves. We deceive ourselves into thinking that because we can have impulses, emotions, thoughts, and beliefs to which no one else is directly privy, we are separate entities. The paradox behind this thinking is that the very foundations of those contents of consciousness we deem our own are in fact inseparable from the social fabric in which we are immersed. Likewise, our ownership of organs and bones encased in skin support the belief that we are isolated, yet they only exist and are still functional because of the environment that nourishes and sustains us. Skin is also porous, not enclosed. This is why Albert Hoffman, the father of LSD, first discovered its effects via its accidental absorption through his fingertips.

Others might argue that the power to deceive one another must indicate that we are separate. First off you need an other for a deception to occur, and second, one is dependent on the other for whatever gain is achieved through the deception. Acting in antisocial ways in private may be self-perceived as sly, yet a deception can quickly propagate a chain of events that can be inconceivably detrimental. Crossing boundaries of morality, for instance, leads to a susceptibility to further moral transgressions, evidenced by moral injury in soldiers (Litz et al., 2009). One may gradually become more easily tempted to engage in antisocial behaviors or become aggressive. This could then lead to a maladaptive cycle that becomes biologically reinforced, leading to a more difficult life marked by paranoia, distrust, guilt, and danger.

One helpful concept from Zen Buddhism is the destructive force of *I, me, and mine* (Austin, 1998). In the Zen tradition, these are emergent properties of the experience of self that are illusory and sources of suffering. The *I* is described as the root of narcissistic traits and selfish thoughts. It is the aspect of us that becomes prideful and stubborn, with a tendency toward confirmation biases, accepting all positive feedback, and shifting blame for all weakness. It can be found in statements like, "I can do this, I can do that, I'm the greatest." This extreme identification of self with all that is positive is empowering but damaging, especially in interpersonal relationships. It is born from the perceived space between ourselves and others and serves as a primitive protector of *me*, the part of ourselves that is reactive and vulnerable. It is prone to be constantly hurt and is always suffering from things happening to it: "Why does this always happen to me?" It plays the victim in every scenario in order to save itself from having to take responsibility. As a result, the *I* tries to accumulate all it can from the environment in order to secure itself. The *mine* is thus possessive, grasping at everything in its path and claiming it as its own, clutching and refusing to let go. Consequently, the *mine* may experience jealousy and disproportionate pain when it has lost something it perceives of value: "This is mine, you're mine, that's mine." The emergent illusion places value on things, so much so that we begin to identify things as who we are. Inevitably, we are bound to suffer, because things are ephemeral by nature.

In agreement with Emersonian thought, it would be more accurate to say that *we are nature experiencing itself in human form,* rather than *a human experiencing forms of nature.* The latter phrasing would mean dissociating oneself from the universe, negating one as being emergent from it. The former gives precedence to that which surrounds us, as well as acknowledging the unique process of self-awareness that exists in everyone. In addition, it may provide the psychological space needed to begin contributing consciously to the navigation of our development. If we are to presuppose that the universe is inherently material, that we are emergent organisms from this universe and by nature we seek and generate meaning, meaning itself becomes a substructure of the universe. To think otherwise is to dissociate ourself from the universe, which contradicts the latter belief. In the belief that all comes from us is also the claim that our psychological experiences are an aspect of the material universe from which we emerge, and if not, at least, an aspect of their interactions. The universe is thus not meaningless as we become the agents of meaning.

AN INTEGRATED THEORY OF SELF-PROCESSES

The term many presupposes the term one, and the
term one presupposes the term many.

—ALFRED N. WHITEHEAD

In their split-brain studies, Gazzaniga and colleagues (1965) found that our right and left hemispheres harbor two functionally distinct consciousnesses; yet individuals with split brains are able to live fairly normal lives. Everything appears to be unified in these patients until some activity elicits conflicting responses and their left hand decides against what the right hand was attempting to do. When we combine this information with recognized clinical disorders such as dissociative identity disorder (DID, formerly known as multiple personality disorder) and schizophrenia, a picture of multiple selves emerges. Individuals suffering from schizophrenia may have fully coherent visual and auditory hallucinations with specific personalities. The difference is that they do not become them, as in the cases of dissociative identity disorder, rather they interact with their hallucinatory presence. Although previously viewed with skepticism in the scientific community, DID is no longer questioned, with ample evidence supporting its validity (Dorahy et al., 2014). The hallmark of DID includes identity confusion, dissociative identities, and amnesia. It has been successfully distinguished from false presentations and other disorders, and found to exist throughout the world. There are actually different neurobiological *and* cognitive profiles during the activation of dissociative identities (ibid). Strasburger and Waldvogel (2015) presented a case whereby the individual had dissociated identities that were blind and others with sight. Using an EEG, the researchers found that their subject exhibited no visual evoked potentials when a blind personality was present. These became normal when identity shifted to a state whereby the subject could see. They concluded that early stage visual suppression may be playing a role. Bhuvaneswar and Spiegel (2013) identified psychophysiological differences in four alter personalities in a

DID subject. Each of them varied on handedness, visual acuity, and pendular nystagmus.

Somnambulism, or sleepwalking, is another good example. A sleepwalker may engage in complex behaviors while in an unconscious state. It is quite clear in these circumstances that the brain-body has a mind of its own that goes beyond one's immediate conscious awareness. In its most extreme (and controversial), there have been several cases whereby people have murdered in their sleep and have been acquitted with a strong defense (absence of motive, aberrant EEGs, passing tests of malingering, turning themselves in when awakened) (Popat & Winslade, 2014). Even if these cases were all proved to be false, somnambulism is commonly known to involve coordinated behaviors with some specific "goal" in mind.

Yet another condition is alien hand syndrome (Sacco & Calabrese, 2010), a disorder whereby an individual loses the sense of ownership of their own hand. Movements occur without their awareness and permission. It seems to have a "will" of its own. These cases usually occur by "lesions to the medial prefrontal lobe, the corpus colosum and the parietal areas, but can also appear in neuro-degenerative diseases such as corticobasal degeneration and may even precede them (e.g., Creutzfeldt-Jakob disease)" (p. 1).

We can further view this phenomenologically from common dream experiences, whereby the dreamer tends to be in either first person or third person, interacting with a world filled with different characters with distinct appearances and personalities within a narrative not of the dreamer's choosing. McGilchrist (2009) notes that "experiential wholes that are completely coherent across all realms affect us at the most conscious as well as unconscious levels" (p. 226).

The notion of multiple selves was speculated long ago by William James (1890), and has received more support from Antonio Damasio (2010) and neuroethological studies (Panksepp, 1998). Panksepp used SELF as an acronym for a simple ego-type life form, representing the first layer. He posited a continuum of selves, each one expanding on the next in "the deep layers of the colliculi and underlying circuits of the periaqueductal gray (PAG)" (p. 312). To better understand his conceptualization, he introduced:

> an image . . . of a tree: most full grown trees have a remarkable canopy of branches and leaves that interact dynamically with the environment. However,

the spreading branches cannot function or survive without the nourishment and support they receive from the roots and trunk. (p. 302)

Evolving this theory, Panksepp and Northoff (2009) suggested that at the very foundation is an interior representation of the body. From this arises the core SELF, which is a nonverbal, raw, somatic-affective interior experience. This would be akin to the seed of the SELF process. The trunk rises with secondary processes, such as non-conscious learning, conditioning, and habit formation; and as the core SELF is incorporated into higher order cognitive processes, its raw feelings are elaborated into a canopy of distinct and phenomenally refined selves. This model was formulated in response to empirical evidence that has accumulated over time. For example, despite damage to many areas of the cortex (which may influence our *tools of consciousness*), we may still have intentionality. However, with even the slightest neuronal insult at the PAG in the brainstem, the intentionality itself becomes lost (Panksepp, 1998). In later writings, three nested hierarchies (each subsequent level houses the next) of consciousness were identified that have a decent correspondence to three selves Damasio (2010) theorizes.

TABLE 4.5: Phases of Consciousness and Self-Processes

Vanderkerckhove & Panksepp (2009)	Damasio (2010)	Damasio (2010) Panksepp & Biven (2012)	Description
Anoetic Consciousness	Protoself	Deep subcortical brainstem, insular and ACC, somatosensory cortex (primary process emotions)	Somatic-affective, interoceptive awareness, felt body states
Noetic Consciousness	Core Self	Upper limbic Superior colliculus Thalamus (Secondary process learning)	Subject-object relationship develops. Thinking linked to external world

Vanderkerckhove & Panksepp (2009)	Damasio (2010)	Damasio (2010) Panksepp & Biven (2012)	Description
Autonoetic Consciousness	Autobiographical Self	Neocortex Default mode network (Tertiary process cognitions)	Awareness of self existing in space and time, mental time travel, introspection, increase in complexity of narrative coherence. Personhood, identity.

A cross-talk between Panksepp, Jung, and Whitehead forms the basis of my notion of self-processes. For Panksepp and Biven (2012), affective states play a role as the self's center of gravity. This is congruent with Jung (1907/1989) who stated "the essential basis of our personality is affectivity. Thought and action, as it were, only symptoms of affectivity" (p. 38). These states, at the subcortical midline structures, can be divided into three different categories: homeostatic/visceral affects (conscious, internal bodily states), instinctual/emotional affect (approach/avoid), and sensorial affect (which relates to basic perceptual experiences with affective value like touch or a surprise sound). He believed we organize ourselves according to the the triggering of these states. Using electrical brain stimulation, he identified basic emotional systems including those that induce *SEEKING, PLAY, CARE, FEAR, RAGE, PANIC/GRIEF,* or *LUST* (Alcaro, Carta, & Panksepp, 2017).

This complements Jung's (1948/1981) theory of *feeling toned* complexes. Jung believed the personal unconscious was populated by agglomerations of elements from experience driven by an emotional core. This emotional core may be related to primary, secondary, or tertiary emotional states. Whereas many states of consciousness may be consciously regulated, there also exist complexes that are "not under the control of the will and for this reason it possesses the quality of psychic autonomy. Its autonomy consists in its power to manifest itself independently of the will and even in direct opposition to conscious tendencies: it forces itself tyrannically upon the conscous mind" (Jung, 1966, p. 131). An emotional event may add onto an existing complex, or create a new one (like a traumatic experience). One example of an active complex would be finding yourself acting contrary to what you intended to do. Thus, it has the ability to inhibit the actualization of your intention. You become compelled to do something else, "to give way to the other, stronger sensations connected with the new complex" (Jung, 1907/1989, p. 41). It may also stimulate action, such as a sudden burst of anger upon meeting a stranger who reminded you of someone you despise. Let me be clear, however: most complexes are working harmoniously. Only when there is dissonance do they become an issue for consciousness to resolve. Complexes may be understood as autonomous representations in direct neural correspondence to unique configurations of affective, sensorimotor, and cognitive systems. Complexes are complex, self-organizing processes (from complexity theory), likely arising from interactions within and between the body-mind and relationships.

Jung's ideas on archetypes are worth considering in this framework. Beyond extensive investigations into recurring themes and symbols in myths, dreams, religious texts, positive symptoms in psychotic patients, and active imagination, how might one test such an idea? One way is by objectively assessing memory advantages after exposure to unknown archetypal symbols in relation to their meanings and mismatched meanings. A study like this was first conducted by Rosen and colleagues (1991), and has been replicated by Huston, Rosen, and Smith (1999), and further improved (by controlling for variables such as ethnicity, descriptive advantage, and cultural transmission among others) upon by Bradshaw and Storm (2013) as well as Brown and Hannigan (2013) who included English and Spanish speakers. All of these studies demonstrated significant results for matched versus mismatched words. Other related ideas include: inherited behavioral patterns (imprinting, innate releasing mechanisms); language acquisition; mother-infant interactions, attachment, regulation theory*; and phylogenetic inheritance. One interesting connection may be epigenetics, which has found that our experience (as well as our ancestors), can modify our gene functioning (Masterpasqua, 2009). Certain epigenetic functions are only triggered when select experiences present themselves. The aforementioned studies in aggregation with other lines of research makes room for psychobiological potentials that may serve as *instincts of imagination* (Alcaro

---

* "A central principle of regulation theory dictates that attachment is the relational unfolding of an evolutionary mechanism." (Schore, 2019, p. 19)

& Carta, 2019), but not for the collective unconscious, as an aspatial/atemporal universal storehouse of archetypes.

I would have to agree with Saunders and Skar (2001) who suggest that *presently*, archetypes may be better understood as recurring classes of complexes. This binds archetypes to *affective fields* within which complex self-processes agglomerate. The specifier of archetype represents the subset of complexes with feeling-tones directly associated to Panksepp's primary affective systems. In parallel to Panksepp's (1998) and Damasio's (2010) localization of an affective protoself beginning at the brainstem, Jung (1958/1989) actually predicted the Self archetype to "lie subcortically in the brain-stem" as ". . . besides being specifically characterized by the ordering and orienting role, its uniting properties are predominantly affective" (p. 270). Image mediates between sensory-affective and higher-order cognitive processes. In fact, Damasio (2010) theorizes that the very development of a core self requires a procession of mental images from the perceptual world to be coherently linked, allowing for there to be a subject-object relation. In relation, Jung (1959) asserted, ". . . there is not a single important idea or view that does not possess historical antecedents. Ultimately, they are founded on primordial archetypal forms whose concreteness dates from a time when consciousness did not think, but only perceived. 'Thoughts' were objects of inner perception, not thought at all, but sensed as external phenomena—seen or heard, so to speak" (p. 33). Certain images become more salient than others due to their perceived value. It is not difficult to consider how the expression of affective fields, in dreams or otherwise, may be constituted by recurring symbolism that represent some form of value. If we follow the idea that mind-matter compose two sides of a coin (dual-aspect monism), or can be collapsed into an occasion, and add a layer of complex narrative sequences that our minds are capable of, what emerges are archetypes.

Jung (1936) never considered archetypes the image themselves, they are *forms without content*, thus more of a psychobiological potential. He specifies, archetypes "might be compared to the crystal lattice that is preformed in the crystalline solution. It should not be confused with the variously structured axial system of the individual crystal" (Jung, 1928/1981, p. 311, footnote). I am well aware that traditional Jungians may view this as a grand deformation of his theory, and it is for this reason that I believe a different, but related, term should be used for this framework. I offer the descriptor *primordial*, which was used as a descriptor for archetypes in his earlier work (Jung, 1954/1959), thus referring to them as *primordial self-processes*. All primordial self-processes have direct connections to the periaqueductal gray (Panksepp & Northoff, 2008), located at the heart of the subcortical midline structures, which may be the ideal foundation for the Jungian Self.* In sum, I view primordial self-processes as psychophysiological predispositions,† adaptive blueprints imagisitically expressed, intimately tied directly to Panksepp's primary affective systems. In this sense, I localize them as rooted in the personal protoself-process. What separates them from a complex is that they do not represent any secondary or tertiary emotional process, but are primary. Unlike instincts, primordial self-processes can discriminate, are temporally selective, and can appear in a variety of forms depending on the culture and epoch. Moreover, their potentials are innate, and enduring; otherwise, they too are elicited by particular experiences, accrue emotional gravity, and may act autonomously.

The exact image or motifs associated with this potential may fluctuate for each person, via the zeitgeist and media. Thus, in agreement with Roesler (2012), it is important to consider both vertical and horizontal transmission when considering archetypes in practice. Although the emphasis may seem to reduce the "depth" in depth psychology, this needn't be so, as it adds a horizon. The use of myths and symbols in practice continue to serve the same purpose, the amplification of interpretations actively connects the client to a much larger sphere of existence—a depth of personal experience and horizon of sociocultural consciousness that extends into a vanishing point.

Integrating ANW's (1927–28/1978) philosophy of the organism, I use the term *conscious self-process* to signify the conscious events we are experiencing at any given moment, and *complex self-process* instead of complexes as an effort to stress dynamism, and the autonomous nature of complexes that make them more like inner personalities. Things are in perpetual flux, and it is important

---

* Jung's archetype of the Self is the central organizing agent for all archetypes, or primordial self-processes. At the brainstem, Jung would likely hypothesize it appears as a two-dimensional mandala, which in fits Panksepp's view of geometric sensory-motor affective map. As it rises into the limbic and cortical levels, it may be psychologically represented as a sage or primordial mother in dream space and myth production.

† In other words, they need not be thought of as existing in some aspatial or atemporal dimension. They may be perfectly understood as rooted in deep layers of our non-conscious neurological functions.

that our language reflects that. Naturally, I also identify the three core layers of self (Damasio, 2010) as the *protoself-process, core self-process,* and *autobiographical self-process.* Finally, when referring to the sum total of conscious and unconscious processes, I use the word *Sum self-process.*

TABLE 4.6: R-MOR Conceptualization of Self-Processes

LEVELS OF ANALYSIS	SUM SELF-PROCESS
Primary level of analysis	Primordial self-processes
Secondary level of analysis	Complex self-processes Conscious self-process
Tertiary level of analysis	Protoself-process Core self-process Autobiographical self-process

We emerge from and are composed of relationships. Physically, there are as many bacterial cells in humans as there are human cells (Sender, Fuchs, & Milo, 2016). Colonies of bacteria have formed symbiotic relationships within our bodies, influencing our immunity, metabolism, and behavior (Shropshire & Bordenstein, 2016). Gilbert, Sapp, and Tauber (2012) concluded that "neither humans, nor any organism, can be regarded as individuals by anatomical criteria" (p. 327). This is reflected psychologically, with our stream of consciousness revealing a cacophony of narratives voiced from different selves. Oliver Sacks (1998) was aware of this as indicated by his reflections on neuropsychology: ". . . living creatures, first and last, have selves—and are free. This is not to deny that systems are involved, but to say that systems are embedded in and transcended by selves" (p. 177). Thus, the inner world is composed of a spatiotemporal society of self-processes. This is akin to Bion's idea that you are never really treating an individual in psychotherapy, but groups of personalities (Ogden, 2008). Underlying these self-processes is likely an integration of affective systems coordinated with higher order cognitive systems. More specifically, there may be a variety of neural loops sustaining or maintaining these self-processes as distinct operating systems depending on the particular process in question. Some of these systems may be found in Table 4.7.

TABLE 4.7: Neural Loops and Selves

NEURAL CIRCUITRY ASSOCIATED TO SELVES	FUNCTION	SOURCE
Cortico-thalamo-striatal-cortical (CSTC) Exc DA (unique to worry), 5HT, GABA, Glu, NE	Worry/obsession (anxious misery, apprehension, expectation)	Fettes, Schulze, and Downar (2017)
Amygdala, insula (<pride), ventral striatum (=), bilateral dorsomedial PFC, mPFC, PCC	Pride, shame, and guilt	Roth, Kaffenberger, Herwig, and Bruhl (2014)
Ventral Loop mPFC, OFC, ventral striatal projections DA and 5-HT	Impulsivity	Mitchell and Potenza (2014)
Dorsal Loop OFC → dorsal striatum → thalamus	Compulsions	Wood and Ahmari (2015)
Insula Striatum vMPFC, amygdala, basal ganglia mesolimbic dopamine system	Cravings	Naqvi, Gaznick, Tranel, and Bechara (2014)
sgPFC and the DMN	Depressive rumination	Hamilton, Farmer, Fogelman, and Gotlib (2015)
Amygdala-Based Fear Circuits Amygdala → ACC Amygdala → OFC Amygdala → VMPFC	Fear, threat detection Panic, phobia Affect of fear	Balaev et al. (2020)

Continued on p. 138

TABLE 4.7 CONTINUED

NEURAL CIRCUITRY ASSOCIATED TO SELVES	FUNCTION	SOURCE
Amygdala → PAG (Periaqueductal grey—in brainstem) Amygdala → Locus Coeruleus	Avoidance, freeze Autonomic output of fear	Adolphs (2013)
Amygdala → Hypothalamus	Endocrine output of fear	Duvarci and Pare (2014)
Amygdala ↔ Parabrachial Nucleus (PBN) receives affective nociceptive information	Increased respiratory rate, increased shortness of breath, increased asthma PBN: Sends affective nociceptive information to amygdala	Silva, Gross, and Graff (2016)
ACC, amygdala + insula Excess NE Decreases of 5-HT	Anxiety	Duval, Javanbakht, and Liberzon (2015)
Bed Nuclei Stria Terminalis + Amygdala	Anticipatory anxiety Maintaining hypervigilance and anxiety Perception of aversive stimulus	Greenberg (2014) Knight and Depue (2019)
Hypothalamic-Pituitary-Adrenal Axis (HPA)	Controls reactions to stress, regulates mood/emotions, sexuality, energy usage, digestion, and the immune system	Long et al. (2020)

ATTACHMENT AND SUBLIMINAL INFLUENCES

Health is the ability to stand in spaces between realities without losing any of them—the capacity to feel like one self while being many.

—Philip Bromberg

We do as we have been done by.

—John Bowlby

Our brains develop in accordance with the quality of relationships shared with our primary caregivers. Harlow's (1959) study on mother-infant relationships in rhesus monkeys and the phenomenon of failure-to-thrive infants by purely psychosocial means illustrate the importance of early relationships (Fojanesi et al., 2017). Ainsworth and Bowlby's seminal work on attachment theory has since found ample support in social neuroscience (Cozolino 2014; Siegel, 1999). The evidence that Schore (2016) has accumulated and integrated through his exhaustive work has found coherence with Solms and Solms (2002) highlighting the inhibitory role of the ventromedial frontal cortex as a reflection of an *internalized, containing mother.* This internalized mother is formed through moment-to-moment interactions as the brain develops (emphasis on right-hemisphere); the quality of which is highly contingent upon levels of attunement between the mother and infant. High levels of misattunement and negative affect may inhibit the proper maturation of developing corticolimbic systems (Schore, 2003b). Attachment styles are expressed through internal working models that children and adults develop over time, directly influencing the way people relate to themselves and others. In this context, attachment may be understood as an early filter. We perceive the world through the lens of our early relationship models, relating to others in the same style in which we were related to and with. The content may manifest in an infinite number of variations, but the process remains relatively the same. Everything we learn in life has the potential to change our perspective on specified situations due to the nature of our minds. This includes not only familial relationships as found in attachment, but also the knowledge and experiences we accrue as we age.

Sometimes information is societally embedded and below our immediate awareness. For example, experiments have found that subliminal messaging can influence the way we consciously process information, cause mood alterations, and even generate changes in our political leanings (Ruch, Züst, & Henke, 2016). Ruch and colleagues (2016) found that after just a few exposures (12 presentations within 6 seconds), subliminal messages could in fact alter our decision making. Whether it is forgotten, stored, or reacted to is mostly decided unbeknownst to us.

Research on implicit biases has been controversial, but it has at least enough evidence to support there exists a bias. The extent to which they impact our behavior is much more difficult to ascertain. Nonetheless there have been some compelling studies. Although the Implicit Association Test (IAT) has been used in hundreds of studies, there has also been question as to its validity and generalizability. In examining racial implicit bias, subjects are asked to press one of two keys associated with a particular category (positive or negative adjective) after exposure to an image or name of a white or black individual. To say the least, findings have favored white over black individuals (Kelly, Roedder, 2008). Outside of the IAT, other studies have been conducted, such as Bertrand and Mullainathan (2003) who distributed near 5,000 resumes from white and black sounding names. Results? "White names receive 50 percent more callbacks for interviews. Callbacks are also more responsive to resume quality for white names than for African American ones" (p. 991). In their systematic review on healthcare professionals, Fitzgerald and Hurst (2017) concluded that "biases are likely to influence diagnosis, treatment decisions and level of care in some circumstances" (p. 1). In implicit biases, there is a discrepancy between the practitioner's conscious intention (to help and care) and their unconscious influences. Using the implicit association test from Harvard, studies have found significant correlations between physicians' implicit bias toward African Americans (AAs) and perceived negative interactions with AA clients. Some examples of determinants included males being less sensitive than females when working with self-harm victims in accident and emergency scenarios and AA clients in the United States being questioned more about smoking. Additionally, when compared to U.S. medical graduates, international graduates judged AA male clients as being of lower socioeconomic status.

THE LAYERING OF SUBJECTIVITY

No problem can be solved from the same level of consciousness that created it.

—ALBERT EINSTEIN

The conscious conceptual world is currently divided into three categories, with every category falling under the umbrella term of mental states: (1) spontaneous thought, (2) rumination and obsessive thought, and (3) goal-directed thought (Christoff et al., 2016). At the root of defining these categories is cognitive control. We possess a spectrum of control over thoughts, some of which are automatic, such as the immediate shift of our thoughts toward a loud noise, and some of which are more deliberate, such as intentionally brainstorming about a topic. For this reason, spontaneous thought has been divided further into three subcategories: dreaming, mind-wandering, and creative thinking. We typically have the least control over our thoughts when we are dreaming. "Mind-wandering has more deliberate constraints than dreaming, but less than creative thoughts and goal-directed thoughts" (Christoff et al., 2016, p. 719).

Thus, when we examine the basis of mental states, we can characterize them within degrees of automaticity or deliberation (cognitive control). Second, we must consider variations in content, whose extreme would be flight of thoughts in manic episodes, with its opposing spectrum being stability, entering rigidity, whose extreme would be obsessive rumination. Thoughts are constantly moving, and topics change just as quickly as they may be introduced. Sometimes we are able to grab the reins in order to achieve some sort of goal, and other times we daydream in flights of fancy.

What do we know about mind wandering in spontaneous thought? When our minds wander, it is common for us to have spontaneous bouts of engagement with internally oriented cognition. We may simply be revisiting a memory or thinking about the future. We also may be analyzing how a social event transpired or reflecting on who we are and who we are becoming. Other times, this automaticity is more deliberate, as we consciously exercise our skills to be of use for the future. If these activities sound familiar to you, it is because they are correlated to the DMN (Soon & Jones, 2013). In relation, Killingsworth and Gilbert (2010) discovered that the more our minds wander, the more likely it is that we are unhappy.

Despite this discovery, some mind wandering has been found to be healthy and even helpful, potentially enhancing creativity (Beaty, Benedek, Kaufmann, & Silvia, 2014). Baird and colleagues (2012) found that mind wandering during simple external tasks may facilitate creative problem solving. Similarly, Levinson, Smallwood, and Davidson's (2012) study found that individuals with higher working memory capacity also reported more mind-wandering during simple tasks without hindering performance. Other advantages were summarized in a review by Smallwood and Schooler (2015), including: improved capacity for delayed gratification via future planning, which has been predictive of positive attributes, such as greater intelligence; enhanced self-reported meaning as a result of thinking about specific remembered or anticipated events; greater meaning in personal experience fostering well-being and enhancing health outcomes; and providing an avenue for mental breaks. Additionally, mind wandering (particularly future-oriented thinking) has been found to reduce undesirable mood states associated with engaging in a boring task (Baird et al., 2012; Ruby, Smallwood, Engen, & Singer, 2013). Lastly, the simulation of negative content promotes preparedness for potential threats.

In mind wandering (MW) processes of self-other and mental time travel intermingle without conscious intention. A release from volitional control may be promoting divergent thinking, and regenerative processes. One related theory comes from Djiksterhuis, Strick, Bos, and Nordgren (2014) who believes that part of the DMN's function (which has been related to mind wandering) may be involved with to what they call *Type 3 processing* in addition to Type 1 (unconscious, fast, associative, automatic, and effortless) and Type 2 (conscious, slow, logical, rule-based, goal-directed, and effortful) processing. They view Type 3 processing as "conscious intermezzi" (p. 360): a form of processing that is largely unconscious, very slow, abstract, exploratory, goal dependent, and largely effortless. They specified that two conscious intrusions bring Type 3 processing to light: (a) the awareness of an unconscious goal when progress becomes difficult, and (b) when an answer to a challenging question arises while doing something completely different, also known as a *eureka moment*. They view Type 3 processing as necessary in creative problem solving and making important decisions. They did, however, specify that working memory involvement is necessary, and as such the DMN is not solely responsible for all Type 3 processing.

Sometimes, mind wandering can turn into fantasies. Cherry (1988) distinguishes between autonomous fantasies and surrogate fantasies. Autonomous fantasies are ones that we have no control over, sometimes they may be fantasies we have that we may never want to act out, in which case one is absolved of responsibility as to where their mind wanders to. This would be outside the jurisdiction of the inner "thought police." It may just be secondary to a natural biological function and our mind wandering to some particular destination does not necessarily mean that the place wandered to is something we would like to live out. In fact, given the disproportionate amount of negative MW, it would make more sense if people would rather steer clear from actualizing many of them. For example, a person might imagine it would feel cathartic to release their wrath upon the boss who has wronged them. Yet it will likely not be enacted, because the person might lose their job. There is also the possibility that the person is convinced the fantasy is the right thing to do, and upon acting upon it, finds that it was in fact better as a fantasy. There are many things we might want to do that are not accepted when living in society, but the mind allows us to imagine them. Surrogate fantasies on the other hand, are ones that we would like to happen in real life. These fantasies are perhaps more deliberate, and as such are likely more within the jurisdiction of our conscience.

When we relegate MW to a lower position of importance, we also detract from its compensatory and regenerative power, which can be highly adaptive in many situations. In a sense we continue to dream when we are awake, this happens in the form of mind wandering, which has been found to occur 46.9% of the time we are awake (Killingsworth & Gilbert, 2010). This is a hefty investment for evolution. MW is a process of the mind, a universal experience, as are perception, dreams, and sleep. If we could conceive of MW as *just as real*, might we begin moving toward a higher state of overall satisfaction? Might MW contain insights, a distinct piece of the puzzle that forms who we are, better understood as it relates to the whole. Learning to discern different types of fantasies and their effect on us requires far more research. We are simultaneously inhabiting different worlds with different rules, and it is simply incorrect to insist that there is only one *real world* and that our daydreams are *solely* a source of what we want to do, but cannot, in *dominant reality*.

APPLICATIONS: TETHERED TO THE UNKNOWN

The only point of importance in any session is the
unknown. Nothing must be allowed to distract from
intuiting that. In any session, evolution takes place. Out
of the darkness and formlessness something evolves.

—W. R. BION

Stress is rampant in today's culture. The necessity to *do* something "useful," otherwise be harassed by pangs of guilt and shame, is an experience common to most in the United States. The value of being, on the other hand, has been cast to the side, left in the shadows. This necessity to *do* can prevent psychological progression. In session it can lead to moments of "stuckness." The client arrives: "I have nothing to say today," or "Is there something for me to do?" Paradoxically, I am usually quite happy when we reach this point. These to me are moments ripe for the picking. Without an agenda, there is a flow of raw affect and cognition more easily accessible. This allows for deeper change, and experience in the moment. These moments may begin by asking them if they would allow their minds to wander and free associate. In particular, mind wandering during simple tasks may help promote creativity and problem solving. Guiding clients' minds to wander in a general direction, such as defining life events, may help construct meaning in their lives. With particularly busy and focused individuals, it would not be a bad idea to ask them to spend some time *spacing out* to give their minds a break. It is important to acquaint very rigid individuals with their inner space of spontaneity and chaos. Asking clients to give some time to let their minds wander may be regenerative and facilitate information processing. If a client feels they have *hit a wall*, time, sleep, and engaging in other tasks may help trigger their associative centers to facilitate the emergence of a solution. In a more concrete suggestion, it may be more beneficial during introspective moments to ask *what* questions as opposed to *why* questions, as suggested by Tasia Eurich (2018). She suggests that *why* questions are a trap, whereas *what* questions are constructive. For example, instead of asking, "Why do I feel this way?" a client can ask, "What am I feeling now? And what can I do to move forward?"

The concept of *reverie* (Ogden, 1997) or bouts of mind wandering elicited in the therapist by clients may be important to familiarize yourself with. The concept of *maternal reverie* was introduced by Bion and further elaborated by Ogden (1997) for their relevance in therapy. Reveries the therapist experiences may not be meaningless; rather, some may be intimately connected to the client's problem. It may be that some specific problem has elicited what seems to be random but in fact may simply have been an experience reached through associative means rather than logical ones. Reverie may be a useful way to engage the DMN. This would be in congruence with research supporting the DMN as a necessary network to toggle in and out of to contextualize information.

SLEEP AND THE VALUE OF DREAMING

Waking consciousness is dreaming—but dreaming
constrained by external reality.

—OLIVER SACKS

Although we have not seen it, we know dark matter exists through its gravitational effects on visible matter and have learned that it outnumbers visible matter by 50 times. Similarly, unconscious processes are known because of their effects on conscious processes, and our brain is known to be involved with far more non-conscious processing than conscious processing. To date, sleep studies have identified four stages of sleep: three are non-rapid eye movement (NREM) and one is REM. These are divided by their characteristic electrophysiological fluctuations. The most vivid dreams tend to occur in REM sleep, with stage 3 being known as the most restorative phase. Contrary to popular belief, although we may have no memory of it upon awakening, during sleep we are still experiencing internal stimuli involving lower resolution perceptual experiences: sensations, thought-like content, and potential *selfless states*. Current theories speculate that, objectively speaking, sleep is necessary for processing memory and facilitating emotion regulation (Windt, Nielsen, & Thompson, 2016).

I categorize sleep as a mechanism within the veil of self due to its contributions (potential and otherwise) to the formation of who we are. Moreover, beyond the obvious experiential impact of sleep deprivation, studies have found significant deficits in several functions, such as memory, attention, executive functioning, and overall alertness (Costa & Periera, 2019). Someone operating from a sleep-deprived state may actually begin to hallucinate if they do not sleep for an extended period of time, as if the brain forces the individual to dream in their waking life. Grotstein (2007) acknowledges that Bion believed we were always dreaming, and in fact dreaming is a part of the evolution of sophisticated thought. He goes on to share that from the Bionian perspective "dreaming functions as a filter that sorts, categorizes, and prioritizes emotional facts that are stimulated by this incoming data, much like the motto of the New York Times: 'All the news that's fit to print' " (p. 264).

Hobson and McCarley (1977) introduced the activation-synthesis hypothesis, suggesting that dreams were the brain's attempt at interpreting random neural activity. This hypothesis has never been satisfactory to me, given the complexity, structure, and adaptive value that dreams tend to carry when considered seriously. I am more inclined to subscribe to Franklin and Zyphur's (2015) hypothesis that dreams have been preserved throughout evolution and arose via natural selection to enhance our potential for adaptation and overall fitness.

We know sleep is necessary, given the consequences of sleep deprivation and the restorative effects of getting a good night's rest. Today we are aware that levels of brain metabolism during REM and wakefulness are quite similar. We also know that up to 70% of NREM sleep may yield dreams and a minority of people deny having any dreams during REM sleep (Nir & Tononi, 2010), meaning dreams do not only occur during REM sleep. Scientists are still debating about the primary function of sleep and dreams, offering the following possibilities:

Biological:
- Sleep-dependent learning and memory reprocessing (Stickgold, Hobson, Fosse, & Fosse, 2001)
- Long-term memory consolidation (Payne & Nadel, 2004)
- Development and maintenance of consciousness and higher order brain functions (problem solving; Hobson, 2009)
- Maintaining and developing our autobiographical narratives and self (Domhoff, 2010)

Psychological:
- Wish fulfillment (Freud, 1900)
- Compensating for imbalanced psychological experiences, expressing concerns, anticipating future developments, and facilitating the process of individuation (Jung, 1967)

- Threat simulation to improve chances of survival (Revonsuo, 2000)
- Facilitating conflict resolution by expressing concerns in the form of images to which we can better relate (Hartmann, 1996)
- Creativity and problem solving increasing chances of survival (Barrett, 2007)

Throughout my practice, there have been multiple instances in which dreams inevitably surface without any prompting. As children, many of us took our dreams quite seriously, and a common parental response was, "Don't worry, it was just a dream." As we get older, our dreams lose significance, partially due to our culture. Other cultures and religious practices place differing degrees of value on dreams. Regardless of our beliefs, I have found it to be quite common for there to be a dream or sets of dreams that become quite significant in our overall inner narrative or mental functioning. Certain dreams have a tendency to stick, and only the interpretive process allows them to unstick. It is for this reason that I find it important to explore ways in which we may understand dreams.

Dreams may not be compatible with science (requiring evidence and measurement), but that is not to say they have no value. In fact, considering dreams as a scientific problem is incongruent with the analysis and understanding of dream images and symbols. Whereas science requires precise specification and accuracy, symbols are composed of multiple meanings and their interpretation is defined by their *productivity*. This means that a single dream may have several interpretations, and all of them are *accurate* to the extent that they are productive in facilitating the integration of self.* In other words, dreams follow William James's (1904/1987) model of pragmatism, which asks,

What concrete difference will its being true make in any one's actual life? How will truth be realized? What experiences will be different from those which would obtain if the belief were false? What, in short, is the truth's cash-value in experiential terms? (p. 573)

Dreaming can be understood as another form of consciousness that requires

---

* Jung conceptualized the self as both the center and sum total of one's conscious and unconscious processes.

its sibling, waking consciousness, to imbue it with meaning. Thompson and Cotlove (2005) identified several models of dream interpretation. According to the wish fulfillment model, which originated with Freud, dreams represent disguised wishes. An individual may also suffer from traumatic dreams, in which the dream reenacts unprocessed trauma that have yet to be integrated into the individual's psyche. There are self-state dreams whose primary motive is to mirror an individual's internal state. According to the model of communication dreams, a dream is directed toward a dreamer, intending to communicate a point. We may also mix these models.

All dreams will to some degree express *day residues* and an integration of sensory output while the person is sleeping (Freud, 1900). This is exemplified in Freud's (1900) dream analysis of the burning child, as he began his interpretation:

> The bright light shining through the open door on to the sleeper's eyes gave him the impression which he would have received if he were wake: namely that a fire had been started near the corpse by a fallen candle. (p. 353)

Conscious cognition tends to be inhibited during sleep, enabling a much freer and more associative kind of thinking (Mattoon, 2006). This process activates a wider range of networks, allowing associations from disparate parts of the mind to interact in novel ways, blending together what waking consciousness kept separate in discrete categories of space, time, and logic.

Freud believed that rational thought was a secondary process emerging from primitive cognitive processes. He posited that this secondary process developed as the infantile ego acquired the capacity to delay its wish for immediate gratification and engage with the constraints of external reality (Mattoon, 2006). In dreams, the individual regresses into a more primitive level of the pleasure principle. Thus, all dreams can be understood as a disguised form of wish fulfillment.

Freud's (1900) trajectory of dream interpretation begins with an instinctual wish, which may be associated with an event from the day that has just passed. Information is subsequently filtered by a mental censor that protects and prevents unacceptable repressed wishes from disturbing the dormant ego. This process subsequently results in a disguise for the dreamer by utilizing what Freud called *primary process*. Through associative chains, one idea can be displaced or condensed into another idea or image. Freud termed the literal substance of the dream *manifest content* and the underlying unconscious meaning the *latent content*. It is as if our conscious experience speaks plainly and our unconscious speaks through poetry.

In contrast, rather than seeing the dream as masked, Jung (1966) asserted that dreams reveal the inner truth and reality of the client as it really is. In this view, the obscurity of dreams stems from its compensatory function. Previously biased views in conscious life would thus be balanced by an opposing view from the unconscious world where meaning is generated via metaphor and symbol rather than linear thought (Mattoon, 2006). In addition to the translation of a dream, Jung was also interested in elaboration. Ultimately, he identified common themes and symbols that appeared to be universal among cultures. In an attempt to access this domain, Jung developed an interpretive approach of amplifying the dream by showing its connection with archetypal themes of mythology. In this way, he created a larger network of meaning through which symbolic themes of a dream might be elucidated. Jung (1969) did not believe that our minds were passive receivers of information; rather, he believed the unconscious mind to be dynamic and autonomous, consisting of built-in *potentials* that influence the way we perceive. We have complexes that can be understood as emotionally charged sets of ideas developed in our own lifetimes from which we operate at times. We are also highly influenced by archetypes or formless psychological instincts inherited from past generations waiting to be realized through experience (Corbett & Stein, 2005). This results in a shared yet uniquely configured psyche.

APPLICATIONS: WHAT DREAMS MAY BECOME

Dreams tell us many an unpleasant biological truth about ourselves and only very free minds can thrive on such a diet. Self-deception is a plant which withers fast in the pellucid atmosphere of dream investigation.

—SIGMUND FREUD

The following steps offer a brief guide to interpreting dreams in psychotherapy:

1. Client recounts the dream.

2. Ask client to retell the dream, in addition to sharing all associations with different characters and objects.

3. Ask client to recount the emotional experiences that have arisen as a narrative in the dream.

4. Consider current, historical, relational, or other meaningful connections in the dream (if interested in archetypal symbolism, see Ronnberg & Martin, 2010).

5. Provide or co-construct an interpretation based on all information given.

In waking life, we experience ourselves as the subject with some control of ourselves as objects. Our brains prevent the internal world from overriding our perceptual processing of the world around us. In dreams, our selves as objects are presented to the self as subject through imaginal experiences. Our internal worlds are presented to us through a narrative format. The previous steps focus on interpreting the experience of the internal world from subject to object. Bollas (1987) reversed this operation to also consider how self as object may be treating the self as subject: "How is the experiencing subject handled as an object by the dream script?" or "How is the dreamer managed as an experiencing subject within his hallucinated scripts?" (p. 47)

Adapted from *The Gestalt Perspective* (Yontef, 1993):

1. Client recounts the dream.

2. Access more information from the dream by having the client retell it from the perspective of several characters or objects within the dream.

3. Co-construct an interpretation (if needed) based on what emerges.

CHAPTER 5.

Social Relationships and Culture

....

The world in which you were born is just
one model of reality. Other cultures are not
failed attempts at being you; they are unique
manifestations of the human spirit.

—WADE DAVIS

Whether we classify ourselves as recluses or social butterflies, we are inevitably influenced by the relationships we foster and the society in which we are immersed. We live in a world where most of us interact daily with many people in a variety of settings. With some, we are extremely comfortable, and we express our thoughts without filters; with others, however, we think carefully before we speak. Sometimes we may even meet someone and in a matter of seconds and decide we dislike the person. Every relationship we are in is partly imagined, with much of our *understanding* of them potentially being a projection of ourselves. At times being in a relationship with another may help us access other parts of ourselves; otherwise, those parts may have remained unconscious. Some relationships may even birth ways of being or behaviors we hadn't thought possible.

The mere presence (real or imagined) of another person can alter the way we think and behave. For instance, it is a well-known phenomenon in social psychology that the presence of observers actually improves a person's speed and performance on tasks that are simple and in which a person is competent and worsens a person's performance on tasks that are novel and complex (Uziel, 2007). The susceptibility to social influences runs deeper than most of us would like to acknowledge.

SOCIOSTASIS ACROSS THE SOCIAL SYNAPSE

Inside is projected outside, as we say. In reality there
is a "psychization" of the object: everything outside
us is experienced symbolically, as though saturated
with a content which we co-ordinate with the psyche.

—ERICH NEUMANN

Cozolino (2014) referred to the *social synapse* as the space through which we are connected to one another. This space is a channel through which information (seen or unseen) is reciprocally transmitted, eventually generating social structures much larger than any individual on their own. *Sociostasis* describes these links, specifically how we "regulate each other's internal biochemistry, emotions and behaviors via conscious and unconscious mechanisms of communication across the social synapse" (p. 173).

One of the central tenets of interpersonal neurobiology is the notion that relationships can be considered our primary environment (Cozolino, 2008). We all evolved from nomadic roots, seeking food, shelter, and safety. When one environment was exhausted, we moved on to another one. The only consistency that resulted in safety was the people with whom we shared the journey. Studies have found that social exclusion (Eisenberger, Lieberman, & Williams, 2003), negative feedback (Eisenberger, Inagaki, Muscatell, Haltom, & Leary, 2011), and social rejection (Kross, Bergman, Mischel, Smith, & Wager, 2011) all recruit neural areas that overlap with regions responsible for processing the affective components of physical pain, in particular the anterior cingulate cortex and the anterior insula. Even though physical pain usually heals, emotional pains may be relived again and again. Meyer, Williams, and Eisenberger (2015) found that relived social pain elicits continued dorsomedial prefrontal cortex activity, in contrast to relived physical pain, which triggers inferior frontal gyrus activation. This finding suggests the existence of a specialized neural pathway that guides the re-experiencing of social versus physical pain. Why does the brain care so much about social rejection? Perhaps because in our evolutionary history social rejection may have been a threat to survival. Being rejected within a group would have substantially decreased a person's chances of procreating with a desired partner or reaching a higher social status. If someone were to be excommunicated from a group, they would have to survive alone, and their chances of survival would drop precipitously.

Our brains also have *mirror neurons,* neurons in the motor cortex that fire when we observe another person performing an action. Case, Abrams, and Ramachandran (2010) found that when we anesthetize the arm at the brachial plexus, we are able to actually experience the sensations of another person being touched. In particular, as the arm is touched, a signal is sent from the brain to the skin receptors. Usually, there is a return signal indicating that it is not the subject's arm being touched but rather the observed arm. However, when the arm undergoes anesthetization, the return signal is not sent. This procedure results in the sensation of the other person's arm being touched, which is a direct result of mirror neurons' functionality. This led Ramachandran (2009) to nickname mirror neurons "Gandhi neurons or empathy neurons" (5:56).

Ramachandran (2009) further argued that rapid evolution in humans can be attributed in part to the emergence of mirror neurons. He stated that instead of a slow evolution that takes years of trial and error and genetic mutations, mirror neurons allow us to empathize with one another and learn immediately. Instead of needing to learn only from our own experiences, we can now also learn from the experiences of others, skipping steps and thereby reaching a Lamarckian form of evolution as opposed to purely Darwinian evolution. Notably, Uddin and colleagues (2005) discovered that neural networks containing mirror neurons, in particular right frontoparietal structures, are active when a person is recognizing their own face. This finding suggests that mirror neurons may have adapted to function beyond mapping out others into the domain of the internal representation of the self as well.

In fact, mirror neurons serve as the foundation for treating individuals with phantom limb pain. A subset of amputees still experiences their lost limb being in pain. To alleviate the pain, one treatment option is mirror therapy, a system of therapy that tricks the visual system into believing a missing arm, which now appears to be reflected by the existing arm in a mirror, has returned. Movements in the existing arm actually create the sensation of movement in the missing arm, and when the existing arm is massaged, the person may actually feel a reduction in pain. Currently, the efficacy of mirror therapy for upper limbs has been shown to be effective (Ezendam, Bongers, & Jannink, 2009), whereas effectiveness for other areas is still being researched.

Of particular relevance is polyvagal theory, which was introduced by Stephen Porges (2011). The tenth cranial nerve, or vagus nerve, is the only nerve that descends into the gut. Polyvagal theory asserts that the vagus nerve, which, among other functions, acts as a subconscious system for detecting threats (neuroception), has also evolved to use social information as a way to self-regulate. Porges posited that there are three neural platforms. (a) The dorsal vagal complex is involved in immobilization. It is part of the parasympathetic nervous system (PNS), engaged with the faint-or-freeze response, such as when animals feign death. This complex works in opposition to (b) the sympathetic-adrenal system, which is involved with mobilizing the body when it is in a state of fight or flight. Humans also have (c) the ventral vagal complex, a newer branch, also part of the PNS, involved with social engagement. It is believed to foster calm behavioral states by inhibiting primitive responses (from the PNS and SNS) by negotiating the safety of the environment via social cues (e.g., faces, intonation of voices). In practice, vagal tone has been understood as a marker of sensitivity to stress. Individuals with PTSD exhibit low vagal tone, which is associated with reduced adaptivity to the environment, as well as poorer emotional and attentional regulation. This theory also helped inspire and support somatically based therapies for PTSD.

SOCIAL PSYCHOLOGY

It is not so much the kind of person a man is as the
kind of situation in which he finds himself that
determines how he will act.

—Stanley Milgram

The very idea that our identity can be molded by our interactions with others was formally noted by Charles Horton Cooley (1902), who labeled this concept *the looking-glass self.* Indeed, sociologists have theorized that we have shared social systems of meaning on which we base our interactions with other individuals. This framework, called *symbolic interactionism*, influences our interpretations of reality and can be altered as a result of the variety of interactions we have with others.

The controversial case of Kitty Genovese, who was raped and murdered despite multiple witnesses, is an example often used to illustrate the *bystander effect*. This notion was first introduced by Darely and Latané (1968), who were interested in the circumstances of her murder. Despite new examinations of the facts of the case, the effect still stands. Put simply, it becomes less likely that someone will assume responsibility to assist a victim when others are present. Moreover, the likelihood decreases further as there are more people involved. One meta-analysis examining bystander literature from the 1960s to 2010 found that diffusion tends to occur when there are five or more bystanders (Fischer et al., 2011). This is beneficial to know in case a person finds themself in a situation where action is necessary, yet no one is acting.

This shift of responsibility also relates to times when someone decides to work less in groups than they would if they were working individually, a phenomenon known as *social loafing* (Karau & Williams, 1993). Underlying these phenomena is a *diffusion of responsibility*, which occurs when responsibility becomes dispersed by the presence of multiple people in a given situation. From the perspective of neural processing, it has been suggested that the presence of others influences how information is processed and how consequences are experienced. What this suggests is that there is not only a self-serving bias but also actual reductions in sense of agency and outcome monitoring (Beyer, Sidarus, Bonicalzi, & Haggard, 2017).

Groups tend to form their own dynamics, generating a gestalt, which signifies that the whole is greater than the sum of its parts. To this date, we know of several illusions and misdirections that arise when people are in immersed in and identified with groups. One of the most commonly known phenomena is *groupthink*. When people identify themselves with certain groups, it becomes easier for polarized ideas and thoughts to emerge. Janis (1991) defined groupthink as a concurrent-seeking tendency, more specifically when the desire for a unanimous decision trumps the realistic evaluation of any given situation. There are several reasons for this phenomenon, including the illusion of invulnerability, belief in the inherent morality of the group, collective rationalization, out-group stereotypes, self-censorship, illusion of unanimity, and direct pressure on dissenters and mindguards.* This is simi-lar to *group polarization,* a phenomenon that characterizes the amplification of attitudes and subsequently risky behaviors people take once they have identi-fied with a particular group (Aronson, 2010).

Intergroup violence has permeated group formations throughout humanity's existence, leading to violence and destruction ranging from racism to religious wars. In-group biases may present as unfavorable beliefs about other groups and dehumanization or distrust of out-group members (Hughes, Ambady, & Zaki, 2017). Indeed, the very identification with a group results in the emergence of social expectations that become wired into our intuitive responses, a phenome-non that has been characterized by the *social heuristics hypothesis* (Rand & Epstein, 2014). Two forms of intergroup conflict are readily identified: in-group defense and out-group aggression. Of interest, De Dreu and colleagues (2016) found that there was less strength and coordination in in-group aggression than in defense. It is theorized that there is a strong evolutionary reason behind this phenomenon, because the mere identification with a group increases survival, and evolution may favor cooperation and coordination over domination and expansion.

As large groups gather and increase in size there emerges a social conscious-ness or a "collective mind . . . in perpetual interaction through the exchange of symbols; they interpenetrate one another. They group themselves accord-ing to their natural affinities; they co-ordinate and systematize themselves" (Durkheim, 1978, p. 103). Systemic faults or situations when there is ambi-guity and an external threat (e.g., pandemic, natural disaster, war) may impel groups to generate their own rules, leading to a higher susceptibility to issues such as groupthink. Political affiliations strengthen as individuals watch the news, and biased information is more readily accepted. As fear increases, indi-viduals may begin unknowingly making decisions influenced by biased infor-mation to the detriment of others in need, as can be seen in the lack of masks available for healthcare professionals who were in direct contact with COVID-19. We attune to social cues in order to direct our own behaviors, and as we see people with worried expressions and shelves of water and toilet paper dwindling, we submit to the pressures of *panic buying.* In contrast, groups of individuals who are not concerned, either due to misinformation or personal-

---

* A member who intentionally omits information that may contradict the group's main idea for the sake of preservation and relinquishing doubt.

ity, disobey the directives of social distancing, allowing the virus to spread and endangering the lives of many more.

CULTURE AND SPIRITUALITY

In this world the unseen has power.

—APACHE PROVERB

Culture is another stratum underlying individual and group behaviors. Culture is influenced by several variables that are passed down to future generations, deeply influencing how people function. This is of extreme relevance today, given our increasingly multicultural population. To begin addressing diversity, Harrell and Bond (2006) proposed a list of three core principles:

1. *The Principle of Community Culture:* Every community has multilayered cultural characteristics and diversity dynamics.

2. *The Principle of Community Context:* There are important historical, sociopolitical, and institutional forces that affect diversity and its dynamics within a community.

3. *The Principle of Self-in-Community:* Our own values, cultural lenses, and identity statuses affect all stages of work with diverse individuals, groups, and communities.

These principles shed light on a variety of invisible forces influencing the narratives that guide identity. Important historical events are preserved through cultural customs, reminding us, in certain cases, of the struggles our ancestors underwent to ensure our continued existence. Political ideologies that pervaded in these times highly influenced individualistic thoughts and actions. Dominant religious ideologies may have caused much strife in individuals whose biological disposition was in conflict with the basis of these ideas.

In one example, a member of a minority culture may struggle through multiple processes before establishing an integrated multicultural identity. When someone from an Eastern culture, raised on the phrase *the nail that stands out gets pounded down* is thrust into a Western culture that proclaims *the squeaky wheel gets the grease*, there inevitably will be a conflict in their ability to thrive.

When basic cultural values are no longer congruent with the demands of the dominant culture, a person's culture may come into question. Poston (1990) posited a biracial identity development model with five stages that remain relevant today.

1. *Personal identity:* In childhood, the person is unaware of ethnic identity in relation to the self.

2. *Choice of group categorization:* The person begins to experience pressure to identify with one group over another due to appearances, group status, influence from parents, and knowledge of culture.

3. *Enmeshment or denial:* The awareness of rejecting the other group for superficial reasons leads to guilt, anger, confusion, and lack of acceptance.

4. *Appreciation:* Still identifying more with one culture over another, the person begins appreciating both instead of harboring dissonant feelings. The person actively seeks more information about the minority group they are associated with.

5. *Integration:* Both cultures are valued equally and successfully unified into one whole.

Beyond these processes, there exist several cultural stereotypes that tend to be magnified and distorted. People operate through psychological models based on what they have learned through social media, family beliefs, friends, education systems, and so on. As a result, preconceptions are generated, influencing the way they may interact with someone of a different culture. There exists an imposition of belief when someone is approached in a particular manner. The projected expectations of how they are *supposed* to be begins a cycle that may highly influence their identity.

Deep beliefs, customs, community, religion, and spirituality all play a role in a person's cultural makeup. It is easy to forget that there are many worldviews vastly different from Western culture, and many survive and continue to flourish alongside it. The following discussion explores fundamental beliefs and ways of being found in different cultures. It is by no means exhaustive; in fact, each example will only illustrate one subculture within the umbrella culture in which many other subcultures exist. I only seek to exemplify the diverse ways in which varied cultures manifest.

Speaking to African-centered psychology, Piper-Mandy and Rowe (2010) operate through a framework termed *Path of the Spirit.* They identify that "in an African worldview, a person is a known, knowing and knowable spirit" (p. 14), journeying through seven cycles: "Before, Beginning, Belonging, Being, Becoming, Beholding, and Beyond" (p. 14), each with its own characteristics and goals. The purpose of the journey is to align with the moral universe, "adhering to the principles of the Ma'at" (p. 16). Aviera (2002) noted that low-acculturated Latinos from Mexico or Central America may believe that struggles are fated (*fatalismo*). He further emphasized the importance of exploring supernatural reasons because "emotional problems may be seen by some as being caused by bad spirits or witchcraft" (p. 1). Chinese culture emphasizes that the "family is the basic unit of society: family is perceived as the 'great self,' and the individual . . . the 'small self'" (Ng & James, 2013, p. 2). In Chinese culture, interpersonal agreement tends to be more important than an individual's needs. According to the tenets of Taoism, the individual seeks to harmonize with nature, promoting *wu-wei* (i.e., doing not doing, akin to flow). Traits such as being adaptable, soft, resilient, and humble are endorsed. Evil is seen as ignorance, degrees of dissonance from nature (Tzu, 2003). Taoists strive to embody that from which we see (what Westerners might call consciousness). The Hindu Advaita Vedanta school, in contrast, views the world as illusory or *Maya,* emphasizing that through spiritual practices they may come in contact with *Brahman,* an eternal truth encompassing the fleeting world (Oldmeadow, 1992). According to Buddhism, by understanding the four noble truths, following the eightfold path, and engaging in dharma practice, one may experience awakening, liberating oneself from anguish (Batchelor, 1997). Voodooists dance to invoke the spirit of the dead, and the beliefs of the Kogi from Northern Colombia revolve around the narrative that their prayers preserve the balance of the cosmos (Davis, 2003).

As is evident, there is a stark contrast between Western civilization and any of the aforementioned cultures. Operating from any of these systems could influence decisions made in any circumstance. The differences among cultures and worldviews not only are apparent in functioning, but also, as would be expected, may manifest in culture-specific disorders. Currently, the *DSM-5* acknowledges the culturally specific syndromes (American Psychiatric Association, 2013, pp. 833–837) shown in Table 5.1.

TABLE 5.1: **Cultural Concepts of Distress in the *DSM-5***

CULTURAL CONCEPTS OF DISTRESS	DESCRIPTION
Ataque de nervios Related to: • Indisposition in Haiti • Blacking out in U.S. • Falling out in West Indies	*Syndrome common in Latino descent* Includes feeling out of control, acute anxiety and panic like symptoms, fainting episodes and potential, suicidal gestures, usually in relation to a stressful event related to the family.
Dhat Syndrome Related to: • Koro in southeast Asia • Shen-k'uei in China (kidney deficiency)	*Syndrome originating from South Asia* The attribution of anxiety, depression, fatigue, and other somatic complaints to semen loss. This idea may have evolved from Hindu systems of medicine, describing semen as an essential fluid whose balance is necessary to maintain health.
Khyal cap Related to: • Pen lom in Laos • Srog rlung gin ad in Tibet • Vata in Sri Lanka • Hwa byung in Korea	*Syndrome found among Cambodians* Anxiety and symptoms of panic attack that arise from a fear of a "wind-like substance" building in the body and may cause difficulties breathing and may eventually enter the head, causing one to faint.
Kufungisisa Related to: • Idioms in Africa, Caribbean, Latin America, East Asian and Native groups	*"Thinking too much"* An idiom of distress originating from the Shona of Zimbabwe. Anxiety, depression, and somatic problems may arise from "thinking too much." This may involve ruminating and worrying.
Maladi moun Related to: • Mal de ojo in Spanish communities • Mal' occhiu in Italian communities	*A cultural explanation in Haitian communities* It is believed that envy and malice may harm others by transmitting mental illnesses or physical disabilities that may severely impact their ability to perform activities of daily living.

CULTURAL CONCEPTS OF DISTRESS	DESCRIPTION
Nervios Related to: • Nevra among Greeks • Nierbi among Sicilians • Nerves in whites in Appalachia and Newfoundland	*An idiom of distress among Latinos* It refers to a range of symptoms such as emotional distress, somatic disturbance, an inability to function, stomach problems, sleeplessness, nervousness, and dizziness.
Shenjing shuairuo Related to: • Ashaktapanna in India • Shinkei-suijaku in Japan	*A syndrome from China translating to, "Weakness of the nervous system"* Three out of five symptom clusters to be met: weakness, emotions, excitement, nervous pain, and sleep. These may arise from occupational or family-related stressors including a loss of face and acute sense of failure. Feeling weak includes deficiencies of Chi when vital forces become this regulated. A person may also feel "vexed," manifesting as irritability and overall distress due to conflicting thoughts and unfulfilled desires.
Susto Related to: • Espanto in Andean region • Latinos in the Caribbean	*"Fright" from Latinos in Mexico, Central America, and South America.* It is not considered an illness. A frightening event may push the soul out of the body and this may result and sickness and misfortune. It may even cause death.
Taijin Kyofusho Related to: • Taein kong po in Korea	*"Interpersonal fear disorder"* Originates in Japan as extreme social anxiety due to the "conviction that one's appearance and actions in social interactions are inadequate or offensive to others."

Although many other culturally related diagnoses exist, all of these examples offer further evidence of the fact that large groups of individuals create a strong sociocultural process. This process, which evolves and exists beyond

the life and death of any single person, then permeates into future generations, driving the way people operate on a fundamental level. Just like the
mind, it is recursive; this field is capable of turning in on itself, altering our
perception and molding our identity. The influence others have on our self and
experience is an inevitable veil that may distort our conscious experience. At
times, this influence can be proactive and other times it brings out the worst in
us. This *dark side* of humanity has indeed been encountered in famous studies
such as Milgram's (1963) experiment on obedience to authority figures and
Zimbardo's (1971) Stanford Prison Experiment. If one lesson has been learned
from this area of study, it is that, given the right circumstances and pressure,
humans have the potential for evil as well as virtue.

THE NOUMENAL-PHENOMENAL AXIS

We adore chaos because we love to produce order.

—MAURITS CORNELIS ESCHER

Given the increasing diversification of the United States, and the importance of
spirituality and religion in many cultures, there exists a need for transpersonal
inclusion. Psychotherapists are in an interesting position, necessitating the
ability to shift not only among treatment frameworks, but also the ability to
empathize and connect with their clients through their spiritual beliefs. Being
able to understand their beliefs will relate to relational dynamics, and any prejudice may be recognized by nonverbal, right hemispheric systems, which may
impact risk the relationship.

In psychodynamic treatment there is a conscious-unconscious axis. I propose that spirituality and all forms of ontology can be conceptualized within
a noumenal-phenomenal axis (N-P axis). I am merely defining the noumenal
as reality outside of sensory-perception. The N-P axis presupposes that there
exists a noumenon that is *unknown*. The idea is that the clinician can use this
uncertainty to their advantage in a clinical setting. Uncertainty allows one to
reassemble their models of reality in correspondence to better empathizing
with their patient. One way is through introducing the noumenal-phenomenal
axis in practice. This agnostic therapeutic stance is a requisite for the pluralistic
viewpoints that exist in the world around us. The atheist may have to more

deeply consider what it would be like to be a Christian, the Christian may have to consider the viewpoint of the Buddhist.

Since the noumenon is unknown, this means that it is just as likely to be inert matter as it is to be a dynamic conceptual process in continual dialogue with the phenomenal world we experience (what some might call God). At the pole of the phenomenal axis there exists material reductionists, non-reductionist materialists, emergentists, and the like. At the center would likely be pantheism, and pan-experientialism, as it enters into the noumenal axis there are pan-psychists, pantheists, all forms of idealism, and at its extreme: God(s). Thus, levels of noumenal or phenomenal activity and involvement in everyday life define the order to which beliefs are distributed. Other differences may include immaterial versus material, monism versus pluralism, spatial versus aspatial, temporal versus atemporal, and so on. Seen in this way, it may be easier for clinicians to approach spiritual matters (that do not encroach on religious counseling). One argument against this is the idea that asymmetry may help generate novel solutions. I agree with this, but in the field, the application of differences spawn greater novelty when there is a dialectic, and a dialectic cannot happen without a better conscious understanding of the other person's point of view.

Imagine an atheist treating someone who was highly religious. They are discussing the importance of religious experiences the client had. If the client believes she was touched by God (and schizophrenia and bipolar disorder are ruled out), it would be very easy to invalidate their experience if one were to operate from the view that it was a result of a series of electrochemical interactions. Microexpressions may detract from an established relationship and work counter to the goals of treatment.

If the clinician were able to suspend their own beliefs and shift their conceptual framework toward the noumenal end, the ability to relate increases. The clinician might tell themselves "Okay, I will temporarily put my beliefs aside, and assume that the noumenon is active, not passive, and immaterial, not material. With this in mind, what might be the next best step?" Some questions you may want to know include: How active is their conception of noumenon? To what degree does it fit into their everyday life and functioning? Some religions stress an external versus an internal locus of responsibility or control; how might these beliefs be contributing to the presenting problem, and what might be a novel solution that respects their beliefs? How does this differ from my own beliefs, and what are the boundaries that I am working within (or what boundaries should I be working without!). When approaching these matters, it is best to adopt a curious, open, and accepting attitude.

APPLICATIONS: WORKING WITH SOCIOCULTURAL DYNAMISM

Each brain reverberated with the ethereal rhythms of its environment; and each contributed its own peculiar theme to the complex pattern of the whole.

—OLAF STAPLEDON

There is no escaping the influences of sociocultural systems. Many of those who choose to isolate themselves do so in reaction to the effects of social influences, inadvertently empowering the status of social impact. Indeed, we even find our ancestors speaking to us on a genetic level, and as our brains develop, they do so in direct interaction with our social and environmental experiences. We are highly social organisms, and the best we can do is to play the hand we have been dealt. Beyond the simple awareness of these emergent maladaptive phenomena, we may also include strategies to promote objectivity.

The underlying recommendations to address groupthink parallel those for group polarization. Janis (1991) suggested tasking all members of a team to critically analyze crucial decisions being made, as opposed to relying solely on the group leader to make decisions. It would be most effective to create an open and safe space where individuals are able to voice their opinions freely and provide views contrary to popular consensus. Multiple meetings may help further address ideas from other group members who have been exposed to novel information. In addition, hiring consulting teams outside the organization may improve objectivity in decision making.

Diffusion of responsibility in workplaces may be achieved via incentive programs and a system that holds each individual accountable for the work they do. Some helpful examples include increasing transparency of work done among team members or reaching a consensus on delegated responsibilities. Highlighting the personal value of work being done and the opportunity for growth may be supportive.

One way to decrease intergroup violence is to promote intergroup trust, which generates affiliation, supports the process of identifying with a group (Baumeister & Leary, 1995), and promotes cooperation that may benefit all (Zaki & Mitchell, 2013). However, there are differences in neurological functioning when generating trust among in-group and out-group members. Trust among in-group members is maintained by the subjective value gleaned from the group, which relates to activity in the striatum and ventromedial prefrontal cortex (Ruff & Fehr, 2014). In contrast, to develop trust with out-group members, we must target top-down processes, such as those mediated by the dorsal anterior cingulate and lateral prefrontal cortex, which have been associated with slower, more deliberate processes involved in the reevaluation of systems (Shenhav, Botvinick, & Cohen, 2013). A study by Hughes and colleagues (2017) provided further support for this dual-process model, further concluding that reduced time to think and access resources resulted in reduced out-group trust. It is also important to consider the sociocultural context in which intergroups are embedded. For instance, when two nations are at war, it is considered socially acceptable to be vocally expressive of ill sentiments, but when compared to racial biases, which are socially unacceptable, neurological correlates are reversed, whereby evaluative cortical regions are engaged (Amodio, Devine, & Harmon-Jones, 2008). Thus, when working with the potential for intergroup violence, it will be important to integrate solutions from group polarization research and provide time for individuals to reflect and evaluate their thoughts and emotions. It may also be helpful to offer groups increased opportunities to be exposed to one another in safe, controlled spaces, as well as to work together toward a specific goal.

In therapy, the analyst Thomas Ogden (2004) described the existence of the *analytic third*, which is an interpersonal field or a third process that is generated by the dialectical tensions of the two subjectivities in continual interaction. The field carries its own unconscious life, illuminated by experiences like projective identification. The two individuals relate to this field differently, and the field itself has the power to structure and influence the relationship. Similar to this concept, Stolorow and Atwood (1996) proposed the *intersubjective field*, whereby the greater relational system mutually shapes experience that arises.

The role of culture is deeply embedded in all of our meaning systems. There exist far too many layers of complexity within culture alone to make any sort of assumption. It is important to harbor an attitude of openness and curiosity, consume information actively to better understand others in different cultures, and monitor our thoughts for potential biases. What might be some biases to be aware of? According to Sue (1996), cultural biases may generally include:

1. *Focus on the individual rather than the family:* In some cultures, the family is more important than the individual.

2. *Verbal expression of emotions rather than nonverbal:* These may result in misattributions and overpathologizing.

3. *Expectation of openness and intimacy:* These may be incongruent with the client's experiences due to culture.

4. *Insight versus denial:* Insight is believed to be very important for growth, but for some cultures, practical interventions and a healthy denial may be more useful.

5. *Competition versus cooperation:* An inclination toward cooperative work may be denigrated by therapists as a lack of assertiveness, when it may simply be culture-based.

6. *Linear time emphasis versus circular:* In some cultures, punctuality is extremely important, and others mark time via events rather than clock time.

7. *Nuclear versus extended family:* Extended families may be seen as nuclear families in many cultures, particularly Latin American and Asian American.

8. *Locus of responsibility:* An internal locus of responsibility and control is counterbalanced by an external locus of responsibility and control.

9. *Emphasis on scientific empiricism:* Quantitativeness, reductionism, and objectivity are not valued to the same degree in all cultures. Many value a more holistic and nonlinear approach.

As may be evident based on the previous description of fundamental beliefs transmitted from one generation to the next, psychotherapy necessarily extends into the domain of spirituality. The goal, however, is not to play the role of a spiritual figure engaging the client in religious discourse or direction, but to seek clarity on the individual's relationship to that which they consider transcendent (Shafranske, 2009). Beliefs may be the primary lens through which someone operates and their primary mode of deriving meaning from their actions. Should this foundation become compromised, it may cause the entire system to topple. Shafranske (2009) suggested that a psychodynamic approach may be useful because "god images reflect influences of culture as well as seminal patterns of relating with parents and significant others" (p. 150), and "religious ideation may reflect emerging dynamics in the client's relationship with the therapist, point to memories or provide narratives to describe states of mind" (p. 151).

There is an intimate relationship among a person's psychological health, culture, and environmental demands that cannot be ignored. Each feeds into the other in a nonlinear fashion. Culture, a societal construction of a variety of individual minds, becomes deeply embedded into our neural circuitry, moving us in ways we often fail to acknowledge. Overall, the sociocultural process is one to consider with great sensitivity and curiosity. Imposition of the therapist's beliefs is damaging, particularly toward those cultures that greatly respect and acquiesce to expert authority. On a large scale, this sort of dominance plays a role in the Westernization of the world, as we begin to lose touch with the beautiful array of cultural diversity that currently exists.

CHAPTER 6.

Existence and Meaning

··

Man is indispensable for the completion of
creation; that, in fact, he himself is the second
creator of the world, who alone has given the
world its objective existence—without which,
unheard, unseen, silently eating, giving birth,
dying, heads nodding through hundreds of
millions of years, it would have gone on in the
profoundest night of non-being down to its
unknown end. Human consciousness created
objective existence and meaning, and man
found his indispensable place in the great
process of being.

—CARL JUNG

Our survival is contingent on our genetic disposition, the accuracy and efficiency of our brain's predictive circuitry, and current environmental pressures. The processing delays inherent in sensing and perceiving the world
around us prevent us from truly living in the present moment. Memory serves
to provide us with a probable selection of future possibilities and as a result is
not an accurate record of history. We generate expectations for everything
that is unknown to us and these expectations drive much of our present-day

functioning and decision making. We are driven by biological and social needs, our mind filtered by heuristics, defenses, distortions, non-conscious paradigms and learned behavior, social influences, and culture. Where is the room for freedom and meaning? Are we just deluded puppets spiraling inevitably toward death?

Embedded in the human experience is our capacity to enter an existential space where we may question the very nature of our existence. With increasing depth, our investigation may begin coloring perception with the sentiment of derealization. In this experiential state, we may feel dread or liberation, such that we feel as if we are closer to the core of *potential and possibility*. These are significant states, the human experiential equivalent of recursion in complex systems theory (ability to change that from which it originates). Freedom, isolation, meaninglessness, and death are the roots to existential approaches in psychotherapy (Yalom & Leszcz, 2005).

It is because we are uncertain that we have the ability to, or the illusion of the ability to, direct choice. If certainty existed, there would be no choice to be made, because all choices would already have been made. In basic statistics and physics there exists the concept of chance. The idea of chance implies that there exists a range of possibilities in the future. In James's (1890) view, consciousness is adaptive, and its advantage is explained quite aptly in the analogy of "dice thrown forever on a table. Unless they be loaded, what chance is there that the highest number will turn up oftener than the lowest?" He goes on to ask: "Can consciousness increase its efficiency by loading its dice?" (James, 1890, p. 64).

This *experience* of free will cannot be denied even if objective freedom proves to be an illusion. In this situation, it is important to remember that our experience as a conscious agent with motivations to change is just as legitimate as an experience of succumbing to bad habits; that our experience of the drive to transcend a maladaptive urge is just as real as the urge. Given that it may facilitate proactive change, the belief in an illusion may be a more productive way of living than yielding to the temptation to submit oneself to what we have decided is a deterministic force. By yielding, we may deny a potential way of being, if we had only believed in it.

Libet (1973, 1999) believed that the 200 msec gap between conscious registration of an event and its behavior was sufficient for us to *veto* an undesirable behavior. Haggard (2008) clarifies that the presupplementary motor area, the

anterior prefrontal cortex, and the parietal cortex have been consistently associated with intention and voluntary control. He posits that that volition may be
experienced as an elicitation of these systems, which involve the classification
of internally generated information that informs impending actions. He views
it as a process that consists of "a series of decisions regarding whether to act,
what action to perform, and when to perform it" (p. 934).

Perhaps it is my upbringing, but I remember very early on in a course on
philosophy of mind questioning the question of free will itself. For the life of
me, I could not understand what the fuss was about. It was a Western idea to
separate mind from body, whereas it was always natural for me to see them as
inextricably linked. When I recognized this discrepancy, the problem came
to me as a linguistic or ideological deception. Might it be that the dissociation
of our self from our biological nature is simply an error that tricks us into
believing we are controlled by our biology when, really, we are our biology?
This is dangerous in many respects. When we do not see our natures as part
of who we are, we create artificial in-group/out-group boundaries. History
offers ample evidence to demonstrate how these dynamics may result interpersonally, and this seems to be a notion that may further extend intrapsychically.
When someone or some part of ourselves is seen as *the other,* we begin to act
defensively, we possibly see others as hostile, and our limbic systems activate.
When we think our ego is separate from all these unconscious processes, we
may treat ourselves cruelly, as if we are waging a battle within rather than
engaging in a respectful form of inner democracy. Furthermore, in the line
of reasoning that we are that readiness potential* rising before an action (as
referred to in Libet's study), the freedom and resolution we may have in implementing some behavior against some other dissonant part of our nature is only
amplified by the decision to identify with the part of us that wishes to transcend. I have always been interested in these questions: To what degree do we
have free will? To what extent can we motivate ourselves to reorganize networks of information into a more coherent fashion? Can free will be influenced
by awareness, knowledge, or wisdom?

While some are shaken by the potential of no free will, the adoption of the
perspective has fortunately not been too difficult for me to digest. It merely

---

* Using an electroencephalogram (EEG), a device measuring electrical activity in the brain, Libet
found a readiness potential (i.e. electrical discharges), preceding any conscious decision.

involves (for me), ejecting out of nature, into the isolated ego, and a reverence for the complex *machinery* that is a human. It must include the acceptance of consciousness as a reflective capacity and the emergence of an exceedingly complex system as result of determined forces. It is not as if subjective experience ceases to exist or that we are haunted by the notion of being a puppet. Moreover, reductionism does not abolish responsibility or morality, because the experience of what is right, wrong, freedom, responsibility, beauty, and meaning is still inherent in all human experience. How would you live your life differently if free will was proven to exist? And if not?

In reaction, I have seen some opt for nihilism, but this track is rarely, if at all, sustainable. Personally, I *accept* my experience of free will as a point of departure from which I operate. At minimum, I consider that we have *pockets of freedom* distributed throughout every day. With a multiplicity of genetic, self, and sociocultural processes, it is very difficult for every choice to be conscious. In fact, many times, we strive to be more conscious, only to be less conscious, as automaticity exerts less effort and energy when things come naturally to us (Solms, 2017). These pockets of freedom are mostly dedicated to solving problems and guiding self-development. When it comes to personal maturation, I am of the mind that experience takes precedence. We begin with the experience that we are aware, that we can think a thought, move a limb, or act in ways that are conducive to our health. In most cases, if we find it within us to suspend and generate an internal dialogue with dissonant self-processes for long enough, while behaving in accordance to what our conscience feels is best, the discordant feelings may become concordant, if not easier to manage, thanks to plasticity. Perhaps it may be more useful to think of yourself as a self-organizing, or self-regulating, organism without invoking the notion of free will.

The biological potential to survive is enhanced by psychological functions propelling us to face the challenges we must confront strategically. This function may even transcend a biological urge, as is seen in purposeful fasting or sexual abstinence. We might even argue that spiritual meaning systems that exist are all in service of this function. In other words, the narratives we have act as a sort of fuel. Narratives—or at least their interpretation—may change. I would go so far as to say that it is a core responsibility for humans to continue weaving these subjective narratives into stronger and more resonant ones in relation to the objective facts uncovered by science. Although there is undoubtedly influence between our experiences and expectations and belief systems, the experience of a transpersonal element may override our predisposition to act in a certain way. Whereas religious individuals may subordinate themselves to god(s), atheists or agnostics may subordinate themselves to the mystery of nature, meaning, desired life stories, greater states of consciousness, their family, friends, or humanity itself. This recognition opens access and redistributes the energy required to make sacrifices necessary for us to thrive. This is one of the reasons why AA meetings are still effective for those suffering from addiction. An addicted person must be able to relegate the god they currently worship (the substance) and promote another.

APPLICATIONS: DISCOVERING DOMINANT BELIEFS THROUGH BEHAVIORS

Intelligence without ambition is a bird without wings.

—Salvador Dali

People have many beliefs. It is important for me to mention that people's ideals may be part of their beliefs, but not necessarily their *dominant* beliefs. Significant disagreements among meaning systems may be found in the unknown and in times of uncertainty or conflict. Those who are aware of their system will adapt better when confronted by the unknown. The unknown covers vastly more territory than the known, and it has the power to produce thoughts within us and guide our behaviors. It is capitalized by those of us prone to endlessly theorize as a means to justify delaying responsibility. For others, uncertainty may be either a source of existential angst or a metaphysical springboard for courage. Individuals with great fear of the unknown may cower in its presence, becoming locked into rigid forms of thinking in order to remain with that which is familiar. Constantly projecting the worst-case scenarios into the future, they petrify in the present. In contrast, individuals oblivious to their relationship with the unknown may charge recklessly into the darkness without awareness of the consequences. Suddenly, they find themselves in a situation that may be beyond recovery. Whether we like it or not, the unknown stirs our imagination, producing thoughts, emotions, and experiences of every kind. For many, the unknown awakens uncertainty, an active veil that we all confront, but also a source of information.

One way to help individuals is to identify their dominant belief system through their behaviors. The behavior is what wins out in the competition happening in the mind among belief systems. Someone suffering from a nasty habit of lying for pleasurable gains may tell themselves that they *believe* that lying for personal gain is bad, and they wouldn't want anyone to lie to them. Yet, in order to receive pleasurable gains, they may suddenly find themselves lying to someone who trusts them. In this case, the dominant belief is that lying for personal gain is acceptable in times of need. When the inconsistency is accentuated, the path and motivation to change may become more easily accessible, as is often found in the efficacy of techniques of motivational interviewing (Rubak, Sandboek, Lauritzen, & Christensen, 2005). It will then be important to locate where they lie on the stages of change (Krebs, Norcross, Nicholson, & Prochaska, 2018) and proceed appropriately. One way clinicians may open the door to this dimension without invoking any particular religion is to explore their clients' dominant beliefs through actions when confronted with uncertainty or inner conflict. What decisions are they making? What do these decisions tell clinicians about their beliefs? A dominant beliefs identification chart can be used to help with this process (see Appendix D).

WHAT IS MEANING?

What is to give light must endure burning.

—VIKTOR FRANKL

What endures in states of extreme suffering and euphoria? Meaning. This chapter explores existing concepts of meaning and methods practitioners have used to help others live a life in accordance with these concepts. The subsequent chapter, Vital Signals, elaborates on meaning, how it may be discovered through *self-transcendent experiences* and how to apply these ideas into practice. I specify the word *conscious* because we also give meaning to things on a nonconscious, perceptual level. Consider the following example:

D y u udrstnd th s?

What we read above is inherently meaningless, yet we put the most likely of words together to form the sentence. We did not have to do so with much deliberation; in fact, it was likely quite automatic for us. This meaning-making system thus exists at a non-conscious level as well as at a conscious level that is involved with making sense of a significant experience. They are connected, just as an important experience may be meaningful only once we make sense of it in our lives.

This chapter will focus on existential meaning. I use the construct of *meaning*, which I am defining as the experience of significance for its applicability to atheism, religion, and spirituality. I assert that in order for something to be meaningful, there is a *making sense of,* a *giving significance to,* and an *attaining significance from.* Whereas I previously described the ego as an observer and liaison, I conceptualize meaning as the North star.

For many of us, there comes a point in life when satisfactory living becomes insufficient. It has been my personal and professional experience that approaching pleasures and avoiding pain becomes humdrum, some individuals deem themselves *bored* with life itself, but I have found that it is rather a dissatisfaction with the way they are *being* in life. As evolutionary traits arise by necessity, so too does an inner necessity give rise to a more conscious existence. Indeed, Rogers (1951) noted that humans have a "basic tendency and striving—to actualize, maintain, and *enhance the experiencing* organism" (p. 487). In other words, there is the need to sustain vitality in their existence in opposition to simply answering an instinctual call, following social pressure, or chasing a pleasure. However, doing so is not an easy task. Habits resist, people judge, and pleasures tempt, and although they may imagine a life that would be much better, there is no guarantee of the results. Most people slide back into the comfort of what is manageable, justify the decision, and never allow their full potential to emerge.

Jung (1954) was also well aware of the difficulty of achieving a fully conscious life and the needs that beckon: "The words 'many are called, but few are chosen' are singularly appropriate here" (p. 173). Earlier he says,

> Personality is the supreme realization of the innate idiosyncrasy of a living being. It is an act of high courage flung in the face of life, the absolute affirmation of all that constitutes the individual, the most successful adaptation to the universal conditions of existence coupled with the greatest possible freedom for self-determination. (p. 171)

Jung also claims that true personality is always a vocation (p. 175). A person must "choose his own way, consciously and with moral deliberation" (p. 174).

One of the core attributes that separates humans from other living organisms is the complex meaning-based systems from which humans operate. Existential philosopher Jean-Paul Sartre (1983) asserted that the world is inherently meaningless and that it is our responsibility to give the world meaning. He stated, "At the end of the infinite series of my efforts, the world will have become necessary because of me and I shall have created myself by means of the world, hence I shall have given myself necessary existence" (p. 555).

Meaning may be generated before the fact, as an aspirational concept put into action, in which case the moment the action occurs, meaning is lived into existence. Meaning may also as arise intuitively, during the fact, as a feeling prompting one to action or formed after the fact with reflection, resulting in attitudinal shifts or deployment of specific behaviors. In the view that meaning is one of the most complex, emergent features of biological interactions, and a phenomenon unique to humans, is it not logical to exercise and expand this dimension of our experience?

Existential psychologist and Holocaust survivor Viktor Frankl (1986) founded logotherapy, a system of psychotherapy, in service of helping people find meaning. In his struggle to survive through various concentration camps, he was inspired by the resilience people could muster when they led a meaningful life. Whereas Freud believed in a *will to pleasure* and Adler and Nietzsche opined on a *will to power*, Frankl argued for the *will to meaning*. He asserted that power and pleasure are to a degree necessary and means to an end, but not the end itself. In a powerful statement Frankl emphasized that:

> Pleasure is not the goal of our aspirations, rather the consequence of attaining them. Pleasure does not loom before us as the goal of an ethical act, rather an ethical act carries pleasure on its back. . . . The pleasure principle overlooks the intentional quality of all psychic activity. (p. 35)

During the extreme conditions of the Holocaust, meaning acted as psychological armor that protected him and others from giving up.

Frankl (1986) asserted that meaning is found in the moment and can be derived in conditions of happiness and suffering, evidenced by several anecdotal accounts of individuals who were able to appreciate life despite being in a concentration camp. This experience was a testament to Nietzsche's (1888) statement, "If we have our own 'why' of life, we shall get along with almost

any 'how' " (para. 1.12). In Frankl's theory (1986), although the mind is contingent on biological processes, it is not dependent upon them. The realm in
which freedom exists is what he termed the *noological dimension* (the mind).
Furthermore, he argued that "freedom predicates responsibility" (p. 53), "guilt
presupposes responsibility" (p. 109), and the "starting point in existential analysis is consciousness of responsibility" (p. 25). By responsibility, he meant the
responsibility to uphold meaning in life and bear the consequences of doing so.

In deconstructing meaning, Frankl (1986) identified four central tenets.
First, there is the acknowledgement of the will to meaning as a primary
concern. Second, the meaning is not an overarching meaning of life, rather,
always, the meaning of our life in the moment. Third, meaning is found
through the pursuit of three values: creative values, which are actualized
by doing; experiential values, which are realized by receiving of the world
(nature, art); and attitudinal values, which are actualized whenever we confront an impasse. When speaking of values, Frankl did not refer to subjective
properties; instead he considered the personal significance of a possibility,
an action, a person, or a thing as they are encountered in everyday life. We
find meaning through what we take from the world in terms of experiencing
values, and we find meaning by taking a stand toward a fate we no longer can
change (Deurzen, 2010).

Meaning is also central to the therapeutic approach developed by Stephen
Hayes (2009), acceptance and commitment therapy (ACT). ACT proposes
that we can identify our core values through certain exercises that may relate
to different dimensions of living and be utilized as guides to living a meaningful life. I am of the mind that both of these methods may be quite successful,
depending on the client. Indeed, people naturally gravitate toward specific
values; some follow their intuition and others need more concrete guides that
may help direct their decision making. If these values are embodied in everyday
living, regardless of the consequence, we have lived in accordance with what
we determine as highest in them in the moment.

In contrast to the preceding ways in which meaning can be facilitated consciously, I will now pivot the conversation to share how meaning may also arise
on an unconscious level. As is evident by the previous discussion of veils, not
only are we not perceiving much of reality, but also the majority of neuroscientists and psychologists alike are well aware that most of what occurs in our
brains is non-conscious.

Whereas Carl Jung's (1973) conceptions of the unconscious may extend beyond mainstream scientific and psychoanalytic comfort (beyond time and space) and have been capitalized upon thoroughly by new age writers, there is no reason to discard elements thereof that are currently acceptable in our cultural climate and may be useful even to those with the most skeptical of minds. In fact, analytical psychology has found empirical support in the form of symptom reduction, improved interpersonal functioning, enhanced personality structure, and increased quality of life. Moreover, these improvements have been found to be stable for up to six years. Research has also shown that clients who underwent Jungian therapy had later rates of healthcare usage below their previous use, as well as below the average population's usage (Roesler, 2013).

Jung (1966) believed that people strive for *wholeness*, and by wholeness he meant the integration of unconscious processes with the conscious. He called this process *individuation*. Murray Stein (2015) succinctly described the process as developing "a conscious relationship to the various aspects of one's personality, not by further identifying with the more prominent features . . . rather by containing them all maximally within consciousness precisely without such identification" (p. 4). The concept of wholeness resonates with the psychotherapeutic goal of promoting healthy degrees of vertical and horizontal neural integration, as opposed to denying some aspect of experience. It "aims at a living co-operation of all factors" (Jung, 1953, p. 174). For example, Gazzaniga and colleagues' (1962) findings suggest that there are multiple operating systems within us, many of which we may be unaware of. To become aware of what these may be as they are expressed psychologically would fall under the principle of individuation, which promotes the establishment of relationships with all domains of the self.

To reconceptualize this from the perspective of meaning, meaning may arise from unconscious processes if they are interpreted consciously. Unconscious matter to be interpreted includes dreams, daydreams, unconscious relational patterns, and forms of art. What we find as meaningful is subjective and productive in its ability to potentiate our individuality, wisdom, and unique contributions to the world. In modern-day terms, we might say that it is the integration of the multiple neural and relational operating systems with the autobiographical self, most of which happens on a non-conscious level, that may help us achieve well-being. Joseph Campbell (1949) suggested that we all have our own personal myths to live out, all of which follow the general structure of recurring mythological patterns that occur throughout the world, regardless of contact, time, or place. Meaning may thus exist in the unknown, the past, or the future, waiting for the right conditions to express itself. One question Jung asked himself was, What is the myth I am living out? This is a profoundly deep question that can be useful to ask ourself or to ask clients who wish to engage in this process.

APPLICATIONS: SELF-CONTROL AND THE QUEST FOR MEANING

Withdraw into yourself and look. And if you do not
find yourself beautiful yet, act as does the creator of
a statue that is to be made beautiful . . . cut away all
that is excessive, straighten all that is crooked, bring
light to all that is overcast, labour to make all one
glow of beauty and never cease chiseling your statue.

—PLOTINUS

Meaning is a product of relationships, and relationships are founded on meaning. In isolation, subjects and objects cease to be, and are rendered meaningless. One requires the other to exist. Meaning is thus a result of relationships between polarities. As has been explored, meaning may be conceptualized and expressed in different ways. Sartre endorses the notion that meaning is created, Frankl that meaning is discovered and derived from the moment, and Hayes suggests that meaning is a process of living a life according to values you consciously decide. Experiential truth is found through the experimentation of different systems, which is for every individual to experience themselves.

Underlying the ability to pursue any conscious direction is self-control (Baumeister & Exline, 2000). Self-control is governed by our capacity to inhibit, which when done successfully develops descending inhibitory tracts. For this reason, I speculate that internal conflicting stimuli may serve the secondary purpose of exercising our ability to inhibit, which may expand our metacognitive capacities. In other words, continued desires need not be seen as a nuisance or evolutionary mistake, but instead as an opportunity to advance our neural development, enabling improved chances for conscious living and the evolution of meaning. To make it clear, every time we inhibit a maladaptive impulse, we assert our freedom by establishing dominance. Importantly, we are not negating the existence of these impulses; rather, we seek to redirect our impulses' purpose toward an integrated response in service of a higher meaning that benefits the entire organism.

With constant reinforcement, pleasurable responses may become automated and eventually habitual. Unfortunately, every time we engage in habitual cycles, we reinforce their existence in our neural pathways, strengthening their connections to a system of the brain associated with regulating our behaviors as a result of pleasure (i.e., the reward center). Sometimes, these habits are not conducive to our long-term goals, in which case we will need to develop appropriate practices to redirect their paths. In a way, we can be like bulls in a bull-fighting ring. We are first released into life, and we begin charging at red veils being held by performers. The veils represent life's promises of some lasting satisfaction, with the performers being the instigators. Most of the time, as soon as we hit the mark, we miss it, or we realize there is another veil waiting for us. Other times, we manage to hit the target and find temporary freedom, only to find there are more waiting for us. It is a cruel game, and eventually life takes us.

The core foundations of self-control stretch back to successful ascetic practices that lead to positive transformation and virtuous behavior (Graiver, 2018). Part of the issue is that matter is undisciplined and, with the nearly infinite amount of unhealthy but pleasurable activities to which we have access, we increase the reservoir of potential maladaptive primitive impulses that may work against health. This rift has us seemingly working against our biology in response to pleasurable behaviors with maladaptive long-term consequences. Our reward system is nearsighted and does not fully account for long-term consequences. It has no moral compass, which is why a short-term pleasure can temporarily blind our ability to plan for the future. Even feelings of guilt have been found to be reinforcing, alongside pride, eliciting responses from the dorsomedial prefrontal cortex, amygdala, insula, and nucleus accumbens. The nucleus accumbens in particular, known as the brain's *reward system,* is even more triggered in guilt and shame than pride (Korb, 2015). By the time we have decided to move away from a maladaptive habit, the difficulty in doing so may be comparable to the difficulty of breaking an addiction, resulting in cravings, withdrawal, and temporary loss of the ability to feel pleasure (i.e., anhedonia). In such cases, the expectation of future reward must be greater than the suffering we must undergo to achieve it. Clinicians must be well-equipped to make these expectations a foreseeable reality and remind clients that there is a state of consciousness greater than what they are currently experiencing.

One method of assistance is to identify clients' ideal value systems and have them actively engage with them. Meaning may be identified and expressed through historical, attitudinal, creative, and experiential means (adapted from Breitbart & Poppito, 2014), each of which may correspond to questions.

Dialogue: Questions to Embellish Meaning

Historical: How do you want to be remembered when you die?

Attitudinal: How do you want to conduct yourself in the face of challenge and suffering?

Creative: What activities express what is meaningful to you?

Experiential: What are some experiences that were meaningful to you?

The following is an adapted exercise used in Acceptance and Commitment Therapy (ACT):

EXERCISE

I typically use a modified form of the ACT's banquet exercise:

"With your eyes closed, imagine X years from now you are at a banquet being held in your honor. Everyone you love, respect, and know well is there to celebrate your excellence. You are seated at the center of the room. You see a single spotlight on a stage with a microphone and stand. You hear footsteps walking up the stage. Someone is about to talk about you. Who might this person be? Imagine you are that person, what would you say?"

You, the clinician, may continue this process with three other speakers about the client. In the meantime, you will be jotting notes and identifying themes throughout. When the third person finishes, you may gently bring the client back into the room with you. Share the purpose of the exercise and actively collaborate with them on identifying three to five (this number may vary) of their core values. For example: if, after collaborating, the values of **h**onesty, **r**esilience, and **h**ealth arise, you may help them form a mnemonic such as **h**eaven **r**esides **h**ere. Once established and discussed in depth, before making any crucial decision in their lives, they may revisit this mnemonic of their values to determine whether their proposed actions are congruent with their values. In this scenario, even if a negative consequence arises as a result of an action, they may be at peace by knowing they still lived that moment in accordance with their values, generating meaning.

• •

The other challenge is that self-control behaviors quickly exhaust our finite reservoir of energy (Baumeister, Vohs, & Tice, 2007). It becomes more difficult to engage in a desired behavior instead of one that is habitual after just one instance of successful self-control. This is reflected in decreased blood glucose levels, which can then be recovered with a glucose drink (the study provided Kool-Aid lemonade with sugar vs. the control group, which received Kool-Aid with Splenda) (Gailliot et al., 2007).

Ego depletion does occur. Luckily, continually exerting self-control does seem to increase our resources or at least increase our resistance in the face of depletion. In addition, exertion in one area seems to generalize onto others. For example, specific efforts to manage finances or engage in physical activity may improve study habits. Moreover, we become better at anticipating the future and conserving our resources with increased self-control behaviors. Finally, other motives (e.g., cash incentives, positive emotions, social goals, humor) may help counteract ego depletion (Baumeister, Tice, Vohs, 2018).

Clinically, if a client is struggling with a maladaptive habit but has been unable to subvert its influence, it may be beneficial to ask the client to engage in the requisite self-control behaviors in other domains of their life to increase the chances of applying self-control to the identified problem.

CHAPTER 7.

The Varieties of Vital Signals

··

*Yet the unseen region in question is not merely
ideal, for it produces effects in this world. When
we commune with it, work is actually done upon
our finite personality, for we are turned . . .
But that which produces effects within another
reality must be termed a reality itself, so I feel
as if we had no philosophic excuse for calling
the unseen . . . unreal.*

—WILLIAM JAMES

To live a life according to personalized principles is likely to fail if they solely inhabit self-consciousness. How common it is to fall short while chasing an ideal in mind! And how quickly we all give up our ideals in favor of accepting our nature as-is! As Kierkegaard (1849/2004) noted long ago, when one attempts to consciously construct a self "rebellion is legitimate at any moment"; furthermore, one "is forever building only castles in the air, and is always only fencing with an imaginary component. All these experimental virtues look very splendid . . . at a whim it can dissolve the whole thing into nothing" (pp. 100–101). The very act of living out a meaningful belief requires cross-talk between circuitry, giving rise to meaning and basic sensory-motor processes necessary to fulfill the corresponding behavior. The concept is just as important as its implementation. Might it be possible to forge ideals that can match or outweigh the experience of an instinctual impulse? The answer to this question lies in meaningful experiences that are *discovered* through their impact to our entire being.

There are several states of interest with varying degrees of direct psycho-physiological experience (Pohling & Diessner, 2016) that are classified as *self-transcendent experiences* (STEs; Yaden, Haidt, Hood, Vago, & Newberg, 2017). Importantly, many of these states overlap; one may be an amplification of another, as a consequence resulting in different behavioral outcomes. They are thus conceived to rest on a *unitary continuum* (Newberg & d'Aquili, 2000). Yaden and colleagues (2017), emphasized that:

> STEs do not consist of practices or activities that may induce experiences of self-transcendence. Such practices include meditation, prayer, yoga, music, dancing, ingesting psychoactive substances and many more . . . while such practice, rituals and activities capable of eliciting STEs are clearly important for the study of these mental states, they would not themselves be considered STEs. (p. 3)

Although I am in agreement with much of their work, this seems to be an unnecessary distinction that results in more confusion, as can be seen even in the very phrasing of the claim. For this reason and for practical purposes, I will continue with the idea that STEs can be reached through passive or active means—a necessary categorization. The other liberty I will take that is incongruent with the literature is the use of the construct *moved*. Some classify being moved as another subcategory (Cova & Deonna, 2013) of lesser magnitude (to awe), but I am using it simply as a descriptor that connects all STEs. These states are all connected by the experience of being temporarily moved from one state of consciousness to encompass another. "Moved" also serves as a more relatable word for clients to use in the context of practice. These states are characterized by decreased self-involvement and higher levels of connectedness.

All STEs are states of interest, but a complete review of the literature would be too vast for the purposes of this book. For this reason, I will necessarily narrow my focus to include *moral elevation, inspiration,* and *awe.* STEs generally occur as we witness another acting with immensely admirable qualities; when we encounter someone with exceptional abilities; and when we become absorbed in the beauty of a natural landscape, person, or art form (Keltner & Haidt, 2003; Thrash & Elliot, 2003).

SELF-TRANSCENDENT STATES

Moved (Cova & Deonna, 2013)
Kama Muta (Schubert, Zickfeld, Seibt, & Fiske, 2018)
Elevation (Algoe & Haidt, 2009)
Environmental epiphanies (Storie & Vining, 2018)
Admiration (Onu, Kessler, & Smith, 2016)
Inspiration (Thrash & Elliot, 2003).
Mindfulness (Vago & Silbersweig, 2012)
Awe (Keltner & Haidt, 2003)
Flow (Csikszentmihalyi, 1990)
Peak experiences (Maslow, 1964)
Mystical experience (Yaden et al., 2016)

• •

Throughout this discussion, I will use a generic example involving the fictional character named "Arthur" in order to help us distinguish between these experiences:

Arthur is an aspiring psychologist. He has a voracious appetite for books related to philosophy, psychology, and neuroscience. Eventually, he stumbles upon a series of books that move him deeply, helping him overcome some of his own challenges in life. He decides to seek out the author, Emrys, and finds him presenting at an event. As the author speaks, Arthur feels as if the presentation is intended specifically for him. The author's tone of voice, prosody, gestures, and overall flow leave Arthur in a state of *awe*. Arthur feels as if his world had gone silent, his everyday sense of self feeling moved to a different state of consciousness. He feels a heightened level of connectedness and humility (Stellar et al.,

2018), a prosocial inclination (Rudd, Vohs, & Aaker, 2012), a dilation of time, and a level of life satisfaction (Piff, Dietze, Feinberg, Stancato, & Keltner, 2015) that he had not experienced since viewing a spectacular view after a strenuous hike.

According to Keltner and Haidt (2003), states of awe involve a perceived vastness that may be conceptual (e.g., complexity, social status) and physical, requiring immediate accommodation. By accommodation they are referring to Jean Piaget's (1973) formulations on accommodation and assimilation. In the process of learning, new information is either incorporated into our pre-existing knowledge base without issue (assimilation) or requires us to adjust our pre-existing knowledge base in order to accommodate the new information. The accommodation that occurs tends to be the diminishment of the sense of our everyday self. There is some semantic concern here, because the interpretation can be both a dissolving of self-boundaries or an expansion (as well as other possible responses). An expansion would imply that people are still aware of their previous selves; they just experience more, resulting in prosocial behaviors. Perhaps it is not even so much the self that expands or contracts, but the *sense* of self that expands. This might clarify some nuances, suggesting that these kinds of experiences are simply *dormant* within us, and a particular configuration of activity may trigger the experience. In any case, the everyday sense of self as an isolated entity is moved into a different experience.

Indeed, the type of knowledge we acquire or to which we attend has a tendency to relate to our personal disposition, as is evidenced by the self-referential effect (Symons & Johnson, 1997). Thus, personality and knowledge revolve around one another. Information can modify our autobiographical self, just as the autobiographical self can modify the information being interpreted. Accordingly, it seems that increasing knowledge or the alteration of our informational structures may lead to a wider variety of experiences.

One theory of awe is that it is a primordial emotion, fashioned by evolution for the purposes of maintaining hierarchical positioning (Keltner & Haidt, 2003). This may occur in the context of an exceptional leader. In Arthur's case this would be Emrys. In contrast, experiences of awe in nature have been theorized to be a response to encountering zones that are strategic due to their vantage point and safety. This finding parallels the fact that people often experience awe in areas with extravagant views (Chirico & Yaden, 2018).

Although these theories are logical, they are not entirely complete. Deep experiences of awe are known to alter how we perceive the world and our-self, fueling transformation (Gaggioli, 2016). Submission may be part of the response, yet if we extend the timeline, we may be *temporarily* submitting our-self in order to learn and eventually embody the traits that moved us. We might argue that this encroaches into the territory of admiration, leading to inspiration, but these technicalities have still yet to be completely agreed upon by the scientific community. Connectedness and humility may moreover be reinterpreted as necessary traits to improve social connectivity, which are important to thriving in social groups. This can be further used for our per-sonal advantage.

On another front, many authors who have basked in the presence of awe in relation to nature have also encountered new standards of functioning in harmony with maintaining such pleasant states of being. The notion of nature as a teacher can be found in ancient Taoist texts and in the writings of Emer-son (1995) and Thoreau (1992). These states may have evolved in humans to motivate them to expand our own capacities, moving us deeper into reality and encouraging flourishing beyond survival. Perhaps this relates to a body of literature that has emerged investigating *environmental epiphanies*. These are experiences classified as experiences "in which one's perception of the essential meaning of their relationship to nature shifts in a meaningful manner" (Storie & Vining, 2018, p. 157). These phenomena are often accompanied by "intense emotions such as awe and wonder, magical experiences, and self-described life-changing moments" (p. 156). Indeed, the benefits of exposure to nature have been supported empirically and even led to the formation of what Jap-anese scientists are calling *shinrin-yoku,* or forest bathing, as a psychological treatment. Research has so far indicated improvements in immune function-ing, cardiovascular and respiratory health, depression and anxiety, and overall mental relaxation, as well as increased feelings of awe in response to forest bathing (Hansen, Jones, & Tocchini, 2017).

The likelihood of experiencing an STE has also been related to character-ological disposition, in particular the personality trait of *openness to experience* (Silvia, Fayn, Nusbaum, & Beaty, 2015). To harness STEs in a therapeutic con-text, I would suggest that there are passive and active recipients of awe, just as there are passive and active ways to experience an STE. Whereas a passive recipient might enjoy the experience, it is the active one who truly receives the benefits. What STEs indicate to me is that, in these states, something *vital* is being transmitted to the whole individual, and it is the responsibility of consciousness to put it into words or action to clarify the direction. Whereas physically we have vital signs, psychophysiologically, we have *vital signals*. The definition of vital as "essential" is just as important as its experience of being "full of energy; lively" (New Oxford American Dictionary, 2010, p. 1934). It is possible that descriptors from these STEs are potential states available to individuals who live in accordance with the vital signals being communicated.

Arthur decides to speak to the author, Emrys, after the presentation. Emrys is flattered by Arthur's experience and compliments. He agrees to allow Arthur to join his practice as an extern and takes on the role of a mentor/supervisor. As time goes on, Arthur's *star-struckness* diminishes and he becomes a licensed psychologist working alongside Emrys. Late one night, while walking back to their respective vehicles in the parking lot, Arthur and Emrys are held at gunpoint by two thieves. Arthur notices that one of them was bald. Arthur freezes in fear and then simply does what he is told. The thieves leave with their money, but Arthur and Emrys are safe. The following day, Arthur reflects on the incident. Upon this reflection, Arthur realizes that Emrys had calmly positioned himself, verbally and physically, in a way that protected Arthur's life and prevented the situation from escalating. He is struck by the *moral beauty* (Diessner, Solom, Frost, Parsons, & Davidson, 2008) of courage, self-sacrifice, and wisdom and feels a sense of *moral elevation*. This experience is similar to what he felt on his first encounter with Emrys, but Arthur notices that this elevation is unrelated to power differentials and is of a lesser magnitude. This elevation then shifts into a deep *admiration* of Emrys's ability to live out his writings and the skills necessary to implement them effectively. Arthur feels *inspired* to embody those character traits that he finds to be so moving.

When we witness an act of virtue, we may experience *moral elevation*. This includes "pleasant feelings of warmth in the chest, feeling uplifted, moved, and optimistic about humanity" (Pohling & Diessner, 2016, p. 3). Moral elevation promotes specific character traits that people find beautiful. Admiration, in contrast, is elicited by skills that exceed what is considered to be standard (Algoe & Haidt, 2009). Admiration supports the acquisition and development of skills in a prosocial manner. Put simply, moral elevation relates to character virtues that exceed standards, whereas admiration relates to abilities that exceed standards.

Inspiration may accompany moral elevation or admiration. Inspiration "implies motivation, which is to say that it involves the energization and direction of behavior; inspiration is evoked rather than initiated directly . . . and involves transcendence of the ordinary preoccupations or limitations of human agency" (Thrash & Elliot, 2003, p. 871). Thrash and Elliot (2003) concluded that inspiration is best described through "evocation, motivation and transcendence" (p. 885). Inspiration may occur as a result of either an external or internal source. For example, it is common that an aspiring professional might be moved and inspired by an expert professional's knowledge, achievements, and character, inspiring the aspirant to ascend to similar heights. Similar to awe, these qualities elicit feelings of connection, vigor, openness, and lucidity (Hart, 1998). There are other, more indirect, ways people can find themselves inspired as well. I can personally recall expansive sensations throughout my upper body, a lightness, an emptiness in my throat, teary eyes, euphoria, connectedness, and a sense of playfulness when I first listened to the band Rodrigo y Gabriela perform live. As a musician myself, I could gauge their technical and artistic excellence. What was conveyed to me in that moment was not that I wanted to play as they do, but rather the potential of beauty that lies within humanity given enough inspiration, dedication, and persistence. Of relevance, the dedication toward the self-discipline necessary to achieve such heights, or "perspiration" (Oleynick, Thrash, Lefew, Moldovan, & Kieffaber, 2014, p. 1), is just as important as inspiration.

Internal inspiration may come from an idea that arises, such as the aha! moments discussed earlier relating to the DMN or even from dreams, as will be illustrated in the following case. Interestingly, this passage by Jung (1963) offers an account of inspiration in a *negative* form:

The first time I experienced this was on a bicycle trip through upper Italy. . . . we had intended to pedal on along the lake and then through the Tessin as far as Faido, where we were going to take the train to Zurich. But in Arona I had a dream which upset our plans. . . . At the very moment of awakening I thought of the book I was working on . . . and had such intense inferiority feelings about the unanswered question that I immediately took the train home in order to get back to work. It would have been impossible for me to get back to continue the bicycle trip and lose another three days. I had to work, to find the answer. (pp. 306–307)

Inspiration can be a powerful motivating force that transcends our regular disposition, causing us to stop whatever it is we are doing to fulfill the direction of our inspiration. When our being is inspired, and we pursue activities that are aligned with the qualities that moved us, this can lead to what Csikszentmihalyi (1990) called *flow*. He coined this term to describe experiences individuals achieve when fully engaged in tasks that are intellectually stimulating and emotionally satisfying. Individuals may become entranced by feelings of bliss, excitement, and deep, often *oceanic* feelings further characterized as elevations of consciousness with *mystic and magical* effects. Accompanying these pleasant moments, people may experience the boundaries of time and space dissipate, harmony, a full use of one's capacities, strength, confidence, spontaneity, flexibility, and mindfulness.

There is a deep connectedness between self-transcendent states and meaning. To revisit the psilocybin experiments from Johns Hopkins (Griffiths et al., 2016), many of which evoke STEs, two-thirds of the participants rated the experience as among the top five most *meaningful* moments of their entire lives. These moments may be transformative, and if we do not mine STEs for all the information they have imparted, we will end up wasting what was a *vital signal* due to ignorance.

One way to understand awe and moral elevation may be as they connect to aspirational states of *being*, whereas admiration and inspiration are connected to aspirational states of *doing*. Some people may refer to these signals as *callings* from the *true self* or *authentic self*. We align ourselves with nature, in congruence with the pressures from natural selection, and we are *rewarded* for doing so. Contrary to the notion that aligning with natural selection would lead to antisocial or Machiavellian behaviors, "an advancement in the standard of morality and an increase in the number of well-endowed men will certainly give an immense advantage to one tribe over another" (Darwin, 1871/2005, p. 872). Vital signals are railroad switches that may guide the train that is us from one direction to another with higher levels of resonance with nature.

DISINTEGRATIVE VITAL SIGNALS

There can be no doubt that a tribe including many members who, from possessing in a high degree the spirit of patriotism, fidelity, obedience, courage and sympathy, were always ready to give aid to each other and to sacrifice themselves for the common good, would be victorious over most other tribes . . . this would be natural selection.

—CHARLES DARWIN

Of particular importance, there are also vital signals that warn us of actions that lead us toward a disintegrative experience of self through psychophysiological discomfort. This can be determined through moral emotions that are other-oriented and self-oriented. The core vital signals here would be the other-oriented moral emotions of disgust, anger, and contempt (Hutcherson & Gross, 2011) and the self-oriented moral emotions of shame, embarrassment, and guilt (Rozin, Lowery, Imada, & Haidt).* All of these emotions are connected by the experience of the violation of values associated with community, autonomy, and divinity (Steiger & Reina, 2017). Moreover, they are set apart from other emotions, such as sadness, due to their primary drive and effects on an individual (Schnall, Haidt, Clore, & Jordan, 2008). I agree with the *social intuitionist model* (SIM), proposed by Haidt (2001), which suggests that there are underlying moral truths that are not rationally achieved; instead, we have a direct feeling or experience. Haidt added the social aspect because it emerges through interpersonal relationships. This is counter to the prevalent rationalist approach, which emphasizes that morality is reached through reasoning. These

---

* Due to the limited research on contempt (Steiger & Reyna, 2016) and embarrassment (Tangney, Stuewig, & Mashel, 2007), I will be excluding them from this discussion.

models conflict on the surface, yet the truth is likely a mixture of the two, depending on the context.

With the introduction of the SIM, evidence has begun to mount in support of its existence; for example, one study found that the experience of physical disgust was positively associated with moral decision making (Schnall et al., 2008). Physical disgust directs animals to avoid or expel food and may elicit a direct reaction from the enteric nervous system. Neuroscientific studies have found that disgust toward rotting food overlaps with moral disgust (e.g., incest, cannibalism) through the insula (Vicario, Rafal, Martino, & Avenanti, 2017). Other ways they connect are through facial expressions (Cannon, Schnall, & White, 2011), descriptions of physical and moral stimuli (Haidt et al., 1997), and the amplification of moral judgments due to physical disgust (Eskine, Kacinik, & Prinz, 2011). This leaves me with the thought that disgust may have undergone a form of exaptation, co-opting its use for morally repugnant ideas in service of adaptive avoidance. The idea that moral disgust sets moral boundaries has also been supported in the research (Chapman & Anderson, 2014).

The visceral reactions people have when accidentally drinking expired milk or smelling a rotting egg self-evidently point to the response of *stop immediately and throw it out*. People's gag reflexes may trigger when thinking of such experiences; they may even be moved to vomit (a very physical sign of exit!). These experiences are interesting to consider because morally repugnant scenarios may lie on a spectrum that can elicit similar experiences of different magnitudes. For example, both the thought of someone having sex with a farm animal and the notion of someone stealing from a blind person may lead to strong feelings of moral disgust, but they likely differ in their amplitude. Moral disgust is a primitive signal conserved through evolution, modified through exaptation, to help direct us in ways that are adaptive to our current culture.

Anger has been highly associated with the left inferior frontal gyrus (Vytal & Hamann, 2010). Individuals exposed to the same moral violation–based scenario may exhibit moral anger or disgust. The experience is mediated by costs to the self, with direct self-involvement increasing the likelihood of moral anger and less or ambiguous cases leading to disgust (Molho, Tybur, Guler, Balliet, & Hofmann, 2017). Molho and colleagues (2017) further found that "anger related positively to higher-cost, physically or verbally aggressive sentiments (direct aggression) . . . disgust related positively to sentiments in favor of lower-cost social exclusion and reputational attacks" (p. 614). Disgust also seems to shift to anger when the finger is pointed at the self rather than at the other.

Moral disgust and anger both act as signals that may lead to further behaviors to enhance or impose boundaries on ourself or others. If an act that would elicit moral anger or disgust were committed by an individual, these inverted feelings may transform into shame, which is a disintegrative experience. It is connected to STEs through necessity of and interactions with the self and a psychophysiological response. Shame is categorized as a self-conscious emotion (Robins & Schriber, 2009). Shame can manifest in two forms: external shame, which involves a perceived social evaluation of oneself, and internal shame, which relates to a devaluation of the self (Gilbert & Procter, 2006). Sedighimornani (2018) elaborated that shame is "an incapacitating emotion that is accompanied by the feeling of being small, inferior, and of shrinking. The self as a whole, is de-valued and considered to be inadequate, incompetent, and worthless" (p. 76). Thus, instead of an expansion of self boundaries with uplifting sensations and feelings, as found in STEs, shame yields a contraction of the self, with an increase of self-involved rumination and negative feelings.

Guilt and shame are both negative assessments; however, shame is directed at the self, whereas guilt is directed at behavior (Lewis, 1971; Tangney, Stuewig, & Mashek, 2007). Overall, research conceptualizes shame and guilt as being more similar than different, with shame being a more severe form of guilt, because guilt may have more potential for constructive self-criticism (Leach, 2017). Shame and guilt are common experiences that often surface in psychotherapy. In this sense, perhaps it may be the therapist's job to help clients revert their experience of shame to guilt when negative evaluations of the self are reframed to describe behaviors instead. Such a process may involve forgiving themselves and using these experiences to direct their consequent behaviors in search of redemption.

Shame-inducing acts may vary; many times they are for potential gains, be it social approval, pleasure, or power. Regrets form in response to an impulsive act and many times clients are able to describe in detail how these experiences manifested in them as they were committing the act. When clients are being helped to process some of these experiences, they have reported feeling a lump in the throat, a coldness or chills throughout the body, a deadening, an emptiness, an experience of dread, paranoia, negative ruminations, a sense of falling apart, an increase in self-involvement, a tightening, and defensiveness. Schore (2019) notes that excessive feelings of shame and disgust lead to parasympathetic hyperarousal, which may result in dissociation or an implosive experience of self. If clients do not work through these experiences, the experiences may become disowned and projected to other people or the world. Similar to STEs, there is something *vital* being communicated. These are very clear *psychophysiological* indicators of what behaviors we should not pursue, and they may be helpful to identify in therapy.

Importantly, the experiences of shame discussed as a disintegrative vital signal must be distinguished from Cozolino's (2015) *social status schema*. He posits that *core shame* may potentially be a result of natural selection. Specifically, we may inherit states of shame that categorize us into a hierarchical position of a beta, to make it easier to follow an alpha. In the context of modern day, what makes us an alpha is very different from what evolution intended. This shame-based sensitivity is typically independent of actual experiences, and may likely be seen in practice as vestigial feelings that need to be understood and challenged. This sort of core shame would not be seen as a vital signal.

REFLECTIONS AND APPLICATIONS: EMBELLISHING VITAL SIGNALS

Truth does not merely "dwell" in the "inner man,"
or rather there is no "inner man," man is in and
toward the world and it is in the world that he knows
himself.

—MAURICE MERLEAU-PONTY

I conceptualize self-transcendent states as vital signals because they are psychophysical signals that can overpower our everyday sense of self. Vital signals are directional anchors for self-processes; they *move* us toward expansive and integrative potential and away from contractive and disintegrative potential. Another purpose of integrating vital signals into practice is to facilitate a growth-oriented cycle; the moved becomes the mover as the mover evokes the moved.

Historically, we have designated anything that may overpower our selves to the realm of religion and spirituality. Whether these potent signals emerge from complex systems in interaction or some unobservable realm is something yet to be solved. In my opinion, the word transcendent is in and of itself somewhat misleading. To transcend something implies a movement *away from*, whereas I am more of the mind that these states move us *deeper into*. I assert this in response to the very fact that the elicited feelings of STEs, such as interconnectedness and the dissolving of self-boundaries, are more aligned with *objective* reality as we know it. We are not isolated entities; rather, we are interconnected processes. In line with Darwin's (1871/2005) assertions, moral emotions are attuned to natural selection, enhancing the group's overall survival. People who exhibit moral beauty and remarkable skills may leave us in awe because they are living examples of individuals who have converted their highest potential into experience—a feat most difficult for the reality in which we live. In fact, they surpass their survival and social goals. Nature does not need to be seen as some primitive force against which we have to work; rather, nature is a collection of pressures that simply need to be guided and adapted to the present circumstance. Our overall fitness is enhanced when we are capable of aligning ourselves with the appropriate vital signals.

For practical purposes, it is of little consequence whether the person or thing that elicits these feelings is genuine; what matters is the experience itself. The experience is real, and it is a response to some projected or perceived trait(s). Caution is warranted here; I am not condoning people blindly following leaders because they are in awe of them. Rather, I am suggesting that people identify and explore the traits they admire, independent of the admired, and work to meet them. We should always tread with caution when these vast experiences are elicited by another, as there may very well be deceptive biases and intentions in the admired that are more than sinister. In this context, whether projected or true, they remain vital signals with measurable effects, both experientially and objectively. They alter the very foundations of our biology as well as the heights of our belief systems. I think it would be wise to treat them with significance, because these experiences clearly impart significance to us. Many of these states need no introduction. How many times have you admired a mentor, felt moved by a particular scene in a movie, been inspired by a character in a book, felt elevated by a genuinely good person, been touched by an act of altruism by a stranger, or been in awe of a performance? On the other end of the spectrum, how many times have you been angered directly by a betrayal, been disgusted after witnessing an injustice, or experienced self-induced shame?

There exists a multiplicity of character truths, and it is important to consider them individually. At the same time, there are general themes that seem to pervade these experiences of being moved that make it a very fascinating subject of study. Beginning with STEs, is it possible to induce states of awe? The following list includes different ways investigators have been able to do so.

- Being in the presence of groves of tall trees[1]
- Virtual reality [2]
- Reading or writing about experiences of awe[3]
- Listening to music or viewing awe-inspiring images[4]
- Altruistic behaviors[5]

References (as cited in Yaden et al., 2017)

1 Piff et al. (2015)
2 Chirico, Yaden, Riva, and Gagglioli (2016)
3 Shiota, Keltner, and Mossman (2007)
4 Prade and Saroglou (2016)
5 Rudd et al. (2012); Van Cappellen, Saroglou, Iweins, Piovesana, and Fredrickson (2013)

Given that these are a select few examples, it will always be important to ask clients to explore their own history in regard to what has produced feelings of awe and tailor the approach thereafter. Moral elevation, admiration, and inspiration will also likely require an individualistic approach in order to identify relevant themes and experiences. Random acts of kindness, video clips demonstrating self-sacrifice or courage, and extremely talented performances may all be contenders, but the best way would be to explore personal experiences in session.

Clients may be given tasks outside of the session that may elicit such feelings during their period of deliberate change. These experiences may further help them relate to the world with more creativity and openness. In session, the therapist may discuss vital signals to reignite the neural circuitry connected to said experiences. The therapist may assign the task of visiting a national park, journaling about the clients' STEs, or viewing a performance by Cirque du

Soleil. Should clients not have the resources or time to visit nature or view a virtuoso pianist play Rachmaninoff's Piano Concerto no. 2 in C minor flawlessly, the therapist may bring the experience to them. Clinicians may also begin integrating the use of technology by including virtual reality. Indeed, virtual reality has been shown to be able to elicit feelings of awe (Chirico, Yaden, Riva, & Gagglioli, 2016). Such immersive experiences include viewing the earth from space, being in a forest, or visiting snow-covered mountains (Chirico, Ferrise, Cordella, & Gagglioli, 2018). If the client is already engaged in practices that have led to STEs, it might be useful to promote their active, conscientious engagement toward what the experiences may mean to them. If they are not, it may be helpful to ask them if they are open to trying some potential STE-eliciting activities, such as: "meditation, prayer, yoga, music, [and] dancing" (Yaden et al., 2017, p. 3).

The following list contains some questions the clinician may ask to help identify and examine these vital signals. Make sure to help the client examine these experiences to get to the root of the signal: experientially, biologically, psychologically, socially, and existentially. Parenthetically, a vital signal would include all states that elicit a significant psychophysiological response and either an expansion or constriction of the self-process. To reiterate, I will simply use the word *moved*, not as a state in and of itself, but in an attempt to capture the connection between all of them.

Dialogue: Questions to Embellish Vital Signals

Integrative Vital Signals

Experiential: What activities or people move you? Why are you moved? What is being communicated? *(Assign tasks to engage in those activities.)*

Biological: How did you sense this inner movement? How did your body respond?

Psychological: What impulses, thoughts, or feelings did you have?

Social: How does this experience relate to your experience of others, or how you would like to relate to others?

Existential: To what value does this experience relate? Toward what direction does the experience point you? In the future, what actions can you see yourself taking that would move you?

Disintegrative Vital Signals

Experiential: What experiences have made you feel morally outraged, angry, or disgusted? What is being communicated? *(Assign tasks to engage in those activities.)*

Biological: What were the physiological sensations you had during those experiences?

Psychological: What impulses, thoughts, or feelings did you have?

Social: How does this experience relate to your experience of others?

Existential: What underlying values are being threatened? What excesses or deficiencies of behaviors or values do these represent? What direction does the experience point you away from?

See Appendix E for extra resource: Vital Signals Identification Chart

One other exercise of importance is living out the identified values one step at a time. Each value can be collapsed into multiple other values, and each contains its own expression as it becomes embodied in the individual. For example, a common value that has arisen is resilience, a construct that may be broken down further into determination, resolve, and strength. To explore the overarching values in depth, I recommend having clients embody one value at a time and explore what this was like in session. After each value has been embodied and explored successfully, the therapist may then facilitate a discussion with clients on how these values, when integrated, may appear in different scenarios and challenges they face commonly.

From a more clinical perspective, it is worth considering who might benefit from such an approach. To my knowledge, research has yet to be conducted on structured approaches integrating STEs into clinical practice. This is likely due to the fact that these states are only now surfacing as important in the realm of science. The following, then, are my general thoughts on the matter. Individuals suffering from anxiety, depression, adjustment, compulsions, and addictions may benefit from the addition of such an approach, but sessions should prioritize safety measures and coping skills (if the client is a risk to themself or others). Inducing states of awe would likely be ideal when symptoms decline to mild levels, at which point the client has sufficient resources to cope without prompting the clinician's concerns. Clients suffering from psychotic symptoms, delusions, or other intense symptoms would likely be excluded from these sorts of activities until their symptoms are controlled. It is best to use this approach as complementary to any other core approaches that have been supported by research.

According to this conceptualization, there is a decisive choice to be made, and that is the choice that is aligned with the vital signals that direct the existential process. What we think we *should* do may be more parentally or societally based, and acting out a maladaptive impulse is often based on reactive physiological processes that are *blind* to context. Vital signals in the form of STEs are often evoked psychophysiological changes; they are experiences greater than the self, and they promote adaptive traits and positive feelings. By consciously articulating these experiences, we are collaborating with that which naturally moves us.

The first step is to identify what values can be derived from vital signals. Figure 7.1 presents a chart inspired by Aristotle's (4th century BCE/1943) *golden mean* and ACT methodology. Aristotle (4th century BCE/1943) notes that "goodness is rare and praiseworthy and noble" (p. 110) because several contextual variables must be considered with every act. Actions must be considered with "the right person, [with] right amount . . . , at the right time, for the right cause, and in the right way" (p. 110). An example of a golden mean is confidence, whose deficiency would lead to submissiveness and its excess to arrogance. It is beneficial to have the two opposites of the signal, as in many cases, people may polarize to the other end in an attempt to discover the mean. Before the following chart can be used, it is very important to have explored what vital signals have been communicated to clients and what values have been established as a result (see Appendix E). The instructions for this chart and its use as a tool for therapy can be found in Appendix F.

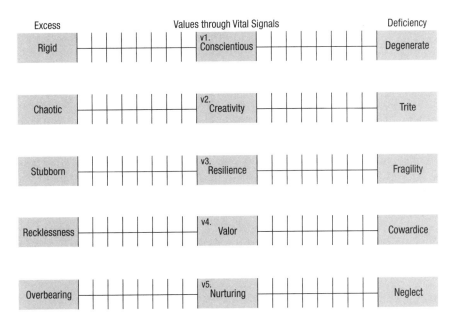

Figure 7.1: Vital Signals Chart

Although there exist shared value systems, these systems may be expressed very differently from one person to the next. Never assume the meaning of a value, nor how it *should be* expressed. Make sure to have the client describe what each value means to them and what it would take for them to move closer to those lived values. When asking clients to describe the associated physical sensations, you may ask them to shift their awareness to the memory of the event, and describe it from the perspective of their bodily experience. I am suggesting making an important shift here; instead of asking the vague question, "What is the right thing to do?" the question becomes, "What is the *vital* thing to do? Can you sense it in your body?" It may also be beneficial to begin with people or characters with whom they've experienced moral elevation or whom they admire before moving into the more abstract domain of awe. Notably, it is the *striving* to live in accordance to values that matters most, and individuals should reward themselves immediately after they have accomplished a behavior that moves them closer to their value system. Anticipate regressions to older habits.

By living a life in accordance with vital signals, what once moved an individual becomes embodied, and the moved becomes the mover. The physical sensations, thoughts, and feelings once exhibited for someone else, may become directed toward the self.

Values are not stagnant. Used in a rigid way, they may actually hinder creative living. As people develop over time and demands change, some of these values may change; thus, it is essentially a process that does not end. Values are also likely different depending on the context (i.e., work, play, relationships). Thus, one may use a different chart for different situations, if needed. People are likely pursuing several values at a time without awareness, yet there tend to be certain values that people are drawn to at any given moment. This is an important experience and perhaps could be understood as a *call to action.*

MYSTICAL EXPERIENCES

Who am I? . . . if other thoughts arise . . . inquire,
"To whom did they arise?"

—BHAGAVAN SRI RAMANA MAHARSHI

Mystical experiences can be considered the crown-jewel of all STEs. One fact to derive from the limits of sensation and perception is that there is an *exterior* reality being limited, a reality that contains and envelops our own, with unknown boundaries. The vividness of our perceptual experience attempts to convince us of its sole reality, but we know this is false. We only experience a fraction of the reality we are a part of. What if we turn our eyes toward the *interior* of reality? Is it possible that the interior follows the patterns of the exterior? Might our state of consciousness reflect only a fraction of what may be potentially experienced? Current trends in science subscribe to the notion that the interior arises from the exterior, especially since we can measure that which is exterior. Yet this is still in debate, and might it be the other way around? We assume that consciousness, the autobiographical self, and meta-cognition emerge from the most advanced and complex processes occurring within the brain, but who are we to assume that nothing else has emerged that may be just as advanced as or even more advanced than these processes?

Mystical experiences are considered to be the pinnacle of STEs, far less frequent, yet their transformative effects and widespread acknowledgment make them worthy of exploring. The Pew Research Center (Heimlich, 2009) estimated that half of the U.S. population claims to have had a mystical experience. A mystical experience is a vital signal that a person simply cannot ignore. The applications section mentioned previously still would be applicable to these sorts of experiences. I have separated them from the previous section due to their profound nature, rendering it necessary to explore other concepts that will be important to consider.

In this section, I am interested in exploring the possibilities of this depth without implicating religion or god. Nature, always many steps ahead of us, is far more complex than any of us can imagine. Of the many philosophers and scientists whose work continues to impact the field of STEs, none have been so successful as William James. I am indebted to James's work, in particular three ideas of his still relevant today: radical empiricism, pluralism, and his transmissive theory of the brain.

To understand the approach of radical empiricism, first we must be acquainted with his view that the world is made of *particulars* and relationships between particulars. In adaptation, I will add that what comes of the relationship between particulars may be similar to that of a gestalt (the whole is greater than the sum of its parts). This assertion echoes the notion that interactions between complex systems are synergistic $(1 + 1 = 3)$.* This phenomenon becomes clear when we recognize that the more closely we examine our experience through science, the more we find that, much of the time, our whole experience tells a very different story from the parts examined in isolation. Thus, we can actually commit errors if we were to infer from a part, as science often does, or make statements about the whole, as philosophy does. By focusing on a particular, or even a few particulars in relation to one another, we may still end up missing the broader picture, the reality that is, or the reality that can be emergent in our experience. What is synergistic, then, may be reduced to mere addition or, in the worst case, subtraction. Following this logic, we

---

* Synergy is also a concept understood in pharmacology when two medications used together may result in effects beyond either medication used on its own.

can integrate the idea of *exaptation*, whereby functions conserved through time may adopt new applications when related to other networks dedicated to alternative, more complex functions. What was once a trait naturally selected for a particular function now acquires additional responsibilities. Parts then relate to one another to generate a whole, and through exaptation, the previous whole becomes itself another part emerging with others to create a new whole. Psychologically, this may occur at a fast pace, as when two previously psychologically *distant* ideas may become integrated and, through further awareness, generate a new whole.

In James's view, life is composed of *pure experience.** This view espouses that "inner experience never originated, or developed out of the unconscious, but that it and the physical universe are co-eternal aspects of one self-same reality, much as concave and convex are aspects of one curve" (James, as cited in Richardson, 2006, p. 447). This perspective challenged Descartes's dualism. James posited that there is no *general stuff* through which all experience is made, emphasizing a *plurality* of things experienced. In his radical empiricist approach, which encompasses what we now call phenomenology, he stated: "an empiricism must neither admit into its constructions any element that is not directly experienced, nor exclude from them any element that is directly experienced" (James, 1904, p. 1160).

Because of his openness to the value embedded in experience, James was accepting of and took very seriously the existence of different states of consciousness, especially as described in transcendent states related to religious and spiritual experiences and those elicited by hallucinogenic substances. People may be transformed by these experiences. In fact, it is well known that many of the world's religions were founded by individuals who had such experiences. James (1902/1987) concluded:

> Our normal waking consciousness, rational consciousness as we call it, is but one special type of consciousness, whilst all about it, parted from it by the filmiest of screens, there lie potential forms of consciousness entirely different. We may go through life without suspecting their existence; but apply the requisite stimulus and at a touch they are there in all their completeness, definite

---

* This may be reminiscent of A. N. Whitehead's PR, and rightfully so, as he acknowledges James as a major influence.

types of mentality which probably have their field of application and adaptation. No account of the universe in its totality can be final which leaves these other forms of consciousness quite disregarded. How to regard them is the question, for they are discontinuous with ordinary consciousness. Yet they may determine attitudes though they cannot furnish formulas, and open a region though they fail to give a map. At any rate, they forbid a premature closing of our accounts with reality. (p. 349)

PERSPECTIVES

In the woods . . . standing on the bare ground—my
head bathed by blithe air, and uplifted into infinite
space—all mean egotism vanishes. I become a
transparent eyeball; I am nothing; I see all.
—RALPH WALDO EMERSON

Most experiences that people consider life changing are external events, such as the case of transcendent experiences, which occur from the internal (e.g., subjective experience) to the external (e.g., behaviors). Life-altering shifts even emerge as a result of dissonant experiences, such as the experience of a trauma or the death of a loved one. The theory that most materialists would espouse is that these experiences arise as a result of specific configurations of neural networks. From a Darwinian perspective, it may be further inferred that because of the effect these states have on enabling us to experientially transcend a prior maladaptive state, they are adaptive, and therefore *written* into our repertoire of possible experiences. As an ever-evolving culture and society, we are all aware of the values that, if embodied, would help us live a meaningful life successfully. Yet what seems to be lacking is the experience necessary for us to live them out. Are these possible routes in order to do so? What does the quality of these experiences tell us about the nature of reality? These states have been documented throughout all of history, regardless of time, place, or religious or spiritual beliefs. Perhaps these states do not demonstrate the existence of a particular deity, but might they point to something else that could be underlying our reality?

The popular view of consciousness is that it is a process that emerges from complex brain functioning. Another view is James's transmission theory, which

still cannot be entirely discredited. In his theory, the brain is not just the producer of information but also a releaser and receiver. James (1898) suggested,

> In the world of physical nature productive function of this sort is not the only
> kind of function with which we are familiar. We have also releasing or permis-
> sive function; and we have transmissive function. . . . In the case of a colored
> glass, a prism, or a refracting lens, we have transmissive function. The energy
> of light, no matter how produced, is by the glass sifted and limited in color, and
> by the lens or prism determined to a certain path and shape. (p. 118)

This analogy posits that what we perceive is restricted and distorted by our
neural processes. In its regulation of information, the brain focuses and limits
the *fabric of reality*. What follows is a unique mental expression of reality in
every individual brain. Assuming there may be depth of energy and information beyond our immediate knowing, the brain, being composed of a specific
arrangement of elements of nature, may be susceptible to the eruption of this
information when appropriate configurations are met.

One of the most famous studies in this domain comes from Beauregard and
Paquette (2006), who viewed the brain activity of Carmelite nuns as they were
subjectively reexperiencing God. They found a number of areas spanning the
depths of the brainstem to the right middle temporal lobe and the prefrontal
cortex. These experiences include a complex variety of top-down and bottom-
up processing. Kohls, Sauer, Offenbacher, and Giordano's (2011) review of
more recent fMRI research in relation to mystical experiences conclude that
"it is not a specific brain site that mediates aspects of these experiences, but
rather the differential spatial and temporal activation of neural pathways and
networks" (p. 1842). This echoes Northoff's (2018) neuro-ecological model.

A release of neurotransmitters from the midbrain, such as endogenous opioids
and dopamine, mediate experiences of bonding and euphoria, whereas alterations in frontal-parietal functioning may lead to the dissolution of the sense of
self (Kohls, Sauer, Offenbacher, & Giordano, 2011). Furthermore, activity in the
right middle temporal lobe may be related to contacting a higher dimension, and
caudate nucleus resulting in feelings of joy and unconditional love (Beauregard &
Paquette, 2006). Thus, mystical experiences may be met with unique configurations of the brain's spatiotemporal dynamics in relation to the world (Northoff,

2018; world-brain relation). This would explain why mystical experiences usually involve drastic psychophysiological changes from normal everyday life, such as in deep meditation or the use of a psychedelic substance. The mystical experience may thus be described as the result of an ongoing interpenetration of complex systems enabling a range of superordinate emergent experiential phenomena.

Since the excitement of mystical experiences has come to the forefront of popular attention, many criticisms have been made against their actual existence. One such critique suggests that mystical states are induced by temporal lobe seizures. This literature remains controversial; for instance, in a recent study of 98 clients with epilepsy, only around half of the subjects reported having some experiences related to mysticism, but none met the criteria for a true mystical experience. In addition, no association was found with any lobe or hemisphere of the brain, demographics, medical history, precipitants, location, or type of seizure (Greyson, Broshek, Derr, & Fountain, 2015).

Another front of criticism is that individuals who have mystical experiences are mentally ill. The problem with attributing transcendent experiences to disorders like schizophrenia is that most accounts come from otherwise healthy individuals, and schizophrenia is a lifelong disorder; it does not simply emerge and then disappear. When there are no substances or extreme psychosocial events to induce a state as such and the individual is able to lead a life of increased functioning and well-being, mystical experiences defy the very criteria for any known mental disorder.

Interestingly, one study by Yaden and colleagues (2016) people with monotheistic religious affiliations scored the lowest on their mystical experiences measure, with members of Eastern religions scoring the highest. Most surprising, they found that atheists actually scored somewhere in the middle. As would be expected, in their analysis of language used to describe mystical experiences, Yaden and colleagues found that people had a tendency to use inclusive language, less third-person language compared to first, and less religious language. The perception of unity on spatial and social dimensions was the underlying experience among all participants.

James (1902/1987) defined mystical states as having four qualities:

- *Ineffability:* Defies expression, no adequate report of its contents can be given in words . . . must be directly experienced . . . more like states of feeling than like states of intellect.

- *Noetic quality:* States of knowledge . . . insight into depths of truths unplumbed by discursive intellect.
- *Transiency:* Cannot be sustained for long (30–60 min), is imperfectly reproduced in memory; but when they recur it is recognized; and from one recurrence to another it is susceptible of continuous development in what is felt as inner richness and importance.
- *Passivity:* May be facilitated voluntarily but mostly received. In this state, own will is in abeyance of a feeling of being grasped and held by a superior power. (p. 343)

Today, mystical experiences are typically measured on seven subscales using the 30-item Mystical-Type Experiences Questionnaire (MEQ30). Presented subsequently are the seven subscales, with one example for each (F. Barrett & Griffiths, 2017; Barrett, Johnson, & Griffiths, 2015):

- *Internal unity:* Experience of pure being or awareness.
- *External unity:* Experience of the insight that "all is one."
- *Noetic quality:* Certainty of encounter with ultimate reality.
- *Sacredness:* Feeling that you experienced something profoundly sacred or holy.
- *Positive mood:* Sense of awe or awesomeness.
- *Transcendence of time and space:* Experience of timelessness.
- *Ineffability:* Sense that the experience cannot be described adequately in words.

People generally reach mystical states through a variety of different traditions and practices, including but not limited to: Buddhist meditation; Christian prayer; Judaic prayer (*tefillah*) and learning (*Talmud Torah*); Sufi learning and love of god through philosophy, intuition, and asceticism; other spiritual practices; and the ingestion of psychedelic substances (Wahbeh, Sagher, Back, Pundhir, & Travis, 2018).

Given the spontaneity of mystical experiences and the difficulty of inducing them in laboratory settings, one way of examining changes in the brain resulting in mystical experiences is through the use of psychedelic drugs, as discussed earlier. Not surprisingly, these experiments (notably those featuring psilocybin) have yielded widespread changes in brain functioning, what researchers are labeling an *entropic* brain state whereby cortical activity is dys-regulated yet with enhanced global connectivity that has been associated with ego dissolution and increased trait openness (Carhart-Harris et al., 2017). In any case, we would expect changes in brain functioning regardless of whether or not we ascribe to the perspective of brain as a producer and receiver.

Overall, the majority of neuroscientists assume that the objective world is composed of physical quantities such as space-time, momentum, spin, charge, and mass. The representative voice of materialism or physicalism may chuckle in reaction to any metaphysics that are directly antagonistic to this concep-tion. The idealist in contrast, scratch their heads in confusion, wondering how lumps of "dead" matter, complex or not, may generate consciousness. The two sides continue to wrestle, while scientist iconoclasts such as Hoffman (2019) and Tononi (2012) seek to rectify the place of consciousness in our universe.

In philosophy, the existence of experiencing realities beyond our own was noted in Plato's (380 BCE/1943) cave allegory around 380 BCE. In short, Plato, through Socrates, likened our view of reality to shadows cast onto a wall of a cave. A fire is lit behind us, and entities come and go. The majority of us are chained to view reality from this perspective, unaware of the existence of a higher reality. If we manage to unshackle ourselves, we might be able to expe-rience a reality beyond the cave within which we are imprisoned.

Plato (380 BCE/1943) believed that outside space and time exists unchang-ing perfect forms that are ideal blueprints for all that we see today. This is what he considered real. Plotinus (1991) likened us to a weak emanation from a source, he called the one, and that human souls were like the derivative of light reflected off the moon from the sun (the light from the sun itself being the source, not the sun). Many religious systems resonate with the belief that there is an atemporal and aspatial place existing beyond our universe, imbued with unchanging virtuous attributes—a source we strive to return to. Some religions suppose we have immortal souls, others suggest immortality is con-tingent upon spiritual practices. William James (1909/1987) concludes from his research that there is a "reasonable probability to the continuity of our consciousness with a wider spiritual environment from which the ordinary prudential man (who is the only man that scientific psychology, so called, takes cognizance of) is shut off" (p. 767).

Jaspers (1959) believed that we can only transcend the subject-object dichotomy through encounters with *cyphers*. Cyphers may present in the form of art, philosophy, and religion. Emerson (1995) and Thoreau (1992) would likely include nature. They are scripts which begin with the feeling of wonder, and open up the possibility of transcendence. In this way, contemplation leads to transparency, which can penetrate the depths of being if directed appropriately. "The cypher is neither object nor subject. It is objectivity which is permeated by subjectivity and in such a way that Being becomes present in the whole" (p. 35). It is more of an experience arrived at through interpretation of something abstract. This experience, however, is ephemeral, as ". . . eternity is in the now and being is in the disappearing" (p. 43).

Whether there are perfect forms (Plato, 380 BCE/1943), a collective unconscious (Jung, 1969), a fabric of meaning (acausal connecting principle, synchronicity; Jung, 1973), universal memory (morphic resonance; Sheldrake, 2017), and/or conscious agents (Hoffman and Prakash, 2020), are all conjectures based off of inferences from interpretations from practice-based observations, and select numbers of studies. The common striving for all of us to see beyond our perceptive faculties into the great unknown itself has been challenged by philosophers like Hannah Arendt (1971), who asked:

> Could it not be that appearances are not there for the sake of the life process but on the contrary, that the life process is there for the sake of appearances? Since we live in an appearing world, is it not much more plausible that the relevant and the meaningful in this world of ours should be located precisely on the surface? (p. 27)

Dan Siegel (2018) believes that transcendent experiences may be arising from the capacity to inhabit two different realities. Incorporating physics and his collaboration with several prominent physicists, he believes that our everyday *normal* waking experience is *Newtonian*, focused on the *macroworld*, and that these transcendent experiences may be attributed to our inner ability to inhabit a *quantum* world, or the *microworld*. In his discussions with quantum physicists, he has come to understand that "energy is the movement from possibility to actuality," and from quantum mechanics, that there may be a "quantum vacuum," a "mathematical space of reality representing the full range of possibilities that may arise into being" (Siegel, 2018, p. 187). He posited that meditative states, such as those brought about by his "Wheel of Awareness" practice and other practices, result in a descent from the peaks of activation to the plateaus of probability and ultimately to this plateau of possibility. It is here, or in his terminology, at the "hub of awareness," where people become fully immersed in the experience of *pure awareness*, which has been described as "empty of form, but full of possibilities," "bliss," "oneness," an interconnectedness where becoming and all that is experienced as an interconnected process. Because of the feedback he has received from experiences touching on this hub of awareness, he has been led to believe it relates to the quantum world. The core descriptor he attributes to the plane of possibility is *verb-like*: distinct from our everyday Newtonian experiences, which has the tendency to discriminate and emphasize *noun-like* experiences.

REFLECTIONS: HORIZONS BEYOND BOUNDARIES

Without change, something sleeps inside us, and
seldom awakens. The sleeper must awaken.

—Frank Herbert

The objective world around us extends far beyond what we can sense and perceive. Only a sliver of information is received and understood, and not passively so; in fact, we do so rather actively. That sliver of information is transformed and filtered through non-conscious processes that actively select what we end up perceiving consciously. We are always more than we are aware of and there is always more happening than we can be conscious of. As soon as we believe we have settled on the ground of knowledge, another stratum appears. As Jaspers noted, when we reach a boundary, we wonder what is beyond it. A *boundary* does "not indicate the end of our possible experiences, since from the boundary point are visible the wide horizons surrounding existence that are not included within our experiential consciousness" (Miron, 2012, p. 12). The idea that our attempts to understand reality is accompanied by the experience of a "receding" reality with an equivalent speed (due to its vastness), is what Jaspers (1971) called the *encompassing*, which "preserves my freedom against knowability" (p. 23).

As is the case with all complex questions outside the grasp of our daily perception and objective tools of measurement, we are left with more questions than answers. Is it possible that nature runs deeper than most of us are aware of, and that we can achieve states that may grant us access? Might it not be too far of a stretch to open ourselves to the possibility of a consciousness that extends beyond our own? Or can these transcendent experiences be explained away by electrochemical interactions in complex systems?

In my conceptualization, meaning is discovered and experiential truths are at least partially created. Objective truth exists, but we are still too poorly equipped to assert that we have encountered any stable ground. Every meaning discovered opens a new narrative, and every narrative successfully integrated births a new truth. Humans are constantly seeking for a specific configuration of internal experiences that may help us transcend resistant problems. Maybe it's not so much about *why* we live, as it is about *how* we live. With certainty, we know that how we conduct ourselves may bring us either strength, meaning, and flow, or emptiness, guilt, and shame. Perhaps it is in the *how* that we may determine our *why*.

We are all individual expressions of nature. If we are to take mystical experiences with due respect, there may very well be deeper wells of experience, unplumbed depths, that reflect a closer alignment with reality than what we ordinarily perceive. We experience our everyday lives as a dispersion of light in clouds, and every so often, the clouds may clear, and we may experience the light with more intensity.

APPLICATIONS: WORKING WITH MYSTICAL EXPERIENCES

Mystical Experiences (ME) are more common than one might expect. They do not discriminate, occurring in atheists and religious folk alike. In working with MEs, one may integrate the noumenal-phenomenal axis (N-P axis). Here is an example: For those on the phenomenal end, mystical experiences may be seen as a superordinate subjective experience emerging from the spatiotemporal dynamics among complex systems including the brain-body and world. On the noumenal end, there are signals emanating from an active noumenon, which are given partial and temporary permission to enter into awareness through an alteration of brain-body activity and receptivity.

Thus, both scenarios require intrinsic neural activity to change; the difference between these approaches is simple: in the materialistic approach, there is an emphasis of giving rise to the experience, whereas in the noumenal approach, there is the emphasis on the receiving of experience. Both are related to a world-brain relation, with the difference being the depths of which the world might extend. MEs are profound to anyone who has experienced them.

It is important to begin with a curious, open, and respectful approach. If the clinician's belief in MEs clearly differ after exploring their client's beliefs, the clinician may slide toward the respective pole on the N-P axis in service of increasing relational attunement. The vital signals charts found in Appendix E and F may work for any demographic.

If working with a spiritual client, it may be useful to consider the work of Bion. The second half of Bion's work was dedicated to the concept of O, a letter used to represent Kant's noumenon.* Interestingly enough, a typical symbol used to represent the Jungian Self, which is roughly synonymous to Bion's later conception of O, is a circle. Bion believed that O cannot be known, only its representation. He likened O (the-thing-in-itself) to a real poppy field, and what we see as a painting of the poppy field (Bion, 1965/1984). In his view, outside our perception is something akin to an abstract platonic form, not inert and static, rather actively trying to incarnate within ourselves and the patient (Grotstein, 2018). The equivalent of this in ANW's work, would be ever purer realizations of the initial aim conditioned by the overarching conceptual process. What emerges within us, however, are veiled by the various layers that develop within us as we become conscious observers. As a result, we only view or expe-

---

* Their conceptualizations are slightly different (Vermote, 2019).

rience adumbrations of O, yet in sketches are truths, which he called *invariants*.

In psychotherapy, Bion recommends that we can be in better contact with O if we operate from a preconceptual viewpoint without memory or desire. In this perspective, we may not be able to see the unknowable reality of our clients, though we can experience it. "In so far as the analyst becomes O he is able to know the events that are evolutions of O" (Bion, 1970/1986, p. 27). He further asserts that "interpretations depend on 'becoming' (since he cannot know O). The interpretation is an actual event in an evolution of O that is common to analyst and analysand" (Bion, 1970/1986, p. 27). For Bion, O is an emotional truth. The ME from this point of view would be a direct experience with O.

For the materialist, one may confine O to unconscious processing. The ME may be a direct experience resulting in a release of neurotransmitters associated with Panksepp's system of SEEKING and CARE.* The patient may then be reacquainting themselves with protoself affect, free of certain veils, thereby experiencing what Bion considers emotional truth.

The aim of therapy from the perspective of MEs is the (re)connecting with that which is transcendent to the individual. The ME may be considered here as an expression of being in the midst of becoming, or an important psychobiological event orienting one toward meaning. The fundamental role of the therapist in this case relates to unpacking the contents of the experience. What did it mean to the individual? What was the message behind the experience? How does this inform or alter present and future behavior?

• •

* This will be elaborated in the chapter on Conscience.

CHAPTER 8.

Veils of Human Experience

Dream delivers us to dream, and there is no end
to illusion. Life is like at train of moods, like a
string of beads, and, as we pass through them,
they prove to be many-colored lenses which
paint the world their own hue.

—RALPH WALDO EMERSON

Underlying thinking and language is a stream of non-conceptual experience, the manifestation of an intricate concatenation of events. Currents of experience flow into the present, each one informing the next. The present is *perpetually perishing*, as soon as it has happened, it passes to serve the co-evolution of the subsequent event. The word *experience* is itself a linguistic abstraction, used to denote the quality of moment-to-moment events, which are not wholly expressible. Nature is accessed through experience, as much as nature produces the experience from which it is accessed.

According to Dewey (1958), experience "recognizes in its primary integrity no division between act and material, subject and object, but contains them both in an unanalyzed totality" (p. 8). "Experience reaches down into nature; it has depth. It also has breadth and to an indefinitely elastic extent. It stretches. That stretch constitutes inference . . . the very existence of science is evidence that experience is such an occurrence that it penetrates into nature and expands without limit through it" (p. 4a-I). "What is really 'in' experience extends much further than that which at any time is known" (p. 20).

Immediate experience is private and it seems to harbor a spatial-temporal structure, meaning that everything appears to us as having a linear sequence in space and time. Experience precedes all that we know, and everything we know about comes from our experiences (of sensations, images, thoughts, and feelings). We thus depend on experience to learn. In science, we observe a phenomenon, and this presents itself to us via experience. Waking consciousness is the experiential interface between the subjective and objective world. Both worlds are exceedingly complex, and because experience is defined by their relationship, everyone harbors experiences that are both familiar and unfamiliar. What we consciously experience relies much on what we attend to, and what we attend to relies on a myriad of BPSE relationships. Theoretically, there is an infinite amount of potential experiences we may have in the immediate moment. Sometimes we detach ourselves from the experience of the moment by hiding in intellectual experience. Other times, we may be swept away by the experience of emotions, codependent on our experience of others, concentrated on the experience of a painful sensation, or joyously in rapture from a meaningful experience. In some of the most memorable of times, our intellectual and emotional needs align with environmental demands, and we find ourselves in experiences of flow (Csikszentmihalyi, 1990). Experience beckons to be unraveled and examined.

When I speak of veils, what is it that is being veiled? Experience. Simone Weil (1947/2002) made an important clarification that "illusions about things in this world do not concern their existence but their value" (p 51). This is precisely what psychotherapy aims to unveil from the perspective of this book. Whether we can unveil what things in themselves actually are may be an important contribution for objective truth, but subjectively, we seek to expose value.

Before information matures into our experiential awareness, it travels through a multiplicity of *self-processes*, each with its own input and output. Information arrives at its destination in a form much like the remainder of a message passed among numerous operators. If we were to match the number of neuronal communications occurring in the brain with the number of activities in which we engage daily, the equivalent of even a few milliseconds of neural activity would exceed our life span. Feedforward and feedback loops in the brain suggest that in order to sense and perceive reality, information must be dissected, integrated, and reinterpreted multiple times. In fact, it is estimated that up to 80% of the brain's energy is dedicated to information produced within the brain, independent of the exterior world (Raichle, 2010). There are, broadly speaking, five phases of perception: the sensing of data, the translation of incoming data into a coherent presentation, the presentation's interaction with predictions that lead to a representation, the unification of representations into a single whole, and its intermingling with the individual's conceptual world.

William Blake (1794) once famously wrote, "If the doors of perception were cleansed, everything would appear to man as it is, infinite" (p. 14). Blake was referring to the doors through which information must travel in order to become known. The unknown structure and process of the universe are felt through our limited senses and filtered through our percepts and concepts, enabling us to partially know reality in a very particular way and from a particular perspective. We see, feel, and attend to only what was—or what we believe was—most adaptive to us.

Information in the brain is processed in parallel, not serially. That being said, a very basic step-by-step process through which information may be filtered may be useful for illustrative purposes. Consider the following:

Since the robbery, Arthur has noticed that his experience of leaving the office at night is different. He sees a bald male wearing a hoodie entering the parking lot he is in. The following is an example of what could happen in this hypothetical story:

1. *Sensing and Perceiving*

    a. A minute fraction of a thing undergoes processing and reprocessing until it is coherently integrated (sensation).

    b. The sensed thing (foreground) is perceived like another thing (grouping), but unlike other things (background).

    c. Sensed thing results in arousal resulting in instinctual reactions (sympathetic nervous system is engaged: approach/ avoid, or fight/flight).

2. *Feeling and Thinking*

   a. Emotion: body is prepared for fight or flight; Arthur feels energized and nervous.

   b. Attention: Arthur is alert and oriented to this figure.

   c. Language: I see a bald human approaching the vicinity wearing an article of clothing that conceals his face.

   d. Memory: I was robbed before; I need to either run away or fight him.

   e. Executive functioning: maybe he is also parked in this lot and is just looking for his car. I will keep my distance until he is no longer a threat and I will have 911 on speed dial since I still have time.

3. *Distorting*

   a. If I am feeling nervous, he must be threatening (emotional reasoning). I remember that one man who robbed me was bald, and I also have a memory of being made fun of as a child by a bald man (biases from history). Bald men bring nothing but trouble (polarized thinking).

   b. Automated belief: all bald men are bad.

   c. Thought: this bald man in the hoodie is going to rob me.

4. *Self-processes*

   a. I *know* he is going to rob me.

   b. That car is *mine*, if he breaks into that car, it is just as bad as hurting me.

   c. I will catch this bad bald man before he strikes and bring justice to the world. I will call 911 before he strikes.

5. *Sociocultural*

   a. I will be praised by the community for making the world a safer place.

b. Emrys would respect my ability to think a few steps ahead.

c. God will protect me (spirituality) and bless me for my actions.

6. *Existence*

a. Preventing crime is an act of intelligence, and bringing justice to this world is meaningful to me.

b. *At 350 milliseconds conscious thought arises:* all bald men are bad, all men in hoodies are suspicious. This man is going to rob me. He is a thief!

c. *At 550 milliseconds a decision is made:* I am calling 911 now before it is too late.

Our immediate experience involves the integration of multiple narratives running simultaneously at any given time. Arthur's veils have guided his final decision to act before any illegal activity has been committed. Another individual might have simply seen the bald man in the hoodie as someone passing by or someone who is going to their own car. We are easily deceived by the veiling of these filters. In combination with an undisciplined imagination, catastrophic projections are inevitable.

It is from this point on that I will present a broad framework with an eponymous title: reassembling models of reality (R-MOR). The R-MOR approach is meant to supplement existing approaches, providing the clinician with another way to conceptualize and intervene. It draws from the findings of this book and acknowledges pluralism as a central stance when working with others. Given the variety of approaches that exist, I invite the clinician to integrate and apply whichever parts of this model make sense and may be useful to them.

Fundamentally, its goal is to assist with the unveiling of the client's experiential truth in service of maturation, lucidity, tolerance of stress, flexibility, and freedom. It involves examining the extent to which their subjective experiences correspond to shared phenomenon, the explication of ambiguous experiences, the recognition of maladaptive heuristics, defenses, distortions and self-regulatory mechanisms, the exposure of illusions and unconscious patterns of relating, the identification and expression of their meaning-systems, and the encouragement and challenge necessary for them to flourish. We help clients refine their perception to behave in ways more congruent with reason, intuition, and their understanding of the reality. The clinician's goal is to facilitate momentum, when movement has been derailed or obstructed.

It is simultaneously a challenge to all clinicians, suggesting it would be wise to consider the idea that there is truth in every particular theory and discipline that may help us understand "the invisible." Learning never ends, similar to the full realization of being. There will always be a vanishing point, yet this point must remain as such if we are to evolve into robust unification of processes.

Awareness and metacognition enable us to be self-regulating organisms. They allow us to strive for adaptive routes that balance approach behaviors with the necessity to conserve energy. With these faculties at our disposal, how might we work with the range of challenges humans face?

The following is but one overarching approach, inspired by the aggregation of information that this book has had to offer. All the applications listed throughout may be incorporated into this approach as the clinician see's fit. There are many other configurations that exist.

Approach

1. Beware of Deceptions

2. Operate from Awareness and Metacognition

3. Listen to Your Conscience and Vital Signals

4. Integrate through Embodied Symbiosis

5. Suffer Consciously

6. Cycle through BPSE to Facilitate Metabolization

DECEPTIONS

*It is only by making physical experiments that we
can discover the intimate nature of matter and its
potentialities. And it is only by making psychological
and moral experiments that we can discover the
intimate nature of mind and its potentialities.*

—ALDOUS HUXLEY

Humans perceive the world as subjects, yet we are also objects composed of the same material that we are perceiving from. Our attempts to sense the reality hidden behind veils, is very much like a game of hide and seek. As a seeker, we must use the tools available to us, such as thoughts that arise within matter. Thoughts arise in the form of language and images, both of which are representations of the world—that is, the world *as represented in the mind*. The very fact that there is something being represented suggests that the mind operates as a symbolic system. The vast majority of thoughts are automated without our consent, just as the heart pumps blood throughout our circulatory system. Their origins are likely out of our awareness, as we are only aware of their content and form once they've marched through the gates of consciousness. Because of this, their presentation is incomplete. What is it that animates a thought? Attention.

It is as if thoughts appear to us dressed in fanciful clothing (emotion), some of which may captivate our attention and others of which do not. In light of this distraction, it may be easy to overlook the story they carry with them (their origins) because of the clothing they are wearing. Once we have attended to a specific thought, are we bound to identify with their superficial and incomplete forms?

The first step is to be aware of these deceptions. The list of deceptions I have compiled is an accumulation of empirically supported findings that have been discussed up to this point. Living in accordance with these lessons is no easy task; yet anything worthwhile seldom ever is. In light of all the twists and turns that information undergoes before it is received by consciousness, I posit that the main precursor to *self-inflicted* suffering is deception. Deception is, for all intents and purposes, that which biases or obfuscates our immediate experience, preventing us from achieving increased levels of well-being. This would include identification with superficial forms of thoughts. The following list summarizes deceptions discussed in previous chapters that may be integrated into our everyday awareness:

1. We see the world as it truly is.

    • Evolution narrows our view physically (we only see what benefits our survival) and psychologically (thoughts revolve around fitness and reproduction). There is much more to the world than our sensory experience would have us believe.

2. We are born as a singular and isolated entity.

    • We are a synthesis of internal and external relationships. We are an interdependent process.

3. Our memories are accurate.

    • They are not; we remember what we attend to, and we only attend to a very limited base of information. We remember the gist of memories, and even this may be false. Memory is more accurately understood as a function to help us anticipate the future.

4. We can excise parts of our psychological makeup that we dislike.

    • We cannot, although we can learn to relate and respond to them differently.

5. We are born in control of our thoughts.

    • We are not. We can guide them, but the majority of thoughts are automated.

6. We are in control of our behaviors.

    • Short-term pleasures easily blind us to long-term consequences (e.g., addictions). Our reward system does not take into account long-term consequences. For this reason, if we want to stop a behavior, a consequence needs to follow swiftly. Self-control is developed through de-identifying and re-relating with the hold that impulses, emotions, and thoughts have on us.

7. We are objective.

- When we are able to think beyond our sense impressions, those thoughts are susceptible to distortions for efficiency and defenses for protection.

8. We are good at predicting the future.

- Just as in emotional forecasting, we do a poor job predicting what may come to pass as a result of our actions. Similar to difficulties gauging how much weight we have lost purely through vision (because we see ourselves everyday), we fall into traps underestimating their neuropsychological consequence (e.g., substance use).

9. Fulfilling desires leads to long-term satisfaction.

- The desire for *more* is a never-ending cycle, despite our continual belief that we will be satisfied after we possess a desired object. As Lacan (cited in Fink, 1997) aptly theorized, desire seeks its own existence (not really the object). The old adage stands: much of satisfaction comes from within.

10. Stress is bad.

- Mild to moderate stress helps us learn and grow; it will always be part of our stories. However, severe levels of stress and chronicity lead to degradation of the neural network and ultimately create suffering.

11. Objective goods are greater than our internal gifts.

- The acts of introspection, meditation, journaling, and other tools from our creative imagination continue to demonstrate benefits. From a financial perspective, emotional well-being rises until we achieve an annual income of $75,000. Life evaluation rises steadily with income, but current emotional well-being does not (Kahneman & Deaton, 2010). Spending money on experiences and others enhances well-being (Mogilner & Norton, 2016).

12. Dreams and reveries are meaningless.

- Our culture has been evolving in a direction that discards the value of subjective experiences in favor of that which is tangible. We have entire domains of experience open for exploration, yet we discard them as irrelevant. Consider that even if dreams ultimately prove to be *meaningless*, the fact that we give meaning to them draws light to aspects of ourselves that we may not regularly have access. At minimum, they promote divergent thinking.

There is a game that is constantly being played, whether we are aware of it or not. For the sake of simplification, the players are our spotlight of awareness and the biological foundations that give rise to this. Some of these foundations are rooting for us, whereas others appear to work against us. Those that work against us are the dissonant thoughts, emotions, and impulses (TEIs) that are incongruent with how we wish to live. In this way humans "ruptured" from a dimension of nature, now capable of pursuing a goal higher than our instincts. These are easily identified by the ensuing feelings of guilt or shame we experience when we are unable to manage them effectively. The objective of this game is to outwit the opponent. As the number of times the opponent is outwitted increases, the higher becomes the likelihood that we will gain self-control, a foundation necessary for living in accordance with our values, regardless of what they are. One of the keys to winning is to be aware that these dissonant responses tend to arise for one or more of three reasons: (1) due to the brain's tendency to seek efficiency, (2) for protection, or (3) as a result of electrochemical imbalances. Clinically, if problem X is not entirely due to chemical imbalances, it may be useful to simply ask the client, "What function might X serve?"

It is always fascinating to me how internal scales of life can be paralleled in social interactions. Exactly as in the social arena, leaders are followed for their charisma, intelligence, and social skills. Leaders are followed because they can see beyond pitfalls that others may ordinarily not notice. Such people have the executive skills to plan ahead and make decisions that are strategic in nature. They have to demonstrate their utility, and people have to feel they deserve the position. This is not unlike gaining self-control. You will not have self-respect if you are continually *outwitted* by your TEIs. You have to continue to outwit them, and by doing so, firmly and steadily, you soon gain the reinforcement of neural pathways. You gain *respect* from internal operating systems in the form of less effortful and higher levels of self-directed guidance. If not, competing forces will continually lead, many of which, if left undirected, will increase the likelihood of a shipwreck.

Thus, another way of viewing our goal as therapists is to help our clients become less *deceived* by these inherent mechanisms. We do so in many ways, whether by increasing insight, challenging irrational thoughts, interpreting a defense mechanism, or offering psychoeducation. We help our clients outwit their maladaptive tendencies by understanding their function and relating them to their former use as protection or by developing structured techniques that balance their logic. It is also vital that we help our clients cultivate more adaptive forms of introspection in order to embody the awareness necessary for change (e.g., approaching their *darker* selves with curiosity and openness).

It is important for me to return to a point I made in the preface; namely, that our neuropsychological foundations have not yet caught up to the rapid progression of society and technology. This is partially why I believe we suffer from these deceptions. They are only deceptive when their existence no longer serves to protect us. Likewise, they are only deceptive insofar as our brain-seeking efficiency is not beneficial to us due to current demands. Our ancestors, for example, never would have predicted the creation of a globally connected virtual system that can provide us with instant gratification—the internet. Might excessive use of this system alter the way we organize information? Or might it generalize to our expectations, perhaps in relationships? How might our inner experience and worlds be altered? These are questions that go beyond the purview of this book, but serve well to illustrate my point.

AWARENESS AND METACOGNITION

Everything is necessary, everything needs only my
agreement, my assent, my loving understanding; then
all is well with me and nothing can harm me.

—HERMANN HESSE

We are the sum of our conscious and non-conscious processes, yet we experience ourselves as that which can *reflect* upon and *regulate* some of these processes. In the second proposition I suggest that it is most adaptive to root oneself in awareness and act through metacognition (AM), toggling within and between BPSE processes as is necessary.

There continues to be controversy as to what awareness exactly is, and this is because we do not entirely know what it is. Any definition could thus limit its possibilities. We do not know what gives rise to awareness, but we can describe characteristics that awareness harbors. Two important features of awareness are consciousness and metacognition. As mentioned earlier, there are many specified types of consciousness that have been categorized into a hierarchical fashion and it is conceptualized differently in medical circles. As such, we can be more specific when we use the word awareness in relation to to higher level consciousness. Consciousness, in this context, refers to the subjective sensation of experience that includes a knowing and a *likeness* (Nagel, 1974), which will be considered a defining feature of awareness. Awareness encapsulates autonoetic consciousness (AC). AC is the capacity to be aware of ourself as a process existing through time (Tulving, 2002) as one projects themselves into the past to recall a memory or into a simulated future. This concept covers the horizontal plane of time. There are, however, other *realms* of projection: vertical dimensions, which relate to different modes of experiencing, such as being in contemplation or when engaged with the environment. Attention is the vehicle for awareness. Spatially, I can shift the awareness to my right hand, and even the tips of my fingers, enhancing my sensory experience of them. I may also attend to an object outside myself, and essentially reduce my awareness of everything else. In these cases, awareness does not vanish from my head, but the focal point changes. Temporally, I have asserted that we confuse the steady experience of awareness with our self; which changes through its development. Awareness can thus be described as having qualities of psychological *timelessness* and *space-lessness*. When someone commits an act of stupidity, it is common for another to say, "He was not aware of the situation." Awareness clearly involves, here, some form of intelligence. For one to cross the bridge from unaware to aware, there is a requisite for awareness to expand. This is intimately connected with metacognition, which is typically characterized by our ability to reflect upon and regulate our mental processes, sometimes simplified as the ability to think about thinking. There is current controversy over whether consciousness led to the rise of metacognition, or vice versa (Timmermans, Schilbach, Pasquali, & Cleeremans, 2012). Cognition accounts for objective neural changes that correlate with monitoring and influencing processes, whereas awareness refers to the actual experience of doing so. Together, they allow us to select or veto an inner signal (or, for those determinists, it affords us the *illusion* of selection or veto). From the systems model of the mind, AM would be the recursive or self-organizing mechanism.

From my viewpoint, AM represents an evolutionary mandate to support survival and social functioning. The responsibilities of AM are to manage high levels of information from other operating systems in the brain and facilitate individuality to support differentiation within groups. Naturally, this comes with an autobiographical self, identity, and preferences, all of which help with both specialization and function in the domain of societal contributions and productivity. In relation to Darwin's (1859/2005) concept of natural selection, my conjecture is that AM contributes to the process of selecting what psychological traits and cultural meaning systems may survive through time. AM accomplishes this as a result of an ability to inhibit or activate neural expressions to deploy specific behaviors and ideas.

To operate from AM is to be able to relate to all dimensions and veils from a healthy distance, preventing oneself from identification or fusion. For example, there is a difference between *being* angry and *feeling* angry. To be angry is to identify ourselves with the emotion, which results in emotional dysregulation, possibly expressed as an inappropriate outburst. To feel angry is to relate to the emotion from a distance as it arises. Thus, AM enables cognitive defusion, an attitude and an empirically supported ACT technique (A-Tjak et al., 2015). We can then make a choice to act out or sublimate in such a way that expresses the feeling with productivity. For us to engage through the filter of self, we run the risk of the *I, me, mine* triad, which also leads to suffering. Thus, if we desire to live a more conscious life, we must be continually reorienting ourself to AM.

MINDFULNESS EXERCISE

Begin by noticing your inhalations and exhalations. Your breath will tether you to the present if your mind wanders. Continue focusing on your breath until you have cleared a space for new images to populate your mind and you feel comfortable engaging in guided practice.

Now in your mind's eye, imagine yourself lying on a sheet over a soft bed of grass. You are at the summit of a mountain, overlooking valleys and mountain ranges that appear to extend indefinitely into the horizon. Your head is resting on a pillow facing upward at the sky. You are watching clouds pass.

The first step is to sense any emotion(s) you may be having in this moment. Once you have identified the emotion, allow it to color the clouds above. Feel free to add other environmental factors as necessary. For the next few minutes, simply watch the clouds, and if your emotions change during this practice, continue projecting them onto the clouds. Notice the colors changing with your feelings as you observe them over time. One emotion observed over time inevitably gives way to another.

If your mind wanders, gently bring it back to the image and your breath (repeat as necessary).

Next, allow your thoughts to populate the clouds passing. Clouds pass through your field of vision at the same rate as your thoughts. View your thoughts as bits of information, and notice the speed at which they come and go. Do they change with this exercise?

Continue to observe your thoughts and emotions in this fashion. Notice how the very act of being able to observe your thoughts and emotions implies that there exists something that transcends them—you, the one observing.

Feel free to stop as you feel fit. Practicing this over time will enable you to be better acquainted with the nature of your thoughts and feelings. The purpose of practicing this exercise is to develop greater levels of connection with awareness and to create a healthy distance between awareness and your thoughts and feelings.

This exercise was inspired by acceptance and commitment therapy (see Stoddard & Afari, 2014, for a variety of different exercises).

• •

The closest evidence that supports the benefits of anchoring ourself in AM can be found in meditative practices.* This by no means excludes other practices that may accomplish the same results. For example, in phenomenology, Husserl (as cited in Van Deurzen, 2010) suggested *bracketing* our presuppositions in an attempt to remain objective. The purpose of this exercise is to suspend all judgments, thus providing the clearest picture of what we have observed. In summarizing phenomenological rules, Van Deurzen (2010) suggested bracketing presuppositions, describing rather than explaining the observed, unbiasing aspects, contextualizing them (horizontalization), and verifying all observations.

In basic breath awareness practice, we are asked to simply focus on our breath. Every time the mind wanders, we bring it back to the breath. When we are focused entirely on our breathing, awareness is tethered to the present moment, and the experience of self is cradled by the quality of immediate awareness. The ephemeral nature of TEIs becomes more salient, becoming seen as separate from the observer. Meditation empowers AM. In an effort to clarify any misconceptions, it is also important to note that being present does not mean we should not think about the past or simulate events in the future, because these acts of mental time travel can be quite advantageous. The difference is to do so consciously versus mindlessly.

One reliable guide that the organism is moving in the right direction is to follow activities that promote mental and physiological harmony. Thus, if our behavior results in the experience of shame and guilt, it is likely that the behavior is not conducive to the harmony of self and others. To date, many studies have documented the myriad benefits of meditation, as shown in Table 8.1.

---

* Although Buddhists will say that consciousness itself is *Maya* or an illusion and that meditation includes transcending consciousness, it is rare to find individuals who have reached this level of enlightenment. That being said, I suggest abiding in AM as a first step and in no way deny the possibility of transcending consciousness itself.

TABLE 8.1: Literature Review: Benefits of Meditation

REFERENCE	MINDFULNESS CHANGES AND BENEFITS
Sood and Jones (2013)	Improved attention Enhanced cognitive flexibility Decreased emotional reactivity Enhanced executive processing Improved conflict monitoring and reactive control Enhanced rational decision making
Lazar et al. (2005)	Brain structure: increased cortical thickness of right medial and superior frontal cortices and the insula, and gray matter density (insula, somatosensory cortex, parietal regions) of mindfulness meditators compared to controls
Vestergaard-Poulsen et al. (2009)	Increased brainstem density
Baer (2003) Y. Jung et al. (2010) Tang et al. (2007)	Enhanced mood and well-being Improved attention and cognitive performance Reduced stress, depressive symptoms, anger, and cortisol levels
Davidson et al. (2003)	Improved immune function
Schutte and Malouff (2014)	Increased telomere length

As AM becomes more differentiated from other systems, we are able to improve objectivity by preventing ourselves from succumbing to the complete identification with any particular process or veil. In mindfulness research (Taren et al., 2017), this may appear as the reconfiguration of the DMN, with increased resting state functional connectivity to areas of the brain (e.g., dorsolateral prefrontal cortex) associated with working memory, decision making, and regulating attention.

AN INTEGRATED THEORY OF CONSCIENCE

Through pride we are ever deceiving ourselves.
But deep down below the surface of the average
conscience a still, small voice says to us, something is
out of tune.

— C. G. JUNG

Conscience is an underdiscussed topic, deserving of more recognition. Carveth's (2015) view parts from Freud's superego (1933), suggesting conscience should considered as a fourth element in structural theory. I agree with him. Superego was originally divided into conscience, self-observation, and ego-ideal (Freud, 1933). Of most relevance here is the ego-ideal, which is that part of us that tells us how we should be (via internalized values of parents or society), and this internal critic causes persecutory guilt. The *still small voice* of conscience, on the other hand, seeks to nurture, and promotes reparative guilt (Carveth, 2013). Sagan (1988) and Carveth (2010) make a case that conscience stems from early experiences of nurturing, and a need to reciprocate it. Conscience from their perspective is morality grounded in love and attachment, whereas the Freudian superego is grounded in Thanatos (i.e., the death drive). It is suggested that conscience developmentally manifests before the superego, as it is observed that at six months infants suckling may simultaneously offer their finger to their mother; or at one year prefer to give their mother food rather than having it themselves (ibid). Schore (2016) makes note that the ego ideal emerges at 18 months, drawing parallels to right-hemispheric orbito-frontal limbic system.* Carveth (2010) views conscience as being "grounded in attachment and love and is beyond both the pleasure and reality principles" (p. 9). These age ranges fit well with Schore's regulation theory (2019), which stresses the importance of early mother-infant bonding and attachment on the development of self.

Panksepp's (1998) affective neural system of CARE and SEEKING coincides with this paradigm. The CARE system is theorized to have evolved through exaptation from the system of LUST, which both involve oxytocin as a core

---

* Which has been commonly associated with empathy and moral behaviors; with dysfunction correlating to sociopathy (Schore, 2016).

neuropeptide regulating these needs and experiences. They are now, however, differentiated systems, with CARE specializing in the promotion of nonsexual tenderness, which also includes endogenous opioids and dopamine. Areas associated with this system include the anterior hypothalamus, paraventricular nucleus, periacqueductal gray (PAG), and dorsal preoptic area with further connections throughout the medial subcortical regions, and the ventral tegmental area, which is at the core of the SEEKING system (Panksepp & Biven, 2012). The SEEKING system, "allows animals to search for, find, and acquire all of the resources that are needed for survival. Arousal of this SEEKING system produces all kinds of approach behaviors, but it also feels good in a special way" (p. 95). It is associated with the ventral tegmental area, dorsolateral hypothalamus, nucleus accumbens (often called the brains reward system), and PAG. The core neurotransmitter linked to this system is dopamine. Following process-oriented thinking, *it is the continuous moment-to-moment interaction between the environment and systems of SEEKING and CARE that gives rise to conscience.* Using ANW's framework, conscience is the continual presence of initial aims in the form of felt ideals ascending into propositional truths.

When one typically thinks of the CARE system, the assumption is the development of nurturing relationships with others. However, awareness and metacognition has enabled us to also pursue interior ideas that nurtures the self-process. Earlier, I linked experiential truth with conscience, more specifically I believe it to be a precursor process that elaborates that which is *meaningful* into the *still small voice.* It was first Frankl (1986) who considered conscience to be an *organ* for perceiving meaning. What humans consider meaningful is always a form of nurture, to one's self-process or to another. I theorize that experiential truth is a relational resonance, beginning (1) as an anoetic "pure" feeling of congruence (e.g., feelings of nurture) that begins in the upper brainstem; (2) it then becomes differentiated as a noetic sense of meaning when connected with secondary emotions in limbic areas; and (3) defined as propositional truth values as it moves up into cortical regions. Prosocial behaviors would be an example of the nurture system in action. Nurturing behaviors are continually found in two-year-olds feeling greater happiness when they give rather than receive, or adults via increases in well-being through prosocial spending (Mogilner & Norton, 2016). Wang, Zhang, and Jia (2019) distinguished between the activation of reward centers and prosocial behaviors, highlighting that prosocial behaviors activate regions such as the left insula (BA 13), left temporal lobe (BA 42), and left superior temporal gyrus (BA 22). They place particular emphasis on the insula, which "may encode intangible advantageous benefits of prosocial behaviors beyond reward-cost computations" (p. 4). BA 42 is the primary region that receives auditory information, and BA 22 relates to speech comprehension. All three regions put together may reflect the internal experience of prosocial behaviors, perhaps even the feeling of being moved or feeling "right," alongside the experience of a *still small voice*. In their review, Barazza and Zak (2013) divided these conscience congruent behaviors into reciprocity, trust, generosity, and altruism. In alignment with the CARE system, they found that though they may elicit some differing neural activity, they were all highly mediated by oxytocin. That which maximizes nurturing experiences or behaviors corresponds to the release of dopamine, opioids, and oxytocin, reinforcing meaningful actions that have been embodied, supporting the quest for experiential truth.* This conceptualization may be led back to a principle in interpersonal neurobiology: *Those who are nurtured best, survive best* (Cozolino, 2012).

Like so many other self-processes, it is entirely possible that the CARE system dedicated to nurturing may become internally represented as conscience when incorporated with an autobiographical self-process/autonoetic consciousness. In my opinion, conscience would be the conscious embodiment of a primordial self-process. Carveth (2013) notes that at its core it is *a feeling*, not a rationally produced decision, which is in line with increasing support from the social intuitionist model (Haidt, 2001; McGilchrist, 2009). This counters moral relativism, which promotes the conscious self-process as moral arbiter, leaving conscience without its rightful place. Carveth (2013) importantly specifies ". . . the ego needs to be empowered to resist the ego-destructive superego†; but cannot hope to replace it as the moral center of the personality: that is the job of conscience. From conscience we derive moral guidance and

---

* Part of the issue of course is that the SEEKING system is blind on its own, and so clinically, there will be many times when the conscience is silenced, and subordinated to some other call.

† A concept developed by Bion (1959), which can be broadly described as times when the superego attacks the ego so harshly that the individual begins a destructive cycle of self-deprecation, criticism, and judgment, possibly leading to self-harm.

strength to expose the immorality of the superego [or id] and, with the help of the ego, to grow up, emancipate ourselves from and overcome it" (p. 15). Thus, at an anoetic level, the feeling of "right" may be felt as consonant experiences from nurturing/being nurtured, in contrast to "wrong," which may have been reflected in the PANIC/GRIEF/sadness system. This may subsequently evolve into productive guilt in the tertiary process. The PANIC system has been observed as a primary support for attachment in mothers with infants; however, this would be through *separation* distress (Panksepp & Biven, 2012).

Earlier, I discussed shame and non-productive guilt as disintegrative vital signals on a continuum, with shame being more severe. Broadly, guilt focuses on a behavior, whereas shame focuses on the self; and shame is associated with social standards leading to a devaluation of self, whereas guilt is connected to personal standards and is more associated to constructive potential. If we continue with Carveth's (2015) paradigm, relating superego with shame and conscience with guilt, might we find some neuroanatomical differences? In one neuroimaging study, Michl and colleagues (2014) discovered the main difference was that guilt elicited activations in the amygdala and insula, and shame in the frontal lobe, specifically the medial and inferior frontal gyrus. Otherwise there was substantial overlap. Further specification will need to focus on productive guilt compared to shame and the various gradations in between. Another reason to justify the separation is that there are many circumstances whereby conscience can be violated, in spite of acting in accordance with the superego (e.g., obedience studies). This leads us to the slippery slopes of immoral morality. In fact, Carveth (2015) further specifies that "without conscience we lack any basis for judging one superego as superior to another . . . we can only distinguish a mature from an immature superego by the standards of conscience" (p. 14). Progress, he asserts, "requires us to progressively quarantine and disempower the superego and strengthen both the conscience and the rational ego" (p. 14).

Frankl (1986) and Jung (Sullivan, 2010) also viewed conscience as a mediator for that which is transcendent and life-affirming. The difference lies in what the transcendent implies. If it is simply transcending the ego, there is agreement. However, as Elio Frattaroli put it: "If there is no higher consciousness there to hear it (and decode its subtle language of feeling), does the still small voice of conscience really make a sound?" (p. xxvi). Nonetheless, there is evidence that oxytocin supports spiritual experiences (Cappellen et al., 2016), alongside dopamine and endogenous opioids (Kohls, Sauer, Offenbacher, & Giordano, 2011). Whether one roots it in the transcendent, or an internalized nurturing relationship, the fact is that in both models, the conscious self-process is relegated to a position below the conscience. The conscious self-process then assumes its rightful role as the perceiver of psychological life, and an inner liaison, with the conscience acting as the compass.

I also posit that there is likely some relation between conscience and STEs as vital signals. The experiences of connectedness, warmth, and peace experienced in STEs is a shared affective platform. The dissolving of the ego may relate to deep-rooted experiences connected to very early attachment experiences, a time when we did not have a well differentiated autobiographical self, but were predominantly an anoetic somato-affective system. Perhaps this involves novel activation-inhibition patterns throughout the frontal-parietal systems, and the release of endogenous oxytocin, opioids, and dopamine. In response to an inquiry about religious experiences, Freud (1930/2010) responded: "We are entirely willing to acknowledge that the oceanic feeling exists in many people and we are disposed to relate it to an early stage in ego-feeling." He concludes that these feelings are associated with the need for religion which arise from "a child's feeling of helplessness and the longing it evokes for a father" (p. 21). As an adult, he proposes they are connected to religion, and may generate feelings of *trance* and *ecstasy*. In the framework of affective neuroscience, he may have been right; it may be a return of the ego to the source of conscience (or perhaps the source of conscience erupting into the ego) through SEEKING, resulting in intense, unhindered oceanic feelings of being nurtured from the CARE system. It seems Panksepp and Biven (2012) are also in alignment with Freud: ". . . we believe that one driving force behind human religions is our affective nature, especially our desperate need for nurturance and understanding, to ward off grief through community, and often with the desire to seek a higher good" (p. 116). In conclusion, I view conscience as a compass, and vital signals as amplifications of magnetic fields orienting us in directions that maximize growth through the SEEKING and CARE systems.

In clinical practice, one must be mindful of the client's beliefs. There is a difference in conceptualizing conscience for those who are spiritual and those who are not. For the former, it is about facilitating increased sensitivity to such signals, whereas in the latter it may be more about the development of systems in relation to conscience. Fortunately, these two conceptualizations promote conscience as a directing process. How does one go about developing a clearer experience of conscience? This can be approached in many ways. For those who are psychodynamic, one may draw the client's awareness to the voice of conscience when it is speaking, versus when the superego is doing so. The continual categorization will likely help the *still small voice* to be properly differentiated and increase its presence. For those who prefer more direct approaches, one may bring up conscience as an active topic in practice, introduce this model, and educate them on the differences. One may then assign them tasks to identify within themselves when conscience is speaking in contrast to superego. For any approach, it is important to explore the client's understanding of conscience, how they interact with it, and what veil processes may be preventing them from living in accordance to it.

EMBODIED SYMBIOSIS

All Nature is linked together by invisible bonds and
every organic creature, however low, however feeble,
however dependent, is necessary to the well-being of
some other among the myriad forms of life.

— GEORGE PERKINS MARSH

The process of awareness and metacognition (AM) is the *pièce de resistance* of self-processes. The conscious self-process is in connection with societies of complex self-processes and primordial self-processes. Together they form the protoself-process, core self-process, and autobiographical self-process. Self-processes are primarily driven by affective systems and are structured through cognitive processes. Prehensions (i.e., bonding) make concrescence (i.e., growing together) possible, allowing for a succession of past events to flow into the present, and amalgamate to form future events in a cyclical fashion. For the organism, events will typically "terminate in a completed unity of operation, termed 'satisfaction'" (Whitehead, 1927–28/1978, p. 219). This termination, or perishing, leads to the transitioning of its activity into objectivity. This is percolation, the process where becoming perishes into being. This is analogous to a present event becoming a past event, embedded in memory to serve the subsequent present event. Although the term concrescence is used to describe how all nature comes into being, we may also use it in relation to mental health.

Several neural systems operate in parallel, giving rise to a unity of feeling which is then expressed as a behavior. The problem is that not all inner processes are united with a single aim, in fact there may be several in conflict with multiple aims. This necessitates the organism to self-regulate and reorganize itself in order to facilitate a particular expression; thus, generating novel prehensions or relationships. This subsequent section relates to the process of embodied symbiosis, which is the relating of the conscious self-process with complex and primordial self-processes in service of experiential truth and meaning.

When a complex self-process is not getting its needs met, its probability of being presented to the conscious self-process multiplies, in which case awareness and the intentional formation of symbiotic relationships will be necessary. In a sense, it is because of discordance that we are conscious. Problematic complex self-processes may occur due to a *premature consolidation* of problematic experiences without solutions (that Solms [2017] relates to repressed memories), or when their functions are not synchronizing appropriately with environmental demands (i.e., its usual mode of functioning has become antiquated). If conscious self-processes fail to meet the needs of complex self-processes in some way, their affective salience may increase until resolution has been met or a psychopathological process ensues. Part of the task of the clinician is then to identify the self-process(es) in question, and facilitate its reconsolidation with new affective, cognitive, and behavioral events. In other words, self-processes are nourished and empowered by novel conceptual paradigms, new emotional experiences, and behavioral applications. Together, this process results in improving one's chances of meeting an experiential truth. This action happens through symbiogenesis (the birth of new symbiotic relationships) or the development of symbiotic relationships, which confers a competitive advantage for the survival of one interior process over another. From this perspective, the purpose of psychotherapy is the refinement of both conscious and unconscious processes through the relationships within, between, and in connection to the environment. This "fine-tuning" leads to the expansion and advancement of unconscious processes, the empowerment of consciousness, and improved adaptation to the environment. In the context of an individual, conscious symbiosis eventually leads to unconscious unification.

Symbiosis is a biological term first championed by botanist Heinrich Anton de Bary (1879) that generally describes the quality of relationships between two or more dissimilar organisms that are in intimate coexistence. Each organism that lives in relation to one another is called a *symbiont*. The impression that there are dissimilar mechanisms existing in the brain-mind is echoed in MacLean's (1990) model of the triune brain, whereby he generalized three systems whose processes operate with pronounced distinction. To put it simply, it is as if a "human, a horse and a crocodile" (Hampden-Turner, as cited in Cozolino, 2010, p. 6) are required to live in the same space. Lynn Margulis (Margulis & Fester, 1991), the mother of symbiosis, proposed the term *holobiont* to stand for the host in relation to all of its symbionts. Because Margulis is an evolutionary biologist, her term refers to all biological forms of symbiosis. I am asserting that just as we are not individuals biologically, neither are we psychologically.

Generally, any enduring relationship will have three potential symbiotic outcomes that are recognized by scientists: mutualistic, commensalistic, and parasitic (Dimijian, 2000). The three categories of symbiotic relationships can be defined as follows:

- *Mutualistic:* All coexisting organisms benefit from their relationships.
- *Commensalistic:* Select organisms benefit and others are left unharmed.
- *Parasitic:* Select organisms benefit and others are harmed.

Organisms living in close proximity likely developed a symbiotic relationship through time; natural selection and environmental pressures guided their coevolutionary relationship, increasing their likelihood of survival. With this relationship persisting as a given, vertical (genetic) and horizontal (environmental) transmission of information favored cooperation, selecting the relationship as a reliable advantage (Fisher, Henry, Cornwallis, Kiers, & West, 2016). Traits no longer necessary were discarded, as the symbiotic relationship became increasingly salient. As a result, there is a spectrum of interdependency among several different organisms. This is similar to the way we operate psychologically, albeit on a much longer timescale. We cannot escape the intimacy of biological, psychological, social, and existential processes (BPSE), but we can cultivate relationships from awareness and metacognition (AM) toward different sensations, beliefs, thoughts, and behaviors. If we nourish the relationships, they grow stronger and more salient. In time, relationships that encourage the embodiment of our values become capable of overpowering relationships that were maladaptive in some way.

The particular relationship we all strive for is *mutualistic symbiosis*, though there will be times when a parasitic relationship must be formed or a commensalistic relationship settled for. The action of updating previous symbiotic relationships or birthing new ones is what I am calling *embodied symbiosis* (ES). To embody means to "1) be an expression of or give a tangible or visible form to (an idea, quality or feeling); 2) to include or contain (something), as a constituent part; 3) form into a body" (New Oxford American Dictionary, 2010, p. 566). When used in combination with symbiosis, the concept may be defined as: cultivating advantageous symbiotic relationships (ASR) within and between the whole human and its environment until they are a form of implicit functioning. Neuropsychologically, ASRs begin as conscious reflection, yet successful (re)consolidation begins operating beneath conscious awareness as a form of pre-reflective mutualism. Importantly, newly formed mutualistic symbiotic relationships are not embodied until they are lived out or expressed behaviorally. This behavioral component is introduced to maximize plastic changes, producing cognitive-affective alterations. Mutualistic relationships extend into the unconscious, conscious, biological, interpersonal, cultural, ecological, and existential. This may thus include the variety of approaches listed throughout this book, depending on what is presented.

Tying this back to earlier chapters, what remains to be central driving forces are conscience and vital signals. Every synchronous action helps form a psychobiological gravity well that increases in its strength and depth, drawing other conceptual models to orbit its periphery. It is thus through inhabiting the existential space (awareness and metacognition) and relating from its process that we find and build upon freedom and meaning.

The concept of symbiosis has been used in a psychological context before, specifically by family therapists Kerr and Bowen (1988), who applied it to relational dynamics within the family, and analyst Margaret Mahler (1968), who applied it to the mother-infant bond. The idea that we internalize relationships and that the quality of these relationships are important for our psychological health is also very much engrained in object-relations theory in psychoanalysis (Greenberg & Mitchell, 1983). If we think about it, the internalization of the therapeutic relationship as a standalone internal object-relation, is itself the establishment of a pre-reflective mutualistic symbiotic relationship.

Embodied symbiosis subsumes all relationships, consequently integrating different paradigms under a single umbrella. Our conscious self may thus relate to these dimensions in a variety of ways and these relationships may be facilitated in consciousness and reflected back to its body and behavior. The question now is, what does this look like? Practically, it may be beneficial to help clients first identify the quality (type of symbiotic relationship) of their current relationships, and collaboratively determine the best path to take (see Appendix G). This integrates a behavioral approach with dynamic and relational theories.

An example of a parasitic relationship involves the blue butterfly *Maculinea arion,* which lays eggs producing smells that mimic the ant species *Myrmica sabuleti.* Ants bring the butterfly eggs into their nest, where the larvae eats food brought by worker ants and continues to eat young ants until the butterflies metamorphize into adults (Gilbert et al., 2012). In the healing process, we help our clients gain deeper insight in service of becoming aware of one-way, unintentional symbiotic relationships (parasitic) and developing two-way (or more), intentional ones. Many times we may be unaware of a parasitic relationship, such as the ants in the previous example. Continuing the analogy, we find that the birth of a bad habit often involves some influence from outside us. As we find them pleasurable (the scent of eggs) we find ourselves unable to stop "feeding" them (engaging in associated behaviors) until the habit has become a full-blown addiction.

Parasitic relationships may also be found interpersonally, and this is quite salient in cases where domestic violence is prevalent. It can be quite helpful for clinicians to educate clients on the different forms of symbiosis and to ask them to classify their relationships accordingly. This strategy may amplify the significance or insignificance of their relationships and help them decide which to nurture and which to end.

Once parasitic relationships are identified in session, we may help clients alter these relationships by the generation of mutualistic relationships to replace them. In therapy, we help clients develop new ways of relating to themselves and their bodies. One typical way to help counter an addiction is to introduce an alternate activity every time the urge presents itself. Exercise is often recommended, coupled with mindfulness. Exercise and mindfulness (see Table 8.1) benefit both mind and body.* Exercise further allows physical

---

* Exercise has been correlated to improvements in learning, memory, attention, and executive functioning; and this is neurophysiologically reflected through increased cerebral blood flow and oxygen, increases in gray matter volume in temporal and frontal regions, and increased brain derived neurotrophic factor (BDNF). Emotionally, decreases in anxiety, depression, and increases in self-control, emotional stability, assertiveness, and sexual satisfaction (Mandolesi et al., 2018). Unique benefits are found in different activities such as aerobics, weight lifting (Dunsky et al., 2017), and yoga (Brunner, Abramovitch, Etherton, 2017; Gothe, Hayes, Temali, & Damoiseaux, 2018).

urges to be released in activity, altering the way clients relate to the physical urge. Mindfulness alters a person's relationship to their mental contents. The parasitic relationship between individual and substance may thus be supplanted or at least mitigated by a new relationship with exercise and mindfulness.

In nature, one famous example often used to describe mutualistic symbiosis is that of the anemone and the clownfish. The clownfish is offered a home and protection; in exchange, the clownfish offers the anemone nutrients and protection from predators. An interpersonal consideration of this is similarly the relationship established in psychotherapy itself. At face value, the client gains a highly trained professional as an ally to help them overcome challenges, and the clinician gains a means to survive. In time, the relationship is internalized, becoming a source for secure attachment, and the client is successfully discharged, leaving both parties empowered (the client with new insight, experience and tools; the clinician with meaning). Of course, there are numerous benefits on both sides that extend beyond what has been mentioned, but the point to be made is the existence of mutualism.

In most cases, successful treatment may end with a multiplicity of mutualistic and commensalistic relationships, or perhaps some clients might have to live with relationships that border parasitic. Embodied symbiosis is no easy task and much of the time involves delayed gratification. When delayed gratification is necessary, it involves suffering through sacrifice. It takes energy and dedication to stop ourself from unhealthy but pleasurable activities in order to promote relationships that will be healthy in the long run.

CONSCIOUS SUFFERING

Anxiety must be considered the starting point of a
well lived life. It is an adventure that all humans go
through. To learn to be anxious in order that he may
not perish by having been in anxiety or by succumbing
in anxiety. Whoever has learned to be anxious in the
right way will have learned the ultimate.

—SØREN KIERKEGAARD

Suffering is the "state of undergoing pain, distress, or hardship" (New Oxford Dictionary, 2010, p. 1739). Any decision that negates the fruition of any particular need, will lead to some degree of suffering. With so many conflicting needs existing in many levels, some degree of suffering is inevitable. When our expectations for important matters does not match the present experience, we suffer. When a biological need must go unmet, we suffer. When we encounter friction in an important relationship, we suffer. When our actions do not meet the standards that we set for ourselves, we suffer. There is only so much in our control. The continual desire for what is yet to be, and seeming lack of appreciation for what actually exists, is so common that I would go so far as to say that this perpetual state of feeling as if the present is insufficient is a part of the human condition. In agreement with Buddhist and Christian wisdom, life is filled with suffering.

Buddhist psychology highlights two levels of suffering, the first is pain that is inevitable, whereas the second includes self-inflicted suffering. This is the level that is important to target, whereas the first level must be acknowledged and accepted. In the modern age, many individuals find themselves "bored" or anxious when left to their own devices. Alone one may find themselves infinitely distracting themselves through technology and/or with others consuming substances to find an excuse to be who they would like to be and express what they would like to express without filters. In other words, we attempt to anesthetize the suffering and we've gotten very good at it. But might this actually be maladaptive?

Although suffering is often initiated by something out of our control, we have the capacity to choose, whether or not we intend to, and how we would, bear the suffering. I use the term conscious suffering to indicate the conscious choice to engage with it as opposed to pushing it away. Davies (2012) makes note that suffering is relational and has been important in pivotal movements throughout history. "Casting off these anesthetics was therefore critical, since only when suffering was fully felt would they do something about removing its cause through social protest or revolution. Suffering was therefore the first step towards liberation from subjugation and towards the development of the self" (p. 37). The author further distinguishes between unproductive suffering and productive suffering (see Davies, 2012, Appendix 2). He borrows from anthropology, and likens stages of productive suffering to "transition rituals." These include:

STAGE	DESCRIPTION OF STAGES (P. 115)	DESCRIPTION OF THE STAGES OF SUFFERING
Separation	"Individuals are separated from their everyday lives and taken into the ritual site" (by an elder).	Suffering may trigger an inner tension that leads to isolation from typical ways of functioning. Individual is transported to new emotional atmosphere (p. 117).
Transition/ Transformation	"In the ritual site individuals are transformed by ritual elders."	Individuals "temporarily cast off their usual preoccupations, quit their station as a 'person of the world and fall by default 'down and out . . . in service of a more self-exploratory and transformative task'" (p. 121). "consciousness arises out of productive suffering" (p. 129).
Reincorporation	"The transformed individuals now re-enter society but at a higher level than the one they occupied before separation."	"Marks our return to the world as somewhat different from before" (p. 164).

He further cites research[*] on depressive realism and pessimism, noting that a depressive disposition and pessimistic outlook tend to be more accurate in their judgments about certain outcomes than their counterparts. A meta-analytic review (Moore & Fresco, 2012), found that there are positive biases in both depressed and nondepressed individuals, but less so in the nondepressed group (d = .14 vs d = .29) overall. Traditional studies that have been replicated in support of depressive realism find differences in sense of control, self-evaluation accuracy, and predictions of future success on skill-based tasks. Davies (2012) concludes that "productive suffering can raise consciousness of

---

[*] Lyn Abramson and Lauren Alloy (1979), Keedwell (2008)

things not apprehended before, such as other people suffering (which develops compassion), hidden personal factors (selfishness, undue confidence, or potentialities, etc.) or sociocultural factors (poverty, social oppression and injustice)" (Davies, 2012, p. 137). Might some experience of suffering help us be in better touch with reality?

In complementary paradigm, Jaspers (1965) introduced the concept of *limit situations*. Limit situations are perceived impasses characterized by antinomies, ambivalence, or conflicting experiences preventing development. These sorts of problems lead many to psychotherapy. Jaspers viewed these limit situations as deeply rooted in existence itself, and necessary for catalyzing maturation. There are several that he lists, including the necessity to *fight*, without which one falls into depression, and submission (e.g., wars, human rights, #MeToo movement); existential *guilt*, where one is not fulfilling their aspirations; *haphazard*, which involves confronting tragic fates as a result of chance; *finality in life*, both personal and universal; and *suffering* relating to present-day learned helplessness. Each of these limit situations may "destroy the home and makes it uninhabitable" (Mundt, 2014, p. 171). Three phases may be expected, according to Kick and Dietz (2008) (as cited in Mundt, 2014): (1) The individual continues to approach the problem from their existing framework, or they avoid, repress and/or manifest symptoms; (2) emotion amplifies due to ambivalence, and the individual is plunged into despair and/or anxiety; (3) the threshold is met, and psychopathology emerges, or one becomes capable of restructuring their internal system in such a way that address the problem with an adaptive novel solution. If the challenge is met, the individual achieves a wider consciousness and depth of feeling.

Stress, in this conceptualization, is a form of suffering, which can be conscious and controlled, or non-conscious and chaotic. It is particularly revealing to know that one of the most robust findings in psychology is that mild to moderate levels of stress are highly conducive for learning (Osborne, Pearson-Leary, & McNay, 2015). We also know that mild to moderate levels of stress to the body via physical exertion are beneficial to our health. And who does not remember the growth pains one endures as they begin to physically mature? It is only extreme levels of stress (such as life-threating events) and chronic stress (such as PTSD, clinical depression or anxiety) that may result in the degradation of neural circuitry. In this context, growth and suffering appears to have an intimate relationship. In fact, for Bion (Vermote, 2019), optimal levels of suffering are a requisite for the emergence of thought. To put it simply, not getting what we want (tolerating absence of a sense object, for example a substance or even a person), especially if it is unattainable or parasitic, forces us to think beyond our existing framework. Suffering promulgates thinking and subsequently, necessary action. In this context, suffering has adaptational value.

Stress is like the subjective tension of freedom expanding or constricting. When we productively suffer for an existential process, we stand up to forces of nature that may impede development, and align ourselves with those forces that encourage becoming. Increased tolerance corresponds to an expansion of inner time (e.g., delayed gratification) and space (e.g., independence from objects). Beginning this process requires us to make this conscious decision on a daily basis, until this choice becomes a habit that is deeply embedded in our neural architecture. Faith or trust in the direction of maturation is necessary for processes of expansion to outweigh constriction. By doing so, we empower character strength and the capacity to endure and transform stress. In this sense, conscious suffering can be considered the soil from which our character grows.

The capacity to tolerate suffering varies from individual to individual. Conscious suffering is about suffering in service of self-growth, adaptation, and the development of a deeper relationship with reality. In the face of suffering, people may react in two ways: (1) they may approach self-growth or self-diminishment or (2) they may avoid self-diminishment or self-growth. The worst response, of course, is to behave in ways that result in the approaching of self-diminishment. Sometimes approaching self-growth is just not within the realm of realistic possibility, so simply avoiding self-diminishment behaviors may be more plausible. At other times, we may default to the avoidance of self-growth, even with opportunities, due to anxiety. I think it is a responsibility for therapists to share with their clients that suffering is an inevitability, but they can choose what to suffer for. Part of the goal here is to help clients identify something that is worth suffering for.

There exists a story* of an emperor moth that is quite apt to conclude this section. It begins with a man finding the cocoon of an emperor moth. He notices that the hole through which the moth must emerge is tiny. As it struggles to emerge, the man, feeling sympathetic, decided to cut off what was left to

---

* The emperor moth story has been attributed to Robert Frost, but its source is hidden to my avail.

help it out. Consequently, the moth emerged underdeveloped, and as a result died before its time. The psychotherapeutic relationship is very much like the cocoon, and its struggle, akin to the suffering necessary for one to flourish.

NEURAL AND PSYCHOLOGICAL INTEGRATION IN PRACTICE

If we can stay with the tension of opposites long enough—sustain it, be true to it—we can sometimes become vessels within which the divine opposites come together and give birth to a new reality.

—MARIE-LOUISE VON FRANZ

Every time there is a conflict and the client makes a decision without thought, the client incurs a simultaneous negation of an aspect of themself. The response is thus not integrated; the client is not answering with the whole of their being. In relation to a craving, we find that it is itself a signal, a biological one seeking its reward. Areas of the brain associated with craving are cited in Table 8.2, involved with motivation, decision making, and environmental cues. Recent research has supported the role of the insula in cravings related to cigarette smoking (Naqvi et al., 2014). Naqvi and colleagues (2014) found that lesions in the insula disrupted cravings, increasing clients' likelihood of quitting. In Naqvi and colleagues' model, they proposed that the "central function of the insula in addiction is to represent the interoceptive effects of drug taking in the service of goal-directed drug seeking" (p. 11). Broadly speaking, interoception is the ability to consciously sense interior bodily signals. Of course, we cannot will the destruction of some area of our brain, nor should we if we could. We can only weaken maladaptive psychological signals; we can never eliminate them entirely (with the exception of the neurologically compromised).

Successfully tolerating a craving requires the suspension of tension, which requires a new combination of inhibition and activation. One way of doing so is by continually eliciting a response from the orbitofrontal cortex to strengthen descending inhibitory tracts in reaction to excessive limbic system activity (He, Rolls, Zhao, & Guo, 2019; Kober et al., 2010). This translates to saying *no* to a specific craving continually. However, we know that for most people with resistant habits, this is not good enough. From a treatment perspective, we could infer from insular alterations that we must involve interoception in order to unlearn the habit. Importantly, to sustain these changes there must also be a reappraisal or viewing the conflict in a new light. Doing so has been found to recruit the dorsolateral prefrontal cortex, dorsomedial prefrontal cortex, ventrolateral prefrontal cortex, and posterior parietal cortex (Buhle et al., 2014). Part of the difficulty is that cravings are mediated by inputs from circuits related to reward, identity, motivation, and environmental pressures. It thus often requires more than mere willpower to stop. Thus, to unlearn a habit we must also have introspection, interoception, and a strategic behavioral and environmental system. Moreover, giving up on a severe craving for a long-term goal requires sacrifice and a degree of suffering. We will not consciously sacrifice and suffer through something unless it somehow benefits the self to a certain threshold or if some goal is perceived as much more important than selfish pleasure (i.e., vital signals). Conscious suffering plays a large role in healing, whether it is related to an addiction or not.

We now arrive at the question, how might we use introspection and interoception to successfully tolerate a craving? There are many ways this may be facilitated, which I will examine now. In session, a client is asked to *hold the tension*, and while the tension is being suspended, the clinician can facilitate the process by actively examining the two sides that are giving rise to the tension. The methods used for examining the two sides are for the purpose of improving the likelihood of navigating past the whirlpools of craving.

Due to the ample amount of literature on strategic behavioral and environmental plans and medications, I will focus on an area that is less discussed. I am referring to psychological strategies to assist with suspending tension successfully in service of symbiosis. It is helpful to clarify that the precursor to a craving toward something is an urge, and in many cases, it is not so much an inappropriate urge as an urge directed at inappropriate objects. When a craving is experienced, we might choose to focus not on the object of craving but the urge itself. Generally speaking, an urge may be understood as a psychophysical representation correlated to an operating system in the brain that attempts to direct the nervous system in some way. One helpful reframe is to view our craving not as a hindrance, but an opportunity to assert our freedom and empower our cortical functions.

Jung (1973) utilized a technique he called *active imagination*, whereby he reached meditative or trancelike states and would engage his conscious self-process with various expressions within himself via writing and drawings. This first method is an adaptation of this technique. Imagination overall, has been found to elicit descending signals from the parietal cortex to the occipital cortex contrary to visual perception which tends to be from the bottom-up (Dentico et al., 2014). The technique is supposed to act as a theoretical bridge enabling consciousness to interact with unconscious contents. The following will be an adaptation of his method to include recent findings in the context of cravings.

Tension arises from the urge and our conscious experience. Timing the tension is advised in cases of addiction and other relevant conflicts. The average amount of time a craving (tobacco) lasts is about 6–10 minutes (Heishman, Singleton, & Moolchan, 2003). Everyone will vary, but it is well known that cravings come in waves. This can be helpful because it allows people to quantify how long they may have to suffer when the craving arises. If the client is in session with the clinician, the clinician may assume this responsibility and set a timer. Ask the client to indicate when the urge has stopped, after which the clinician will stop the timer. The client will then continue these exercises independently, timing themselves as they go along to find out the average time their cravings last.

1. The client begins by sensing the urge. The client drops into the urge without fulfilling it and begins to describe its sensations. As the client focuses on it, the client *watches* the urge from the perspective of consciousness.

2. The client is then asked to label the sensation and any accompanying feelings. This in and of itself may be helpful in reducing limbic activation, as has been found in studies examining *affect labeling* (Lieberman et al., 2007).

3. The next step is to give, or to allow a form to emerge resulting in a partitioning of a diffuse experience. By form, I mean to literally encourage the client's creativity in associating an image with it. This will be helpful at the subsequent times the craving arises, as the client may conjure up this form again in the future and engage in this exer-

cise more easily. The instant separation of the craving from themself may be an added bonus.

4. The client is then asked to engage in dialogue (with curiosity and openness) with the urge in its represented form.

Theoretically, by engaging in this activity, the open dialogue would be engaging the client's cortical systems with subcortical systems, with the hope of strengthening descending inhibitory tracts from the prefrontal cortex (He et al., 2019). This cross talk may be amplified further by the continued holding of bodily sensations to slowly become more and more tolerable. There is simultaneously an exploration of other subsystems that these symbols might be engaging. Eventually, what is anticipated is a functional relationship between these systems overall: an adaptive integration. If the tension is held long enough, the capacity to bear stress increases and there emerges a new experience and relationship that integrates the opposites. As Marion Woodman (1982) so elegantly put it,

Integration requires chewing the primitive material in order to digest it. To bring consciousness to the instincts, to allow the ego to recognize them and yet not act them out impulsively, is to put the rider on the horse and let the rider make the decision. (p. 91)

A similar method was conceived by Gestalt therapists. Their method is more experiential and pertains more to dream analysis (Yontef, 1993), yet it can be adapted to more conscious systems. The client is asked to present the dreams as if they were happening now and asked to engage in dialogue with different characters in the dream, even taking on the roles of these characters by perceiving the world through their minds. In the context of a conscious urge, the client may be asked to speak from that urge, giving it a voice to better understand where its roots may lie.

If the compulsion is found to be too challenging to hold, I recommend engaging in cognitive enhancement tasks, targeting inhibitory control (Berkman, Kahn, & Merchant, 2014), utilizing meditative techniques, or supplanting the tension with exercise or another activity. Of course, in severe cases, we cannot deny the utility of certain medications, especially when reward systems are already highly reinforced and there is an abundance of available resources that may trigger such arousal; in that case behavioral activation would be of extreme importance as well.

Humans have multiple layers of functioning. We have primitive drives, such as aggression and sexuality, and more advanced forms of functioning, such as logic and metacognition. If we consider these functions as a means to an end and generalize the goal of specific behaviors produced from these drives, it may help to simplify what may be of most benefit when these functions are lived out. I, too, am of the mind that a balanced—and I would add integrated—attitude would result in the highest level of benefits (Table 8.2). To Jung (1969), part of this process entails the integration of the shadow, or aspects of ourselves that we reject. Integration does not entail acting out all impulses and desires, it means learning how to hold the tides of primitive affect and redistribute their energy for something meaningful. History has taught us that humans are capable of supreme evil as well as supreme virtue. The recognition that we are capable of such atrocities allows us to not succumb to them, to recognize them in others, and to have the courage to take preventative measures.

TABLE 8.2: Integrated Response

	BALANCED QUALITIES	EXCESS VIA CRAVING FOR POWER, GRATIFICATION, OR DYSREGULATION OF NEURAL CIRCUITRY
Primitive drives (Aggression, sexuality)	Attack or defend for survival Procreation, adequate sex life	Physical abuse, violence Sexual abuse, violence. Addictions, infidelity
Advanced functions (Consciousness, logic)	Effective future planning High-level negotiation tactics Emotional intelligence Guided expression of impulses Delayed gratification Empathy, compassion Spontaneity, play	Manipulation Exploitation Emotional abuse Poor impulse control Rigidity Burnout Chaos

Benefits of Integrating Qualities

- Recognizing the exploitation of self and others. Energy is rerouted from survival mechanisms to increase potency for effective and measured actions. Increased assertiveness, effective use of aggression.

- Sacrificing aspects of self that hinder development. Suppression of immediate gratification in service of long-term benefits and well-being.

- Rerouting excess sexual energy as motivation to find a partner or for creativity in sex life.

- Expression of sexual and aggressive tendencies for the creation of art, improving physical endurance, or other forms of meaning.

Davies (2012) suggested that " . . . aggressive powers are not inherently 'destructive' or 'constructive,' but as 'destructive' or 'constructive' depending upon how they are expressed. Aggression becomes destructive when it is hampered from removing, for whatever reason, the impediments of realization, for this leads to its flowing out in the wrong direction—either towards ourselves or indiscriminately towards others. It becomes constructive on the other hand, when it is aimed at removing certain life-impeding obstacles to the realization of our tendency for a greater life" (p. 97).

MAINTAINING SUSPENSION OF CONFLICT: PREVENTING ACTING OUT

Remember:

- Suspending tension is not necessarily a hindrance, but an opportunity to assert your freedom, empower your frontal lobes, and advance your functioning.
- When limbic activity is prevalent, there is a narrowing of awareness, resulting in poorer decisions. Therefore, have a list of reasons at your disposal to read over again in moments of vulnerability.
- Activities: Exercise, meditate, journal, introspect, art.
- "This too shall pass."

Ask yourself:

- It may feel good, but does it live well? (Hayes, 2009)
- Can I survive through this? Will holding the tension kill me?
- What will my suffering bring me?

••

Information travels through many veils and may exist on one, two, or several different planes of human experience. We all have had the experience of gaining wisdom from a past experience or learning an intellectual concept that we know would make our lives better, yet we have been unable to put it into practice. It is not until the lesson has permeated every dimension, which sometimes requires several instances of trial and error, that we are able to do so.

In a useful metaphor, Ouspensky (2001) asserted that if one:

> gives way to all his desires, or panders to them, there will be no inner struggle, in him, no "friction," no fire. But if for the sake of attaining a definite aim, he struggles with the desires that hinder him—he will then create a fire which will gradually transform his inner world into a single whole. (p. 43)

It is important to continue learning about ourselves, others, and the world through experience. It is dangerous to believe that being mindful is sufficient to work through entangled tension and psychological turmoil. Although mindfulness may be a helpful and powerful tool, it is still a simple method to better orient ourself while working through these issues. It is easy to conceive of a person who is mindful, but whose mind is full of veils propagating maladaptive signals. The raw psychological materials to work with would then be impotent. Even meaning systems evolve with time, and what we prioritized ten years ago may be vastly different from what is important to us today. We learn through various mediums, including education, self-reflection, relationships, play, and psychotherapy.

One narrative sequence that has spoken to me, the Greek story of Hephaistos the blacksmith, was brought to light by Murray Stein (2015). In particular, Stein interprets the duties of a blacksmith, with fire representing "the fires of creativity" (p. 132), and the resultant forging of divine objects for the gods as the result of his skill in containing fire and using it and other materials strategically to create something beautiful. We all hold tension of different kinds, whose source stems from some unmet will to pleasure, meaning, power, relationship, and truth. Humans are diverse, and my experience working with others has taught me that not only are all these drives present in everyone, but also they differ in their presence in different stages of life. Tension intimates the potential for transformation or collapse. Yet transformation does not necessarily imply one that is positive, nor does a collapse imply something negative. Results are uncertain, and this is the challenge.

It is both comforting and discomforting to know that we are all born with the full repertoire of life. The gradations of which depend on genetics, relationships, and personal pursuits. We begin with the seeds of psychopathy, narcissism, and instability, as well as that of virtue, compassion, and altruism. The flow of becoming provides us with continual opportunities to nurture select seeds, steering the direction of what continually comes into being. Part of the solution lies in the awareness of those seeds which, if nourished, may bring immediate gratification at the expense of others. The second half of the solution relates to acting strategically, so as to harness the power of these parasitic affective-cognitive structures towards protection, self-defense, and offense, if ever needed. This is no easy task, as it requires considerable amount of self-awareness, creativity, behavioral planning, and moral deliberation and grit. Although the process begins with acknowledgment and acceptance of the existence of these energies, the behavioral expression is what nurtures seeds, and this process, when not conducive to our living must be inhibited. Primal energic experiences of predation, aggression and sexuality unfettered become disciplined, inwardly harnessed in service of meaning. To actively build on the world of truth, is a conscious decision, and what it takes to become a modern-day knight.

CYCLING

Perhaps all the dragons in our lives are princesses
who are only waiting to see us act, just once, with
beauty and courage. Perhaps everything that
frightens us is, in its deepest essence, something
helpless that wants our love.

—RAINER MARIA RILKE

Stressful experiences may lead to a form of mental colorblindness. Consider the analogy of our four types of photoreceptors: rods, S-cones, M-cones, and L-cones corresponding to biological, psychological, sociocultural, and existential processes. The susceptibility to polarizing into select BPSE processes are amplified in the face of challenges. Vision is compromised if we were only utilizing rods; with the full spectrum of color vision being redistributed once signals from other photoreceptors are functional.

The technique I am adding is what I call *cycling*. It is an exercise that promotes integration through the discharge and/or metabolization of energy and information. One may use the chart on Appendix A to help localize a client's level of psychological development post-session, in order to guide the decision to engage in this exercise. This may be particularly useful to engage alpha functioning, and if the client's development of thought is localizable between movements 2–5. Essentially, it is a semi-structured method involving the *cycling* of information within BPSE processes while suspending some form of tension related to a resistant obstacle. It thus relates to groups of techniques guided by the goal of integration. Modern approaches might include Siegel's (2012) technique of asking the clients to process the sensations, images, feelings, and thoughts (SIFT) associated with tension and to explore each of these dimensions in depth. From the perspective of the clinician, Cozolino (2014) suggested the method he calls *shuttling*, whereby a therapist pivots their attention between their psychological, physical, and social cognitive processes (imagined perspective of the client) in order to more fully explore the emergent possibilities of information.

The intent of cycling is to actively elicit (or cycle through) responses from distributed networks throughout cortical and subcortical neural regions and the autonomic nervous system. The following technique is an exercise anchored in imagery that may assist with the metabolization of information spanning sensorimotor domains to the symbolic. The exercise targets functions correlated to specific regions of interest (ROI): (1) bodily sensations (ROI: somatosensory cortex, autonomic nervous system); (2) interoception (ROI: insula); (3) images (ROI: precuneus, frontal, and DMN); (4) emotion (ROI: limbic); and (5) verbal expression (ROI: frontal-temporal lobes).

Cycling begins with an image derived from a particular problem. Mental imagery evokes a vast array of input signals from and output signals to neural real estate dedicated to sense impressions, memory, emotion, and higher order symbolic processing (see Skottnik & Linden, 2019). This makes the use of imagery a strong candidate for mediating, processing, and integrating information.

The act of symbolizing a particular trouble builds psychological distance that may assist with an objective deconstruction and reappraisal of inner relationships. Building a healthy distance from emotions is in congruence with *cognitive defusion* in ACT, mindfulness approaches, focusing, the psychodynamic observing ego, and the analytical stance during active imagination.

One would begin the exercise after discussing a resistant problem. The instructions may be as follows:

"I would like you to begin by closing your eyes. Take a few deep breaths, and clear your mind of any clutter. In this free space, picture a blank canvas. Let your mind wander on that canvas. Direct the wandering toward the general atmosphere of the problem: this may include any related sensations, feelings, and thoughts. Continue until your mind settles on an image that best represents the problem at hand. When you have it in mind, describe it to me, and let me know what it means to you."

After determining the symbolic meaning of the image:

"All problems evolve; I'd like you to bring the image to life by allowing it to move and evolve as is necessary. Keep this in mind as I ask you some questions."

A. Are you sensing any bodily experiences as you hold it in mind?
B. What is the emotional atmosphere to it?
C. Let's return our focus to the image, have there been any changes?

"Keep this living image in mind, it may be helpful for us to revisit it in the future."

One may notice that the instructions stress spontaneity as opposed to a conscious construction of an image. The purpose of this is to access information reverberating around the frontiers of conscious and unconscious processes. The use of the word *atmosphere* is meant to evoke the broadening of one's search for associated processing. This attempts to touch on activity in Bion's *contact barrier,* the Markov blanket, preconscious, and/or border zones as described by Gendlin. Neuropsychologically, mind wandering is intended to recruit the

DMN. In this case, we are engaging the client in a brief instance of open monitoring (consciously watching their minds wander) on the blank canvas, which is intended to create a psychological distance from their problem.

Cycling begins with a shared mental image for the clinician and client to refer to throughout treatment. The clinician should ask questions until the symbolic value of the image has been made clear. Asking what objects represent and how they are interacting with one another may be a good start. Thus, the patient moves from engaging the DMN to intentional higher order symbolic systems (frontal activity) and abstract reasoning. The patient synthesizes a meaningful image which becomes a symbol for a specified problem. The clinician may use the mental image as an anchor, returning to it when clinically relevant. Questions may undergo "re-cycling" as novelty is introduced into the mental image. Cycling can be seen as an activity that assists with the tolerance of suffering and frustration.

The subsequent questions are quite self-explanatory and may be elaborated by need. The following mnemonic may help you remember the entire process: I-SEE = Image, Sensation, Emotion, Evolution (exercise concludes with the evolved image). For Self-Directed questions, see Appendix H. It is important to precede processing somatic experiences and emotions with an emphasis on the dynamic nature of the mental image, enabling the image to evolve with the problem. In addition, it preemptively foreshadows changes, potentially instilling hope.

Question A shifts awareness to exteroceptive and interoceptive somatic experiences in relation to the mental image, processing them as needed. This may be beneficial for those with especially strong visceral and bodily reactions, with the mental representation further acting as a system insulating overwhelming bodily experiences. In Question B, the word *atmosphere* is introduced again in relation to emotions. Here the idea is to reinforce some objective distance, enabling the patient to have the feeling without identifying with it, thus viewing it with more clarity. It is also meant to "widen the net" that is being cast. Once the focus on emotion and somatic experiences have been processed, the clinician returns to the image, asking the patient to note any potential changes that have occurred throughout.

Psychodynamic-oriented clinicians may be interested in adding some of their own reveries and knowledge of mythology to amplify the interpretation of the image as it relates to the patient's disposition, history, and current experiences. This approach would focus on enhancing the productivity of its interpretation, further facilitating a co-construction of new narratives. CBT-oriented clinicians may ask patients to rate their level of distress before and after the exercise. They may track the progression and change according to different versions of the image that emerge from session to session.

The exercise capitalizes on a state of stress that may facilitate neuroplasticity. Neuroplasticity is sensitive to a sense of urgency and focus, mild to moderate levels of stress, activating mood and cognition, and the co-construction of new personal narratives (Cozolino, 2010). This is the importance of introducing this exercise at a heightened state of arousal. Theoretically, cycling will activate several different operating systems within the brain, potentially facilitating a process of psychological symbiosis and neural integration. The structure comes from BPSE, which, when explored in depth, can help collapse conflicting responses into its supporting subsystems that are not readily apparent, further providing an overarching system that includes processing of all dimensions. Clinical intuition, spontaneity, and techniques form the line of questioning. Open-ended questions that evoke elaboration are advised.

Sometimes cycling may be short, other times long. Cycling offers a cognitive strategy. It is simple enough that the client may learn and adopt this form of processing chaotic feelings or tensions when they are present. The necessity to switch between modes of thinking may additionally prove useful in enhancing cognitive flexibility, a necessary executive function for anyone who has become rigid due to their circumstances. Indeed, there has been some investigation into how psychotherapy can improve clients' cognition (Hui-Li et al., 2019).

Dialogue

The patient was a 45-year-old female executive, with a tendency to intellectualize. She presented to my office at the suggestion of her friends and family, to assist with processing a divorce. She would have bouts of emotional discharge that would last a few seconds, then revert to an intellectual conversation. My first approach was to ask questions to "stay with the emotion," but those attempts remained as attempts. She was used to taking control of situations where she had lost power.

I decided to try a different approach outside of rational thinking, and introduced cycling. During the initial phase of cycling, the patient's mind had wandered quite quickly to an image of a pit that descended into darkness. This was the best representation of her problem. She stated that the darkness represented the emptiness that she felt inside with her husband gone.

(**C** = Clinician, **P**= Patient)

C: All problems evolve; I'd like you to bring the image to life by allowing it to move and evolve as is necessary. Keep this in mind as I ask you some questions.

P: Okay.

C: Are you sensing any bodily experiences as you hold the image in mind?

P: There is this deep empty feeling at the pit of my stomach.

C: Could you tell me more about this empty feeling?

P: It's almost like nausea, without anything to throw up. *(very symbolic; she is well defended, repressing unpleasant emotions)*

C: Is there a color to the emptiness you are experiencing?

P: Just black, the darkness of a black hole, it's the dark pit.

C: Is there a sound to it? *(integrating other senses to amplify awareness)*

P: Hmm . . . theres a ringing sound, like when you've come back from a loud bar into a completely silent room.

C: Stay with these experiences for a bit *(helping process through awareness and increase her capacity to tolerate painful experiences)*

P: *(10-15 seconds)* Okay . . . it's unpleasant. *(she reached her threshold)*

C: Listen to your body. If this emptiness had a message for you, what would it say?

P: That my husband is gone, and I will never see him again. *(said this void of emotion)*

C: Are there any emotions you can detect within you right now?

P: Well . . . anger, I'm holding onto anger.

C: Tell me more about the anger you are holding onto.

P: I'm just holding tightly onto the comfort that was, and the fact that I don't want to let it go angers me. I try my best not to let it affect me, since he is not worth feeling this way for. *(there is a hint of aggression as she ended the statement)*.

C: Anything else in the emotional atmosphere?

P: Well, there's a sort of desperation. I am worried about never finding another person again, which is why I want him back. At the same time, I know it's not worth it.

C: It must be difficult, holding onto such conflicting feelings.

P: Yes, the right answer is clear to me, but it's followed by fear, I think.

C: How do you feel this desperation?

P: I don't. I know it's there, but I am not feeling it really. I think I should feel it, but I can only sense its presence from a distance.

C: Where is the desperation stored?

P: I keep it stored away in my mind.

C: Okay, let's return to the image of the dark pit. I simply want you to observe it now, and let me know if anything changes.

P: Okay. *(about 15 seconds of silence)* It's getting blurry *(5 seconds)* . . . and now I am seeing things coming out of it. They are like geometric figures floating up to the surface *(something is coming out from nothing).*

C: Stay with it for a while longer, and feel free to open your eyes when you feel comfortable doing so.

After about 30 seconds, she opened her eyes. Her eyes had a hint of melancholy and the presence in the room had changed. To me it felt calm yet heavy, something needed to be unburdened. I often felt a weight of sadness for her and at this juncture I felt sadness without weight. When I asked her how she was feeling, her eyes suddenly welled up and she started crying. She cried in silence, speechless, and continued for a duration that exceeded all other attempts. She subsequently reported feeling temporarily at peace.

We concluded the session, and I simply told her: "Keep this living image in mind, it may be helpful for us to revisit it in the future."

Throughout the session we both referred back to the image during relevant times. It had undergone several changes, eventually leaving the dark pit entirely. Other images were also generated in relation to other problems. The idea crossed my mind of her having an interior art gallery of live paintings, some of which had been completed, and others which were still in the process of maturing.

CONCLUDING REFLECTIONS

It is something to be able to paint a particular
picture . . . more glorious to carve and paint the very
atmosphere through which we look . . . we are tasked
to make our lives, even in their details, worthy of
contemplation of our most elevated and critical hour.

—HENRY THOREAU

Processes of human experience and the veils within form the very fabric from which we operate. The non-conscious interactions between sense-perception and our expectations continually erupt into the beauty of natural forms, as if in revolt against their fragility and limitations. The challenges our species has endured led to the incorporation of higher levels of consciousness, enabling us to see beyond the visible. In turn, the "raw" material of reality, now witnessed in higher degrees and from multiple dimensions, conforms to the internal biases embedded in veils: a responsibility, a price paid for the gift of complexity. Every day we seek to align and manage the variety of voices we hear from different systems operating within us. We sway between passive and active positions when navigating our lives. We act, deceived by internal signals that shout, confusing that which is loud with that which is adaptive. Sometimes, heeding the beckon of the softest whisper is necessary in order for us to blossom. The consequences of our actions reciprocate, either confirming or humbling the certainty of our decisions. Experiential truths are further unveiled, as if evolving with the clarity of signals we receive. Throughout our life span, demands change, challenges are met, and our priorities shift. As we mature, we become more adept at discerning which signals are healthy for us. We learn to distinguish between the appropriate and subtle to not-so-subtle excesses that parts of our being desire in specific contexts. Many times, signals clash, providing us with the necessary tension to learn and grow, just as dissonance may accentuate mellifluous rhythms in a musical piece. Conscious suffering is a necessary struggle, that while unpleasant, moves us toward a proper balance between authenticity to life and authenticity to self. We co-create our lives in a mystery, seeking union between objective truth and character truths in our efforts to root ourselves in what seems to be an ever-changing ground. Signals from multiple processes converge in our awareness, in part determining the path we will take, and in part inviting us to make that determination.

    Our craving for certainty has yielded a culture ever fearful of uncertainty. Yet it is uncertainty that teaches us to think, enabling freedom, movement, and growth. As Siegel (2012) conceptualized, mental disorders are broadly a result of too much chaos or too much rigidity, with the optimal flow being somewhere in between. Some degree of chaos—or better yet uncertainty—allows room for growth, and some degree of rigidity—or better yet structure—creates the stability to endure a challenge. Yet, it is *not in knowing* where we find ourselves rooting for the hero, as much as how the hero defines his own truth in the face of *not knowing*. And it is through these actions that he attains what Joseph Campbell (1949) refers to as *the ultimate boon*.

Consciousness is an orphan; born from darkness, in a land it believes to be foreign. In darkness, it is light, and is thus granted with vision. On its path, it notices that certain experiences and actions enlivened its light, whereas others dimmed its brilliance. It also finds that it is the friction, or resistance from these experiences that amplifies its light within. After many trials and errors, it decided friction, although unpleasant, was necessary. Choosing to pursue radiance over luster, it based its existence on actions that nourished its light. On its journey, it finds the land is within a kingdom, that kingdom in a country, and that country in a world. Its world is but one world, populated by a myriad of lifeforms, connected to and sustained by billions of other worlds. As its radiance grew, its spark became a sun, and it realized that the world had always been its home, and every entity its parents.

Afterword

BY DANIEL J. SIEGEL, M.D.

If you are reading these words, you have likely either completed reading Aldrich Chan's in-depth tour of the science of mental life and would like to reflect on the experience a bit more, or perhaps you have turned to the end of the book to gain some input on whether or not to read this comprehensive exploration of the mind and know something of its relevance for your clinical practice, or your life. For these and many other possible reasons, let me have the honor of offering you a few reflections on this important work, *Reassembling Models of Reality: Theory and Clinical Practice*.

I have known the author, as a student and now colleague, for many years. Aldrich Chan is a deep thinker who assembles many perspectives into his approach to working with patients in his neuropsychology practice. Well-versed in the science and philosophy of mind, experienced as a clinician working in mental health, our capable guide curates a tour of the fundamental processes that shape how energy flow becomes constructed into information that forms what we perceive, how we feel, ways we think and believe, and even our organized approaches to how we behave. These processes that transform energy—such as sound or light—from outside the body into the electrochemical energy patterns within the brains of our body—in our gut, heart, and head—act like constructive filters that shape virtually everything we experience in our conscious and even nonconscious mental lives.

As a therapist and someone who has worked in the cross-disciplinary framework of Interpersonal Neurobiology for decades, I can say that Chan's work is a welcome addition to our Norton Professional IPNB library, offering an innovative way of synthesizing across various disciplines and offering mental health professionals a unique and important way of deepening their clinical understanding of the mind and enhancing their therapeutic interventions.

As human beings, we often take for granted that what we perceive and feel is accurate; what we think correct. But as therapists working with our own mind, and the minds our clients, we know from direct experience that mental life is shaped by both internal processes, such as the networks of the nervous system, and by relational processes, such as those in one-on-one connections we have with each other or within our experience of belonging (or not) to our larger communities and culture in which we live. Here in this book, you have a deep dive into a wide range of sciences that explore the "veils" of the mind: the mental filters that shape our fundamental ways of experiencing being alive.

Here is a quote from the book itself that exemplifies this goal: "In its regulation of information, the brain focuses and limits the *fabric of reality*. What follows is a unique mental expression of reality in every individual brain."

Our work as therapists is to help the individuals we work with open their lives to new, more adaptive, health-promoting ways of living. As psychotherapists, we begin with the "mind" of the person, focusing on their emotional life, the sensations of their body, their patterns of thought, their habits of behavior. We dive deeply into their memories of experience, their focus of attention, their narratives that reveal what has meaning for them and how they've come to make sense—or not—of their lived experience.

The veils of the mind are the filters that shape everything initially derived from the most fundamental inputs of how we receive sensation (from the outside world or from the interior signals of the body) to how we perceive, conceive, and believe that then shape how we make meaning, create identity, and belonging in the world. These "top-down" mental constructions are ubiquitous in human life; and this book will take you on a fabulous, detailed, multidisciplinary journey into what we know now about these filtering constructive processes that don't just shape our experience of reality. They can, at times, imprison us in patterns of adaptation from the past.

The human brain is open to change across the lifespan based on the experiences that induce neuroplastic changes in the connections, and then function, of the brain itself. One form of experience that shapes neuroplasticity is relational communication; another form is self-reflection. Here you have learned, or will learn, how to shape your therapeutic relationship and invite the processes of self-reflection that can change the engrained filters that may be imprisoning the client's mental life within unhealthy cognitive and emotional habits, limiting their experience of well-being.

What rests beneath imprisoning filters? What life can we expect when we come to see more clearly, learn to live more authentically, love more fully? One can propose that the chaos and rigidity (or both) that we hear from our patients, the patterns of the ways clients suffer in their lives that bring them to therapy, are due to a blockage in something we can simply call "integration." Integration is the linking of differentiated parts of a system, and when present, it emerges with a sense of harmony that is flexible, adaptive, coherent, energized, and stable. Integration, then, can be seen as the basis of mental health. Opening the veils of the mind that are leading to chaos and rigidity enables new veils (new and more flexible filters) to be created that are more integrative—and therefore more health-promoting. The result? A more integrative life in which, more than simply reducing symptoms of chaos and rigidity, you as a therapist are inviting a more fulfilling, meaningful, connected life.

One of the restrictive filters constructed in modern times is the illusion of a separate self, reinforced by social media, inadvertently encouraged by education and even parenting, and sadly promoted by some views of science that "mind is only what the brain does"; that mind is simply a synonym for brain activity. When we use the tools of this book to reveal these restricting veils and instead open to a more integrative experience of *selfing*—of becoming a self more like a dynamic ever-changing verb than a fixed noun—the process of psychotherapy offers the opportunity to live a more vibrant and connected life, one filled not only with purpose and presence, but also with compassion and resilience. This book is a resource that will help you discover, uncover, and liberate your clients from restrictive veils as they learn, with your guidance, to reassemble them in more integrative ways that will be of benefit to them, and to the larger relational worlds in which we all live.

References

Abela, A. R., Duan, Y., & Chudasama, Y. (2015). Hippocampal interplay with the nucleus accumbens is critical for decisions about time. *European Journal of Neuroscience, 42*(5), 2224–2233. https://doi.org/10.1111/ejn.13009

Abramov, I., Gordon, J., Feldman, O., & Chavarga, A. (2012a). Sex and vision I: Spatio-temporal resolution. *Biology of Sex Differences, 3*(1). https://doi.org/10.1186/2042-6410-3-20

Abramov, I., Gordon, J., Feldman, O., & Chavarga, A. (2012b). Sex and vision II: Color appearance of monochromatic lights. *Biology of Sex Differences, 3*(1). https://doi.org/10.1186/2042-6410-3-21

Ackerman, J. M., Nocera, C. C., & Bargh, J. A. (2010). Incidental haptic sensations influence social judgments and decisions. *Science, 328*(5986), 1712–1715. https://doi.org/10.1126/science.1189993

Adolphs, R. (2013). The biology of fear. *Current Biology, 23*(2), R79–R93. https://doi.org/10.1016/j.cub.2012.11.055

Alcaro, A., & Carta, S. (2019). The "Instinct" of imagination. A neuro-ethological approach to the evolution of the reflective mind and its application to psychotherapy. *Frontiers in Human Neuroscience, 12*. https://doi.org/10.3389/fnhum.2018.00522

Alcaro, A., Carta, S., & Panksepp, J. (2017). The affective core of the self: A neuro-archetypical perspective on the foundations of human (and animal) subjectivity. *Frontiers in Psychology, 8*. https://doi.org/10.3389/fpsyg.2017.01424

Algoe, S. B., & Haidt, J. (2009). Witnessing excellence in action: The "other-praising" emotions of elevation, gratitude, and admiration. *The Journal of Positive Psychology, 4*(2), 105–127. https://doi.org/10.1080/17439760802650519

Allen, J. B., Kenrick, D. T., Linder, D. E., & McCall, M. A. (1989). Arousal and attraction: A response-facilitation alternative to misattribution and negative-reinforcement models. *Journal of Personality and Social Psychology, 57*(2), 261–270. https://doi.org/10.1037/0022-3514.57.2.261

American Psychiatric Association. (2013). *Diagnostic and statistical manual of mental disorders* (5th ed.). Washington, DC: Author.

Amit, E., Hoeflin, C., Hamzah, N., Fedorenko, E. (2017). An asymmetrical relationship between verbal and visual thinking: converging evidence from behavior and fMRI. *Neuroimage, 152*, 619–627.

Amodio, D. M., Devine, P. G., & Harmon-Jones, E. (2008). Individual differences in the regulation of intergroup bias: The role of conflict monitoring and neural signals for control. *Journal of Personality and Social Psychology, 94*(1), 60–74. https://doi.org/10.1037/0022-3514.94.1.60

Andrews-Hanna, J., Reidler, J., Sepulcre, J., Pulin, R., & Buckner, R. (2010). Functional-anatomic fractionation of the brain's default network. *Neuron, 65*, 550–562. https://doi.org/10.1016/j.neuron.2010.02.005

Anticevic, A., Cole, M. W., Murray, J. D., Corlett, P. R., Wang, X. J., & Krystal, J. H. (2012). The role of default network deactivation in cognition and disease. *Trends in Cognitive Sciences, 16*(12), 584–592. https://doi.org/10.1016/j.tics.2012.10.008

Apocalypse. (2010). In *The New Oxford American Dictionary* (3rd ed.). New York, NY: Oxford University Press.

Arendt, H. (1971). *The life of the mind*. New York, NY: Harcourt.

Aristotle. (1943). *On man in the universe* (L. R. Loomis, ed.). Roslyn, NY: Walter J. Black.

Aronson, E. (2010). *Social psychology*. Upper Saddle River, NJ: Prentice Hall.

A-Tjak, J. G., Davis, M. L., Morina, N., Powers, M. B., Smits, J. A., & Emmelkamp,

P. M. (2015). A meta-analysis of the efficacy of acceptance and commitment therapy for clinically relevant mental and physical health problems. *Psychotherapy and Psychosomatics, 84*(1), 30–36. https://doi.org/10.1159/000365764

Austin, J. H. (1998). *Zen and the brain: Toward an understanding of meditation and consciousness.* Boston, MA: MIT Press.

Auvray, M., Myin, E., & Spence, C. (2010). The sensory-discriminative and affective-motivational aspects of pain. *Neuroscience and Biobehavioral Reviews, 34,* 214–223. https://doi.org/10.1016/j.neubiorev.2008.07.008

Auvray, M., & Spence, C. (2008). The multisensory perception of flavor. *Consciousness and Cognition, 17*(3), 1016–1031. https://doi.org/10.1016/j.concog.2007.06.005

Aviera, A. (2002). Culturally sensitive and creative therapy with Latino clients. *California Psychologist, 35*(4), 18–25. Retrieved from https://latinxtherapy.com/wp-content/uploads/2018/11/aviera.pdf

Baer, R. A. (2003). Mindfulness training as a clinical intervention: A conceptual and empirical review. *Clinical Psychology: Science and Practice, 10*(2), 125–143. https://doi.org/10.1093/clipsy.bpg015

Bahcall, N. (2015). Hubble's Law and the expanding universe. *Proceedings of the National Academy of Sciences, 112*(11), 3173–3175. https://doi.org/10.1073/pnas.1424299112

Baird, B., Smallwood, J., Mrazek, M. D., Kam, J. W., Franklin, M. S., & Schooler, J. W. (2012). Inspired by distraction: Mind wandering facilitates creative incubation. *Psychological Science, 23*(10), 1117–1122. https://doi.org/10.1177/0956797612446024

Baker, M. D., Jr., Sloan, H. N., Hall, A. D., Leo, J., & Maner, J. K. (2015). Mating and memory: Can mating cues enhance cognitive performance? *Evolutionary Psychology, 13*(4), 1–6. https://doi.org/10.1177/1474704915623280

Balaev, V., Ivanitsky, A., Portnova, G., Tetereva, A., Ushakov, V., & Marynova, O. (2020). Longitudinal changes of resting-state functional connectivity of amygdala following fear learning and extinction. *International Journal of Psychophysiology, 149,* 15–24. https://doi.org/10.1016/j.ijpsycho.2020.01.002

Barazza, J., & Zak, P. (2013). Oxytocin instantiates empathy and produces prosocial behaviors. In E. Choleris, D. W. Pfaff, & M. Kavaliers (Eds.), *Oxytocin, vasopressin and related peptides in the regulation of behavior.* New York, NY: Cambridge University Press.

Barrett, D. (2007). An evolutionary theory of dreams and problem-solving. In D. L. Barrett & P. McNamara (Eds.), *The new science of dreaming: Cultural and theoretical perspectives on dreaming* (Vol. 3, pp. 133–153). New York, NY: Praeger/Greenwood.

Barrett, F. S., & Griffiths, R. R. (2017). Classic hallucinogens and mystical experiences: Phenomenology and neural correlates. In A. L. Halberstadt, F. X. Vollenweider, & D. E. Nichols (Eds.), *Behavioral neurobiology of psychedelic drugs* (pp. 393–430). https://doi.org/10.1007/7854_2017_474

Barrett, F. S., Johnson, M. W., & Griffiths, R. R. (2015). Validation of the revised Mystical Experience Questionnaire in experimental sessions with psilocybin. *Journal of Psychopharmacology, 29*(11), 1182–1190. https://doi.org/10.1177/0269881115609019

Bartsch, T., Döhring, J., Rohr, A., Jansen, O., & Deuschl, G. (2011). CA1 neurons in the human hippocampus are critical for autobiographical memory, mental time travel, and autonoetic consciousness. *Proceedings of the National Academy of Sciences, 108*(42), 17562–17567. https://doi.org/10.1073/pnas.1110266108

Bastian, B., Jetten, J., & Stewart, E. (2013). Physical pain and guilty pleasures. *Social Psychological and Personality Science, 4*(2), 215–219. https://doi.org/10.1177/1948550612451156

Batchelor, S. (1997). *Buddhism without beliefs.* New York, NY: Berkley.

Bateman, A., & Fonagy, P. (2010). Mentalization based treatment for borderline personality disorder. *World Psychiatry, 9*(1), 11–15. https://doi.org/10.1002/j.2051-5545.2010.tb00255.x

Batty, C. (2014). The illusion confusion. *Frontiers in Psychology, 5,* 231. https://doi.org/10.3389/fpsyg.2014.00231

Baumeister, R. F., & Exline, J. J. (2000). Self-control, morality, and human strength. *Journal of Social and Clinical Psychology, 19*(1), 29–42. https://doi.org/10.1521/jscp.2000.19.1.29

Baumeister, R. F., & Finkel, E. (2010). *Advanced social psychology: The state of the science.* New York, NY: Oxford University Press.

Baumeister, R. F., & Leary, M. R. (1995). The need to belong: Desire for interpersonal attachments as a fundamental human motivation. *Psychological Bulletin*, *117*(3), 497–529. https://doi.org/10.1037//0033-2909.117.3.497

Baumeister, R. F., Tice, D. M., Vohs, K. D. (2018). The Strength Model of Self-Regulation: Conclusions From the Second Decade of Willpower Research. *Perspectives on Psychological Science.*, Vol. 13 (2): 141–145.

Baumeister, R. F., Vohs, K. D., & Tice, D. M. (2007). The strength model of self-control. *Current Directions in Psychological Science*, *16*(6), 351–355. https://doi.org/10.1111/j.1467-8721.2007.00534.x

Beaty, R. E., Benedek, M., Kaufman, S. B., & Silvia, P. J. (2015). Default and executive network coupling supports creative idea production. *Scientific Reports*, *5*, 10964. https://doi.org/10.1038/srep10964

Beaumont, J. (2008). *Introduction to neuropsychology* (2nd ed.). New York, NY: Guilford.

Bechara, A., Damasio, H., & Damasio, A. (2000). Emotion, decision making, and the orbitofrontal cortex. *Cerebral Cortex*, *10*(3), 295–307, 1047–3211. https://doi.org/10.1093/cercor/10.3.295

Beck, A. T., Rush, A. J., Shaw, B. F., & Emery, G. (1979). *Cognitive therapy of depression*. New York, NY: Guilford Press.

Beck, D. M., Rees, G., Frith, C. D., & Lavie, N. (2001). Neural correlates of change detection and change blindness. *Nature Neurosci. 4*, 645–650.

Bekris, L., Yu, C., Bird, T., & Tsuang, D. (2010). Genetics of Alzheimers Disease. *Journal Geriatric Psychiatry Neurology, 23*(4), 213–227.

Ben-Naim, S., Marom, I., Krashin, M., Gifter, B., & Arad, K. (2017). Life with a partner with ADHD: The moderating role of intimacy. *Journal of Child and Family Studies*, *26*(5), 1365–1373. https://doi.org/10.1007/s10826-016-0653-9

Benoit, R. G., Gilbert, S. J., & Burgess, P. W. (2011). A neural mechanism mediating the impact of episodic prospection on farsighted decisions. *Journal of Neuroscience*, *31*(18), 6771–6779. https://doi.org/10.1523/jneurosci.6559-10.2011

Benton, T. R., Ross, D. F., Bradshaw, E., Thomas, W. N., & Bradshaw, G. S. (2006). Eyewitness memory is still not common sense: Comparing jurors, judges and law enforcement to eyewitness experts. *Applied Cognitive Psychology*, *20*(1), 115–129. https://doi.org/10.1002/acp.1171

Bergeman, C. S., Chlpuer, H. M., Plomin, R., Pedersen, N. L., McClearn, G. E., Nesselroade, J. R.,...McCrae, R. R. (1993). Genetic and environmental effects on openness to experience, agreeableness, and conscientiousness: An adoption/twin study. *Journal of Personality*, *61*(2), 159–179. https://doi.org/10.1111/j.1467-6494.1993.tb01030.x

Berkman, E. T., Kahn, L. E., & Merchant, J. S. (2014). Training-induced changes in inhibitory control network activity. *The Journal of Neuroscience, 34*, 149–157. https://doi.org/10.1523/jneurosci.3564-13.2014

Bertolo, H. et al. (2003). Visual dream content, graphical representation and EEG alpha activity in congenitally blind subjects. *Cogn. Brain Res. 15*, 277–284.

Bertrand, M., & Mullainathan, S. (2003). Are Emily and Greg More Employable Than Lakisha and Jamal?: A Field Experiment on Labor Market and Discrimination. *The American Economic Review*, 991–1013.

Beyer, F., Sidarus, N., Bonicalzi, S., & Haggard, P. (2017). Beyond self-serving bias: diffusion of responsibility reduces sense of agency and outcome monitoring. *Social Cognitive and Affective Neuroscience*, *12*(1), 138–145. https://doi.org/10.1093/scan/nsw160

Bhuvaneswar, C., & Spiegel, D. (2013). An eye for an I: A 35-year-old woman with fluctuating oculomotor deficits and dissociative identity disorder. *International Journal of Clinical and Experimental Hypnosis*, *61*(3), 351–370. https://doi.org/10.1080/00207144.2013.784115

Bianconi, E., Piovesan, A., Facchin, F., Beraudi, A., Casadei, R., Frabetti, F., . . . Canaider, S. (2013). An estimation of the number of cells in the human body. *Annals of Human Biology, 40*(6), 463–471. https://doi.org/10.3109/03014460.2013.807878

Bion, W. R. (1959). Attacks on linking. *International Journal of Psychoanalysis, 40*, 308–315.

Bion, W. R. (1963/1984). Elements of psychoanalysis. London: Karnac.

Bion, W. R. (1965/1984). Transformations. London: Karnac.

Bion, W. R. (1970/1986). Attention and interpretation. London: Karnac.

Bion, W. R. (1983). *Learning from experience*. Lanham, MD: Rowman and Littlefield.

Blackstad, T. (1965). Commisural connections of the hippocampal region in the rat, with special reference to their mode of termination. *Journal of Comparative Neurology, 105,* 417–537. https://doi.org/10.1002/cne.901050305

Blake, W. (1794). *The marriage of heaven and hell*. New York, NY: Dover Publications.

Blakemore, S., Wolpert, D., & Frith, C. (2000). Why can't you tickle yourself. *Neuroreport, 11*(11), R11–R16.

Blankenburg, F., Ruff, C. C., Deichmann, R., Rees, G., & Driver, J. (2006). The cutaneous rabbit illusion affects human primary sensory cortex somatotopically. *PLoS biology, 4*(3), e69. https://doi.org/10.1371/journal.pbio.0040069

Blum, K., Chen, A. L. C., Braverman, E. R., Comings, D. E., Chen, T. J., Arcuri, V.,...Lubar, J. (2008). Attention-deficit-hyperactivity disorder and reward deficiency syndrome. *Neuropsychiatric Disease and Treatment, 4*(5), 893–918. https://doi.org/10.2147/ndt.s2627

Blumenfeld, H. (2010). *Neuroanatomy through clinical cases* (2nd ed.). Sunderland, MA: Sinauer Associates.

Boccia, M., Piccardi, L., & Guariglia, P. (2015). The meditative mind: A comprehensive meta-analysis of MRI studies. *BioMed Research International, 2015,* 1–11. https://doi.org/10.1155/2015/419808

Boldrini, M., Fulmore, C. A., Tartt, A. N., Simeon, L. R., Pavlova, I., Poposka, V.,...Mann, J. J. (2018). Human hippocampal neurogenesis persists throughout aging. *Cell Stem Cell, 22*(4), 589–599.

Bollas, C. (1987). *The Shadow of the Object: Psychoanalysis of the Unthought Known*. London, UK: Free Association Book.

Boroditsky, L. (2001). Does language shape thought? Mandarin and English speakers' conceptions of time. *Cognitive Psychology, 43*(1), 1–22. https://doi.org/10.1006/cogp.2001.0748

Bouchard, T. J., Jr., & McGue, M. (2003). Genetic and environmental influences on human psychological differences. *Journal of Neurobiology, 54*(1), 4–45. https://doi.org/10.1002/neu.10160

Bower, J., Davis, C. (2012). Bayesian Just-So Stories in psychology. *Psychological Bulletin, 138*(3), 389–414.

Bowins, B. (2010). Repetitive maladaptive behavior: Beyond repetition compulsion. *The American Journal of Psychoanalysis, 70*(3), 282–298. https://doi.org/10.1057/ajp.2010.14

Bradley, F. H. (1893). *Library of philosophy. Appearance and reality: a metaphysical essay*. Swan Sonnenschein & Co. https://doi.org/10.1037/12950-000

Bradshaw, S., & Storm, L. (2013). Archetypes, symbols and the apprehension of meaning. *International Journal of Jungian Studies, 5*(2), 154–176. https://doi.org/10.1080/19409052.2012.685662

Breitbart, W., & Poppito, S. (2014). *Individual meaning-centered psychotherapy for clients with advanced cancer*. New York, NY: Oxford University Press.

Brewer, J. A., Worhunsky, P. D., Gray, J. R., Tang, Y.-Y., Weber, J., & Kober, H. (2011). Meditation experience is associated with differences in default mode network activity and connectivity. *Proceedings of the National Academy of Sciences of the United States of America, 108*(50), 20254–20259. https://doi.org/10.1073/pnas.1112029108

Brown, G. P., MacLeod, A. K., Tata, P., & Goddard, L. (2002). Worry and the simulation of future outcomes. *Anxiety, Stress and Coping, 15,* 1–17. https://doi.org/10.1080/10615800290007254

Brown, J. (2001). Microgenetic theory: Reflections and prospects. *Neuropsychoanalysis, 3*(1), 61–74. https://doi.org/10.1080/15294145.2001.10773337

Brown, J. (2017). *Reflections on mind and the image of reality*. Eugene, OR: Resource Publications.

Brown, J. M., & Hannigan, T. P. (2008). An empirical test of Carl Jung's collective unconscious (archetypal) memory. *Journal of Border Educational Research, 5,* 114–120.

Brown, J. W. (1976). Consciousness and pathology of language. In R. W. Rieber (Ed.), *Neuropsychology of language: Essays in honor of Eric Lenneberg* (pp. 72–93). New

York, NY: Plenum Press. https://doi.org/10.1007/978-1-4684-2292-4_4

Brown, J. W. (2018). The mind and brain in time: implications for modern neuropsychology. *Acta Neuropsychologica, 16*(1), 99–116. https://doi.org/10.5604/01.3001.0011.7067

Brown, M. W., & Eldridge, M. A. (2008). Perirhinal cortex: Neural representations. In H. Eichenbaum (Ed.), *Memory systems* (pp. 169–186). Amsterdam, The Netherlands: Elsevier.

Brunner, D., Abramovitch, A., & Etherton, J. (2017). A yoga program for cognitive enhancement. *PloS ONE, 12*(8), e0182366.

Buccione, I., Fadda, L., Serra, L., Caltagirone, C., & Carlesimo, G. A. (2008). Retrograde episodic and semantic memory impairment correlates with side of temporal lobe damage. *Journal of the International Neuropsychological Society, 14*(6), 1083–1094. https://doi.org/10.1017/s1355617708080922

Buckner, R., Hanna, J., & Schacter, D. (2008). The brain's default network: Anatomy, function and relevance to disease. *Annals of the New York Academy of Sciences, 1124*, 1–38. https://doi.org/10.1196/annals.1440.011

Buff, C., Brinkmann, L., Bruchmann, M., Becker, M. P., Tupak, S., Herrmann, M. J., & Straube, T. (2017). Activity alterations in the bed nucleus of the stria terminalis and amygdala during threat anticipation in generalized anxiety disorder. *Social Cognitive and Affective Neuroscience, 12*(11), 1766–1774. https://doi.org/10.1093/scan/nsx103

Buhle, J. T., Silvers, J. A., Wager, T. D., Lopez, R., Onyemekwu, C., Kober, H.,...Ochsner, K. N. (2014). Cognitive reappraisal of emotion: a meta-analysis of human neuroimaging studies. *Cerebral Cortex, 24*(11), 2981–2990. https://doi.org/10.1093/cercor/bht154

Bushdid, C., Magnasco, M. O., Vosshall, L. B., & Keller, A. (2014). Humans can discriminate more than 1 trillion olfactory stimuli. *Science, 343*(6177), 1370–1372. https://doi.org/10.1126/science.1249168

Buss, D. M., Haselton, M. G., Shackelford, T. K., Bleske, A. L., & Wakefield, J. C. (1998). Adaptations, exaptations, and spandrels. *American Psychologist, 53*(5), 533–548. https://doi.org/10.1037/0003-066x.53.5.533

Buzsaki, G., Kaila, K., & Raichle, M. (2007). Inhi-

bition and brain work. *PMC, 56*(5), 771–783. https://doi.org/10.1016/j.neuron.2007.11.008

Campbell, J. (1949). *The hero with a thousand faces.* Princeton, NJ: Princeton University Press.

Cannon, P. R., Schnall, S., & White, M. (2011). Transgressions and expressions: Affective facial muscle activity predicts moral judgments. *Social Psychological and Personality Science, 2*, 325–331. https://doi.org/10.1177/1948550610390525

Cappellen, P. V., Way, B. M., Isgett, S. F., & Fredrickson, B. L. (2016). Effects of oxytocin administration on spirituality and emotional responses to meditation. *Social Cognitive and Affective Neuroscience, 11*(10), 1579–1587. https://doi.org/10.1093/scan/nsw078

Carabotti, M., Scirocco, A., Maselli, M., & Severi, C. (2015). The gut-brain axis: Interactions between microbiota, central and enteric nervous systems. *Annals of Gastroenterology, 28*, 203–209.

Carhart-Harris, R. L., Erritzoe, D., Williams, T., Stone, J. M., Reed, L. J., Colasanti, A.,... Nutt, D. J. (2012). Neural correlates of the psychedelic state as determined by fMRI studies with psilocybin. *Proceedings of the National Academy of Sciences USA, 109*(6), 2138–2143. https://doi.org/10.1073/pnas.1119598109

Carhart-Harris, R. L., Muthukumaraswamy, S., Roseman, L., Kaelen, M., Droog, W., Murphy, K.,...Nutt. D. J. (2016). Neural correlates of the LSD experience revealed by multimodal neuroimaging. *Proceedings of the National Academy of Sciences USA, 113*(17), 4853–4858. https://doi.org/10.1073/pnas.1518377113

Carhart-Harris, R. L., Roseman, L., Bolstridge, M., Demetriou, L., Pannekoek, J. N., Wall, M. B.,...Leech, R. (2017). Psilocybin for treatment-resistant depression: fMRI-measured brain mechanisms. *Scientific Reports, 7*(1). Retrieved from https://www.nature.com/articles/s41598-017-13282-7/

Carlson, C. A., Gronlund, S. D., & Clark, S. E. (2008). Lineup composition, suspect position, and the sequential lineup advantage. *Journal of Experimental Psychology: Applied, 14*(2), 118–128. https://doi.org/10.1037/1076-898x.14.2.118

Caruana, D., Alexander, G., & Dudek, S.

(2017). New insights into the regulation of synaptic plasticity from an unexpected place: Hippocampal area CA2. *Learning and Memory, 19*(9), 391–400. https://doi.org/10.1101/lm.025304.111

Caruso, E. M. (2010). When the future feels worse than the past: A temporal inconsistency in moral judgment. *Journal of Experimental Psychology: General, 139*(4), 610–624. https://doi.org/10.1037/a0020757

Caruso, E. M., Gilbert, D. T., & Wilson, T. D. (2008). A wrinkle in time: Asymmetric valuation of past and future events. *Psychological Science, 19,* 796–801. https://doi.org/10.1111/j.1467-9280.2008.02159.x

Carveth, D. L. (2010). Superego, conscience, and the nature and types of guilt. *Modern Psychoanalysis, 35*(1), 1–25.

Carveth, D. L. (2013). *The still small voice: Psychoanalytic reflections on guilt and conscience.* London: Karnac Books.

Carveth, D. L. (2015). The immoral superego: Conscience as the fourth element in the structural theory of the mind. *Canadian Journal of Psychoanalysis / Revue Canadienne de Psychanalyse, 23*(1), 206–223.

Case, L. K., Abrams, R. A., & Ramachandran, V. S. (2010). Immediate interpersonal and intermanual referral of sensations following anesthetic block of one arm. *Archives of Neurology, 67*(12), 1521–1523. https://doi.org/10.1001/archneurol.2010.290

Castelhano, J., Bernardino, I., Rebola, J., Rodriguez, E., & Castelo-Branco, M. (2015). Oscillations or synchrony? Disruption of neural synchrony despite enhanced gamma oscillations in a model of disrupted perceptual coherence. *Journal of Cognitive Neuroscience, 27*(12), 2416–2426. https://doi.org/10.1162/jocn_a_00863

Cavanna, A., & Trible, M. (2006). The precuneus: A review of its functional anatomy and behavioral correlates. *Brain, 129*(3), 564–583. https://doi.org/10.1093/brain/awl004

Cecchetto, C., Lancini, E., Bueti, D., Rumiati, R. I., & Parma, V. (2019). Body odors (even when masked) make you more emotional: Behavioral and neural insights. *Scientific Reports, 9*(1), 1–14. https://doi.org/10.31234/osf.io/h6f23

Chalmers, A. (2013). *What is this thing called sci-ence?* (4th ed.). Queensland, Australia: University of Queensland Press.

Chalmers, D. (1996). *The conscious mind.* New York, NY: Oxford University Press.

Chan, A. (2016). *The fragmentation of self and others: The role of the default mode network in PTSD* (Doctoral dissertation). Retrieved from Proquest Dissertations & Theses. (UMI No. 10102804)

Chan, A., & Siegel, D. (2017). Play and the default mode network: Interpersonal neurobiology. In T. Marks-Tarlow, D. J. Siegel, & M. Solomon (Eds.), *Play & creativity in psychotherapy* (pp. 39–50). New York, NY: W. W. Norton.

Chapman, H. A., & Anderson, A. K. (2014). Trait physical disgust is related to moral judgments outside of the purity domain. *Emotion, 14*(2), 341–348. https://doi.org/10.1037/a0035120

Cheng, C., Chan, P., Liu, C., & Hsu, S. (2016). Auditory sensory gating in clients with bipolar disorders: A meta-analysis. *Journal of Affective Disorders, 203,* 199–203. https://doi.org/10.1016/j.jad.2016.06.010

Chien, Y., Hsieh, M., & Gau, S. (2019). P50-N100-P200 sensory gating deficits in adolescents and young adults with autism spectrum disorders. *Progress in Neuropsychopharmacology and Biological Psychiatry, 95.* https://doi.org/10.1016/j.pnpbp.2019.109683

Cherry, C. (1988). When is fantasizing morally bad? *Philosophical Investigations, 11*(2), 112–132.

Chirico, A., Ferrise, F., Cordella, L., & Gaggioli, A. (2018). Designing awe in virtual reality: An experimental study. *Frontiers in Psychology, 8,* 1–14. https://doi.org/10.3389/fpsyg.2017.02351

Chirico, A., & Yaden, D. B. (2018). Awe: A self-transcendent and sometimes transformative emotion. In H. C. Lench (ed.) *The Function of Emotions* (pp. 221–233). Cham, Switzerland: Springer.

Chirico, A., Yaden, D. B., Riva, G., & Gaggioli, A. (2016). The potential of virtual reality for the investigation of awe. *Frontiers in Psychology, 7,* 1766. https://doi.org/10.3389/fpsyg.2016.01766

Chomsky, N. (1959). A review of B. F. Skinner's *Verbal behavior. Language, 35,* 26–58.

Chomsky, N. (1986). *Knowledge of language: Its nature, origin, and use.* New York, NY: Praeger.

Christoff, K., Irving, Z., Fox, K., Spreng, N., & Andrews-Hanna, J. (2016). Mind-wandering as spontaneous thought: A dynamic framework. *Nature Reviews Neuroscience, 17,* 718–731. https://doi.org/10.1038/nrn.2016.113

Chudnoff, E. (2012). Awareness of Abstract Objects. *Noûs, 47*(4), 706–726. https://doi.org/10.1111/j.1468-0068.2011.00851.x

Clark, A. (2013). Whatever next? Predictive brains, situated agents and the future of cognitive science. *Behavioral and Brain Sciences, 36,* 181–204.

Cobb, J. B. (2015). *Whitehead word book: A glossary with alphabetical index to technical terms in process and reality.* Anoka, MN: Process Century Press.

Cooley, C. H. (1902). *Human nature and the social order.* New York, NY: Scribner.

Corbett, L., & Stein, M. (2005). Contemporary Jungian approach to spiritually oriented psychotherapy. In L. Sperry & E. Shafranske (Eds.), *Spiritually oriented psychotherapy* (pp. 1019–1518), Washington, DC: American Psychological Association. https://doi.org/10.1037/10886-003

Costa, A., & Pereira, T. (2019). The effects of sleep deprivation on cognitive performance. *European Journal of Public Health, 29*(supp. 1). https://doi.org/10.1093/eurpub/ckz034.096

Cova, F., & Deonna, J. (2013). Being moved. *Philosophical studies, 169,* 447–466. https://doi.org/10.1007/s11098-013-0192-9

Cozolino, L. (2008). *The healthy aging brain: Sustaining attachment, attaining wisdom.* New York, NY: W. W. Norton & Company.

Cozolino, L. (2010). *The neuroscience of psychotherapy: Healing the social brain.* New York, NY: W. W. Norton & Company.

Cozolino, L. (2014). *The neuroscience of human relationships: Attachment and the developing social brain* (2nd ed.). New York, NY: W. W. Norton & Company.

Cozolino, L. J. (2016). *Why therapy works: Using our minds to change our brains.* W. W. Norton & Company.

Cramer, P. (2015). Defense mechanisms: 40 years of empirical research. *Journal of Personality Assessment, 97*(2), 114–122. https://doi.org/10.1080/00223891.2014.947997

Crick, F., & Koch, C. (1998). Constraints on cortical and thalamic projections: The no-strong-loops hypothesis. *Nature, 391*(6664), 245–250. https://doi.org/10.1038/34584

Crick, F., & Koch, C. (2005). What is the function of the claustrum? *Phil Trans R Soc Lond B Biol. Sci, 360*(1458), 1271–1279.

Csikszentmihalyi, Mihaly. (1990). *Flow: The psychology of optimal experience.* New York: Harper & Row.

Cuijpers, P., Reijnders, M., & Huibers, M. J. (2019). The role of common factors in psychotherapy outcomes. *Annual Review of Clinical Psychology, 15,* 207–231. https://doi.org/10.1146/annurev-clinpsy-050718-095424

Damasio, A. (1999). *The feeling of what happens: Body and emotion in the making of consciousness.* Fort Worth, TX: Harcourt College Publishers.

Damasio, A. (2003) *Looking for Spinoza.* New York, NY: Houghton Mifflin Harcourt.

Damasio, A. (2010). *Self comes to mind.* New York, NY: Random House.

D'Angiulli, A., Runge, M., Faulkner, A., Zakizadeh, J., Chan, A., & Morcos, S. (2013). Viviness of visual imagery and incidental recall of verbal cues, when phenomenological availability reflects long-term memory accessibility. *Frontiers in Psychology, 4*(1), 1–18.

Daniels, J. K., Bluhm, R. L., & Lanius, R. A. (2013). Intrinsic network abnormalities in posttraumatic stress disorder: Research directions for the next decade. *Psychological Trauma: Theory, Research, Practice, and Policy, 5*(2), 142–148. https://doi.org/10.1037/a0026946

Darley, J. M., & Latané, B. (1968). Bystander intervention in emergencies: Diffusion of responsibility. *Journal of Personality and Social Psychology, 8*(4, Pt.1), 377–383. https://doi.org/10.1037/h0025589

Darwin, C. (1871/2005). *From so simple a beginning: The four great books of Charles Darwin* (E. O. Wilson, ed.). New York, NY: W. W. Norton.

Davidson, R. J., Kabat-Zinn, J., Schumacher, J., Rosenkranz, M., Muller, D., Santorelli,

S. F., ... Sheridan, J. F. (2003). Alterations in brain and immune function produced by mindfulness meditation. *Psychosomatic Medicine*, *65*(4), 564–570. https://doi.org/10.1097/01.psy.0000077505.67574.e3

Davies, J. (2012). *The importance of suffering*. New York, NY: Routledge.

Davis, W. (2003, February). *Dreams from endangered cultures* [Video file]. https://www.ted.com/talks/wade_davis_dreams_from_endangered_cultures/transcript?language=en

Daviss, W. B. (2008). A review of co-morbid depression in pediatric ADHD: Etiologies, phenomenology, and treatment. *Journal of Child and Adolescent Psychopharmacology*, *18*(6), 565–571. https://doi.org/10.1089/cap.2008.032

de Bary, A. (1879). *Die erscheinung der symbiose*. Strassburg, Germany: Trübner.

De Dreu, C. K., Gross, J., Méder, Z., Giffin, M., Prochazkova, E., Krikeb, J., & Columbus, S. (2016). In-group defense, out-group aggression, and coordination failures in intergroup conflict. *Proceedings of the National Academy of Sciences USA*, *113*(38), 10524–10529. https://doi.org/10.1073/pnas.1605115113

Dennett, D. (1991). *Consciousness explained*. New York, NY: Penguin.

Dentico, D. et al. (2014). Reversal of cortical information flow during visual imagery as compared to visual perception. *Neuroimage*, *100*, 237–243.

De Ridder, D., Kroese, F., Adriaanse, M., & Evers, C. (2014). Always gamble on an empty stomach: Hunger is associated with advantageous decision making. *PloS One*, *9*(10). https://doi.org/10.1371/journal.pone.0111081

Deurzen, E. (2010). *Everyday mysteries: A handbook of existential psychotherapy*. New York, NY: Routledge.

Deutsch, D., Henthorn, T., & Dolson, M. (2004). Speech patterns heard early in life influence later perception of the tritone paradox. *Music Perception: An Interdisciplinary Journal*, *21*(3), 357–372. https://doi.org/10.1525/mp.2004.21.3.357

Dewey, J. (1958). *Experience and nature* (2nd ed.). New York, NY: Dover Publications.

Diessner, R., Solom, R., Frost, N., Parsons, L. & Davidson, J. (2008). Engagement with beauty: Appreciating natural, artistic, and moral beauty. *The Journal of Psychology*, *142*(3), 303–329.

Dijksterhuis, A., Strick, M., Bos, M. W., & Nordgren, L. F. (2014). Prolonged thought: Proposing Type 3 processing. In S. J. Sherman, B. Gawronskii, & Y. Trope (Eds.), *Dual-process theories of the social mind* (pp. 355–370). New York, NY: Guilford Press.

Dimijian, G. (2000). Evolving together: The biology of symbiosis, part 1. *BUMC Proceedings*, *13*, 217–226. https://doi.org/10.1080/08998280.2000.11927678

Domhoff, G. W. (2010). *The case for a cognitive theory of dreams*. Retrieved from http://dreamresearch.net/Library/domhoff_2010.html

Dorahy, M. J., Brand, B. L., Şar, V., Krüger, C., Stavropoulos, P., Martínez-Taboas, A., Lewis-Fernández,. R., Middleton, W. (2014). Dissociative identity disorder: An empirical overview. *Australian & New Zealand Journal of Psychiatry*, *48*(5), 402–417. https://doi.org/10.1177/0004867414527523

Doyle, A. C., & Goodenough, S. (1985). *A study in scarlet: A Sherlock Holmes murder mystery*. London, UK: Peerage Books.

Dugas, M. J., Gagnon, F., Ladouceur, R., & Freeston, M. H. (1998). Generalized anxiety disorder: A preliminary test of a conceptual model. *Behaviour Research and Therapy*, *36*(2), 215–226. https://doi.org/10.1016/s0005-7967(97)00070-3

Dunsky, A., et al. (2017). The effects of a resistance vs. an aerobic single session on attention and executive functioning in adults. *PloS One*, *12*(4), e0179799.

Durkheim, E. (1978). *On institutional analysis* (M. Traugott, trans.). Chicago, IL: University of Chicago Press.

Duquette, P. (2017). Increasing our insular world view: Interoception and psychopathology for psychotherapists. *Front. Neurosci.*, *11*, 135.

Duval, E. R., Javanbakht, A., & Liberzon, I. (2015). Neural circuits in anxiety and stress disorders: a focused review. *Therapeutics and clinical risk management*, *11*, 115–126. doi:10.2147/TCRM.S48528

Duvarci, S., & Pare, D. (2014). Amygdala microcircuits controlling learned fear. *Neuron*,

82(5), 966–980. https://doi.org/10.1016/j. neuron.2014.04.042

Eastman, T. E., & Keeton, H. (2003). *Physics and Whitehead: Quantum, process, and experience.* Albany, NY: State University of New York Press.

Ebbinghaus, H. (1880). *Urmanuskript "Ueber das Gedächtniß."* Passau, Germany: Passavia Universitätsverlag.

Ebbinghaus, H. (1885a). *Memory: A contribution to experimental psychology.* New York, NY: Teachers College Press.

Ebbinghaus, H. (1885b). *Über das Gedächtnis.* Leipzig, Germany: Dunker.

Edelman, G. M. (2003). Naturalizing consciousness: A theoretical framework. *Proceedings of the National Academy of Sciences USA, 100*(9), 5520–5524. https://doi.org/10.1073/pnas.0931349100

Eisenberger, N. I., Inagaki, T. K., Muscatell, K. A., Byrne Haltom, K. E., & Leary, M. R. (2011). The neural sociometer: Brain mechanisms underlying state self-esteem. *Journal of Cognitive Neuroscience, 23*(11), 3448–3455. https://doi.org/10.1162/jocn_a_00027

Eisenberger, N. I., Lieberman, M. D., & Williams, K. D. (2003). Does rejection hurt? An fMRI study of social exclusion. *Science, 302*(5643), 290–292. https://doi.org/10.1126/science.1089134

Elliot, A. J., & Maier, M. A. (2014). Color psychology: Effects of perceiving color on psychological functioning in humans. *Annual Review of Psychology, 65*, 95–120. https://doi.org/10.1146/annurev-psych-010213-115035

Embody. (2010). In *The New Oxford American Dictionary* (3rd ed.). New York, NY: Oxford University Press.

Emerson, R. (1995). *Essays and poems.* London, UK: J.M. Dent Orion.

Epictetus (1916). *The discourses of Epictetus: With the Encheiridion and fragments.* (G. Long, trans.). London: G. Bell and Sons.

Epperson, M. (2004). *Quantum mechanics and the philosophy of Alfred North Whitehead.* New York, NY: Fordham University Press.

Epstein, J. N., Casey, B. J., Tonev, S. T., Davidson, M. C., Reiss, A. L., Garrett, A.,...Vitolo, A. (2007). ADHD- and medication-related brain activation effects in concordantly affected parent–child dyads with ADHD. *Journal of Child Psychology and Psychiatry, 48*(9), 899–913. https://doi.org/10.1111/j.1469-7610.2007.01761.x

Ernst, A., & Frisén, J. (2015). Adult neurogenesis in humans-common and unique traits in mammals. *PLoS Biology, 13*(1). https://doi.org/10.1371/journal.pbio.1002045

Eskine, K. J., Kacinik, N. A., & Prinz, J. J. (2011). A bad taste in the mouth: Gustatory disgust influences moral judgment. *Psychological Science, 22*(3), 295–299. https://doi.org/10.1177/0956797611398497

Essential. (2010). In *The New Oxford American Dictionary* (3rd ed.). New York, NY: Oxford University Press.

Eurich, T. (2018). *Insight: The surprising truth about how others see us, how we see ourselves, and why the answers matter more than we think.* New York, NY: Penguin Random House.

Ezendam, D., Bongers, R., & Jannink, M. (2009). Systematic review of the effectiveness of mirror therapy in upper extremity function. *Disability Rehabilitation, 31*(26), 2135–2149. https://doi.org/10.3109/09638280902887768

Fair, D. A., Cohen, A. L., Dosenbach, N. U., Church, J. A., Miezin, F. M., Barch, D. M., & Schlaggar, B. L. (2008). The maturing architecture of the brain's default network. *Proceedings of the National Academy of Sciences USA, 105*(10), 4028–4032. https://doi.org/10.1073/pnas.0800376105

Fang, T.-mei. (1986). *The Chinese view of life: The philosophy of comprehensive harmony.* Taipei, Taiwan: Linking Pub. Co.

Farovik, A., Dupont, L., & Eichenbaum, H. (2009). Distinct roles for dorsal CA3 and CA1 in memory for sequential nonspatial events. *Learning & Memory, 17*(1), 12–17. https://doi.org/10.1101/lm.1616209

Farrant, M., & Nusser, Z. (2005). Variations on an inhibitory theme: phasic and tonic activation of GABA A receptors. *Nature Reviews Neuroscience, 6*(3), 215–229. https://doi.org/10.1038/nrn1625

Farthing, G. W. (1992). *The psychology of consciousness.* Englewood Cliffs, NJ: Prentice-Hall.

Ferreira, M. R., Reisz, N., Schueller, W., Servedio, V. D., Thurner, S., & Loreto, V. (2020). Quantifying exaptation in scientific evolution. *The Frontiers Collection Understanding Innovation Through Exaptation,* 55–68. https://doi.org/10.1007/978-3-030-45784-6_5

Ferro, A. (2005) Bion: Theoretical and clinical observations. *International Journal of Psychoanalysis, 86*, 1535–1542.

Fettes, P., Schulze, L., Downar, J. (2017). Cortico-striatal-thalamic loop circuits of the orbitofrontal cortex: Promising therapeutic targets in psychiatric illnesses. *Front. Syst. Neurosci., 11*(25), 1–23.

Feynman, R. P. (1988). *What do YOU care what other people think? Further adventures of a curious character.* New York, NY: Norton.

Fink, B. (1997). *A clinical introduction to Lacanian psychoanalysis: Theory and technique.* Cambridge, MA: Harvard University Press.

Fischer, P., Krueger, J. I., Greitemeyer, T., Vogrincic, C., Kastenmüller, A., Frey, D.,... Kainbacher, M. (2011). The bystander-effect: A meta-analytic review on bystander intervention in dangerous and non-dangerous emergencies. *Psychological Bulletin, 137*(4), 517–537. https://doi.org/10.1037/a0023304

Fisher, R. M., Henry, L. M., Cornwallis, C. K., Kiers, E. T., & West, S. A. (2017). The evolution of host-symbiont dependence. *Nature Communications, 8*(1), 1–8. https://doi.org/10.1038/ncomms15973

Fitzgerald, C., & Hurst, S. (2017). Implicit bias in healthcare professionals: A systematic review. *BMC Medical Ethics, 18*(1). https://doi.org/10.1186/s12910-017-0179-8

Fojanesi, M., Gallo, M., Russo, F., Valentini, M., Spaziani, M., Radicioni, A.,...Biondi, M. (2017). Exploring the correlation between perceived attachment security and levels of GH hormone in a sample of children with non-organic failure to thrive: Preliminary findings. *European Psychiatry, 41*, S234–S235. https://doi.org/10.1016/j.eurpsy.2017.01.2249

Fox, N. A., & Henderson, H. A. (2000). Does infancy matter? Predicting social behavior from infant temperament. *Infant Behavior and Development, 22,* 445–455. https://doi.org/10.1016/s0163-6383(00)00018-7

Frankl, V. (1986). *The doctor and the soul: From psychotherapy to logotherapy.* New York, NY: Vintage Books.

Franklin, M. S., & Zyphur, M. J. (2015). The role of dreams in the evolution of the human mind. *Evolutionary Psychology, 3*(1). https://doi.org/10.1177/147470490500300106

Freud, S. (1894). The neuro-psychoses of defense. In J. Strachey (Ed. & Trans.), *The standard edition of the complete psychological works of Sigmund Freud* (Vol. 3). London, UK: Hogarth Press.

Freud, S. (1900). *The interpretation of dreams* (J. Crick, trans.). London, UK: Oxford University Press.

Freud, S. (1920). *Beyond the pleasure principle* (J. Strachey, A. Freud, A. Strachey, & A. Tyson, trans.). London, UK: Hogarth Press

Freud, S. (1933). New introductory lectures on psychoanalysis. In J. Strachey (Ed. & trans.), *The standard edition of the complete psychological works of Sigmund Freud* (Vol. 22). London, UK: Hogarth Press.

Friston, K. (2009). The free-energy principle: a rough guide to the brain? *Trends in Cognitive Sciences, 13*(7), 293–301. https://doi.org/10.1016/j.tics.2009.04.005

Gaggioli, A. (2016). Transformative experience design. In A. Gaggioli, A. Ferscha, G. Riva, S. Dunne, & I. Viaud-Delmon (Eds.), *Human computer confluence: Transforming human experience through symbiotic technologies* (pp. 96–121). Berlin, Germany: De Gruyter Open.

Gailliot, M. T., Baumeister, R. F., DeWall, C. N., Maner, J. K., Plant, E. A., Tice, D. M., & Brewer, L. E. (2007). Self-control relies on glucose as a limited energy source: Willpower is more than a metaphor. *Journal of Personality and Social Psychology, 92*(2), 325–336. https://doi.org/10.1037/0022-3514.92.2.325

Galley, J. D, Nelson, M. C., Yu, Z., Dowd, S. E., Walter, J., Kumar, P. S.,...Bailey, M. T. (2014). Exposure to a social stressor disrupts the community structure of the colonic mucosa-associated microbiota. *BMC Microbiology, 14*(1). https://doi.org/10.1186/1471-2180-14-189

Gazzaniga, M. S. (2005). Forty-five years of split-brain research and still going strong. *Nature Reviews Neuroscience, 6*(8), 653–659. https://doi.org/10.1038/nrn1723

Gazzaniga, M. S., Bogen, J. E., & Sperry, R. W. (1962). Some functional effects of sectioning the cerebral commissures in man. *Proceedings of the National Academy of Sciences USA, 48*(10), 1765–1769. https://doi.org/10.1073/pnas.48.10.1765

Gazzaniga, M. S., Bogen, J. E., & Sperry, R. W. (1965). Observations on visual perception after disconnexion of the cerebral hemispheres in man. *Brain, 88*(2), 221–236. https://doi.org/10.1093/brain/88.2.221

Geldard, F. A., & Sherrick, C. E. (1972). The cutaneous "rabbit:" A perceptual illusion. *Science, 178*(4057), 178–179. https://doi.org/10.1126/science.178.4057.178

Gendlin, E. (1962/1997). *Experiencing and the creation of meaning.* Evanston, Illinois: Northwestern University Press.

Gendlin, E. (1996). Focusing-oriented psychotherapy. New York, NY: The Guilford Press.

Gerkin, R. C., & Castro, J. B. (2015, July). The number of olfactory stimuli that humans can discriminate is still unknown. eLife, 4, 1–15. https://doi.org/10.7554/eLife.08127

Gibson, J. (1979). *The theory of affordances: The ecological approach to visual perception.* Boston, MA: Houghton Mifflin.

Gilbert, P., & Procter, S. (2006). Compassionate mind training for people with high shame and self-criticism: Overview and pilot study of a group therapy approach. *Clinical Psychology and Psychotherapy, 13*, 353–379. https://doi.org/10.1002/cpp.507

Gilbert, S. F., Sapp, J., & Tauber, A. I. (2012). A symbiotic view of life: We have never been individuals. *The Quarterly Review of Biology, 87*(4), 325–341. https://doi.org/10.1086/668166

Griffin, D. R. (1989). *Archetypal process: self and divine in Whitehead, Jung, and Hillman.* Evanston, Illinois: Northwestern University Press.

Gold, E., & Zahm, S. (2018). *Buddhist psychology & gestalt therapy integrated.* Portland, Oregon: Metta Press.

Gordan, S. (2013). *Neurophenomenology and its applications to psychology.* Springer.

Gothe, N. P., Hayes, J. M., Temali, C., & Damoiseaux, J. S. (2018). Differences in brain structure and function among yoga practitioners and controls. *Frontiers in Integrative Neuroscience, 12.*

Gould, S. J., & Vrba, E. S. (1982). Exaptation—a missing term in the science of form. *Paleobiology, 8*(1), 4–15. https://doi.org/10.1017/s0094837300004310

Goulden, N., Khusnulina, A., Davis, N. J.,

Bracewell, R. M., Bokde, A. L., McNulty, J. P., & Mullins, P. G. (2014). The salience network is responsible for switching between the default mode network and the central executive network: Replication from DCM. *Neuroimage, 99,* 180–190. https://doi.org/10.1016/j.neuroimage.2014.05.052

Graiver, I. (2018). *Asceticism of the mind.* Toronto, Canada: Pontifical Institute of Mediaeval Studies.

Green, L., & Myerson, J. (2004). A discounting framework for choice with delayed and probabilistic rewards. *Psychological Bulletin, 130*(5), 769–792. https://doi.org/10.1037/0033-2909.130.5.769

Green, S. A., Hernandez, L., Bookheimer, S. Y., & Dapretto, M. (2017). Reduced modulation of thalamocortical connectivity during exposure to sensory stimuli in ASD. *Autism Research, 10*(5), 801–809. https://doi.org/10.1002/aur.1726

Greenberg, J., & Mitchell, S. (1983). Object relations in psychoanalytic theory. Cambridge, MA: Harvard University Press.

Greenberg, et al. (2014). Sex differences in stress-induced social withdrawl: role of brain derived neurotrophic factor in the bed nucleus of the strai terminalis. *Frontiers in Behavioral Neuroscience, 7:223.* 10.3389/fnbeh.2013.00223

Greenwald & Banaji (1995). Implicit social cognition: Attitudes, self-esteem, and stereotypes. *Psychological Review, 102*(1), 4–27.

Gregoriou, G. G., Gotts, S. J., Zhou, H., & Desimone, R. (2009). High-frequency, long-range coupling between prefrontal and visual cortex during attention. *Science, 324*(5931), 1207–1210. https://doi.org/10.1126/science.1171402

Greyson, B., Broshek, D. K., Derr, L. L., & Fountain, N. B. (2015). Mystical experiences associated with seizures. *Religion, Brain & Behavior, 5*(3), 182–196. https://doi.org/10.1080/2153599x.2014.895775

Griffin, D. R. (1989). *Archetypal process: self and divine in Whitehead, Jung, and Hillman.* Evanston, Illinois: Northwestern University Press.

Griffiths, R. R., Johnson, M. W., Carducci, M. A., Umbricht, A., Richards, W. A., Richards, B. D.,...Klinedinst, M. A. (2016). Psilocybin produces substantial and sustained decreases in depression and anxiety in clients with life-threatening cancer: A randomized double-blind trial. *Journal of Psychopharmacology, 30*(12), 1181–1197. https://doi.org/10.1177/0269881116675513

Griskevicius, V., Tybur, J. M., Sundie, J. M., Cialdini, R. B., Miller, G. F., & Kenrick, D. T. (2007). Blatant benevolence and conspicuous consumption: When romantic motives elicit strategic costly signals. *Journal of Personality and Social Psychology, 93*(1), 85–102. https://doi.org/10.1037/e633982013-262

Grotstein, J. S. (2019). *Beam of intense darkness: Wilfred Bion's legacy to psychoanalysis.* Routledge.

Grunwald, T., Boutros, N. N., Pezer, N., von Oertzen, J., Fernández, G., Schaller, C., & Elger, C. E. (2003). Neuronal substrates of sensory gating within the human brain. *Biological Psychiatry, 53*(6), 511–519. https://doi.org/10.1016/s0006-3223(02)01673-6

Haidt, J., Rozin, P., McCauley, C., & Imada, S. (1997). Body, psyche, and culture: The relationship between disgust and morality. *Psychology and Developing Societies, 9*(1), 107–131. https://doi.org/10.1177/097133369700900105

Haggard, P. (2008). Human volition: Towards a neuroscience of will. *Nature Reviews Neuroscience, 9*(12), 934–946. https://doi.org/10.1038/nrn2497

Haidt, J. (2001). The emotional dog and its rational tail: A social intuitionist approach to moral judgment. *Psychological Review, 108*(4), 814–834. https://doi.org/10.1037/0033-295x.108.4.814

Hameroff, S., & Penrose, R. (1996). Orchestrated reduction of quantum coherence in brain microtubules: A model for consciousness. *Mathematics and Computers in Simulation, 40*(3–4), 453–480. https://doi.org/10.1016/0378-4754(96)80476-9

Hamilton, J., Farmer, M., Fogelman, P., & Gotlib, I. (2015). Depressive rumination, the default-mode network, and the dark matter of clinical neuroscience. *Biological Psychiatry, 78*(4), 224. doi: 10.1016/j.biopsych.2015.02.020

Hansen, M. M., Jones, R., & Tocchini, K. (2017). Shinrin-yoku (forest bathing) and nature therapy: A state-of-the-art review. *International Journal of Environmental Research and Public Health, 14*(8). https://doi.org/10.3390/ijerph14080851

Harlow, H. F. (1959). Love in infant monkeys. *Scientific American, 200*(6), 68–75.

Harper, L. (2005). Epigenetic inheritance and the intergenerational transfer of experience. *Psychological Bulletin, 131*(3), 340–360. https://doi.org/10.1037/0033-2909.131.3.340

Harrell, S., & Bond, M. (2006). Listening to diversity stories: Principles for practice in community research and action. *Am J Community Psychology, 37,* 365–376.

Harris, M., Macinko, J., Jimenez, G., & Mullachery, P. (2017). Measuring the bias against low-income country research: An implicit association test. *Globalization and Health, 13*(80).

Harrison, N.A., Gray, M.A., Gianoros, P.J., & Critchley, H.D. (2010). The embodiment of emotional feelings in the brain. *The Journal of Neuroscience, 30*(38), 12878–12884.

Hart, T. (1998). Inspiration: Exploring the experience and its meaning. *Journal of Humanistic Psychology, 38,* 7–35. https://doi.org/10.1177/00221678980383002

Hartmann, E. (1996). Outline for a theory on the nature and functions of dreaming. *Dreaming, 6*(2), 147–170. https://doi.org/10.1037/h0094452

Harvey, P. D., & Penn, D. (2010). Social cognition: The key factor predicting social outcome in people with schizophrenia? *Psychiatry, 7*(2), 41–44.

Hass, L. (2008). *Merleau-Ponty's philosophy.* Bloomingdale and Indianapolis: Indiana University Press.

Hatemi, P. K., Gillespie, N. A., Eaves, L. J., Maher, B. S., Webb, B. T., Heath, A. C.,... Montgomery, G. W. (2011). A genome-wide analysis of liberal and conservative political attitudes. *The Journal of Politics, 73*(1), 271–285. https://doi.org/10.1017/s0022381610001015

Hawkins, J., & Blakeslee, S. (2004). *On intelligence.* New York, NY: Times Books.

Hayes, S. (2009, December). *BigThink.com interview with Steve Hayes.* Retrieved from https://contextualscience.org/bigthinkcom_interview_with_steve_hayes_december_2009

He, H. L., Zhang, M., Gu, C. Z., Xue, R. R., Liu, H. X., Gao, C. F., & Duan, H. F. (2019). Effect of cognitive behavioral therapy on improving the cognitive function in major and minor depression. *The Journal of Nervous and Mental Disease, 207*(4), 232–238. https://doi.org/10.1097/nmd.0000000000000954

He, N., Rolls, E. Zhao, W., & Guo, S. (2019). Predicting human inhibitory control from brain structural MRI. *Brain Imaging and Behavior.* https://doi.org/10.1007/s11682-019-00166-9

Heimlich, R. (2009). *Mystical experiences.* Retrieved from https://www.pewresearch.org/fact-tank/2009/12/29/mystical-experiences/

Heishman, S. J., Singleton, E. G., & Moolchan, E. T. (2003). Tobacco craving questionnaire: Reliability and validity of a new multifactorial instrument. *Nicotine & Tobacco Research, 5*(5), 645–654. https://doi.org/10.1080/1462220031000158681

Helmond, P., Overbeek, G., Brugman, D., & Gibbs, J. C. (2015). A meta-analysis on cognitive distortions and externalizing problem behavior: Associations, moderators, and treatment effectiveness. *Criminal Justice and Behavior, 42*(3), 245–262. https://doi.org/10.1177/0093854814552842

Hertzog, C., & Shing, Y. (2010). *Handbook of lifespan development: Memory development across the life span.* New York, NY: Springer.

Herz, R. (2005). Odor-associative learning and emotion: Effects on perception and behavior. *Chemical Senses, 30*(suppl. 1), i250–i251. https://doi.org/10.1093/chemse/bjh209

Hirst, W., Phelps, E. A., Buckner, R. L., Budson, A. E., Cuc, A., Gabrieli, J. D.,…Meksin, R. (2009). Long-term memory for the terrorist attack of September 11: Flashbulb memories, event memories, and the factors that influence their retention. *Journal of Experimental Psychology: General, 138*(2), 161–176. https://doi.org/10.1037/a0015527

Hobson, J. A. (2009). REM sleep and dreaming: towards a theory of protoconciousness. *Nature Reviews Neuroscience, 10,* 803–813. https://doi.org/10.1038/nrn2716

Hobson, J. A., & McCarley, R. W. (1977). The brain as a dream state generator: An activation synthesis hypothesis of the dream process. *American Journal of Psychiatry, 134,* 1335–1348. https://doi.org/10.1176/ajp.134.12.1335

Hoffman, D. (2019). *The case against reality: Why evolution hid the truth from our eyes.* New York, NY: W. W. Norton & Company.

Hoffman, D., & Prakash, C. (2020). Objects of consciousness. *Frontiers in Psychology. 5*(577), 1–22.

Holmes, J., & Nolte, T. (2019). "Surprise" and the Bayesian Brain: Implications for psychotherapy theory and practice. *Frontiers in Psychology, 10*(592), 1–13.

Hopkins, R. (2016). Sartre. In Amy Kind (Ed.), *The Routledge Handbook of Philosophy of Imagination.* New York, NY: Routledge.

Hubble, E. (1929). A relation between distance and radial velocity among extra-galactic nebulae. *Proceedings of the National Academy of Sciences USA, 15*(3), 168–173. https://doi.org/10.1073/pnas.15.3.168

Hughes, B. L., Ambady, N., & Zaki, J. (2017). Trusting outgroup, but not ingroupmembers, requires control: Neural and behavioral evidence. *Social Cognitive and Affective Neuroscience, 12*(3), 372–381. https://doi.org/10.1093/scan/nsw139

Hurovitz, C., Dunn, S., Domhoff, G., and Fiss, H. (1999). The dreams of blind men and women: a replication and etension of previous findings. *Dreaming, 9*(2/3).

Hussein, B. A. S. (2012). The Sapir-Whorf hypothesis today. *Theory and Practice in Language Studies, 2*(3), 642–646.

Husserl, E. (1900/1999). *The essential Husserl.* D. Welton (ed.). Bloomington, IN: Indiana University Press.

Husserl, E. (1954). The crisis of European sciences and transcendental phenomenology: an introduction to phenomenological philosophy, *Husserliana,* vol. VI. Walter Biemel. (Ed.). The Hague: Nijhoff

Hutcherson, C. A., & Gross, J. J. (2011). The moral emotions: A social-functionalist account of anger, disgust, and contempt. *Journal of Personality and Social Psychology, 100*(4), 719–737. https://doi.org/10.1037/a0022408

Jackson, R. R., & Cross, F. R. (2013). A cognitive perspective on aggressive mimicry. *Journal of Zoology, 290*(3), 161–171. https://doi.org/10.1111/jzo.12036

James, W. (1890). *The Principles of Psychology Vols. 1–2.* New York, NY: Pantianos Classics.

James, W. (1898). *The will to believe and other essays in popular philosophy and human immortality.* New York, NY: Pantianos Classics.

James, W. (1904). Does "consciousness" exist? *The Journal of Philosophy, Psychology and Scientific Methods, 1*(18), 477–491. https://doi.org/10.2307/2011942

James, W., & Kuklick, B. (1996). *Writings: 1902–1910.* Literary Classics of the United States.

Janis, I. (1991). Groupthink. In E. Griffin (Ed.), *A first look at communication theory* (pp. 235–246). New York, NY: McGraw-Hill.

Jaspers, K. (1951/2003). *Way to wisdom: An introduction to philosophy.* New Haven: Yale University Press.

Jaspers, K. (1959). *General psychopathology* (Vol. 1–2). Baltimore, MD: Johns Hopkins University Press.

Jaspers, K. (1959). *Truth and symbol.* Lanham, MD: Rowman and Littlefield.

Jaspers, K. (1971). *Philosophy of existence* (R. Grabau, trans.). Berlin: Walter de Gruyter.

Johansson, R., Town, J. M., & Abbass, A. (2014). Davanloo's Intensive Short-Term Dynamic Psychotherapy in a tertiary psychotherapy service: Overall effectiveness and association between unlocking the unconscious and outcome. *PeerJ, 2.* https://doi.org/10.7717/peerj.548

Johnson, K. V. A. (2020). Gut microbiome composition and diversity are related to human personality traits. *Human Microbiome Journal, 15.* https://doi.org/10.1016/j.humic.2019.100069

Jonas, P., & Lisman, J. (2014). Structure, function, and plasticity of hippocampal dentate gyrus microcircuits. *Frontiers in Neural Circuits, 8.* https://doi.org/10.3389/fncir.2014.00107

Joo, E. Y., Tae, W. S., Lee, M. J., Kang, J. W., Park, H. S., Lee, J. Y.,...Hong, S. B. (2010). Reduced brain gray matter concentration in clients with obstructive sleep apnea syndrome. *Sleep, 33*(2), 235–241. https://doi.org/10.1093/sleep/33.2.235

Jung, C. (1936). The concept of the collective unconscious. In Collected works (Vol. 9i). Routledge & Kegan Paul.

Jung, C. G. (1954). *The development of personality.* Princeton, NJ: Princeton University Press.

Jung, C. G. (1957). *The transcendent function* (A. R. Pope, trans). Zurich, Switzerland: Students' Association, C.G. Jung Institute.

Jung, C. G. (1960). *The psychogenesis of mental disease* (Vol. 3). London: Routledge & Kegan Paul.

Jung, C. G. (1963). *Memories, dreams, reflections* (R. & C. Winston, trans., A. Jaffé, ed.). New York, NY: Crown Publishing Group/ Random House.

Jung, C. (1966). *Two essays on analytical psychology.* Princeton, NJ: Princeton University Press.

Jung, C. G. (1966). *The practice of psychotherapy* (2nd ed.). Princeton, NJ: Princeton University Press.

Jung, C. G. (1967). *The collected works of C.G. Jung* (Vol. 8). Princeton, NJ: Princeton University Press.

Jung, C. G. (1973). *Synchronicity: An acausal connecting principle* (R. F. C. Hull, trans.). Princeton, NJ: Princeton University Press.

Jung, C. (1980). *The archetypes and the collective unconscious* (2nd ed.). Princeton, NJ: Princeton University Press.

Jung, C. G. (2009). *The red book: Liber novus* (S. Shamdasani, Ed.). New York, NY: W. W. Norton.

Jung, C. G., & Hull, R. F. C. (1975). The psychological foundations of the belief in spirits. In R. Hull & G. Adler (Eds.), *Collected Works of C.G. Jung, Volume 8: Structure and dynamics of the psyche* (Vol. 8). Princeton, NJ: Princeton University Press. doi:10.2307/j.ctt5hhr1w

Jung, Y. H., Kang, D. H., Jang, J. H., Park, H. Y., Byun, M. S., Kwon, S. J.,...Kwon, J. S. (2010). The effects of mind–body training on stress reduction, positive affect, and plasma catecholamines. *Neuroscience Letters, 479*(2), 138–142. https://doi.org/10.1016/j.neulet.2010.05.048

Kahneman, D., & Deaton, A. (2010). High income improves evaluation of life but not emotional well-being. *Proceedings of the National Academy of Sciences USA, 107*(38), 16489–16493. https://doi.org/10.1073/pnas.1011492107

Kahneman, D., & Tversky, A. (1973). On the psychology of prediction. *Psychological Review, 80*(4), 237–251. https://doi.org/10.1037/h0034747

Kahneman, D., & Tversky, A. (1984). Choices, values, and frames. *American Psychologist*, *39*(4), 341–350. https://doi.org/10.1037/0003-066x.39.4.341

Kant, I. (1929). *Critique of pure reason* (N. K. Smith, trans.). Boston, MA: Bedford.

Kapur, N., Ellison, D., Smith, M. P., McLellan, D. L., & Burrows, E. H. (1992). Focal retrograde amnesia following bilateral temporal lobe pathology: A neuropsychological and magnetic resonance study. *Brain*, *115*(1), 73–85. https://doi.org/10.1093/brain/115.1.73

Karau, S. J., & Williams, K. D. (1993). Social loafing: A meta-analytic review and theoretical integration. *Journal of Personality and Social Psychology*, *65*(4), 681–706. https://doi.org/10.1037/0022-3514.65.4.681

Kastrup, B. (2019). *The idea of the world: A multi-disciplinary argument for the mental nature of reality*. Alresford, England: John Hunt Publishing.

Kelly, D. & Roedder, E. (2008). Racial cognition and the ethics of implicit bias. *Philosophy Compass*, *3*(3), 522–540.

Keltner, D., & Haidt, J. (2003). Approaching awe: A moral, spiritual, and aesthetic emotion. *Cognition and Emotion*, *17*, 297–314. https://doi.org/10.1080/02699930302297

Kernberg, O. F. (2016). The four basic components of psychoanalytic technique and derived psychoanalytic psychotherapies. *World Psychiatry*, *15*(3), 287–288. https://doi.org/10.1002/wps.20368

Kerr, M. E., & Bowen, M. (1988). *Family evaluation*. New York, NY: W. W. Norton & Company.

Khedr, E. M., Hamed, E., Said, A., & Basahi, J. (2002). Handedness and language cerebral lateralization. *European Journal of Applied Physiology*, *87*(4–5), 469–473. https://doi.org/10.1007/s00421-002-0652-y

Kierkegaard, S. (1843/1985). *Fear and trembling*. Alastair Hannay (trans.) London: Penguin Classics.

Kierkegaard, S. (1849/2004). *The sickness unto death*. Alastair Hannay (trans.) London: Penguin Classics.

Kierkegaard, S. (1980). *The concept of anxiety: A simple psychologically orienting deliberation on the dogmatic issue of hereditary sin*. Princeton, NJ: Princeton University Press.

Killingsworth, M. A., & Gilbert, D. T. (2010). A wandering mind is an unhappy mind. *Science*, *330*(6006), 932–932. https://doi.org/10.1126/science.1192439

Kim, D.-J., Bolbecker, A. R., Howell, J., Rass, O., Sporns, O., Hetrick, W. P., Breier A., & O'Donnell, B. F. (2013). Disturbed resting state EEG synchronization in bipolar disorder: A graph-theoretic analysis. *NeuroImage: Clinical*, *2*, 414–423. https://doi.org/10.1016/j.nicl.2013.03.007

Kim, H. N., Yun, Y., Ryu, S., Chang, Y., Kwon, M. J., Cho, J.,...Kim, H. L. (2018). Correlation between gut microbiota and personality in adults: A cross-sectional study. *Brain, Behavior, and Immunity*, *69*, 374–385. https://doi.org/10.1016/j.bbi.2017.12.012

Kirchoff, M., Parr, T., Palacios, E., Friston, K., & Kiverstein, J. (2018). The Markov blankets of life: autonomy, active inference and the free energy principle. *Journal R. Soc. Interface*, *15*, 20170792.

Klein, C. (2014). The brain at rest: What it is doing and why that matters. *Philosophy of Science*, *81*(5). https://doi.org/974-985.10.1086/677692

Knickmeyer, R. C., Gouttard, S., Kang, C., Evans, D., Wilber, K., Smith, J. K.,...Gilmore, J. H. (2008). A structural MRI study of human brain development from birth to 2 years. *Journal of Neuroscience*, *28*(47), 12176–12182. https://doi.org/10.1523/jneurosci.3479-08.2008

Kniffin, K. M., Yan, J., Wansink, B., & Schulze, W. D. (2017). The sound of cooperation: Musical influences on cooperative behavior. *Journal of Organizational Behavior*, *38*(3), 372–390. https://doi.org/10.1002/job.2128

Knight, L., & Depue, B. (2019). New frontiers in anxiety research: The translational potential of the bed nucleus of the stria terminalis. *Frontiers in Psychiatry*, Vol. 10, Article 510, 1–7.

Kobayashi, M., Kikuchi, D., & Okamura, H. (2009). Imaging of ultraweak spontaneous photon emission from human body displaying diurnal rhythm. *PLoS One*, *4*(7). https://doi.org/10.1371/journal.pone.0006256

Kober, H., Mende-Siedlecki, P., Kross, E. F., Weber, J., Mischel, W., Hart, C. L., & Ochsner, K. N. (2010). Prefrontal–striatal pathway underlies cognitive regulation of craving. *Proceedings of the National Academy of Sciences USA*, *107*(33), 14811–14816. https://doi.org/10.1073/pnas.1007779107

Korb, A. (2015). *The upward spiral: Using neuroscience to reverse the course of depression, one small change at a time*. Oakland, CA: New Harbinger Publications.

Kraus, B. J., Robinson II, R. J., White, J. A., Eichenbaum, H., & Hasselmo, M. E. (2013). Hippocampal "time cells": Time versus path integration. *Neuron, 78*(6), 1090–1101. https://doi.org/10.1016/j.neuron.2013.04.015

Krebs, P., Norcross, J. C., Nicholson, J. M., & Prochaska, J. O. (2018). Stages of change and psychotherapy outcomes: A review and meta-analysis. *Journal of Clinical Psychology, 74*(11), 1964–1979. https://doi.org/10.1002/jclp.22683

Kroll, J. F., & Dussias, P. E. (2017). The benefits of multilingualism to the personal and professional development of residents of the US. *Foreign Language Annals, 50*(2), 248–259. https://doi.org/10.1111/flan.12271

Kross, E., Berman, M. G., Mischel, W., Smith, E. E., & Wager, T. D. (2011). Social rejection shares somatosensory representations with physical pain. *Proceedings of the National Academy of Sciences USA, 108*(15), 6270–6275. https://doi.org/10.1073/pnas.1102693108

Kruger, J., Wirtz, D., & Miller, D. T. (2005). Counterfactual thinking and the first instinct fallacy. *Journal of Personality and Social Psychology, 88*(5), 725–735. https://doi.org/10.1037/0022-3514.88.5.725

Kuhn, T. S. (2012). *The structure of scientific revolutions* (4th ed.). Chicago, IL: University of Chicago Press.

Lacey, E. P. (1998). What is an adaptive environmentally induced parental effect? In T. Mousseau & C. W. Fox (Eds.), *Maternal effects as adaptations* (pp. 54–66). New York, NY: Oxford University Press.

Lachaux, J. P., Rodriguez, E., Martinerie, J., Adam, C., Hasboun, D., & Varela, F. J. (2000). Gamma-band activity in human intracortical recordings triggered by cognitive tasks. *European Journal of Neuroscience, 12*, 2608–2622. https://doi.org/10.1046/j.1460-9568.2000.00163.x

Lacy, J. W., & Stark, C. E. (2013). The neuroscience of memory: Implications for the courtroom. *Nature Reviews Neuroscience, 14*(9), 649–658. https://doi.org/10.1038/nrn3563

Langeslag, S. (2018). Effects of organization and disorganization on pleasantness, calmness and the frontal negativity in the event-related potential. *Plos One, 13*(8): e0202726

Latzman, R. D., Taglialatela, J. P., & Hopkins, W. D. (2015). Delay of gratification is associated with white matter connectivity in the dorsal prefrontal cortex: a diffusion tensor imaging study in chimpanzees (Pan troglodytes). *Proceedings of the Royal Society B: Biological Sciences, 282*(1809). https://doi.org/10.1098/rspb.2015.0764

Laughlin C., McManus J., & d'Aquili, E. (1990). *Brain, symbol and experience: Toward a neurophenomenology of consciousness*. New York: Columbia University Press.

Lazar, S. W., Kerr, C. E., Wasserman, R. H., Gray, J. R., Greve, D. N., Treadway, M. T.,... Rauch, S. L. (2005). Meditation experience is associated with increased cortical thickness. *Neuroreport, 16*(17), 1893–1897. https://doi.org/10.1097/01.wnr.0000186598.66243.19

Leach, C. (2017). Understanding shame and guilt. In L. Woodyatt, E. L. Worthington, Jr., M. Wenzel, & B. J. Griffin (Eds.), *Handbook of the psychology of self-forgiveness* (pp. 17–28). Cham, Germany: Springer. https://doi.org/10.1007/978-3-319-60573-9_2

Ledoux, J. E., & Brown, R. (2017). A higher-order theory of emotional consciousness. *Proceedings of the National Academy of Sciences, 114*(10). https://doi.org/10.1073/pnas.1619316114

Lee, S.-K., Lee, C.-M., & Park, J.-H. (2015). Effects of combined exercise on physical fitness and neurotransmitters in children with ADHD: A pilot randomized controlled study. *Journal of Physical Therapy Science, 27*(9), 2915–2919. https://doi.org/10.1589/jpts.27.2915

Lefebvre, E., & D'Angiulli, A. (2019). Imagery-mediated verbal learning depends on vividness-familiarity interactions: the possible role of dualistic resting state network activity interference. *Brain Sciences, 9*(143), 1–19.

Leflot, G., Onghena, P., & Colpin, H. (2010). Teacher–child interactions: relations with children's self-concept in second grade. *Infant and Child Development, 19*(4), 385–405. https://doi.org/10.1002/icd.672

Leto, L., & Feola, M. (2014). Cognitive impairment in heart failure clients. *Journal of Geriatric Cardiology, 11*(4), 316–328. https://doi.org/10.11909/j.issn.1671-5411.2014.04.007

Leuzinger-Bohleber, M., Arnold, S., & Solms, M. (2017). *The unconscious: A bridge between psychoanalysis and cognitive neuroscience*. Milton Park, England: Routledge.

Levenson, H. (2003). Time-limited dynamic psychotherapy: An integrationist perspective. *Journal of Psychotherapy Integration, 13*(3–4), 300–333. https://doi.org/10.1037/1053-0479.13.3-4.300

Levine, P. A., & Frederick, A. (1997). *Waking the tiger: Healing trauma: The innate capacity to transform overwhelming experiences.* Berkeley, CA: North Atlantic Books.

Levinson, D. B., Smallwood, J., & Davidson, R. J. (2012). The persistence of thought: Evidence for a role of working memory in the maintenance of task-unrelated thinking. *Psychological Science, 23*(4), 375–380. https://doi.org/10.1177/0956797611431465

Levy, D. J., Thavikulwat, A. C., & Glimcher, P. W. (2013). State dependent valuation: The effect of deprivation on risk preferences. *PloS One, 8*(1). https://doi.org/10.1371/journal.pone.0053978

Lewis, H. B. (1971). *Shame and guilt in neurosis.* New York, NY: International University Press.

Lezak, M., Howieson, D., Bigler, E., & Tranel, D. (2012). *Neuropsychological assessment* (5th ed.). New York, NY: Oxford University Press.

Li, W., Mai, X., & Liu, C. (2014). The default mode network and social understanding of others: What do brain connectivity studies tell us? *Frontiers in Human Neuroscience, 8*(14), 1–15. https://doi.org/10.3389/fnhum.2014.00074

Libet, B. (1973). Electrical stimulation of cortex in human subjects and conscious sensory aspects. In A. Iggo (Ed.), *Somatosensory system: Handbook of sensory physiology* (Vol. 2, pp. 743–790). Berlin, Germany: Springer. https://doi.org/10.1007/978-3-642-65438-1_20

Libet, B. (1999). Do we have free will? *Journal of Consciousness Studies, 6*(8–9), 47–57.

Libet, B., Wright, E. W., & Gleason, C. A. (1982). Readiness-potentials preceding unrestricted: Spontaneous vs. pre-planned voluntary acts. *Electroencephalography and Clinical Neurophysiology, 54,* 322–335. https://doi.org/10.1016/0013-4694(82)90181-x

Lieberman, M. D., Eisenberger, N. I., Crockett, M. J., Tom, S. M., Pfeifer, J. H., & Way, B. M. (2007). Putting feelings into words. *Psychological Science, 18*(5), 421–428. https://doi.org/10.1111/j.1467-9280.2007.01916.x

Lisle, D., & Goldhammer, A. (2003). *The plea-sure trap: Mastering the hidden force that undermines health and happiness.* Summertown, TN: Healthy Living Publications.

Litz, B. T., Stein, N., Delaney, E., Lebowitz, L., Nash, W. P., Silva, C., & Maguen, S. (2009). Moral injury and moral repair in war veterans: A preliminary model and intervention strategy. *Clinical Psychology Review, 29*(8), 695–706. https://doi.org/10.1016/j.cpr.2009.07.003

Liuzza, M. T., Lindholm, T., Hawley, C. B., Gustafsson Sendén, M., Ekström, I., Olsson, M. J., & Olofsson, J. K. (2018). Body odour disgust sensitivity predicts authoritarian attitudes. *Royal Society Open Science, 5*(2). https://doi.org/10.1098/rsos.171091

Loewenstein, D. A., Acevedo, A., Luis, C., Crum, T., Barker, W. W., & Duara, R. (2004). Semantic interference deficits and the detection of mild Alzheimer's disease and mild cognitive impairment without dementia. *Journal of the International Neuropsychological Society, 10*(1), 91–100. https://doi.org/10.1017/s1355617704101112

Loftus, E. F. (1979). *Eyewitness testimony.* Cambridge, MA: Harvard University Press.

Loftus, E. F. (2005). Planting misinformation in the human mind: A 30-year investigation of the malleability of memory. *Learning & Memory, 12*(4), 361–366. https://doi.org/10.1101/lm.94705

Long, M., Verbeke, W., Ein-Dor, T., & Vrtička, P. (2020). A functional neuro-anatomical model of human attachment (*NAMA*): Insights from first- and second-person social neuroscience. *Cortex, 126,* 281–321. 10.1016/j.cortex.2020.01.010

Long, Z., Duan, X., Xie, B., Du, H., Li, R., Xu, Q.,...Chen, H. (2013). Altered brain structural connectivity in post-traumatic stress disorder: a diffusion tensor imaging tractography study. *Journal of Affective Disorders, 150*(3), 798–806. https://doi.org/10.1016/j.jad.2013.03.004

Lopes da Silva, F. (2003). Visual dreams in the congenitally blind. *Trends in Cognitive Sciences, 7*(8), 328–330.

Luebbert, M. C., & Rosen, D. H. (1999). Evolutionary memory. In D.H. Rosen & M.C. Luebbert (Eds.), *Evolution of the psyche* (pp. 139–149). Praeger.

MacLean, P. D. (1990). *The triune brain in evolution: Role in paleocerebral functions.* New York, NY: Plenum Press.

Maddock, R., Garrett, A., & Buonocore, M. (2003). Posterior cingulate cortex activation by emotional words: fMRI evidence from a valence decision task. *Human Brain Mapping, 18*(1), 30–41. https://doi.org/10.1002/hbm.10075

Mahler, M. S. (1968). *On human symbiosis and the vicissitudes of individuation, Vol. 1: Infantile psychosis.* New York, NY: International Universities Press.

Malmberg, K., & Xu, J. (2007). On the flexibility and the fallibility of associative memory. *Memory and Cognition, 35*(3), 545–556. https://doi.org/10.3758/bf03193293

Mandolesi, L., Polverino, A., Montuori, S., Foti, F., Ferraioli, G., Pierpaolo Sorrentino, P., & Sorrentino, G. (2018). Effects of physical exercise on cognitive functioning and wellbeing: Biological and psychological benefits. *Frontiers in Psychology, 9,* 509.

Margulis, L., & Fester, R. (Eds.). (1991). *Symbiosis as a source of evolutionary innovation: speciation and morphogenesis.* Boston, MA: MIT Press.

Markowsky, G. (2017). Information theory. In *Encyclopedia Britannica.* Chicago, IL: Encyclopedia Britannica, Inc.

Marks-Tarlow, T. (2012). *Clinical intuition in psychotherapy: The neurobiology of embodied response.* New York, NY: W. W. Norton & Company.

Mars, R., Neubert, F., Noonan, M., Sallet, J., Toni, I., & Rushworth, M. (2012). On the relationship between the "default mode network" and the "social brain." *Frontiers in Human Neuroscience, 6*(189), 1–9. https://doi.org/10.3389/fnhum.2012.00189

Maslow, A. H. (1964). *Religions, values, and peak-experiences.* Columbus, OH: Ohio State University Press.

Mason, L., Peters, E., Williams, S. C., & Kumari, V. (2017). Brain connectivity changes occurring following cognitive behavioral therapy for psychosis predict long-term recovery, *Translational Psychiatry, 7,* e1001.

Masterpasqua, F. (2009). Psychology and epigenetics. *Review of General Psychology, 13*(3), 194–201. https://doi.org/10.1037/a0016301

Mateos-Aparicio, P., & Rodriguez-Moreno, A. (2019). The impact of studying brain plasticity. *Frontiers of Cellular Neuroscience, 3,* Article 66, 1–5.

Mattoon, M. (2006). Dreams. In R. Papadopoulos (Ed.), *The handbook of Jungian psychology, theory, practice and applications* (pp. 244–259). New York, NY: Routledge.

McGilchrist, I. (2009). *The master and his emissary.* New Haven, CT: Yale University Press.

McGurk, H., & MacDonald, J. (1976). Hearing lips and seeing voices. *Nature, 264,* 746–748. https://doi.org/10.1038/264746a0

McKinney, K. (2011). The effects of adrenaline on arousal and attraction. *Scholars: McKendree University Online Journal of Undergraduate Research, 17.* Retrieved from https://www.mckendree.edu/academics/scholars/issue17/mckinney.htm

Melloni, L., Molina, C., Pena, M., Torres, D., Singer, W., & Rodriguez, E. (2007). Synchronization of neural activity across cortical areas correlates with conscious perception. *Journal of Neuroscience, 27*(11), 2858–2865. https://doi.org/10.1523/jneurosci.4623-06.2007

Merleau-Ponty, M. (1945/2014). *Phenomenology of perception* (D. Landes trans.). New York, NY: Routledge.

Merleau-Ponty, M. (1968). *The Visible and the Invisible* (A. Lingis, trans.). New York, NY: Routledge.

Mesle, C. R. (2008). *Process-relational philosophy: An introduction to Alfred North Whitehead.* West Conshohocken, PA: Templeton Press.

Meyer, M., Williams, K., & Eisenberger, N. (2015). Why social pain can live on: Different neural mechanisms are associated with reliving social and physical pain. *Plos One, 10*(6), 1–20. https://doi.org/10.1371/journal.pone.0128294

Michl, P., Meindl, T., Meister, F., Born, C., Engel, R. R., Reiser, M., & Hennig-Fast, K. (2012). Neurobiological underpinnings of shame and guilt: a pilot fMRI study. *Social Cognitive and Affective Neuroscience, 9*(2), 150–157. https://doi.org/10.1093/scan/nss114

Milgram, S. (1963). Behavioral study of obedience. *The Journal of Abnormal and Social Psychology, 67*(4), 371–378. https://doi.org/10.1037/h0040525

Millière, R., Carhart-Harris, R. L., Roseman, L., Trautwein, F. M., & Berkovich-Ohana, A. (2018, September). Psychedelics, meditation, and self-consciousness. *Frontiers in Psychology, 9.* https://doi.org/10.3389/fpsyg.2018.01475

Miltner, W. H. R., Braun, C., Arnold, M., Witte, H., & Taub, E. (1999). Coherence of gamma-band EEG activity as a basis for associative learning. *Nature, 397*(6718), 434–436. https://doi.org/10.1038/17126

Miron, R. (2012). *Karl Jaspers: From selfhood to being.* New York: Value Inquiry Book Series.

Mischel, W., Shoda, Y., & Rodriguez, M. L. (1992). Delay of gratification in children. In G. Lowenstein & J. Elster (Eds.), *Choice over time* (pp. 147–164). New York, NY: Russell Sage Foundation.

Mišić, B., Dunkley, B. T., Sedge, P. A., Costa, L. D., Fatima, Z., Berman, M. G., Doesburg S.M., Mcintosh A.R., Grodecki R., Jetly R., Pang E.W., & Taylor, M. J. (2016). Post-traumatic stress constrains the dynamic repertoire of neural activity. *The Journal of Neuroscience, 36*(2), 419–431. https://doi.org/10.1523/jneurosci.1506-15.2016

Mitchell, J., Banaji, M., & Macrae, N. (2005). The link between social cognition and self-referential thought in the medial prefrontal cortex. *Journal of Cognitive Neuroscience, 17*(8), 1306–1315. https://doi.org/10.1162/0898929055002418

Mitchell, M., & Potenza, M., (2014). Recent insights into the neurobiology of impulsivity, *Curr Addic Rep., 1*(4), 309–319.

Miyazaki, M., Hirashima, M., & Nozaki, D. (2010). The "cutaneous rabbit" hopping out of the body. *Journal of Neuroscience, 30*(5), 1856–1860. https://doi.org/10.1523/jneurosci.3887-09.2010

Moffitt, T.E., Houts, R., Asherson, P., Belsky, D. W., Corcoran, D. L., Hammerle, M.,... Caspi, A. (2015). Is adult ADHD a childhood-onset neurodevelopmental disorder? Evidence from a four-decade longitudinal cohort study. *American Journal of Psychiatry, 172*(10). https://doi.org/10.1176/appi.ajp.2015.14101266

Mogilner, C., & Norton, M. I. (2016). Time, money, and happiness. *Current Opinion in Psychology, 10,* 12–16. https://doi.org/10.1016/j.copsyc.2015.10.018

Molho, C., Tybur, J. M., Güler, E., Balliet, D., & Hofmann, W. (2017). Disgust and anger relate to different aggressive responses to moral violations. *Psychological Science, 28*(5), 609–619.

Molyneux, R. J., & Ralphs, M. H. (1992). Plant toxins and palatability to herbivores. *Rangeland Ecology & Management/Journal of Range Management Archives, 45*(1), 13–18. https://doi.org/10.2307/4002519

Moore, M., & Fresco, D. (2012). Depressive realism: a meta-analytic review. *Clinical Psychology Review, 32,* 496–509.

Moran, D. (2015). Everydayness, historicity, and the world of science: Husserl's lifeworld reconsidered. The phenomenological critique of mathematisation and the question of responsibility. In L. Ucnik, I. Chvatik, A. Williams (Eds.), *Contributions to phenomenology* (pp. 107–132). Springer International Publishing.

Morein-Zamir, S., Soto-Faraco, S., & Kingstone, A. (2003). Auditory capture of vision: Examining temporal ventriloquism. *Cognitive Brain Research, 17*(1), 154–163. https://doi.org/10.1016/s0926-6410(03)00089-2

Murre, J. M., & Dros, J. (2015). Replication and analysis of Ebbinghaus' forgetting curve. *PloS One, 10*(7). https://doi.org/10.1371/journal.pone.0120644

Nagel, T. (1974). What is it like to be a bat? *The Philosophical Review, 83*(4), 435–450.

Nagel, T. (2012). *Mind and cosmos: Why the materialist neo-Darwinian conception of nature is almost certainly false.* New York, NY: Oxford University Press.

Naqvi, N. H., Gaznick, N., Tranel, D., & Bechara, A. (2014). The insula: A critical neural substrate for craving and drug seeking under conflict and risk. *Annals of the New York Academy of Sciences, 1316,* 53–70. https://doi.org/10.1111/nyas.12415

Neisser, U. (1997). The roots of self-knowledge: Perceiving self, it, and thou. In J. G. Snodgrass & R. L. Thompson (Eds.), *The self across psychology: Self-recognition, self-awareness, and the self-concept, Annals of the New York Academy of Sciences* (Vol. 818, pp. 18–33). New York, NY: New York Academy of Sciences. https://doi.org/10.1111/j.1749-6632.1997.tb48243.x

New, A. S., & Barbara, S. (2010). An opioid deficit in borderline personality disorder:

Self-cutting, substance abuse, and social dysfunction. *American Journal of Psychiatry, 167*(8), 882–885. https://doi.org/10.1176/appi.ajp.2010.10040634

Newberg, A. B., & d'Aquili, E. G. (2000). The neuropsychology of religious and spiritual experience. *Journal of Consciousness Studies, 7*(11–12), 251–266. https://doi.org/10.1016/b978-012417645-4/50073-0

Newen, A., & Vogeley, K. (2003). Self-representation: Searching for a neural signature of self-consciousness. *Consciousness and Cognition, 12,* 529–543. https://doi.org/10.1016/s1053-8100(03)00080-1

Ng, C. T. C., & James, S. (2013). "Directive approach" for Chinese clients receiving psychotherapy: Is that really a priority? *Frontiers in Psychology, 4.* https://doi.org/10.3389/fpsyg.2013.00049

Nietzsche, F. W. (1998). *Twilight of the idols, or, How to philosophize with a hammer* (D. Large, trans.). New York, NY: Oxford University Press.

Nir, Y., & Tononi, G. (2010). Dreaming and the brain: From phenomenology to neurophysiology. *Trends in Cognitive Sciences, 14*(2), 88–100. https://doi.org/10.1016/j.tics.2009.12.001

Northoff, G. (2016). *Neuro-philosophy and the healthy mind.* New York, NY: W. W. Norton & Company.

Northoff, G. (2016). Neuroscience and whitehead I: Neuro-ecological model of brain. *Axiomathes, 26*(3), 219–252. https://doi.org/10.1007/s10516-016-9286-2

Northoff, G. (2011). *Neuropsychoanalysis in practice: Brain, self and objects.* Oxford: Oxford University Press.

Northoff, G. (2018). *The spontaneous brain: From the mind-body to the world-brain problem.* Cambridge, MA: MIT Press.

Northoff, G. (2016). Neuroscience and whitehead I: Neuro-ecological model of brain. *Axiomathes, 26*(3), 219–252. https://doi.org/10.1007/s10516-016-9286-2

Northoff, G. (2016). *Neuro-philosophy and the healthy mind.* New York, NY: W. W. Norton & Company.

Northoff, G., & Bermpohl, F. (2004). Cortical midline structures and the self. *Trends in Cognitive Sciences, 8*(3), 102–107. https://doi.org/10.1016/j.tics.2004.01.004

Northoff, G., Wainio-Theberge, S., & Evers, K. (2019). Is temporo-spatial dynamics the "common currency" of brain and mind? In quest of "spatiotemporal neuroscience." *Physics of Life Reviews.* https://doi.org/10.1016/j.plrev.2019.05.002

Nowak, A., Vallacher, R. R., Tesser, A., & Borkowski, W. (2000). Society of self: The emergence of collective properties in self-structure. *Psychological Review, 107*(1), 39–61. https://doi.org/10.1037/0033-295x.107.1.39

Odinot, G., Wolters, G., & van Koppen, P. J. (2009). Eyewitness memory of a supermarket robbery: A case study of accuracy and confidence after 3 months. *Law and Human Behavior, 33*(6), 506–514. https://doi.org/10.1007/s10979-008-9152-x

Ogden, T. H. (1997). Reverie and metaphor: Some thoughts on how I work as a psychoanalyst. *International Journal of Psycho-Analysis, 78,* 719–732. https://doi.org/10.1002/j.2167-4086.2004.tb00156.x

Ogden, T. H. (2004). The analytic third: Implications for psychoanalytic theory and technique. *The Psychoanalytic Quarterly, 73*(1), 167–195.

Ogden, T.H. (2008). Bion's four principles of mental functioning. *Fort Da, 14*(2), 11–35.

Oizumi, M., Albantakis, L., Tononi, G. (2014). From the phenomenology to the mechanisms of consciousness: Integrated Information Theory 3.0. *PLoS Comput Biol 10*(5): e1003588. doi:10.1371/journal.pcbi.10035888

Oldmeadow, H. (1992). Sankar's doctrine of maya, *Asian Philosophy, 2*(2).

Oleynick, V. C., Thrash, T. M., LeFew, M. C., Moldovan, E. G., & Kieffaber, P. D. (2014). The scientific study of inspiration in the creative process: Challenges and opportunities. *Frontiers in Human Neuroscience, 8.* https://doi.org/10.3389/fnhum.2014.00436

O'Mara, S. (2005). The subiculum: What it does, what it might do, and what neuroanatomy has yet to tell us. *Journal of Anatomy, 207*(3), 271–282. https://doi.org/10.1111/j.1469-7580.2005.00446.x

Onu, D., Kessler, T., & Smith, J. R. (2016). Admiration: A conceptual review. *Emotion Review, 8*(3), 218–230.

Osborne, D. M., Pearson-Leary, J., & McNay, E. C. (2015). The neuroenergetics of stress hormones in the hippocampus and implications for memory. *Frontiers in Neuroscience, 9*. https://doi.org/10.3389/fnins.2015.00164

Otterbring, T., & Sela, Y. (2020). Sexually arousing ads induce sex-specific financial decisions in hungry individuals. *Personality and Individual Differences, 152*. https://doi.org/10.1016/j.paid.2019.109576

Ouspensky, P. D. (2001). *In search of the miraculous* [Kindle edition]. Retrieved from http://www.amazon.com

Park, H., Correia, S., Ducorps, A., & Tallon-Budry, C. (2014). Spontaneous fluctuations in neural responses to heartbeats predict visual detection. *Nature Neuroscience, 17*, 612–618.

Pąchalska, M., Lipowska, M., & Lukaszewska, B. (2007). Towards a process neuropsychology: Microgenetic theory and brain science. *Acta Neuropsychologica, 5*(4), 228–245.

Panek, R. (2011). *The 4 percent universe: Dark matter, dark energy, and the race to discover the rest of reality.* New York, NY: First Mariner Books.

Panizzon, M. S., Vuoksimaa, E., Spoon, K. M., Jacobson, K. C., Lyons, M. J., Franz, C. E.,...Kremen, W. S. (2014). Genetic and environmental influences on general cognitive ability: Is G a valid latent construct? *Intelligence, 43*, 65–76. https://doi.org/10.1016/j.intell.2014.01.008

Panksepp, J. (1998). *Affective neuroscience: The foundations of human and animal emotions.* New York, NY: Oxford University Press.

Panksepp, J. (2012) *The archaeology of the mind, neuroevolutionary origins of human emotion.* W. W. Norton.

Panksepp, J., & Northoff, G. (2009). The trans-species core SELF: The emergence of active cultural and neuro-ecological agents through self-related processing within sub-cortical-cortical midline networks. *Consciousness and Cognition, 18*(1), 193–215. https://doi.org/10.1016/j.concog.2008.03.002

Panksepp, J., & Solms, M. (2012). What is neuropsychoanalysis? Clinically relevant studies of the minded brain. *Trends in Cognitive Sciences, 16*(1), 6–8. https://doi.org/10.1016/j.tics.2011.11.005

Papanicolaou, A. C., Simos, P. G., Castillo, E. M., Breier, J. I., Katz, J. S., & Wright, A. A. (2002). The hippocampus and memory of verbal and pictorial material. *Learning & Memory, 9*(3), 99–104. https://doi.org/10.1101/lm.44302

Patel, R., Spreng, R. N., Shin, L. M., & Girard, T. A. (2012). Neurocircuitry models of posttraumatic stress disorder and beyond: A meta-analysis of functional neuroimaging studies. *Neuroscience & Biobehavioral Reviews, 36*(9), 2130–2142. https://doi.org/10.1016/j.neubiorev.2012.06.003

Payne, B. K., Vuletich, H. A., & Lundberg, K. B. (2017). The bias of crowds: How implicit bias bridges personal and systemic prejudice. *Psychological Inquiry, 28*(4), 233–248.

Payne, J. D., & Nadel, L. (2004). Sleep, dreams and memory consolidation: The role of the stress hormone cortisol. *Learning and Memory, 11*, 671–678. https://doi.org/10.1101/lm.77104

Peirce, C. (1891). The architecture of theories. *The Monist, 1*(2), 161–176.

Pennycook, G., & Thompson, V. A. (2017). Base-rate neglect. In R. F. Pohl (Ed.), *Cognitive illusions: Intriguing phenomena in thinking, judgment and memory* (pp. 44–61). New York, NY: Routledge/Taylor & Francis Group.

Perls, F. (1947). *Ego, hunger, and aggression.* New York, NY: Vintage Books/Random House.

Perner, J. (2000). Memory and theory of mind. In F.I.M. Craik & E. Tulving (Eds.), *Oxford handbook of memory* (pp. 297–312). New York: Oxford University Press.

Perry, A. N., Westenbroek, C., & Becker, J. B. (2013). The development of a preference for cocaine over food identifies individual rats with addiction-like behaviors. *PloS One, 8*(11). https://doi.org/10.1371/journal.pone.0079465

Perry, J. C., & Cooper, S. H. (1986). A preliminary report on defenses and conflicts associated with borderline personality disorder. *Journal of the American Psychoanalytic Association, 34*(4), 863–893. https://doi.org/10.1177/000306518603400405

Peters, J., & Buchel, C. (2010). Episodic future thinking reduces reward delay discounting through an enhancement of prefrontal-mediotemporal interactions. *Neuron, 66*, 138–148. https://doi.org/10.1016/j.neuron.2010.03.026

Petersen, S. E., & Posner, M. I. (2012). The attention system of the human brain: 20 years after. *Annual Review of Neuroscience, 35*, 73–89. https://doi.org/10.1146/annurev-neuro-062111-150525

Piaget, J. (1973). *The child and reality: Problems of genetic psychology* (A. Rosin, trans.). New York, NY: Grossman.

Piaget, J., & Cook, M. T. (1952). *The origins of intelligence in children*. New York, NY: International University Press.

Piff, P. K., Dietze, P., Feinberg, M., Stancato, D. M., & Keltner, D. (2015). Awe, the small self, and prosocial behavior. *Journal of Personality and Social Psychology, 108*(6), 883–899. https://doi.org/10.1037/pspi0000018

Pinto, Y., van Gaal, S., Lange, F., Lamme, V., & Seth, A. (2015). Expectations accelerate entry of visual stimuli into awareness. *Journal of Vision, 15*(8), 13.

Piper-Mandy, E., & Rowe, T. D. (2010). Educating African-centered psychologists: Towards a comprehensive paradigm. *Journal of Pan African Studies, 3*(8), 5–23.

Plato. (1943). *Plato's The republic* (B. Jowett, Trans.). New York, NY: Books, Inc.

Plomin, R., DeFries, J. C., Knopik, V. S., & Neiderhiser, J. M. (2016). Top 10 replicated findings from behavioral genetics. *Perspectives on Psychological Science, 11*(1), 3–23. https://doi.org/10.1177/1745691615617439

Plotinus, Mackenna, S., & Dillon, J. M. (1991). *The enneads*. London, England: Penguin.

Pohling, R., & Diessner, R. (2016). Moral elevation and moral beauty: A review of the empirical literature. *Review of General Psychology, 20*(4), 412–425. https://doi.org/10.1037/gpr0000089

Popat, S., & Winslade, W. (2015). While you were sleepwalking: science and neurobiology of sleep disorders & the enigma of legal responsibility of violence during parasomnia. *Neuroethics, 8*, 203–214.

Pöppel, E. (1988). *Mindworks: Time and conscious experience*. New York, NY: Harcourt Brace Jovanovich.

Popper, K. R. (1968). *Conjectures and refutations: The growth of scientific knowledge*. New York, NY: Harper & Row.

Porges, S. W. (2011). *The polyvagal theory: Neurophysiological foundations of emotions, attachment, communication, and self-regulation*. New York, NY: W. W. Norton.

Poston, C. (1990). The biracial identity development model: A needed addition. *Journal of Counseling and Development, 69*, 152–155.

Prade, C., & Saroglou, V. (2016). Awe's effects on generosity and helping. *The Journal of Positive Psychology, 11*, 522–530.

Puputti, S., Hoppu, U., & Sandell, M. (2019). Taste sensitivity is associated with food consumption behavior but not with recalled pleasantness. *Foods, 8*(10). https://doi.org/10.3390/foods8100444

Purves, D., Augustine, G. J., Fitzpatrick, D., Katz, L. C., Lamantia, A. S., McNamara, J. O., & Williams, S. M. (2001). *Neuroscience* (2nd ed.). Sunderland, MA: Sinauer Associates.

Raichle, M. E. (2010). Two views of brain function. *Trends in Cognitive Sciences, 14*(4), 180–190. https://doi.org/10.1016/j.tics.2010.01.008

Raichle, M. E., MacLeod, A. M., Snyder, A. Z., Powers, W. J., Gusnard, D. A., & Shulman, G. L. (2001). A default mode of brain function. *Proceedings of the National Academy of Sciences USA, 98*(2), 676–682. https://doi.org/10.1073/pnas.98.2.676

Ramachandran, V. S. (2009, November). *The neurons that shaped civilization* [Video file]. Retrieved from http://www.ted.com/talks/vs_ramachandran_the_neurons_that_shaped_civilization

Rand, D. G., & Epstein, Z. G. (2014). Risking your life without a second thought: Intuitive decision-making and extreme altruism. *PLoS One, 9*. https://doi.org/10.1371/journal.pone.0109687

Rebollo, I. et.al. (2017). Stomach-brain synchrony reveals a novel, delayed-connectivity resting-state network in humans. *eLife, 7*: e33321

Rendina, H. J., Millar, B. M., Dash, G., Feldstein Ewing, S. W., & Parsons, J. T. (2018). The somatic marker hypothesis and sexual decision making: Understanding the role of Iowa Gambling Task performance and daily sexual arousal on the sexual behavior of gay and bisexual men. *Annals of Behavioral Medicine, 52*(5), 380–392. https://doi.org/10.1093/abm/kax006

Reuter, M. (2010). The Great Exaptation. Around the fundamental idea of evolutionary psychology. *Ecological Questions, 13*, 89. https://doi.org/10.12775/v10090-011-0050-3

Revonsuo, A. (2000). The reinterpretation of dreams: An evolutionary hypothesis of the function of dreaming. *Behavioral and Brain Sciences, 23*(6), 877–901. https://doi.org/10.1017/s0140525x00004015

Reyna, V. F., & Brainerd, C. J. (1995). Fuzzy-trace theory: An interim synthesis. *Learning and individual Differences, 7*(1), 1–75. https://doi.org/10.1016/1041-6080(95)90031-4

Richardson, R. (2006) *William James: In the maelstrom of American modernism*. New York, NY: First Mariner Book.

Rnic, K., Dozois, D. J. A., & Martin, R. A. (2016). Cognitive distortions, humor styles, and depression. *Europe's Journal of Psychology*, *12*(3), 348–362. https://doi.org/10.5964/ejop.v12i3.1118

Robins, R., & Schriber, R. (2009). The self-conscious emotions: How are they experienced, expressed, and assessed? *Social and Personality Psychology Compass*, *3*(6): 887–898.

Rochat, P. (2003). First levels of self-awareness as they unfold early in life. *Consciousness and Cognition, 12*(4), 717–731. https://doi.org/10.1016/S1053-8100(03)00081-3

Roesler, C. (2013). Evidence for the effectiveness of Jungian psychotherapy: A review of empirical studies. *Behavioral Science, 3,* 562–575. https://doi.org/10.3390/bs3040562

Rogers, C. R. (1951). *Client-centered therapy: Its current practice, implications, and theory.* Boston, MA: Houghton Mifflin.

Ronnberg, A., & Martin, K. (2010). *The book of symbols: Reflections on archetypal images.* Cologne, Germany: Taschen.

Rosen, D. H., Smith, S. M., Huston, H. L., & Gonzalez, G. (1991). Empirical study of associations between symbols and their meanings: Evidence of collective unconscious (archetypal) memory. *Journal of Analytical Psychology*, *36*(2), 211–228. https://doi.org/10.1111/j.1465-5922.1991.00211.x

Roth, L., Kaffenberger, T., Herwig, U., & Bruhl, A. B. (2014). Brain activation associated with pride and shame. *Neuropsychobiology, 69*(2), 95–106.

Roy, D. (2000) *Towards a process psychology: A model of integration.* Oregon, IL: Quality Books.

Roy, D. E. (2017). Can Whitehead's philosophy provide an adequate theoretical foundation for today's neuroscience? *Process Studies, 46*(1), 128–151. https://doi.org/10.5840/process20174617

Rozin, P., Lowery, L., Imada, S., & Haidt, J. (1999). The CAD triad hypothesis: a mapping between three moral emotions (contempt, anger, disgust) and three moral codes (community, autonomy, divinity). *Journal of Personality and Social Psychology*, *76*(4), 574–586. https://doi.org/10.1037/0022-3514.76.4.574

Rubak, S., Sandboek, A., Lauritzen, T., & Christensen, B. (2005). Motivational interviewing: A systematic review and meta-analysis. *British Journal of General Practice, 55*(513), 305–312. Retrieved from https://bjgp.org/content/55/513/305.short

Ruby, F. J., Smallwood, J., Engen, H., & Singer, T. (2013). How self-generated thought shapes mood—the relation between mind-wandering and mood depends on the socio-temporal content of thoughts. *PloS One, 8*(10). https://doi.org/10.1371/journal.pone.0077554

Ruch, S., Züst, M. A., & Henke, K. (2016). Subliminal messages exert long-term effects on decision-making. *Neuroscience of Consciousness*, *2016*(1). https://doi.org/10.1093/nc/niw013

Rudd, M., Vohs, K. D., & Aaker, J. (2012). Awe expands people's perception of time, alters decision making, and enhances well-being. *Psychological Science*, *23*(10), 1130–1136. https://doi.org/10.1177/0956797612438731

Ruff, C. C., & Fehr, E. (2014). The neurobiology of rewards and values in social decision making. *Nature Reviews Neuroscience*, *15*(8), 549–562. https://doi.org/10.1038/nrn3776

Ruisch, B., Anderson, R., Inbar, Y., & Pizarro, D. (2016). *Taste sensitivity predicts political ideology*. Retrieved from https://pdfs.semanticscholar.org/3afb/54b90c11b768e941a4e-f5e2e0c56fffcc6b3.pdf

Rusznack, Z., Henskens, W., Schofield, E., Kim, W., & Fu, Y. (2016). **Adult neurogenesis and gliogenesis: Possible mechanisms for neurorestoration**. *Experimental Neurobiology, 25*(3), 103–112.

Rutter, J., & Friedberg, R. (1999). Guidelines for the effective use of Socratic dialogue in cognitive therapy. In VandeCreek L. & Jackson T.L. (Eds.), *Innovations in clinical practice: A source book* (Vol. 17, pp. 481–490). Sarasota, FL: Professional Resource Press.

Sacco, L., Calabrese, P. (2010). Alien hand syndrome: a neurological disorder of will. *Schweiz Arch Neurol Psychiatr.*, *161*(2), 60–63.

Sacks, O. (1998). *A leg to stand on.* New York, NY: Simon & Schuster.

Sartre, J.-P. (1936/2012). *The imagination* (K. Williford and D. Rudrauf, trans.). London: Routledge.

Sartre, J.-P. (1940/2004). *The imaginary* (J. Webber, trans.). London: Routledge.

Sartre, J.-P. (1943/1969). Being and nothingness: An essay on phenomenological ontology (H. Barnes, trans.). London: Routledge.

Sartre, J.-P. (1983). *Notebooks for an ethics* (D. Pellaner, trans.). Chicago, IL: University of Chicago Press.

Saunders, P., & Skar, P. (2001). Archetypes, complexes and self-organization. *Journal of Analytical Psychology, 46*(2), 305–323. https://doi.org/10.1111/1465-5922.00238

Saxe, R. (2006). Why and how to study theory of mind with fMRI. *Brain Research, 1079*(1), 57–65. https://doi.org/10.1016/j.brainres.2006.01.001

Scarmeas, N., & Stern, Y. (2003). Cognitive reserve and lifestyle. *Journal of Clinical and Experimental Neuropsychology, 25*(5), 625–633. https://doi.org/10.1076/jcen.25.5.625.14576

Schacter, D. L., & Addis, D. R. (2007a). The cognitive neuroscience of constructive memory: remembering the past and imagining the future. *Philosophical Transactions of the Royal Society B: Biological Sciences, 362*(1481), 773–786. https://doi.org/10.1098/rstb.2007.2087

Schacter, D. L., & Addis, D. R. (2007b). The ghosts of past and future: A memory that works by piecing together bits of the past may be better suited to simulating future events than one that is a store of perfect records. *Nature, 445*(27). https://doi.org/10.1038/445027a

Schacter, D. L., Addis, D. R., Hassabis, D., Martin, V. C., Spreng, R. N., & Szpunar, K. K. (2012). The future of memory: remembering, imagining, and the brain. *Neuron, 76*(4), 677–694. https://doi.org/10.1016/j.neuron.2012.11.001

Schwartz, M. (2017). *The possibility principle: How quantum physics can improve the way you think, live, and love.* Louisville, CO: Sounds True.

Schlittmeier, S. J., Hellbrück, J., Thaden, R., & Vorländer, M. (2008). The impact of background speech varying in intelligibility: Effects on cognitive performance and perceived disturbance. *Ergonomics, 51*, 719–736. https://doi.org/10.1080/00140130701745925

Schnall, S., Haidt, J., Clore, G. L., & Jordan, A. H. (2008). Disgust as embodied moral judgment. *Personality and Social Psychology Bulletin, 34*(8), 1096–1109. https://doi.org/10.1177/0146167208317771

Schore, A. N. (2003a). *Affect regulation & the repair of the self.* New York: W. W. Norton.

Schore, A. N. (2003b). *Affect dysregulation & disorders of the self.* New York: W. W. Norton.

Schore, A. N. (2016). *Affect regulation and the origin of the self: The neurobiology of emotional development.* London: Routledge.

Schore, A. (2019). *Right brain psychotherapy.* New York, NY: W. W. Norton & Company.

Schubert, T., Zickfeld, J., Seibt, B., & Fiske, A. (2018). Moment-to-moment changes in feeling moved match changes in closeness, tears, goosebumps, and warmth: Time series analyses. *Cognition and Emotion, 32*(1), 1–11. https://doi.org/10.1080/02699931.2016.1268998

Schuck, S. E., & Crinella, F. M. (2005). Why children with ADHD do not have low IQs. *Journal of Learning Disabilities, 38*(3), 262–280. https://doi.org/10.1177/00222194050380030701

Schultz, H., Sommer, T., & Peters, J. (2015). The role of the human entorhinal cortex in a representational account of memory. *Frontiers in Human Neuroscience, 9*(628). https://doi.org/10.3389/fnhum.2015.00628

Schutte, N. S., & Malouff, J. M. (2014). A meta-analytic review of the effects of mindfulness meditation on telomerase activity. *Psychoneuroendocrinology, 42*, 45–48. https://doi.org/10.1016/j.psyneuen.2013.12.017

Seidman, L. J., Valera, E. M., Makris, N., Monuteaux, M. C., Boriel, D. L., Kelkar, K. …Faraone, S. V. (2006). Dorsolateral prefrontal and anterior cingulate cortex volumetric abnormalities in adults with attention-deficit/hyperactivity disorder identified by magnetic resonance imaging. *Biological Psychiatry, 60*(10), 1071–1080. https://doi.org/10.1016/j.biopsych.2006.04.031

Sedighimornani, N. (2018). Shame and its features: Understanding of shame. *European Journal of Social Sciences Studies, 3*(3), 75–107. Retrieved from https://oapub.org/soc/index.php/EJSSS/article/view/442

Semenza, C. (2017). The unconscious in cognitive science. In M. Leuzinger-Bohleber, S.

Arnold, & M. Solms (Eds.), *The unconscious: A bridge between psychoanalysis and cognitive neuroscience.* London: Routledge.

Sender, R., Fuchs, S., & Milo, R. (2016). Revised estimates for the number of human and bacterial cells in the body. *PloS Biology, 14*(8), e1002533.

Sengupta, J. (2009). Visceral Pain: The Neurophysiological Mechanism. *Handbook of experimental pharmacology.* (194): 31–74.

Seth, A. K., & Friston, K. J. (2016). Active interoceptive inference and the emotional brain. *Philosophical Transactions of the Royal Society B: Biological Sciences, 371*(1708). https://doi.org/10.1098/rstb.2016.0007

Sever, R. W., Vivas, A. C., Vale, F. L., & Schoenberg, M. R. (2018). Wada asymmetry in clients with drug-resistant mesial temporal lobe epilepsy: Implications for postoperative neuropsychological outcomes. *Epilepsia Open, 3*(3), 399–408. https://doi.org/10.1002/epi4.12250

Shafranske, E. P. (2009). Spiritually oriented psychodynamic psychotherapy. *Journal of Clinical Psychology, 65*(2), 147–157. https://doi.org/10.1002/jclp.20565

Shapiro, D. (2000). *Dynamic of character.* New York, NY: Basic Books.

Sheldon, S., McAndrews, M. P., & Moscovitch, M. (2011). Episodic memory processes mediated by the medial temporal lobes contribute to open-ended problem solving. *Neuropsychologia, 49*(9), 2439–2447. https://doi.org/10.1016/j.neuropsychologia.2011.04.021

Sheldrake, R. (2017). Science and spiritual practices. Berkeley, CA: Counterpoint.

Shenhav, A., Botvinick, M. M., & Cohen, J. D. (2013). The expected value of control: An integrative theory of anterior cingulate cortex function. *Neuron, 79*(2), 217–240. https://doi.org/10.1016/j.neuron.2013.07.007

Sherman, M., Kanai, R., Seth, A., & VanRullen, R. (2016). Rhythmic influence of top-down perceptual priors in the phase of prestimulus occapital alpha oscillations. *Journal of Cognitive Neuroscience, 28*(9), 1318–1330.

Sherrat, T. (2008). The evolution of Mullerian mimicry. *Naturwissenschaften, 95*, 681–695.

Shiota, M. N., Keltner, D., & Mossman, A. (2007). The nature of awe: Elicitors, appraisals, and effects on self-concept. *Cognition and Emotion, 21*, 944–963. https://doi.org/10.1080/02699930600923668

Shropshire, J. D., & Bordenstein, S. R. (2016). Speciation by symbiosis: The microbiome and behavior. *MBio, 7*(2). https://doi.org/10.1128/mBio.01785-15

Shulman, G. L., Fiez, J. A., Corbetta, M., Buckner, R. L., Miezin, F. M., Raichle, M. E., & Petersen, S. E. (1997). Common blood flow changes across visual tasks: II. Decreases in cerebral cortex. *Journal of Cognitive Neuroscience, 9*(5), 648–663. https://doi.org/10.1162/jocn.1997.9.5.648

Siegel, D. (1999). *The developing mind: How relationships and the brain interact to shape who we are.* New York, NY: Guilford Press.

Siegel, D. (2010a). *The mindful therapist.* New York, NY: W. W. Norton & Company.

Siegel, D. (2010b). *Mindsight: The new science of personal transformation.* New York, NY: Bantam Books.

Siegel, D. (2012). *Pocket guide to interpersonal neurobiology.* New York, NY: W. W. Norton & Company.

Siegler, R. S. (1998). *Children's thinking* (3rd ed.). Upper Saddle River, NJ: Prentice Hall.

Silva, B., Gross, C., & Graff, J. (2016). The neural circuits of innate fear: detection, integration, action, and memorization. *Learning and Memory, 23*, 544–555.

Simons, D. J., & Chabris, C. F. (1999). Gorillas in our midst: Sustained inattentional blindness for dynamic events. *Perception, 28*(9), 1059–1074. https://doi.org/10.1068/p28105

Sin, M. T. A., & Koole, S. L. (2013). That human touch that means so much: Exploring the tactile dimension of social life. *Mind Magazine, 2*. Retrieved from https://www.in-mind.org/article/that-human-touch-that-means-so-much-exploring-the-tactile-dimension-of-social-life

Skinner, B. F. (1948). "Superstition" in the pigeon. *Journal of Experimental Psychology, 38*(2), 168–172. https://doi.org/10.1037/h0055873

Skottnik, L. & Linden, D. (2019). Mental imagery and brain regulation–new links between psychotherapy and neuroscience. *Frontiers Psychiatry, 10*, 779.

Sliney, D. H. (2016). What is light? The visible spectrum and beyond. *Eye, 30*(2), 222–229. https://doi.org/10.1038/eye.2015.252

Smallwood, J., Brown, K. S., Baird, B., & Schooler, J. W. (2012). Cooperation between the default mode network and the frontal-parietal network in the production of an internal train of thought. *Brain Research, 1428*, 60–70. https://doi.org/10.1016/j.brainres.2011.03.072

Smallwood, J., & Schooler, J. W. (2015). The science of mind wandering: Empirically navigating the stream of consciousness. *Annual Review of Psychology, 66*, 487–518. https://doi.org/10.1146/annurev-psych-010814-015331

Smith, V., Mitchell, D., & Duncan, J. (2018). Role of the default mode network in cognitive Transitions. *Cerebral Cortex, 28,* 3685–3596. https://doi.org/10.1093/cercor/bhy167

Snowdon, D. A. (1997). Aging and Alzheimer's disease: Lessons from the Nun Study. *The Gerontologist, 37*(2), 150–156. https://doi.org/10.1093/geront/37.2.150

Solano, M. B. (Producer). (1983). Francisco Varela: "What we do and what we see is not separate" [Video file]. Amsterdam, Netherlands: Foundation Asset.

Solms, K., Solms, M. (2002). *Clinical studies in neuropsychoanalysis: Introduction to a depth neuropsychology* (2nd ed.). London: Karnac.

Solms, M. (2017). What is "the unconscious," and where is it located in the brain? A neuropsychoanalytic perspective. *Annals of the New York Academy of Sciences, 1406*, 90–97.

Solms, M., Turnbull, O. (2002). *The brain and the inner world: An introduction to the neuroscience of subjective experience.* New York: Other Press LLC.

Sood, A., & Jones, D. T. (2013). On mind wandering, attention, brain networks, and meditation. *EXPLORE: The Journal of Science and Healing, 9*(3), 136–141. https://doi.org/10.1016/j.explore.2013.02.005

Sowell, E. R., Petersen, B. S., Thompson, P. M., et al. (2003). Mapping cortical change across the human life span. *Nature Neurosci., 6,* 309–315.

Spellman, T., Gordon, J. (2015). Synchrony in schizophrenia: A window into circuit-level pathophysiology. *Current Opin Neurobiol,* 17–23.

Spence, C., & Squire, S. (2003). Multisensory integration: maintaining the perception of synchrony. *Current Biology, 13*(13), R519–R521. https://doi.org/10.1016/s0960-9822(03)00445-7

Spreng, R. N., & Grady, C. L. (2009). Patterns of brain activity supporting autobiographical memory, prospection and theory of mind, and their relationship to the default mode network. *Neuroscience, 22*(6), 1112–1123.

Spreng, R. N., Mar, R. A., & Kim, A. S. (2009). The common neural basis of autobiographical memory, prospection, navigation, theory of mind, and the default mode: A quantitative meta-analysis. *Journal of Cognitive Neuroscience, 21*(3), 489–510. https://doi.org/10.1162/jocn.2008.21029

Sridharan, D., Levitin, D. J., & Menon, V. (2008). A critical role for the right fronto-insular cortex in switching between central-executive and default-mode networks. *Proceedings of the National Academy of Sciences USA, 105*(34), 12569–12574. https://doi.org/10.1073/pnas.0800005105

Steiger, R. L., & Reyna, C. (2017). Trait contempt, anger, disgust, and moral foundation values. *Personality and Individual Differences, 113*, 125–135. https://doi.org/10.1016/j.paid.2017.02.071

Stein, M. (2015). *The principle of individuation: Toward the development of human consciousness.* Wilmette, IL: Chiron Publications.

Stellar, J. E., Gordon, A., Anderson, C. L., Piff, P. K., McNeil, G. D., & Keltner, D. (2018). Awe and humility. *Journal of Personality and Social Psychology, 114*(2), 258–269. https://doi.org/10.1037/pspi0000109

Stenfors, C. U. D., Hanson, L. M., Theorell, T., & Osika, W. S. (2016). Executive cognitive functioning and cardiovascular autonomic regulation in a population-based sample of working adults. *Frontiers in Psychology, 7*(10). https://doi.org/10.3389/fpsyg.2016.01536

Stern, D. (1985). *The interpersonal world of the infant: A view from psychoanalysis and developmental psychology.* New York, NY: Basic Books.

Stevenson, R. J., Prescott, J., & Boakes, R. A. (1999). Confusing tastes and smells: How odours can influence the perception of sweet and sour tastes. *Chemical Senses, 24*(6), 627–635. https://doi.org/10.1093/chemse/24.6.627

Stickgold, R., Hobson, J. A., Fosse, R. & Fosse, M. (2001). Sleep, learning and dreams: Off-line memory reprocessing. *Science, 294,* 1052–1057.

Stoddard, J., & Afari, N. (2014). *The big book of ACT metaphors.* Oakland, CA: New Harbinger Publications, Inc.

Stolorow, R. D., & Atwood, G. E. (1996). The intersubjective perspective. *Psychoanalytic Review, 83*(2), 181–194.

Storie, M., & Vining, J. (2018). From oh to aha: Characteristics and types of environmental epiphany experiences. *Human Ecology Review, 24*(1), 155–175. https://doi.org/10.22459/her.24.01.2018.08

Strasburger, H., & Waldvogel, B. (2015). Sight and blindness in the same person: Gating in the visual system. *Psych Journal, 4,* 178–185.

Strawson, G. (2006). Realistic monism, why physicalism entails panpsychism. *Journal of Consciousness Studies, 13*(10), 3–31.

Strawson, Suchy, Y., Holmes, L. G., Strassberg, D. S., Gillespie, A. A., Nilssen, A. R., Niermeyer, M. A., & Huntbach, B. A. (2019). The impacts of sexual arousal and its suppression on executive functioning. *The Journal of Sex Research, 56*(1), 114–126.

Suddendorf, T., & Corballis, M. (1997). Mental time travel and the evolution of the human mind. *Genetic, Social and General Psychology Monographs, 123*(2), 133–167.

Sue, D. W. (1996). Multicultural counseling and therapy (MCT) theory. In D. W. Sue, A. E. Ivey, & P. B. Pedersen (Eds.), *A theory of multicultural counseling and therapy* (pp. 813–827). Belmont, CA: Thomson Brooks/Cole.

Sue, D. W., Ivey, A. E., & Pedersen, P. B. (1996). *A theory of multicultural counseling and therapy.* Belmont, CA: Thomson Brooks.

Sugita, Y., & Suzuki, Y. (2003). Audiovisual perception: Implicit estimation of sound-arrival time. *Nature, 421*(6926). https://doi.org/10.1038/421911a

Sullivan, B. S. (2010). *The mystery of analytical work: Weavings from Jung and Bion.* New York: Routledge.

Supekar, K., Uddin, L. Q., Prater, K., Amin, H., Greicius, M. D., & Menon, V. (2010). Development of functional and structural connectivity within the default mode network in young children. *Neuroimage, 52*(1), 290–301. https://doi.org/10.1016/j.neuroimage.2010.04.009

Sutin, A. R., Stephan, Y., & Terracciano, A.

(2018). Facets of conscientiousness and risk of dementia. *Psychological Medicine, 48*(6), 974–982. https://doi.org/10.1017/s0033291717002306

Swanson, L. (2016). The predictive processing paradigm has roots in Kant. *Frontiers in Systems Neuroscience, 10,* 79. https://doi.org/10.3389/fnsys.2016.00079

Symington, J., Symington, N. (1996). *The clinical thinking of Wilfred Bion.* London: Routledge.

Symons, C. S., & Johnson, B. T. (1997). The self-reference effect in memory: A meta-analysis. *Psychological Bulletin, 121*(3), 371–394. https://doi.org/10.1037/0033-2909.121.3.371

Silvia, P. J., Fayn, K., Nusbaum, E. C., & Beaty, R. E. (2015). Openness to experience and awe in response to nature and music: Personality and profound aesthetic experiences. *Psychology of Aesthetics, Creativity, and the Arts, 9*(4), 376–384.

Tamietto, M., & Gelder, B. (2010). Neural bases of the non-conscious perception of emotional signals. *Nature Reviews Neuroscience,* 1–13

Tang, Y. Y., Ma, Y., Wang, J., Fan, Y., Feng, S., Lu, Q., ... Posner, M. I. (2007). Short-term meditation training improves attention and self-regulation. *Proceedings of the National Academy of Sciences USA, 104*(43), 17152–17156. https://doi.org/10.1073/pnas.0707678104

Tangney, J., Stuewig, J., & Mashek, D. (2007). Moral emotions and moral behavior. *Annual Review of Psychology, 58,* 345–372. https://doi.org/10.1146/annurev.psych.56.091103.070145

Tanovic, E., Gee, D., & Joorman, J. (2018). Intolerance of uncertainty: Neural and psychophysiological correlates of the perception of uncertainty as threatening. *Clinical Psychology Review, 60,* 87–99.

Taren, A. A., Gianaros, P. J., Greco, C. M., Lindsay, E. K., Fairgrieve, A., Brown, K. W., ... Creswell, J. D. (2017). Mindfulness meditation training and executive control network resting state functional connectivity: A randomized controlled trial. *Psychosomatic Medicine, 79*(6), 674–683. https://doi.org/10.1097/PSY.0000000000000466

Taylor, J. B. (2016). *My stroke of insight.* New York, NY: Penguin Books.

Taylor, S. E., Pham, L. B., Rivkin, I. D.,

& Armor, D. A. (1998). Harnessing the imagination: Mental simulation, self-regulation, and coping. *American Psychologist*, *53*(4), 429–439. https://doi. org/10.1037/0003-066x.53.4.429

TheHallOfRecords. (2011). *Alan Watts – Tribute to Carl Jung* [Video file]. Retrieved from https://www.youtube.com/watch?v=BgN8m_gIXB8

Thompson, J., & Cotlove, C. (2005). *The therapeutic process*. Lanham, MD: Rowman and Littlefield.

Thoreau, H. D. (1992). *Walden; and, Resistance to civil government: Authoritative texts, Thoreau's journal, reviews, and essays in criticism.* New York, NY: W. W. Norton.

Thrash, T. M., & Elliot, A. J. (2003). Inspiration as a psychological construct. *Journal of personality and social psychology*, *84*(4), 871–889. https://doi. org/10.1037/0022-3514.84.4.871

Tillfors, M., Furmark, T., Marteinsdottir, I., Fischer, H., Pissiota, A., Långström, B., & Fredrikson, M. (2001). Cerebral blood flow in subjects with social phobia during stressful speaking tasks: A PET study. *American Journal of Psychiatry*, *158*(8), 1220–1226. https://doi. org/10.1176/appi.ajp.158.8.1220

Timmermans, B., Schilbach, L., Pasquali, A., & Cleermans, A. (2012). Higher order thoughts in action: Consciousness as an unconscious re-description process. *Philosophical Transactions of the Royal Society B, 367*, 1412–1423. https://doi.org/10.1098/rstb.2011.0421

Tranel, D., Damasio, A. (1985). Knowledge without awareness: An autonomic index of facial recognition by prosopagnosics. *Science, 228*(4706m), 1453–1454

Tononi, G. (2012). The integrated information theory of consciousness: an updated account. *Arch Ital Biol, 150*(2–3), 56–90. https://doi. org/10.4449/aib.v149i5.1388.

Tononi, G., Boly, M., Massimini, M., Koch, C. (2016). Integrated information theory: From consciousness to its physical substrate. *Nat Rev Neurosci, 17*, 450–461. https://doi. org/10.1038/nrn.2016.44

Toyomaki, A., Hashimoto, N., Kako, Y., Tomimatsu, Y., Koyama, T., & Kusumi, I. (2015). Different P50 sensory gating measures reflect different cognitive dysfunctions in schizophrenia. *Schizophrenia Research: Cognition*, *2*(3), 166–169. https://doi.org/10.1016/j. scog.2015.07.002

Tulving, E. (2002). Episodic memory: From mind to brain. *Annual Review of Psychology*, *53*(1), 1–25. https://doi. org/0084-6570/02/0201-0001

Tzu, L. (2003). *Tao Te Ching: An illustrated journey.* (S. Mitchell, trans.). Islington, UK: Frances Lincoln.

Twito, L., Israel, S., Simonson, I., & Knafo-Noam, A. (2019). The motivational aspect of children's delayed gratification: Values and decision making in middle childhood. *Frontiers in Psychology*, *10*. https://doi. org/10.3389/fpsyg.2019.01649

Uddin, L. Q., Kaplan, J. T., Molnar-Szakacs, I., Zaidel, E., & Iacoboni, M. (2005). Self-face recognition activates a frontoparietal "mirror" network in the right hemisphere: An event-related fMRI study. *Neuroimage*, *25*(3), 926–935. https://doi.org/10.1016/j. neuroimage.2004.12.018

Uziel, L. (2007). Individual differences in the social facilitation effect: A review and meta-analysis. *Journal of Research in Personality*, *41*(3), 579–601. https://doi.org/10.1016/j. jrp.2006.06.008

Vaillant, G. (2011). Involuntary coping mechanisms: a psychodynamic perspective. *Dialogues in Clinical Neuroscience, 13*(3), 366–370. Retrieved from https://www.ncbi. nlm.nih.gov/pmc/articles/PMC3182012/

Van Boven, L., & Ashworth, L. (2007). Looking forward, looking back: Anticipation is more evocative than retrospection. *Journal of Experimental Psychology: General, 136*(2), 289–300. https://doi. org/10.1037/0096-3445.136.2.289

Van Cappellen, P., Saroglou, V., Iweins, C., Piovesana, M., & Fredrickson, B. L. (2013). Self-transcendent positive emotions increase spirituality through basic world assumptions. *Cognition and Emotion, 27*, 1378–1394. https://doi.org/10.1080/02699931

Van Deurzen, E. (2010). *Everyday mysteries: A handbook of existential psychotherapy.* New York, NY: Routledge.

Vanderkerckhove, M., & Panksepp, J. (2009). The flow of anoetic to noetic and autonoetic consciousness: a vision of unknowing (anoetic) and knowing (noetic consciousness) in the remembrance of things past and imagined futures. *Consciousness and Cognition, 18*, 1053–8100.

Van der Kolk, B. A. (2014). *The body keeps the score: Brain, mind, and body in the healing of trauma.* New York: Viking.

Vago, D. R., & Silbersweig, D. A. (2012). Self-awareness, self-regulation, and self-transcendence (S-ART): A framework for understanding the neurobiological mechanisms of mindfulness. *Frontiers in Human Neuroscience, 6.* https://doi.org/10.3389/fnhum.2012.00296

Varela, F. J. (1996). Neurophenomenology: A methodological remedy for the hard problem. *Journal of Consciousness Studies, 3*(4), 330–349.

Varela, F., Thompson, E., & Rosch, E. (2016). *The embodied mind: Cognitive science and human experience.* Cambridge, MA: Massachusetts Institute of Technology Press.

Vestergaard-Poulsen, P., van Beek, M., Skewes, J., Bjarkam, C. R., Stubberup, M., Bertelsen, J., & Roepstorff, A. (2009). Long-term meditation is associated with increased gray matter density in the brain stem. *Neuroreport, 20*(2), 170–174. https://doi.org/10.1097/WNR.0b013e328320012a

Vermote, R. (2019) Reading Bion, *Routledge,* New York, NY

Vi, C. T., & Obrist, M. (2018). Sour promotes risk-taking: An investigation into the effect of taste on risk-taking behaviour in humans. *Scientific Reports, 8*(1), 1–8. https://doi.org/10.1038/s41598-018-26164-3

Vicario, C. M., Rafal, R. D., Martino, D., & Avenanti, A. (2017). Core, social and moral disgust are bounded: a review on behavioral and neural bases of repugnance in clinical disorders. *Neuroscience & Biobehavioral Reviews, 80,* 185–200. https://doi.org/10.1016/j.neubiorev.2017.05.008

Von Franz, M. L. (1992). *Psyche and matter.* Boulder, CO: Shambhala.

Vytal, K., & Hamann. (2010). Neuroimaging support for discrete neural correlates of basic emotions: A voxel-based meta-analysis. *Journal of Cognitive Neuroscience, 22,* 2864–2885. https://doi.org/10.1162/jocn.2009.21366

Wagemans, J., Elder, J. H., Kubovy, M., Palmer, S. E., Peterson, M. A., Singh, M., & von der Heydt, R. (2012). A century of Gestalt psychology in visual perception: I. Perceptual grouping and figure–ground organization. *Psychological Bulletin, 138*(6), 1172–1217. https://doi.org/10.1037/a0029333

Wahbeh, H., Sagher, A., Back, W., Pundhir, P., & Travis, F. (2018). A systematic review of transcendent states across meditation and contemplative traditions. *Explore, 14*(1), 19–35. https://doi.org/10.1016/j.explore.2017.07.007

Walczyk, J. J., Sewell, N., & DiBenedetto, M. B. (2018). A review of approaches to detecting malingering in forensic contexts and promising cognitive load-inducing lie detection techniques. *Frontiers in Psychiatry, 9.* https://doi.org/10.3389/fpsyt.2018.00700

Walker, D. B., Walker, J. C., Cavnar, P. J., Taylor, J. L., Pickel, D. H., Hall, S. B., & Suarez, J. C. (2006). Naturalistic quantification of canine olfactory sensitivity. *Applied Animal Behaviour Science, 97*(2–4), 241–254. https://doi.org/10.1016/j.applanim.2005.07.009

Wang, H., Zhang, J., & Jia, H. (2019). Separate Neural Systems Value Prosocial Behaviors and Reward: An ALE Meta-Analysis. *Frontiers in Human Neuroscience, 13,* https://doi.org/10.3389/fnhum.2019.00276

Weber, M. (2006). *Whitehead's pancreativism: The basics.* Berlin: Walter De Gruyter & Co.

Weber, M. (2008). Process and individuality. In Pachalska M., & Weber, M. (Eds.) *Neuropsychology and Philosophy of Mind in Process.* Frankfurt: Ontos Verlag. https://doi.org/10.1515/9783110329438.401

Weber, M., & Desmond, W. (2008). *Handbook of Whiteheadian process thought* (Vol. 1–2). Frankfurt: Ontos Verlag.

Weil, S. (1947/2002). *Gravity and grace.* New York, NY: Routledge.

Wells, G. L., Memon, A., & Penrod, S. D. (2006). Eyewitness evidence: Improving its probative value. *Psychological Science in the Public Interest, 7*(2), 45–75. https://doi.org/10.1111/j.1529-1006.2006.00027.x

Whitehead, A. N., Griffin, D. R., & Sherburne, D. W. (1985). *Process and reality: An essay in cosmology.* New York, NY: The Free Press.

Whitehead, A. N. (1968). *Modes of thought.* New York, NY: The Free Press.

Whitehead, A.N. (1927–28/1978). *Process and reality.* New York, NY: The Free Press

Wilson, E. O. (1999). *Consilience: The unity of knowledge.* New York, NY: Vintage.

Wilson, T. D., & Gilbert, D. T. (2003). Affective forecasting. *Advances in Experimental Social*

Psychology, 35(35), 345–411. https://doi. org/10.1016/s0065-2601(03)01006-2

Wilson, M., & Daly, M. (2004). Do pretty women inspire men to discount the future? *Proceedings of the Royal Society of London. Series B: Biological Sciences, 271*(suppl. 4), S177–S179. https://doi.org/10.1098/rsbl.2003.0134

Windt, J. M., Nielsen, T., & Thompson, E. (2016). Does consciousness disappear in dreamless sleep? *Trends in Cognitive Sciences, 20*(12), 871–882. https://doi.org/10.1016/j.tics.2016.09.006

Witter, M. P., Naber, P. A., Van Haeften, T., Machielsen, W. C., Rombouts, S. A., Barkhof, F., ... & Lopes da Silva, F. H. (2000). Cortico-hippocampal communication by way of parallel parahippocampal-subicular pathways. *Hippocampus, 10*(4), 398–410. https://doi.org/10.1002/1098-1063(2000)10:4<398::aid-hipo6>3.3.co;2-b

Wood, J., & Agmari, S. (2015) A framework for understanding the emerging role of cortico-limbic-ventral striatal networks in OCD-Associated Repetitive Behaviors. *Front. Syst. Neurosc., 9*, Art. 171, 1–22.

Woodman, M. (1982). *Addiction to perfection: The still unravished bride: a psychological study.* Toronto, Canada: Inner City Books.

Wu, T., Dufford, A. J., Mackie, M. A., Egan, L. J., & Fan, J. (2016). The capacity of cognitive control estimated from a perceptual decision making task. *Scientific Reports, 6.* https://doi.org/10.1038/srep34025

Wu, Y. T., Teale, J., Matthews, F. E., Brayne, C., Woods, B., Clare, L., & Ageing Study Wales research team. (2016). Lifestyle factors, cognitive reserve, and cognitive function: results from the Cognitive Function and Ageing Study Wales, a population-based cohort. *The Lancet, 388.* https://doi.org/10.1016/s0140-6736(16)32350-9

Yaden, D. B., Eichstaedt, J. C., Schwartz, H. A., Kern, M. L., Le Nguyen, K. D., Wintering, N. A., ... & Newberg, A. B. (2016). The language of ineffability: Linguistic analysis of mystical experiences. *Psychology of Religion and Spirituality, 8*(3), 244–252. https://doi.org/10.1037/rel0000043

Yaden, D. B., Haidt, J., Hood, R. W., Vago, D. R., & Newberg, A. B. (2017). The varieties of self transcendent experience. *Review of*

General Psychology, 21(2), 143–160. https://doi.org/10.1037/gpr0000102

Yalom, I. D., & Leszcz, M. (2005). *The theory and practice of group psychotherapy.* New York, NY: Basic Books.

Yano, J. M., Yu, K., Donaldson, G. P., Shastri, G. G., Ann, P., Ma, L., ... & Hsiao, E. Y. (2015). Indigenous bacteria from the gut microbiota regulate host serotonin biosynthesis. *Cell, 161*(2), 264–276. https://doi.org/10.1016/j.cell.2015.02.047

Yassa, M. A., Hazlett, R. L., Stark, C. E., & Hoehn-Saric, R. (2012). Functional MRI of the amygdala and bed nucleus of the stria terminalis during conditions of uncertainty in generalized anxiety disorder. *Journal of Psychiatric Research, 46*(8), 1045–1052. https://doi.org/10.1016/j.jpsychires.2012.04.013

Yontef, G. M. (1993). *Awareness, dialogue, and process.* Highland, NY: Gestalt Journal Press.

Yontef, G., & Jacobs, L. (2010). Gestalt therapy. In R. Corsini & D. Wedding (Eds.), *Current psychotherapies* (9th ed., pp. 342–382). Belmont, CA: Brooks/Cole-Thompson Learning.

Zaki, J., & Mitchell, J. P. (2013). Intuitive prosociality. *Current Directions in Psychological Science, 22*(6), 466–470. https://doi.org/10.1177/0963721413492764

Zanarini, M. C., Weingeroff, J. L., & Frankenburg, F. R. (2009). Defense mechanisms associated with borderline personality disorder. *Journal of Personality Disorders, 23*(2), 113–121. https://doi.org/10.1521/pedi.2009.23.2.113

Zheng, H., Luo, J., & Yu, R. (2014). From memory to prospection: what are the overlapping and the distinct components between remembering and imagining. *Frontiers in Psychology, 5*(856), 1–14.

Zhou, B., Feng, G., Chen, W., & Zhou, W. (2018). Olfaction warps visual time perception. *Cerebral Cortex, 28*(5), 1718–1728. https://doi.org/10.1093/cercor/bhx068

Zimbardo, P. G. (1971). *The power and pathology of imprisonment. Congressional Record. (Serial No. 15, 1971-10-25). Hearings before Subcommittee No. 3, of the Committee on the Judiciary, House of Representatives, Ninety-Second Congress, First Session on Corrections, Part II, Prisons, Prison Reform and Prisoners' Rights: California.* Washington, DC: U.S. Government Printing Office.

APPENDIX A: Metabolizing Experience: Movements 1–8

MOVEMENT	NEUROANATOMICAL CORRELATES	PSYCHOLOGICAL CORRELATE	DESCRIPTION
Movement 1) Transduction sensory-affect processing, expectational influences[1] Registering sensory and affective information[2]	Upper brain stem, and limbic systems[3] Sense receptors, primary and secondary sensory areas and sensory-perceptual associative regions[2] Medial-temporal structures, hippocampus, temporo-parietal region, PFC[4]	Protoself processes Sensory gating, habituation[4] Markov blanket*	Sensory information converted into narrow band of neural signals. Signals interact with non-conscious expectations of the brain (among many others, this includes rapid feedback and feedforward affective-limbic signaling, and sensory gating).
Movement 2) Primary sensory and emotional data in non-conscious systems	Upper brain stem, and limbic systems[3] Right-hemisphere amygdala biased circuits and autonomic nervous system[5, 6] Pulvinar, hippocampus, superior colliculus[5]	Beta elements (Bion)[7] Protoself processes Markov blanket*	Raw sensory and emotional data. Not yet thoughts. Non-conscious experiencing No subject-object differentiation.

* "A Markov blanket is a set of states that separates the internal or intrinsic states of a structure from extrinsic or external states… it describes a spatial boundary…[which] comprises sensory and active states" (Palacios et al., 2020, p. 123)

Movement 3) Perceptual processing[2, 8] Mental imagery[9]	Secondary/ Tertiary sensory areas and sensory-perceptual associative regions[2] Broad-band synchronization within the thalamo-cortical system Hippocampus[10]	Alpha elements (Bion)[7] Alpha function Transform raw data into thought. Data is organized and made mean-ingful to observer (Bion)[7] Protoself pro-cesses, complex self-processes Gestalt laws[8] Markov blanket*	Proto-thought Image-emotion synthesis Beginning of subject-object differentiation
Movement 4) Associative, non-linear based thought processes dominant. Some basic structure	Dreams REM: Different from waking state, frontal and posterior areas less coherent in most frequencies, and posterior areas and left/right brain more coherent[8] Default mode network[11] (DMN) Thalamo-cortical system continues to function as normal in dreaming[12] DLPFC deactivated in REM sleep[12] Hippocampus[10]	Dream thought, dreams, myth (Bion)[7] Protoself processes Complex self-processes Autobiographical self-process (PCA) Markov blanket*	Thinking with representations[13] Dream recollec-tion, personal description of an event May include fleeting asso-ciations[14] and Mind-wandering and spontaneous thoughts
Movement 5) Linear thought formation	Reverberating neural circuits. Layers [1, 2, 6] and 5 of neocortex[15] Left frontal-hippocampal[6] DMN11 and frontal-parietal[16]	Preconception (Bion)[7] Contact barrier (conscious/ unconscious) PCA Markov blanket*	Intrinsic information with an expectation before meeting its corresponding experience. "Like a variable without a value" (Symington, Symington, 1996, p. 40)[17]

Movement 6) Forming of abstract thought	Layers 3, 4 of neocortex[15] Bottom-up, top-down convergence zones Frontal -Parietal (FTP)[16], Temporal, Hippocampus[10]	Conception (Bion)[7]: can still return to pre-conception PCA Markov blanket*	The meeting of expectation and experience. Variable develops a value, "becomes saturated, therefore a constant" (Symington, Symington, 1996, p. 40)[17]
Movement 7) Fully formed abstract thought	Frontal -parietal (FTP)[16], temporal, hippocampus[10] Dorsolateral prefrontal cortex (DLPFC) Left-hemisphere, posterior inferior frontal regions[18] Hippocampus[10]	Concept (Bion)[7] Verbal and nonverbal conceptual knowledge[18] PCA, Markov blanket*	Higher order symbolic representation "Derived from conception, by purifying it of anything that would stop it from representing the truth"[17]
Movement 8) Abstract relational reasoning	Relational reasoning: FTP, DLPFC, parietal cortex[19]	Scientific deductive system (SDS) Relational reasoning[19] PCA, Markov blanket*	SDS: Linking higher order abstract representations into a scientific hypothesis
Movement 9) Abstract mathematical reasoning	Physics reasoning: Lateral prefrontal cortices, parietal cortices, central executive network (CEN)[20] Algebra: Left frontal gyri, horizontal intraparietal sulci, posterior superior parietal lobules, precuneus[21] Calculus: Horizontal intraparietal sulcus, posterior superior parietal lobe, posterior cingulate gyrus[22]	Symbolic algebra Physics reasoning[20] Algebraic calculus (AC) (Bion)[7] PCA, Markov blanket*	Symbolic algebra: Using alphanumeric equations as representations of problems AC: an unsaturated generalizable principle. Reasoning not tied to senses.

1. Geisler, W. S., & Diehl, R. L. (2003). A Bayesian approach to the evolution of perceptual and cognitive systems. *Cognitive Science, 27*(3), 379-402. doi:10.1207/s15516709cog2703_3

2. Whishaw, I. Q., & Kolb, B. (2015). *Fundamentals of human neuropsychology.* Worth Custom Publishing.

3. Boutros, N., Mears, R., Pflieger, M., Moxon, K., Ludowig, E., & Rosburg, T. (2008). Sensory gating in the human hippocampal and rhinal regions: Regional differences. *Hippocampus, 18*(3), 310-316. doi:10.1002/hipo.20388

4. Grunwald, T., Boutros, N. N., Pezer, N., Oertzen, J. V., Fernández, G., Schaller, C., & Elger, C. E. (2003). Neuronal substrates of sensory gating within the human brain. Biological Psychiatry, 53(6), 511–519. https://doi.org/10.1016/s0006-3223(02)01673-6

5. Tamietto, M., & Gelder, B. D. (2010). Neural bases of the non-conscious perception of emotional signals. *Nature Reviews Neuroscience, 11*(10), 697-709. doi:10.1038/nrn2889

6. Cozolino, L. (2010). *The neuroscience of psychotherapy: Healing the social brain.* New York, NY: WW Norton & Company.

7. Bion, W. R. (1963/1984) Elements of psychoanalysis, London, Karnac

8. Tononi, G. (1998). Complexity and coherency: integrating information in the brain. *Trends in Cognitive Sciences, 2*(12), 474–484. doi.org/10.1016/s1364-6613(98)01259-5

9. Skottnik, L., Linden, D. (2019) Mental Imagery and Brain Regulation – New Links Between Psychotherapy and Neuroscience. *Frontiers Psychiatry*, vol. 10, 779

10. Cornelius, J. T. (2017). The hippocampus facilitates integration within a symbolic field. *The International Journal of Psychoanalysis, 98*(5), 1333–1357. https://doi.org/10.1111/1745-8315.12617

11. Raichle, M. E., MacLeod, A. M., Snyder, A. Z., Powers, W. J., Gusnard, D. A., & Shulman, G. L. (2001). A default mode of brain function. *Proceedings of the National Academy of Sciences USA, 98*(2), 676–682. https://doi.org/10.1073/pnas.98.2.676

12. Tononi, G., & Koch, C. (2008). The neural correlates of consciousness: An update. *Annals of the New York Academy of Sciences, 1124,* 239–261. doi.org/10.1196/annals.1440.004

13. Solms, M. (1995). New Findings on the Neurological Organization of Dreaming: Implications for Psychoanalysis. *The Psychoanalytic Quarterly, 64*(1), 43-67. doi:10.1080/21674086.1995.11927443

14. Mason, M. F., Norton, M. I., Horn, J. D. Van, Wegner, D. M., Grafton, S. T., Macrae, C. N., Mason, M. F., Norton, M. I., Horn, J. D. Van, Wegner, D. M., Grafton, S. T., & Macrae, C. N. (2007). Wandering minds: Stimulus-independent thought. *Science,* 315(January), 393–395. doi.org/10.1126/science.1131295

15. Hawkins, J., & Blakeslee, S. (2004). *On intelligence.* New York, NY: Times Books.

16. Smallwood, J., Brown, K. S., Baird, B., & Schooler, J. W. (2012). Cooperation between the default mode network and the frontal-parietal network in the production of an internal train of thought. *Brain Research, 1428*, 60–70. https://doi.org/10.1016/j.brainres.2011.03.072

17. Symington, J., Symington, N. (1996) The Clinical Thinking of Wilfred Bion, *Routledge*, New York, NY.

18. Binder, J. R., Westbury, C. F., Mckiernan, K. A., Possing, E. T., & Medler, D. A. (2005). Distinct Brain Systems for Processing Concrete and Abstract Concepts. *Journal of Cognitive Neuroscience, 17*(6), 905-917. doi:10.1162/0898929054021102

19. Hinton, E., Dymond, S., Hecker, U. V., & Evans, C. (2010). Neural correlates of relational reasoning and the symbolic distance effect: Involvement of parietal cortex. *Neuroscience, 168*(1), 138-148. doi:10.1016/j.neuroscience.2010.03.052

20. Brewe, E., Bartley, J. E., Riedel, M. C., Sawtelle, V., Salo, T., Boeving, E. R., Bravo, E. I., Odean, R., Nazareth, A., Bottenhorn, K. L., Laird, R. W., Sutherland, M. T., Pruden, S. M., & Laird, A. R. (2018). Toward a neurobiological basis for understanding learning in University modeling instruction physics courses. *Frontiers in ICT, 5.* https://doi.org/10.3389/fict.2018.00010

21. Lee, K., Lim, Z. Y., Yeong, S. H., Ng, S. F., Venkatraman, V., & Chee, M. W. (2007). Strategic differences in algebraic problem solving: Neuroanatomical correlates. *Brain Research, 1155*, 163-171. https://doi.org/10.1016/j.brainres.2007.04.040

22. Krueger, F., Spampinato, M. V., Pardini, M., Pajevic, S., Wood, J. N., Weiss, G. H., Landgraf, S., & Grafman, J. (2008). Integral calculus problem solving: An fMRI investigation. *NeuroReport: For Rapid Communication of Neuroscience Research, 19*(11), 1095–1099. https://doi.org/10.1097/WNR.0b013e328303fd85

23. Palacios, E. R., Razi, A., Parr, T., Kirchhoff, M., & Friston, K. (2020). On Markov blankets and hierarchical self-organisation. *Journal of Theoretical Biology, 486*, 110089. https://doi.org/10.1016/j.jtbi.2019.110089

APPENDIX B: Defense Mechanisms

NEUROTIC DEFENSES:	EXAMPLE(S):
Controlling: Regulating the environment in order to avoid discomfort Psychologically controlling parenting: " . . . pressuring the child to think, act, and feel in particular ways, such as the use of guilt induction, love withdrawal, and shaming."[1]	Due to his own fears and anxiety, a father keeps his daughter's cell phone at night and audits all of her activity, even though there has been no evidence of any inappropriate interactions or searches.
Displacement: Shifting an individual's emotions or drives from an idea/object to another.[2]	Someone who has a bad day may take out their aggression on a pet dog.
Externalization: Projecting the individual's own personality, impulses, conflicts, emotions, and ways of thinking onto the outside world; people.[3]	A judgmental individual may perceive others as judgmental instead, and themself as uncritical.
Repression: Curbs ideas before reaching consciousness; but not forgotten.[4]	Memories of an abuse that occurred in an individual's childhood are forgotten but still influencing their ability to form stable relationships.
Isolation: Separating or repressing ideas from affect.[5]	A Holocaust victim may recall details from memories, but may not express the associated emotions.
Intellectualization: Avoiding feelings and affective expression by focusing on logical details and facts.[6]	A client diagnosed with a disease focuses on the intellectual components to avoid the emotional aspect of their situation.
Rationalization: Offering rational justifications on incongruent values, beliefs, behaviors, and/or attitudes.[7]	An individual cheats on his spouse, and justifies this behavior via the perceived notion that she is unaffectionate.

NEUROTIC DEFENSES:	EXAMPLE(S):
Reaction formation: Adopting traits, feelings, beliefs that are opposite to what you believe.[8]	After committing a crime, the individual begins judging others harshly on morality while preaching the importance of being a paragon of virtue
Sexualization: Endowing an object with sexual significance.[9]	After many failed attempts at sexual relationships, a woman begins to find hairbrushes sexually arousing.
Repetition compulsion: Repeating an internalized event behaviorally and psychologically.[10]	Because of emotional neglect from her father, a woman finds herself engaging in relationships with men who are emotionally distant.
MATURE DEFENSES:	**EXAMPLE(S):**
Altruism: Pleasure in serving others to manage their own pain.[11]	After the stock market crashed, the investor felt angry and sad. While walking home, he passed a homeless man begging for money. He decided to buy him lunch, and he felt better.
Anticipation: Realistic and goal-directed planning for future inner discomfort. The individual anticipates a dreadful outcome.[12]	After receiving several indicators, verified by others, that he was to be let go from his company, a man began actively searching for new jobs.
Asceticism: Renouncing pleasurable experiences by assigning moral values to them. This renunciation is received with gratification.[13]	After engaging in self-exploration, she found that her tendency to eat unhealthy foods ran counter to her values. She felt empowered and satisfied with the control she subsequently developed over her eating behaviors.
Humor: An individual who focuses on funny aspects of a situation or experience to prevent uncomfortable thoughts and feelings.[14]	The comedian expressed his anger toward institutional policies by creating a humorous act related to it.
Sublimation: Channeling instincts into socially acceptable outlets.[15]	In order to deal with his sexual desires, an artist paints erotica.

MATURE DEFENSES:	EXAMPLE(S):
Suppression: Postponing, minimizing, and controlling uncomfortable thoughts or feelings.[16]	Despite feeling a desire to yell at his boss, a man decides to inhibit that desire in order to secure his job, instead choosing to express that desire more constructively.

NARCISSISTIC DEFENSES:	EXAMPLE(S):
Denial: Consciously avoiding painful thoughts; refusing to examine uncomfortable realities.[17]	A couple who claims their relationship is "OK" when it is actually in trouble.
Distortion: Redesigning an individual's external reality to suit their inner need.[18]	A child tells her parents that she passed the test, when in fact she did not.
Primitive idealization: Imposing more negative or positive qualities on an external object than they possess.[19]	A girlfriend who is infatuated with her new boyfriend experiences him as absolutely perfect, even though he has been abusive at times.
Projection: Attributing one's inner qualities to another person. The individual may act on these perceptions.[20]	A teenager is angry that his parents don't listen to him when he is the one not listening to them.
Projective identification: Places unwanted qualities or pressures onto another person to experience similar feelings.[21]	An individual who has recently put on weight decides to body shame another individual. The other individual subsequently begins to feel insecure about her weight.
Splitting: Viewing external objects as "all good" or "all bad" without considering all of their qualities.[22]	A woman diagnosed with borderline personality disorder may believe she will "always" be abandoned by others, despite the many signs that her friends and family have demonstrated otherwise.

IMMATURE DEFENSES:	EXAMPLE(S):
Acting out: Expressing extreme behaviors to avoid affect; acting on impulse.[23]	A child throws a temper tantrum because she doesn't want to go to bed.

IMMATURE DEFENSES:	EXAMPLE(S):
Blocking: Inhibited thoughts and feelings similar to repression, except the tension is felt.[24]	In a moment of vulnerability, the man blocks this expression because he was taught that men should avoid weakness.
Hypochondriasis: Exaggerating somatic illness in order to avoid responsibilities and feelings of guilt.[25]	In a moment of anxiety, the client experiences a headache and believes he has a tumor. He begins learning all that he can about tumors.
Identification: The opposite of projection; the individual conforms to the aspects of another object/person for approval.[26]	The interviewee begins to adopt the same mannerisms and body language as the interviewer, despite his true feelings for the interviewer, in the hope that he will be liked and hired.
Introjection: The internalization of an expectation from others.[27]	A man kept being denied a raise and did not know why. His work was strong and his productivity was high. He was recommended to be more assertive, which confused him because he had always been taught, "Keep your head down and focus on the quality of your work."
Passive-aggressive behavior: Aggression that is indirectly expressed that affects others more than the self.[28]	After being told by his spouse that he was not cleaning the dishes correctly, he began to spend an inordinate amount of time cleaning them, making sure it would interfere with time they would usually spend together.
Regression: Returning to earlier functioning to avoid uncomfortable situations.[29]	An individual suffers a mental breakdown and begins to suck his thumb after hearing the news of the death of a loved one. Includes: childlike behaviors, self-destructive acting out, dissociative experiences, pursuit of sexual affairs, and reckless drug and alcohol usage.
Schizoid fantasy: Withdrawal in self to obtain gratification; resolve conflict.[30]	A schizoid client claims (part playfully) he is riding a horse down a hospital hallway, but he is actually on a bicycle. The fantasy is symbolic and necessary as a transitional space, enabling him to safely traverse a space that might be considered dangerous.

IMMATURE DEFENSES:	EXAMPLE(S):
Somatization: Individuals react with bodily symptoms rather than psychic derivatives.[31]	A man began having seizures after experiencing a traumatic event. Upon further investigation there was found to be no medical cause or malingering.

1. Mabbe, E., Vansteenkiste, M., Brenning, K., De Pauw, S., Beyers, W., & Soenens, B. (2019). The moderating role of adolescent personality in associations between psychologically controlling parenting and problem behaviors: A longitudinal examination at the level of within-person change. *Developmental Psychology, 55*(12), 2665–2677. https://doi.org/10.1037/dev0000802.supp

2. Ponder, J. (2019). Patients' use of dogs as objects of identification, projection, and displacement. *Psychoanalytic Psychology, 36*(1), 29–35. https://doi.org/10.1037/pap0000164

3. Guterman, O., & Neuman, A. (2020). Parental attachment and internalizing and externalizing problems of Israeli school-goers and homeschoolers. *School Psychology, 35*(1), 41–50. https://doi.org/10.1037/spq0000342

4. Boag, S. (2020). Reflective awareness, repression, and the cognitive unconscious. *Psychoanalytic Psychology, 37*(1), 18–27. https://doi.org/10.1037/pap0000276

5. Békés, V., Perry, J. C., & Starrs, C. J. (2017). Resilience in holocaust survivors: a study of defense mechanisms in holocaust narratives. *Journal of Aggression, Maltreatment & Trauma, 26*(10), 1072–1089. https://doi.org/10.1080/10926771.2017.1320344

6. Diehl, M., Chui, H., Hay, E. L., Lumley, M. A., Grühn, D., & Labouvie-Vief, G. (2014). Change in coping and defense mechanisms across adulthood: Longitudinal findings in a European American sample. *Developmental Psychology, 50*(2), 634–648. https://doi.org/10.1037/a0033619

7. Vranka, M. A., & Bahník, Š. (2016). Is the emotional dog blind to its choices? An attempt to reconcile the social intuitionist model and the choice blindness effect. *Experimental Psychology, 63*(3), 180–188. https://doi.org/10.1027/1618-3169/a000325

8. Cohen, D., Kim, E., & Hudson, N. W. (2018). Religion, repulsion, and reaction formation: Transforming repellent attractions and repulsions. *Journal of Personality and Social Psychology, 115*(3), 564–584. https://doi.org/10.1037/pspp0000151

9. Behm-Morawitz, E., & Schipper, S. (2016). Sexing the avatar: Gender, sexualization, and cyber-harassment in a virtual world. *Journal of Media Psychology: Theories, Methods, and Applications, 28*(4), 161–174. https://doi.org/10.1027/1864-1105/a000152

10. Holowchak, M. A., & Lavin, M. (2015). Beyond the death drive: The future of "repetition" and "compulsion to repeat" in psychopathology. *Psychoanalytic Psychology*, *32*(4), 645–668. https://doi.org/10.1037/a0037859

11. Hauser, D. J., Preston, S. D., & Stansfield, R. B. (2014). Altruism in the wild: When affiliative motives to help positive people overtake empathic motives to help the distressed. *Journal of Experimental Psychology: General*, *143*(3), 1295–1305. https://doi.org/10.1037/a0035464

12. Neubauer, A. B., Smyth, J. M., & Sliwinski, M. J. (2018). When you see it coming: Stressor anticipation modulates stress effects on negative affect. *Emotion*, *18*(3), 342–354. https://doi.org/10.1037/emo0000381.supp

13. Sosik, J. J., & Cameron, J. C. (2010). Character and authentic transformational leadership behavior: Expanding the ascetic self toward others. *Consulting Psychology Journal: Practice and Research*, *62*(4), 251–269. https://doi.org/10.1037/a0022104

14. Besser, A., & Zeigler-Hill, V. (2011). Pathological forms of narcissism and perceived stress during the transition to the university: The mediating role of humor styles. *International Journal of Stress Management*, *18*(3), 197–221. https://doi.org/10.1037/a0024826

15. Sperber, E. (2014). Sublimation: Building or dwelling? Loewald, Freud, and architecture. *Psychoanalytic Psychology*, *31*(4), 507–524. https://doi.org/10.1037/a0038079

16. Dworkin, J. D., Zimmerman, V., Waldinger, R. J., & Schulz, M. S. (2019). Capturing naturally occurring emotional suppression as it unfolds in couple interactions. *Emotion*, *19*(7), 1224–1235. https://doi.org/10.1037/emo0000524

17. Lannin, D. G., Bittner, K. E., & Lorenz, F. O. (2013). Longitudinal effect of defensive denial on relationship instability. *Journal of Family Psychology*, *27*(6), 968–977. https://doi.org/10.1037/a0034694

18. Ramsay, J. R. (2017). The relevance of cognitive distortions in the psychosocial treatment of adult ADHD. *Professional Psychology: Research and Practice*, *48*(1), 62–69. https://doi.org/10.1037/pro0000101

19. Morry, M. M., Kito, M., & Dunphy, L. (2014). How do I see you? Partner-enhancement in dating couples. *Canadian Journal of Behavioural Science / Revue Canadienne Des Sciences Du Comportement*, *46*(3), 356–365. https://doi.org/10.1037/a0033167

20. Zoubaa, S., Dure, S., & Yanos, P. T. (2020). Is there evidence for defensive projection? The impact of subclinical mental disorder and self-identification on endorsement of stigma. *Stigma and Health*. https://doi.org/10.1037/sah0000217

21. Jurist, E. (2019). Review of core concepts in contemporary psychoanalysis: Clinical, research evidence, and conceptual critiques. *Psychoanalytic Psychology*, *36*(2), 200–202. https://doi.org/10.1037/pap0000217

22. Kramer, U., de Roten, Y., Perry, J. C., & Despland, J. N. (2013). Beyond splitting:

Observer-rated defense mechanisms in borderline personality disorder. *Psychoanalytic Psychology, 30*(1), 3–15. https://doi.org/10.1037/a0029463

23. Vaillant, G. E. (2011). Involuntary coping mechanisms: A psychodynamic perspective. *Dialogues in Clinical Neuroscience, 13*(3), 366–370. Retrieved from https://www.ncbi.nlm.nih.gov/pmc/articles/PMC3182012/

24. Malone, J. C., Cohen, S., Liu, S. R., Vaillant, G. E., & Waldinger, R. J. (2013). Adaptive midlife defense mechanisms and late-life health. *Personality and Individual Differences, 55*(2), 85–89. https://doi.org/10.1016/j.paid.2013.01.025

25. Weck, F., Neng, J., Richtberg, S., Jakob, M., & Stangier, U. (2015). Cognitive therapy versus exposure therapy for hypochondriasis (health anxiety): A randomized controlled trial. *Journal of Consulting and Clinical Psychology, 83*(4), 665–676. https://doi.org/10.1037/ccp0000013

26. Oreg, S., & Sverdlik, N. (2011). Ambivalence toward imposed change: The conflict between dispositional resistance to change and the orientation toward the change agent. *Journal of Applied Psychology, 96*(2), 337–349. https://doi.org/10.1037/a0021100

27. Koestner, R., Losier, G. F., Vallerand, R. J., & Carducci, D. (1996). Identified and introjected forms of political internalization: Extending self-determination theory. *Journal of Personality and Social Psychology, 70*(5), 1025–1036. https://doi.org/10.1037/0022-3514.70.5.1025

28. Liu, E., & Roloff, M. E. (2015). Exhausting silence: Emotional costs of withholding complaints. *Negotiation and Conflict Management Research, 8*(1), 25–40. https://doi.org/10.1111/ncmr.12043

29. Kaplan, M. (2016). Clinical considerations regarding regression in psychotherapy with patients with conversion disorder. *Psychodynamic Psychiatry, 44*(3), 367–384. https://doi.org/10.1521/pdps.2016.44.3.367

30. Orcutt, C. (2017). Schizoid fantasy: Refuge or transitional location? *Clinical Social Work Journal, 46*(1), 42–47. https://doi.org/10.1007/s10615-017-0629-2

31. Challa, S. A., Graziano, R., Strasshofer, D. R., White, K. S., Sayuk, G. S., & Bruce, S. E. (2020). Perceived sleep quality mediates the relationship between posttraumatic stress and somatic symptoms. *Psychological Trauma: Theory, Research, Practice, and Policy.* https://doi.org/10.1037/tra0000561

APPENDIX C: Cognitive Distortions

DESCRIPTION	EXAMPLE(S)	POTENTIAL SOLUTIONS
All-or-nothing thinking: Thinking in black-and-white categories regarding self and others.[2]	"I failed my exam, I am a failure at life."	What does it mean to be a failure? Examine the evidence for and against. Cost-benefit analysis: Reflect the advantages and the disadvantages of these negative thoughts and feelings. Does this thought or feeling benefit you? Why or why not?
Overgeneralization: Viewing a single negative event as a never-ending cycle of misfortune or failure. Overgeneralizing consists of utilizing words such as "always" and "never."[3]	You forget to do the dishes once and your partner says: "You always forget to the do the dishes!" You suffer from insomnia and you tell yourself: "I never get good sleep!"	Keep a written record of times you go to bed and the quality of sleep. Actually quantify it. Thinking in shades of gray: Evaluate findings on a range of 0 to 100; this allows us to analyze these findings or experiences as a partial success and not a complete failure.
Mental filter: Dwelling on a single, negative detail to the point where positives are overlooked.[4]	Thinking, "I'm doing very poorly at work" after receiving one negative customer satisfaction report.	The double standard method: Instead of talking to oneself in a harsh, critical way, try speaking in the way a close friend or loved one would—with compassion and understanding.

DESCRIPTION	EXAMPLE(S)	POTENTIAL SOLUTIONS
Discounting the positive: Believing that our positive qualities or characteristics "don't count" or aren't "good enough."[4]	"I'm not a valued employee at my place of work"—although this person always arrives to work on time and prepared.	The survey method: If we believe we are not valued employees, we may ask our co-workers if they feel the same way (survey them).
Jumping to conclusions: Making decisions with certainty based on lacking information.[5] There are two different features of this distortion: Mind reading—concluding that someone is reacting negatively to you Fortune telling—predicting that bad things will happen.[4] "Fortune telling" is also similar to the cognitive distortion "illusion of control" among gamblers: the perceived ability to control gambling outcomes.[6]	"When the teacher laughed during my drama performance, it wasn't because they thought it was funny. It was because they thought it was so stupid." "If I bring my lucky rabbit's foot to the casino tonight, I'll win big playing poker."	Examine the evidence: Ask people you trust, suspend critical judgments before concluding they are true without evidence, ask for constructive feedback. Examine the evidence for this decision. For example, an individual may analyze the times they had brought their lucky rabbit's foot to the casino, but still didn't win.
Magnification/ minimization: Placing an overemphasis on the negatives and underemphasis on the positives.[7]	"It's no big deal. Everyone breaks the law." "I'm totally going to fail that test."	Identifying the distortion: Write down negative thoughts in order to identify the distortion; making it easier to think about what is being experienced in a more positive way.

DESCRIPTION	EXAMPLE(S)	POTENTIAL SOLUTIONS
Emotional reasoning: Basing reasoning on the way that one feels.[8]	"If I feel anxious, it's because there is danger." "If I feel disgusted, it must be contagious."	The experimental technique: If you feel anxious and believe there is danger, evaluate the situation. For example, in an episode of panic and feeling as if a heart attack will occur, doing jumping jacks will prove that the heart is healthy and working properly.
Should statements: Criticizing oneself with "shoulds" and "shouldn'ts."[4]	"I shouldn't have been so stupid." "I should just leave it be and forget about it."	The semantic method: Reframing these thoughts into more positive ones. For example, instead of telling myself, "I shouldn't have been so stupid," it would be better to say, "Next time, I will be more mindful of certain situations."
Labeling: Attaching negative, paradoxical labels to oneself.[4]	"I'm a failure." "I'm nobody."	Define terms: Identifying one's personal labels, and then defining them. For example, what is a "failure"? What makes one a "nobody"? The goal is to show that these definitions aren't relatable to the person.
Personalization/ blame: Holding oneself or others personally accountable for events that were out of their control.[9] Ultimately, personalization leads to feelings of resentment and guilt.[4]	"If only I were more affectionate, he wouldn't have cheated on me."	Reattribution: Enables a person to realize that mistakes do not define who they are as a person. For example, if a man believes he is a bad father, he should try to come up with factors that contributed to coming up with this belief, instead of blaming himself for the entire situation. This insight provides solutions.

1. del Pozo, M. A., Harbeck, S., Zahn, S., Kliem, S., & Kröger, C. (2018). Cognitive distortions in anorexia nervosa and borderline personality disorder. *Psychiatry Research, 260,* 164–172. https://doi.org/10.1016/j.psychres.2017.11.043

2. Çelik, C., & Odacı. H. (2013). The relationship between problematic internet use and interpersonal cognitive distortions and life satisfaction in university students. *Children and Youth Services Review, 35*(3), 505–508. https://doi.org/10.1016/j.childyouth.2013.01.001

3. Takano, K., Boddez, Y., & Raes, F. (2016). I sleep with my mind's eye open: Cognitive arousal and overgeneralization underpin the misperception of sleep. *Journal of Behavior Therapy and Experimental Psychiatry, 52,* 157–165. https://doi.org/10.1016/j.jbtep.2016.04.007

4. Burns, D. D. (1999). *The feeling good handbook.* New York, NY: Plume.

5. So, S. H. W., Siu, N. Y. F., Wong, H. L., Chan, W., & Garety, P. A. (2016). "Jumping to conclusions" data-gathering bias in psychosis and other psychiatric disorders—Two meta-analyses of comparisons between patients and healthy individuals. *Clinical Psychology Review, 46,* 151–167. https://doi.org/10.1016/j.cpr.2016.05.001

6. Ciccarelli, M., Griffiths, M. D., Nigro, G., & Cosenza, M. (2017). Decision making, cognitive distortions and emotional distress: A comparison between pathological gamblers and healthy controls. *Journal of Behavior Therapy and Experimental Psychiatry, 54,* 204–210. https://doi.org/10.1016/j.jbtep.2016.08.012

7. Pace, U., D'Urso, G., & Zappulla, C. (2019). Hating among adolescents: Common contributions of cognitive distortions and maladaptive personality traits. *Current Psychology.* https://doi.org/10.1007/s12144-019-00278-x

8. Verwoerd, J., de Jong, P. J., Wessel, I., & van Hout, W. J. (2013). "If I feel disgusted, I must be getting ill": Emotional reasoning in the context of contamination fear. *Behaviour Research and Therapy, 51*(3), 122–127. https://doi.org/10.1016/j.brat.2012.11.005

9. Hazama, K., & Katsuka, S. (2016). Cognitive distortions among sexual offenders against women in Japan. *Journal of Interpersonal Violence, 34*(16), 3372–3391. https://doi.org/10.1177/0886260516669544

APPENDIX D: Dominant Beliefs Identification Chart

BEHAVIOR	DOMINANT BELIEF	IDEAL BELIEF	IDEAL BEHAVIOR

APPENDIX E: Vital Signals Identification Chart

DATE AND EXPERIENCE	PHYSICAL SENSATIONS	THOUGHTS AND FEELINGS	DERIVED VALUE(S) OR DIRECTIONS

APPENDIX F: Vital Signals Application Chart

Previously, you identified experiences that have moved you deeply. From these experiences, you derived values that may act as a compass for you. This chart allows you to apply the knowledge gained from those experiences directly to your life and track your progress toward moving in those directions. The first step is to fill in those identified values in the center column. The second step is to identify words that express an excess and deficiency of that value. For example, if your value was confidence, its excess might be arrogance and its deficiency might be submissiveness. Now dot a line in each row that best describes where you feel and think you are right now. Finally, ask yourself: what actions might move you from your dot to the next line closer to the values? Fill out these responses in the second chart.

Excess	Values through Vital Signals	Deficiency
	v1.	
	v2.	
	v3.	
	v4.	
	v5.	

VALUES	BEHAVIOR 1	BEHAVIOR 2	BEHAVIOR 3
V1			
V2			
V3			
V4			
V5			

APPENDIX G: Symbiotic Relationships

SYMBIONT (internal or external)	CURRENT SYMBIOTIC RELATIONSHIP (e.g., mutualisitic, commensalistic, parasitic)	DESIRED SYMBIOTIC RELATIONSHIP (DSR)	PATH TO DSR

APPENDIX H: Self-Directed Cycling

....

Instructions:

Reasoning ability is sensitive to a variety of experiences. In the midst of an emotional challenge, blood flow in the brain may be redirected to areas that are not helpful for thinking clearly. One way to cope is to have a default strategy. The following strategy is called cycling. It is a structured method aimed to help process challenging experiences, and assist with informed decision-making.

Order of Self-Directed Questions

- What image (or word) would best represent this challenge?
- What are my senses telling me?
- What feelings am I having?
- What thoughts am I having?
- What would I tell a friend in my position?
- What do I want to do in the moment? What are the consequences?
- What decision would be most aligned with my values? What are the consequences?
- Has my experience of this situation changed?
- Is the image (or word) still an accurate representation? If not, how has the image (or word) changed?

Index

ABOUT THE AUTHOR

Aldrich Chan, Psy.D., is a neuropsychologist and founder of the Center for Neuropsychology and Consciousness (CNC), a private practice in Miami, Florida, that provides neuropsychological and psychological services. In addition to his practice, he is an adjunct professor for Pepperdine University and conducts research on the default mode network (DMN) and trauma at the University of Miami.